OpenVMS Performance Management

TUNING TECHNIQUES FOR OPENVMS VAX
AND OPENVMS AXP, 2ND EDITION

OpenVMS Performance Management

Tuning Techniques for OpenVMS VAX and OpenVMS AXP, 2nd Edition

James W. Coburn

CBM
BOOKS

Trademark Acknowledgments

DEC is a registered trademark and Alpha AXP, DCL, DECnet, DECUS, DECwindows, ESE-20, Files-11, HSC, KDM-50, KDM-70, LAVc, Local-Area VAXcluster, OpenVMS, OpenVMS AXP, OpenVMS VAX, RA70, RA81, RA92, VAX, VAXcluster, VAX/VMS, VAX RMS, VMS, VMScluster are all trademarks of Digital Equipment Corporation.

All other trademarks are the property of their respective owners.

Library of Congress Cataloging-in-Publication Data

Coburn, James W., 1953-
    [VMS performance management]
    OpenVMS performance management: tuning techniques for open
    VMS/VAX and openVMS/AXP / James W. Coburn. — 2nd ed.
        p. cm.
    Previous ed. published under title: VMS performance management.
    Includes index.
    ISBN 1-878956-40-X
    1. VAX computers. 2. VAX/VM I. Title. II. Title: VMS
    performance management.
QA76.8.V32C63 1994
005.4'449—dc2   94-15516
                                                             CIP

Please address comments and questions to the publisher:

CBM Books
101 Witmer Road
Horsham, PA 19044
(215)957-1500 FAX(215)957-1050

Editor: Eric Schoeniger
Editorial Coordinator: Debbie Hiller
Production Manager: Patty Wall

Cover Design: Tim Kraft

Contents

List of Figures

List of Tables

List of Equations

Preface

The first edition of this book was developed and published before the release of Digital Equipment Corp.'s Reduced Instruction Set Computing (RISC) platform, Alpha AXP. All of the material that was in the first edition is included in this book. In many places revisions have been made to account for the newer hardware and software releases that have been made for OpenVMS VAX. In addition, this book covers the relevant topics for performance management for OpenVMS AXP.

This book covers the underlying concepts of OpenVMS within the context of performance management. It provides detailed procedures for developing the tools and skills needed to tune OpenVMS systems effectively. These procedures will help you analyze and correctly modify your system's resource use. The book also describes in detail how to change system parameters when your analysis determines that adjusting system parameter settings would result in higher system performance. Also discussed are the side effects to watch for that could lower system performance.

This book is written for both the beginning and the advanced OpenVMS system manager. The intent is to provide an understanding of how OpenVMS works and how to apply this understanding to performance management. Regardless of whether you are using OpenVMS VAX or OpenVMS AXP, performance problems can often be readily solved once you understand how the system works.

System managers responsible for managing the performance of their OpenVMS systems but who need more information than is available in the Digital manual set should find this book a useful guide. It includes many of the tricks and "hidden information" I have discovered over the years.

This book contains the basics of the first edition and also includes many updates that are the results of feedback from the DECUS presymposium seminar "VMS Performance Management." Over the last several years of giving this seminar in Europe, North America, and the Far East, I have received invaluable feedback from the hundreds of attendees. In this second edition I have tried to address the great number of suggestions for changes and also the requests for further information in many areas.

Note that the first edition was called *VMS Performance Management*, while this edition is titled *OpenVMS Performance Management*. In July 1992, Digital changed the name of its operating system to reflect its conformance with various industry standards. Contrary to popular belief, OpenVMS is not in itself a new product, but simply a renaming of the original; therefore, the name change is essentially retroactive, and all references to *VMS* and *VAX/VMS* become *OpenVMS* and *OpenVMS VAX*. Similarly, *VAXcluster* has become *VMScluster*, since a cluster can now include both VAX and Alpha AXP systems. I have tried to use *OpenVMS* and *VMScluster* throughout this edition; however, it is sometimes necessary to use *VMS* and *VAXcluster* to distinguish between earlier and later versions of the product. In any case, *VMS* and *OpenVMS* are essentially the same and can be used interchangeably.

If you have any questions that you would like to ask me about subjects covered in this book, or, if you have suggestions for future revisions, please contact me at the address below:

Jim Coburn
P.O. Box 200015
Austin, Texas 78720-0015

HOW THIS BOOK IS ORGANIZED

This book contains ten chapters and fourteen appendices.

Chapter 1, "Introduction to Performance," provides an overview of performance terms, tuning, and the skills you need to correctly tune your system.

Chapter 2, "Files-11 ODS-2 Structure Overview," describes the basics of XQP, the OpenVMS file management system.

Chapter 3, "File System Analysis," explains how to use the available tools to collect and analyze data on your system's file management system.

Chapter 4, "File System Tuning," explains how to use the results of your analysis to modify the performance behavior of the file management system.

Chapter 5, "How To Build a Better Disk," discusses the superset of problems addressed by file fragmentation. Included are methods for building an optimal disk, one much better than that created by mere defragmentation.

Chapter 6, "Basic System Tuning," describes the basic terms and system parameters that relate to the tuning of your memory system.

Chapter 7, "Memory System Analysis," explains how to use available tools to collect and analyze data on your memory management system.

Chapter 8, "Memory System Tuning," details how to use the results of your analysis to modify your memory management system for optimal performance.

Chapter 9, "Static Versus Dynamic Tuning," discusses the new and exciting field of dynamic tuning, including the potential for dynamic tuning under various system configurations.

Chapter 10, "SYSGEN and Other Concerns," discusses many items that do not fit into the other chapters. Much of this information is included at the request of DECUS seminar attendees and feedback from those who purchased the first edition of this book.

Appendix A, "PMS Dump Program," shows a program written in DEC C that dumps out the values of selected performance data. This is Version 1 of a program to collect performance-related data.

Appendix B, "Output from Dump Command," contains the DCL command and associated output for dumping out a file header.

Appendix C, "Page Monitor," contains a DCL program you can use to help analyze memory and faulting on your system. Also included in this appendix is a DEC C program that allows you to get information about programs on any or all nodes in your VMScluster.

Appendix D, "Page File Utilization," shows several methods for monitoring page file use. Included are commands that can be used with the System Dump Analyzer to extract page file information. Also included is a DEC C program that allows you to dump out the majority of the information available about page file usage.

Appendix E, "Dump Logical Names," is a set of programs written in DEC C that dumps out the internal structures of the logical name tables.

Appendix F, "Show Memory," shows several ways to look at the memory allocation for your system. Examples of how to get the information for both OpenVMS VAX V6.0 and OpenVMS AXP V1.5 are included.

Appendix G, "MODPARAMS File," contains a listing for a starting point in setting up your master MODPARAMS.DAT file. This file is set up to work on both OpenVMS VAX and OpenVMS AXP systems.

Appendix H, "Simple Tuner," contains the DEC C source code for a simple dynamic tuner. This tuner will correct the problems encountered when trying to use AWSA.

Appendix I, "Memory Checking," contains the DEC C source code for a simple daily memory-checking program. Once you have upgraded to OpenVMS VAX V6.0 or OpenVMS AXP, this program will no longer be needed.

Appendix J, "MSCP Information Program," contains the DEC C program that allows you to dump out the entire MSCP database for performance analysis.

Appendix K, "Monitor System Program," contains the entire source listing for a fairly complicated performance data program. While not everything needed for a "commercial" product is supplied, enough data and code are supplied to allow use in monitoring your system. It should be fairly easy to expand the functionality of this program into a much higher level data collection program.

Appendix L, "Dump Resource Names," is a set of programs written in DEC C that dumps out the internal structures of the resource name tables. These tables directly affect lock performance on your machine.

Appendix M, "AST Control," is a set of programs that allows you to queue an AST to another process. With the release of OpenVMS AXP, this is now a much harder process. This program shows many of the "undocumented" features needed to be able to build system executive images.

Appendix N, "Home Block," is a DEC C program that allows you to dump out the contents of a volume's home block.

Acknowledgments

While it is almost impossible to name all the people who contributed to this book, I will attempt to recognize those who provided major input.

I learned and developed most of my VMS skills while working as an engineer for Schlumberger Well Services at the Austin Systems Center. I would like to thank Bob Olsen, Doug Bordner, and Kevin Kennedy at Schlumberger for allowing me the time to develop the materials required for this book.

In addition to supplying the basis of several chapters and helping to get the DECUS seminars started, Bill Davy of RAXCO Inc. supplied much-needed technical feedback. Without Bills help and support, this project would never have been possible.

Credit is also due to Dr. J. W. White of Modular Mining Systems for getting me started in the field and for his support during my early years of using VMS.

Finally, thanks to my wife Denise for her help and understanding. She provided a lot of input and reviewed and edited all of my work. This book would not have been possible without her effort and support.

Introduction to Performance

T HE GOAL OF PERFORMANCE MANAGEMENT IS TO MAXIMIZE THE PRODUCTIVITY OF A given amount of hardware while maintaining an acceptable level of user productivity. To do this, you must understand how system resources are being used.

Applications such as graphical human interfaces, simulation packages, financial analysis, and seismic processing, just to name a few, require fast response times and high throughput in order to satisfy the user. Fast hardware is not enough to achieve good performance. Both the application and the underlying operating system must be fast and efficient. The majority of this book deals with how to make the underlying operating system fast and efficient. In some cases I will also show how to add efficiency to your applications.

Only when you truly understand how resources are being consumed can you effectively modify consumption. Usually, a few key programs are responsible for the majority of resource use. Thus, no amount of improvement to a program using only 1 percent of resources will reflect favorably on overall performance. Likewise, a 10 percent improvement to a single program that uses 50 percent of available resources can result in a noticeable overall performance gain. Improvements come from good usage habits on the part of both users and developers. All elements of the overall system must work together effectively to yield high performance.

SYSTEM TUNING

System tuning consists of making adjustments to system parameters in an attempt to realize the best performance over time. To effectively tune a system, you must:

- Understand how the components that make up OpenVMS work together.

- Determine how resources are being used.

- Determine how to differentiate between normal and abnormal system behavior.

- Know how to modify user behavior to use the system resources effectively.

- Know how to evaluate the effectiveness of tuning.

System parameter adjustments cannot cure problems caused by unreasonable expectations, hardware problems or limitations, improper system management, or poor program design or implementation. However, in many cases system parameter adjustment is the only option available.

System parameters that can be adjusted include SYSGEN parameters, process quotas, and file system parameters. Such adjustments will result in big improvements only in mistuned systems. If system parameter settings were derived exclusively from the use of AUTOGEN, your system could be mistuned.

SYSTEM ANALYSIS

The major step in improving performance is knowing how to analyze the operation of the system to determine how resources are being used. Consequently, the key word in performance is analysis. Until you understand what is going on, you cannot correct it. The real benefit comes from establishing realistic performance goals and understanding your system. You need to become familiar with your workload and its characteristics, including:

- Total system loads.

- Typical response times.

- Peak access times.

- Areas that are likely to become bottlenecks.

- Users' goals.

Remember, your objective is not only to solve the performance problem but also to solve it in such a way that the user knows that the problem has been solved.

DATA COLLECTION TOOLS

Many tools can be used to collect performance data. In this book I will discuss many of these tools, concentrating on those that are readily available at little or no cost, such as:

- MONITOR.

- DCL commands.

- Accounting tools.

- In-house tools.

SOFTWARE EFFICIENCY

There seems to be an attitude today that designing and implementing software for efficiency is too costly. This attitude leads to programs that work poorly. A basic requirement for any program is a good design, and an integral part of any design is efficiency. This does not mean writing everything in assembly language, nor does it mean packing every last bit into every available location, which can actually cause your program to run more slowly.

Some of the basic requirements for software efficiency will be covered in later chapters. How to implement some of the most cost-effective performance improvements will be shown. A large amount of the available application software is inefficient and can be greatly improved. Remember, many OpenVMS users have no regard for the amount of resources they consume or for their impact on other users.

One of the most common and costly mistakes made in software development can be attributed to an attitude that says, "Let's get it working; we'll worry about performance later." While you can make performance improvements after the fact, high-performance software is designed and developed, not patched or modified.

Also keep in mind that for most cases, the more standard and the more complex the language used to develop the program, the lower the efficiency of the code. If all you want to do is write to a terminal, the code developed in VAX C or FORTRAN using standard I/O calls will be significantly slower than the equivalent code written in MACRO-32/64. However, there are tradeoffs. While the MACRO-32/64 code is highly efficient, the amount of time to maintain and support the code as the system evolves will closely approximate the inverse of the performance increase. Gaining efficiency by coding in a low-level or nonstandard language is not a valid long-term performance solution.

A FIRST STEP

Performance of an OpenVMS system can be measured in many ways. The most commonly accepted measure of performance is user satisfaction. If the users of the system do not perceive that the system is performing in a satisfactory manner, then the system is not correct. Remember, in some cases the users' perception exceeds the ability of the system. No amount of tuning can provide a level of service that is not possible for the current hardware/software configuration.

TRADITIONAL OPTIONS FOR INCREASING PERFORMANCE

There are four traditional options for increasing performance:

1. Buy more memory.

2. Buy more CPU.

3. Buy more disk.

4. Distribute the workload.

In many cases these options work, and they do not require a high degree of expertise to implement. The first three options listed are usually used in response to a perception of insufficient resources. If resources actually are insufficient, these options are good choices. If the available resources are not being used efficiently, these options will still work but will not be cost-effective solutions.

The fourth option listed is not an option in the same sense as the other three. To be able to distribute workload, you must have unused resources, which implies that you have already "bought more."

Another performance option often used is that of upgrading your hardware to compensate for poor code design. The worst part of this solution is that it works, at least to some extent. Instead of correcting the performance problem or redesigning a poorly implemented or designed program, the "sins" of the past are passed on to future generations. Even today there are major programs that are essentially "ports" of working programs from the PDP-11 series of processors. Algorithms and methods that work superbly on the 16-bit PDP-11 platform are not necessarily well-suited for the VAX or AXP environment of today.

PERFORMANCE TERMS

We will use many terms throughout this book. Just to make sure everyone is talking about the same the same thing, I will give some simple definitions of some of the basic performance terms.

Resource — What everyone wants and there is not enough of to go around, such as memory, CPU, and disk.

Workload — The amount of resources users consume simultaneously.

Response Time — The time it takes for the system to respond to the user.

Throughput — The amount of work performed per unit of time.

Bottleneck — What occurs when the first resource reaches saturation.

USER BEHAVIOR

What you do not know may kill your system. All of the following abuses can cause major performance degradation:

- Users running "tickle" programs to defeat inactive job killers.
- Resetting all file protections on login/logout.

- Improper use of monitoring programs.

Although it is difficult to modify user behavior, in many cases this can be the critical step in tuning your system. Make sure you know what is really happening, not what you suspect or what someone else tells you. In addition, realize that seemingly innocent usage can have a major impact on performance.

If your users are doing the following, you have a problem:

```
Compile  !A large number of small files
Library  !Put all object files in the library
Delete   !Delete all object files
Link     !Now you are in trouble
```

The deletion of the large number of very fragmented object files just created will leave your disk extent cache pointing to a large number of small fragments. By default, the linker does a contiguous best try, and the severely fragmented cache will cause your link to take much longer and consume more system resources. The worst case is that you could end up with a severely fragmented executable file, and there is a performance penalty for running fragmented executable files.

Another example of both user behavior and "what you don't know" is the default actions of using the Motif graphical user interface (GUI). If your users are using heavy resource consumption login procedures via LOGIN.COM, then you might have a problem. By default your login procedure (SYS$LOGIN:LOGIN.COM) is executed twice upon each login. Unless you take active steps to bypass this "feature," you can expend large amounts of time executing a second invocation of SYS$LOGIN:LOGIN.COM upon each login.

If you use Digital's MONITOR program to do remote monitoring of systems, you need to understand how the remote monitoring facility works. There is no extra overhead on the monitored node to collect data for more than one requesting node. However, there is still extra network load to send the data to each requesting node. For those using medium-size or large clusters, there is a major performance problem with using remote monitoring. To allow a single data collector to run on a node and service all requests for monitor data, the collector collects all possible monitor data at the minimum interval. All data is sent to the requesting node, and it is the responsibility of the requesting node to select the data it requires. Thus, if you issue the command:

```
$ MONITOR DISK/ITEM=ALL/INTERVAL=600
```

and you are running on a node called ASC131, only a minimum amount of data will be collected.

However, if you issue the command:

```
$ MONITOR/NODE=ASC131 DISK/ITEM=ALL/INTERVAL=600
```

while you are using remote monitoring, all data for node ASC131 must be collected at the minimum interval and sent via the Ethernet to your local node. If ASC131 has a large number of balance set slots, then it is possible for the data collected to require 10 to 30 percent of the Ethernet bandwidth to send the data to your node. In a large cluster, I have measured 50 to 70 percent of the Ethernet bandwidth being used to support remote monitoring!

Files-11 ODS-2 Structure Overview

FILES-11 ON-DISK STRUCTURE LEVEL 2 (ODS-2) IS THE STANDARD FILE STRUCTURE for OpenVMS. The file system is responsible for maintaining the structure and integrity of data stored on disk.

Following are the major tasks of the file system; when discussing ODS-2 from a performance viewpoint, I will focus on the first four items:

- The mapping of logical blocks to virtual blocks.

- Free space management.

- Directory file management.

- Basic file operations.

- File integrity.

- Translating RMS data requests.

While a large portion of the code for the file system is dedicated to ensuring data integrity, overall performance is a secondary issue for the file system. Unfortunately for OpenVMS performance, but fortunately for its users, the primary objective for the file system has been accomplished. Now that we have a highly reliable file system, the user community is putting increasing significance on the overall performance of the file system.

BASIC TERMS

In this section I will give some definitions and a quick review of the basic components of the file system.

FILE SYSTEM MAPPING

There are four levels of mapping to go from user information to the disk media locations:

1. User files map user information to virtual blocks (files).

2. Files-11 ODS-2 maps virtual blocks to logical blocks.

3. Device drivers map logical blocks to physical blocks.

4. The hardware and software on a disk map physical blocks to the track/cylinder/sector information.

VOLUME

A volume is the basic unit of the file system. In almost all cases, a volume refers to a single disk storage device. However, a volume can consist of multiple disk storage devices bound together into a single logical volume. A volume consists of an ordered set of logical blocks, where a logical block is an array of 512 bytes of 8 bits each. Logical blocks are numbered from zero to n-1, where n is the number of blocks on the volume. This number is called the logical block number (LBN). Files-11 can handle volumes that contain up to 232 blocks.

CLUSTERS

Logical blocks are grouped into clusters. A cluster consists of a set number of blocks for a volume. All Files-11 access to logical blocks is done in terms of clusters. The number of logical blocks in a cluster is referred to by the term *volume cluster factor* or *bitmap storage cluster factor*.

IDENTIFICATION

The file system recognizes a volume by the contents of its home block. The home block is almost always mapped to logical block 1 of the volume. However, because LBN 1 might be defective, the home block might be mapped to another LBN. The selection of the alternate block number takes into account the geometry of the volume and the trend of volume LBN failures. The home block contains the information necessary to describe the volume to Files-11, that is, structure and version levels, cluster factors, maximum number for files, and so on. Appendix N contains the code necessary to produce a listing of the home block information for a volume. The home block also contains the volume label (an ASCII character string) to identify the volume. Table 2-1 shows the listing of a typical home block.

LBN of home (that is, this) block	1
LBN of alternate home block	767
LBN of alternate index file header	409986
Volume structure level	
Structure version number	1
Main structure level	2
Storage bitmap cluster factor	3
VBN of home (that is, this) block	2
VBN of alternate home block	9
VBN of alternate index file header	10
VBN of index file bitmap	13
LBN of index file bitmap	409221
Maximum number files on volume	102287
Index file bitmap size, in blocks	25
Number reserved files on volume	9
Disk device type	0
Relative volume number of this volume	0
Count of volumes in set	0
Volume characteristics	
Turn off high-water marking	
Volume owner UIC	[1,4]
Volume security mask	00000000
Volume protection	0000
Default file protection	FA00
Default file record protection	FE00
First checksum	0CF8
Volume creation date	30-DEC-1991 13:35:44.81
Default window size	7
Default LRU limit	3
Default file extend	5
Minimum file retention period	20 00:00:00.00
Maximum file retention period	30 00:00:00.00
Volume revision date	17-NOV-1858 00:00:00.00
File lookup table FID	0000
Lowest struclev on volume	
Structure version number	0
Main structure level	0
Highest struclev on volume	
Structure version number	0
Main structure level	0
Spare (310 bytes)	
Pack serial number	0
Structure (volume set name)	
Volume name	ASC513_4609X
Volume owner name	
Volume format type	DECFILE11B
Spare (2 bytes)	
Second checksum	17272

Table 2-1. Home Block Data Listing

Another important function of the home block is that it contains a pointer to the index file, indexf.sys. This block of data contains the information needed to access all files on the volume.

FILES

The file system treats each file as a set of virtually contiguous logical blocks (VBN) numbered from 1 to n, where n is the highest block allocated by the file. All VBNs have corresponding LBNs. A logical block and a virtual block describe the same physical unit of storage, 512 8-bit bytes. There is no guarantee that the underlying logical blocks are also contiguous. Files get their structure from the working of Files-11.

MAPPING

Files-11 maps virtual to unique logical blocks. It is the responsibility of the device driver to map logical blocks to physical blocks on the device. At this time, OpenVMS does not support unallocated virtual blocks.

ACP VERSUS XQP

The early versions of VAX/VMS used a file system ancillary control process (ACP). This meant that each request that used that file system required a process context switch to the ACP as well as a context switch back to the requesting process when the request was finished. Thus, the ACP suffered significant overhead due to its separate process context. Also, as the size of OpenVMS VAX systems increased, the ACP suffered from being a systemwide bottleneck because all processes' requests were handled by a single ACP.

With the release of VAX/VMS V4.0, VAXclusters were introduced. This introduction forced a major change in how the file system requests were handled. The extended QIO processor (XQP) was introduced to perform the following tasks:

- Eliminate the ACP bottleneck due to context switching and single process thread of operation.

- Provide synchronization between processes in the VAXcluster environment.

- Provide distributed file system data structures in the VAXcluster environment.

The XQP handles file system function requests on a per-user basis. Each process maps the XQP code in its P1 image section and maintains process private data that pertains to running the XQP for that process. This provides the functionality that the file system activity of any one process has no major impact on that of any other process on the system. Thus, the XQP converted the single-threaded ACP into a multithreaded cluster synchronized file system.

FILE IDENTIFICATION

A file identifier (file ID, or FID) is a set of numbers that uniquely defines a file on a volume. As shown in Figure 2-1, if you execute a DCL command $ DIR/FILE, you will see the file ID as a triple set of numbers (n,m,i), where:

- n = the file number. This number is used as an offset into the index file to obtain the file header information.

- m = the file sequence number. Once a file has been deleted, its file ID is available for reuse. Each time a file ID is reused, the file sequence number is incremented.

- i = the relative volume number. For a bound volume set, this number is the relative volume in the set on which the file header is located. For nonvolume sets, this number is zero.

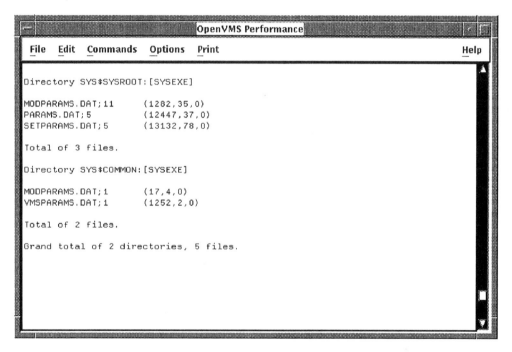

Figure 2-1. How To Display File IDs

FILE HEADER

A file ID is used to locate the file header for a file. The file header contains all information about a file that is needed to access the file, including pointers to where the file's data is located. A file header is fixed in size at 512 bytes. If all information needed to describe the file does not fit in 512 bytes, multiple headers will be used.

11

These extra headers are called extension headers. There is at least one file header for each file on the disk. A zero-length file consists of just a file header block and no data space allocated to the file. Everything about a file that is not data is in the file header block. File headers have the following characteristics:

- The first file header is located by using the file ID as an offset into the index file.

- There is no user data in the file header block.

- The primary file header block contains a back pointer to the directory in which the file resides. If the file is in multiple directories, the back pointer is to the primary directory, with a bit set indicating that there are others.

- File header blocks contain file IDs; creation and modification dates; file attributes; the access control list (ACL), if any exists; and mapping pointers.

- If all information does not fit into one file header block, multiple blocks can be used. There will be a forward link to the next file header block, called an extension file header.

Figure 2-2 shows how the file ID is used to locate the file header in the indexf.sys file.

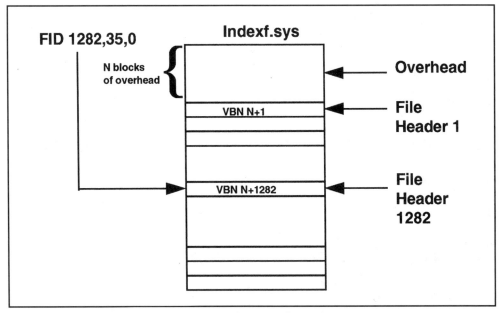

Figure 2-2. File ID to File Header

KEY FILES

The first twelve files (file IDs 1 through 12) are predefined (see Table 2-2). They are known as reserved files. These files are unique in that their file identifiers are known constants. The exact number of these files can vary depending on the particular volume. Even though there are reserved files that are not used by OpenVMS for Files-11 ODS-2, you should not delete any of these reserved files.

File	Description
[000000]INDEXF.SYS	Index File
[000000]BITMAP.SYS	Bitmap File
[000000]BADBLK.SYS	Bad Blocks File
[000000]000000.DIR	Master File Directory
[000000]CORIMG.SYS	Not Used by ODS-2
[000000]VOLSET.SYS	Volume Set Description File
[000000]CONTIN.SYS	Standard Continuation File
[000000]BACKUP.SYS	Not Used by ODS-2
[000000]BADLOG.SYS	Pending Bad Block Log File
[000000]FREFIL.SYS	OpenVMS Disk Striping
[000000]STRIPE$DATA.SYS	OpenVMS Disk Striping
[000000]STRIPE$VOLS.SYS	OpenVMS Disk Striping

Table 2-2. Key Files

INDEX FILE

File specification	*[000000]INDEXF.SYS*
File ID	*(1,1,0)*

The index file is the root of the file system. This file contains a bitmap, which tells which blocks (file headers) in the index file are in use. The index file bitmap is cached by the XQP.

Located starting at logical block 1, the home block is in the start of the index file and contains key volume information. Contained in the home block are the volume label and a pointer to the starting block of the rest of the index file.

All of the file header blocks are contained in the index file. The index file is extended in blocks of 1,000 (increased to a multiple of the cluster factor). Since the default size of indexf.sys is sixteen blocks and you can have only approximately fifty extents, it is possible to have large-capacity disks run out of file header space before they run out of free space. If this happens, you will be required to reinitialize the disk to fix the problem. The default extension algorithm has been changed with OpenVMS V6.0, and this problem will not occur for drives that are reinitialized using OpenVMS V6.0.

BITMAP FILE

File specification	*[000000]BITMAP.SYS*
File ID	*(2,2,0)*

The bitmap file contains the storage control block in the first logical block of the file. This block contains summary information about the volume. Some of the information it contains is:

- Structure level.

- Cluster size.

- Volume size in blocks.

- Current volume status.

- Time of last mount.

The rest of the blocks of the bitmap file contain the storage bitmap. The bitmap file must be contiguous.

The storage bitmap contains one bit for each cluster on the volume. For example, if the disk cluster size were three, then the bitmap would have one bit for every three blocks on the disk to indicate whether that cluster were allocated or free. A zero bit means that the corresponding cluster on the disk is allocated. A 1 bit means that the corresponding cluster is free. While in most cases zero is used to specify free and 1 means used, there is a reason for the inverting of the normal meanings. When a page of memory is allocated on OpenVMS, the default is to give the requester a page filled with initial values of zero. Using the modified scheme, a programming error would leave clusters marked allocated that were really free. While this is bad, the inverse — clusters marked free that are allocated — is a real disaster.

BAD BLOCKS FILE

File specification	*[000000]BADBLK.SYS*
File ID	*(3,3,0)*

The bad blocks file comprises the blocks on the disk that are not to be used by the file system. The contents are not a list of the bad blocks; they are the bad blocks themselves.

Blocks are allocated to the bad block file in one of three ways:

1. If cluster size does not exactly divide the disk size, the blocks in the last partial cluster are allocated to the bad blocks file so that they will not be accessed.

2. If a bad block is detected in a cluster not currently allocated to a file, the file system allocates that cluster to the bad blocks file.

3. If a bad block is detected in a cluster that is currently allocated to a file, additional work is required to get the bad block into the bad blocks file. See the Pending Bad Blocks File section of this chapter.

The advantage of the bad blocks file is that by allocating the blocks that should not be used to a file, no special code is needed in the XQP to avoid them. They are avoided just like any other blocks in any other file.

MASTER FILE DIRECTORY

File specification	*[000000]000000.DIR.*
File ID	*(4,4,0)*

The Master File Directory (MFD) contains itself, the index file, all the other reserved files as entries, and all user top-level file directories. You can create files in this directory if you wish. While the MFD is the root of the directory tree, it is also a valid Files-11 directory and can be used as such. This also means that the MFD is of the same format as any other directory file.

SYSTEM CORE IMAGE

File specification	*[000000]CORIMG.SYS.*
File ID	*(5,5,0)*

This file is not currently used by OpenVMS. It is used for ODS-1 structured disks (RSX).

VOLUME SET DESCRIPTOR FILE

File specification	*[000000]VOLSET.SYS*
File ID	*(6,6,0)*

The volume set descriptor file describes the nature of the volume set to which the volume belongs. It also contains the list of names of volumes contained in the volume set and the name of the volume set itself.

Multiple disks can be combined to form one logical volume. Each volume of a volume set has all of the structures found on a single volume. Before the introduction of large disk devices, it was fairly easy to have programs that contained database files that were larger than the largest single disk available. To allow these programs to run on OpenVMS VAX, volume sets were introduced. Volume sets allow the system to bind together several disk drives into one large virtual disk.

Files can span volume sets. If so, there is a separate file header in the index file each time the file crosses a volume. This is one of the big performance hits for using volume sets. In the worst case, you would need one file header for each extent, assuming that each time the file was extended, the next extent was not on the underlying disk drive to which the current extent was mapped. This leads to huge overhead and very long access time for these types of files.

CONTINUATION FILE

File specification	[000000]CONTIN.SYS
File ID	(7,7,0)

This file allows a multivolume file to be written sequentially with only one volume mounted at a time.

BACKUP JOURNAL FILE

File specification	[000000]BACKUP.SYS
File ID	(8,8,0)

This file is not currently used.

PENDING BAD BLOCKS FILE

File specification	[000000]BADLOG.SYS
File ID	(9,9,0)

If a suspected bad block is detected and the block is allocated to a file, the system will not be able to allocate the block to the bad blocks file, since a block can be allocated to only one file at any time. To work around this, an entry made in the badlog.sys file will be used to keep track of the file containing the suspected bad block. When this file is deleted, the information in badlog.sys is used to place the suspected bad block in the badblk.sys file.

DISK STRIPING RESERVED FILES

Disk Striping Driver for OpenVMS is a layered product, available from Digital, that decomposes an individual I/O request into multiple I/O requests that are then processed concurrently on multiple disk drives. The result is an increased data rate and an overall reduction in the disk seeks. To implement striping, several disks are bound together into a stripe set. In implementing this function, three new reserved files were created: frefil.sys, Striping Data File, and Striping Description File.

FREFIL.SYS

File specification	*[000000]FREFIL.SYS*
File ID	*(10,10,0)*

The frefil.sys file currently is not used. It is a holdover from the initial release of Disk Striping Driver for OpenVMS software.

STRIPING DATA FILE

File specification	*[000000]STRIPE$DATA.SYS*
File ID	*(11,11,0)*

This file is used to take up the free space in the index file so that no nonstriped files can be created. To ensure the integrity of the stripe set, you cannot write any file directly to the underlying disk drives.

STRIPING DESCRIPTION FILE

File specification	*[000000]STRIPE$VOLS.SYS*
File ID	*(12,12,0)*

The striping set description file describes the nature of the stripe set to which the volume belongs. It contains the list of names of volumes contained in the stripe set.

XQP CACHES

A large amount of disk-based data is required to run the file system. A large number of disk accesses are needed to access this data, but can be avoided by keeping frequently used information in memory. Since memory access of data is dramatically faster than disk access, the XQP keeps caches to speed up file system operations.

The following caches are in paged pool:

- Bitmap cache.
- File header cache.
- Directory data cache.
- Directory index cache.

The following caches are kept in nonpaged pool:

- File identifier cache.
- Extent cache.
- Quota cache.

Therefore, if you set the SYSGEN ACP cache parameters in paged pool to build large caches, make sure your system working set size is large enough that you do not replace XQP disk accesses with page file accesses. For information about detecting and correcting these types of problems, see Chapters 3 and 4.

Do not confuse the XQP caches with RMS caches. The XQP caches file headers, directory blocks, and bitmap file blocks. It also caches directory indexes and free space extents. The XQP is not a general data cache.

The OpenVMS lock manager is used to keep caches synchronized clusterwide.

It is important to remember that the XQP is the basic file system. The file system is mainly concerned with what the files are and where they are. On the other hand, RMS is the record management system. It is mainly concerned with the contents of the files, that is, the records.

FILE HEADER CACHE

Access to a file is controlled by the File Control Block (FCB). The information needed to construct the FCB is located in the file header. To greatly decrease the time needed to open a file, the XQP maintains a cache of file headers. In addition to speeding up file opens, the performance decrease caused by window turns is also decreased, since the file header contains all the mapping information for the file. In addition to opens, any access of the file's attributes requires access to the file header. The size of the file header cache is controlled by the SYSGEN parameter ACP_HDRCACHE. Each entry in the File Header Cache requires its own lock.

BITMAP CACHE

To optimize free space allocation and to minimize I/O operations, the XQP maintains a Bitmap Cache. This cache contains blocks of the bitmap.sys files. Because most free space is allocated from the extent cache on a well-tuned system, and because of the large size of the bitmaps themselves, it is hard to effectively tune the bitmap cache. The size of this cache is controlled by the SYSGEN parameter ACP_MAPCACHE. Only on a heavily fragmented system can you really benefit from the bitmap cache. If you cache the entire bitmap on a volume that is heavily fragmented, performance gains will be seen in the following situations:

- When the file system makes multiple passes over the bitmap cache trying to cache a reasonable amount of disk space in the extent cache.

- When trying to allocate either a contiguous file or extend a contiguous file.

- When satisfying a contiguous-best-try allocation request.

EXTENT CACHE

The extent cache contains a list of known free extents that can be used. An extent is a pointer (consisting of a starting LBN and the size of the fragment starting at this LBN) that maps a contiguous area of disk space. This cache is allocated on a per-disk basis at volume mount time.

The extent cache attempts to maintain a certain fraction of the total volume free space in the cache. SYSGEN parameter ACP_EXTCACHE specifies the maximum number of entries in the cache. In addition, only a certain percentage of the free space on a volume can be contained in the cache. Equation 2-1 shows how the SYSGEN parameter ACP_EXTLIMIT is used to control how many extents are in the cache.

$$\frac{ACP\_EXTLIMIT}{10} \leq percent\ of\ volume\ free\ space\ in\ the\ cache$$

Equation 2-1. Extent Cache Limits

Because of this limitation, on volumes with large amounts of contiguous free space the cache will not contain many entries.

When the file system tries to allocate an extent, the extent cache is used first. If the cache allocation fails, the storage bitmap cache is used; then, if needed, the storage bitmap itself. After the allocation, an attempt is made to refill the extent cache from the bitmap cache, then from the bitmap itself. When the file system returns extents, they are added to the extent cache. If the cache becomes too large, some extents are purged back into the bitmap.

FILE ID CACHE

This cache contains a list of unused file identifiers. This allows the file system not to have to scan the indexf.sys bitmap when allocating new file headers or when freeing used file headers (usually at file creation or deletion). This cache is also allocated on a per-volume basis at mount time. The size of the cache is specified by the SYSGEN parameter ACP_FIDCACHE.

QUOTA CACHE

The quota cache is used to cache disk quota entries. This cache is not used unless you have disk quotas enabled for the volume. This cache is also allocated on a per-volume basis at mount time. The SYSGEN parameter ACP_QUOCACHE specifies the maximum number of quota entries that may be cached. This parameter can be overridden by the mount command.

DIRECTORY FILES

Directory files are just appendages to the real file structure contained in the index file. However, the XQP has a lot of code to make directories work. Directories are nearly indistinguishable from other files. Directories contain file names and file IDs. Once the file ID is known, the rest of the information can be gained from the index file.

Directory files have the following characteristics:

- They are organized sequentially with variable-length records.

- The FCH$V_DIRECTORY bit is set to 1 in the file characteristics field of its header to indicate that it is a directory. This prevents accidental deletion of a nonempty directory.

- They are always created with the extension .DIR;1 and will not function correctly without this extension.

- Records are in alphabetical order of the filenames, with multiple versions of a file stored in one record unless there are so many versions that they will not all fit into one block. In this case a second record is created to store the additional versions in another block. A maximum of sixty-two versions can be entered in one record.

- Subdirectories are file entries in the parent directory.

- Directories must be contiguous.

- If a directory expands, it may have to be moved, since it **must** remain contiguous.

DIRECTORY CACHING

Four directory caches are maintained for directory information: Directory Index Cache, Directory Data Cache, RMS Data Cache, and RMS Path Cache. The XQP maintains the two directory caches, and RMS maintains the other two.

XQP DIRECTORY CACHING

Blocks for a given directory are flushed when the directory is updated. Reads are cached, writes are not. **When a directory file is updated anywhere on a cluster, all of that directory's blocks are flushed from the XQP cache clusterwide.**

DIRECTORY INDEX CACHE

The first XQP cache is the Directory Index Cache. This cache maintains copies of directory blocks in memory (ACP_DINDXCACHE SYSGEN parameter). One page of this is allocated for each open directory if the cache is large enough. The entries are the first fifteen characters of the filename of the last entry in each directory data block. The maximum number of entries per page is thirty-three. If all files in a directory start with the same fifteen characters, this cache loses its effectiveness. This cache allows the file system to do a hashed search of a directory for a given file instead of having to do a linear search of the entire directory.

As the directory file grows in size, the allocation of space for each entry will change. Equation 2-2 shows how the entry size is calculated.

$$Entry\ Size = MAX\{\ 1, (15 - \frac{Size\ of\ Directory}{120}\ )\}$$

Equation 2-2. DINDX Entry Sizing

This result implies that if your mail area directory is larger than 1,200 blocks, all cache entries will have the same value. The resulting search times for a linear lookup result in very poor mail response times.

DIRECTORY DATA CACHE

The second XQP cache is the Directory Data Cache (ACP_DIRCACHE SYSGEN parameter). FCBs for directory files are stored here along with directory data blocks for open directories. This means that the cache contains the contents of recently referenced directories. The number of directory data blocks allowed here depends only on the cache size. ACP_MAXREAD is used to control the maximum number of blocks that will be read into the Directory Data Cache by the XQP per I/O request.

RMS DIRECTORY CACHING

RMS does the directory access if files are being accessed with a wildcard character, as is the case with search lists. RMS maintains two of its own caches. RMS flushes all RMS directory cache entries for a volume when the XQP does any of the following on a volume:

- Supersedes a directory.

- Removes a directory name.

- Clears the directory bit in the file header.

- Mounts the volume.

Thus, running BACKUP on a volume in record mode will cause an RMS cache invalidation each time BACKUP records the data of last backup for each directory file.

RMS DATA CACHE

The first RMS cache is the data cache, which contains the contents of the current directory, if the used portion of the directory is less than 128 blocks. If a directory is larger than 128 blocks, RMS attempts to cache it but runs out of room. In this case a separate operation for each directory entry must be performed, and each operation requires at least three I/Os.

RMS PATH CACHE

The other RMS cache is a path cache, which allows repeated use of a directory tree without accessing and reading through the intervening directories each time. The RMS Path Cache is a list of directory names and file IDs that RMS has recently processed. The purpose of this cache is to reduce the number of calls RMS must make to the XQP when RMS is processing the same subdirectories multiple times.

XQP FUNCTIONS

XQP functions are performed at the queue I/O (QIO) request level. No matter what language or facility you use, including RMS, the functions in Table 2-3 are always done by calls to the XQP.

Function	Description
CREATE	Create a new file.
ACCESS	Open a file.
DEACCESS	Close a file.
MODIFY	Change file header information, such as dates, attributes, and ACL information.
EXTEND	Allocate more space to a file.
TRUNCATE	Deallocate space from a file.
DELETE	Delete a file.

Table 2-3. XQP Functions

WINDOW TURNS

OpenVMS keeps up to ACP_WINDOW mapping pointers for an open file in memory in the window control block (WCB). If a file exists in more than ACP_WINDOW pieces and an access is done to a piece not mapped in memory, then a window turn is performed. That is, the file header block is reaccessed to get new mapping information. Information about how to detect window turns is contained in Chapter 3. What to do about window turns is covered in Chapter 4.

Table 2-4 is the listing of your file's complete mapping pointers. Assume that ACP_WINDOW is set to 3. Your program opens the file. Then the file system will map the first three extents into the WCB for the open file:

- WCB 1 maps VBN 1-24.

- WCB 2 maps VBN 25-30.

- WCB 3 maps VBN 31-33.

Your program reads three blocks starting at VBN 4. Then your program issues an I/O to read three blocks starting at VBN 36. However, first the file system must perform a window turn to load the appropriate mapping pointer into the WCB for your file. Loading the WCB can take several I/Os, depending on the state of the File-11 caches.

LBNs	Size	VBNs
2002	21	1-24
160	6	25-30
30001	3	31-33
171	30	34-63

Table 2-4. File's Mapping Pointers

SPLIT I/OS

An I/O request cannot read across a mapping pointer directly. If you request data that resides in more than one mapping pointer, the device driver will split your single I/O into several I/Os that request the same data but only request data from a single mapping pointer for each I/O. There is no feedback to your process that this has occurred.

In Table 2-4, when your program issues an I/O to read sixteen blocks starting at VBN 26, the file system must issue three reads to satisfy your program's request: one to LBN 160 for five blocks, one to LBN 30001 for three blocks, and one to LBN 171 for eighteen blocks.

Although this is only an example, unless you have taken active steps to reduce the fragmentation of your files, most of the files on your OpenVMS disks will be much like this. The reason for this is that the file system, by default, allocates disk clusters on a first-fit basis.

There are a number of reasons for this default action:

1. Originally, there were few spare CPU cycles or extra memory to attempt to create files in any other manner. First-fit is a very fast and low-overhead method. This method also makes efficient use of the Files-11 caches.

2. In a multiuser environment, the value of file continuity is decreased. While one user is reading a file sequentially, another user can also be reading a file sequentially. OpenVMS will time-share the access to the file system. Without a way for the two files being accessed to be located in contiguous disk VBN, there will still be seeks as the LBNs of the different files are accessed in a random pattern. If the two files are located at opposite ends of the disk, the fact that both files are contiguous will not prevent the disk heads from seeking the entire width of the disk if the I/Os being serviced are switched from one file to the other.

3. If the files being accessed are not being accessed sequentially, and if the files are very large, then the order of I/Os will cause the disk heads to seek, reducing the value of the contiguous nature of the files.

QUEUE I/O REQUEST

The $QIO call issues (queues) an I/O request to a channel. $QIO operates only on assigned I/O channels (for example, $ASSIGN), and the request completes asynchronously, that is, it returns to the calling code immediately after the request is queued. It is the responsibility of the calling code to synchronize the I/O completion with other events.

One or more of the following process quotas are required to issue an I/O request:

DIOLM (Direct I/O Limit) — A direct I/O is performed directly from a device into or out of the user's virtual memory that has been locked into physical memory. A process with a direct I/O in progress cannot be swapped out or deleted.

BIOLM (Buffered I/O Limit) — A buffered I/O, on the other hand, is buffered via nonpaged pool, thus allowing the user process to be swapped or even deleted.

BYTLM (Buffered I/O Byte Limit) — The buffered I/O byte limit is the maximum number of bytes of nonpaged system dynamic memory that a user's job can use at any one time. The amount used for an I/O will depend on the exact I/O being processed. Buffered I/O is a major consumer of BYTLM.

CHANNELCNT (Channel Count) — The channel count is the total number of I/O channels available to a process. An I/O channel is required before you can make a connection between a user process and an output device.

ASTLM (Asynchronous System Trap Limit) — The asynchronous system trap limit is the number of outstanding ASTs that a process can have at any time. ASTs are the mechanism for signaling asynchronous events to a process.

A shortage in any one of these quotas can cause the QIO either to fail or to enter a resource wait state.

RMS FUNCTIONS

Anything that RMS does that resembles XQP functions is done by RMS making QIO calls to the XQP.

VMSCLUSTER I/O

There are additional I/O issues unique to VMSclusters. In this section I will cover some of the I/O-related issues for clusters. If the system you are tuning is not part of a cluster, you can skip the rest of this chapter.

MSCP

Working in conjunction with the Distributed Lock Manager, the Mass Storage Control Protocol (MSCP) server lets the system manager provide simultaneous read and write access to those disks by all cluster nodes that have the disks mounted. As of OpenVMS V5.4, MSCP load balancing is implemented. Bear in mind that once an MSCP link is established (a device is mounted), MSCP will not dynamically reassign the serving node, regardless of how the MSCP load balance has changed, if you are running OpenVMS VAX V5.5-2 or earlier.

HOW MSCP WORKS

To be able to understand and analyze MSCP, some background information about how MSCP buffers are used is needed. The procedure, briefly, is as follows.

When an I/O request is sent to a device that is not local to the requesting node, the requesting node sends its request for I/O to the MSCP server on the node that serves that disk. When the MSCP server processes an I/O request, it places the data into its own special memory buffer before sending it over the hardware connection to the requesting node (CI, NI, and so on). The amount of space in the MSCP buffer area reserved for the requesting node is determined by an algorithm within the MSCP code.

This algorithm takes into account the total amount of MSCP buffer space and allocates what it considers a reasonable percentage of this space for the requested I/O. The algorithm computes both a maximum fragment size (the highest number of buffer pages it will reserve for a single I/O request) and a minimum fragment size (the lowest number of contiguous buffer pages that must be available to service any I/O request).

MSCP Terms

There are three performance/monitoring terms associated with MSCP. To explain these terms, I will give a simplistic example of an MSCP I/O.

1. **Fragmented Request Rate** — The I/O from the requesting node needs sixty-four blocks of data from the disk. The MSCP server has only 128 pages in its buffer. (SYSGEN MSCP_BUFFER was set to 128, the default.) Since the server has to consider that other nodes may also have I/O requests, it will not give away the entire buffer to any one request. Based on this rather small buffer size, the algorithm might decide that it can safely give out only thirty-two of these pages to satisfy the I/O request; that is, the algorithm computes a maximum fragment size of 32. MSCP sees that the I/O request (sixty-four blocks) will not fit into its maximum fragment size, so it divides the I/O request size by two. Thus, the sixty-four-block I/O request has to be fragmented into two data transfers of thirty-two blocks each.

2. **Extra Fragment Rate** — If the MSCP buffer area does not have enough contiguous space to fulfill the thirty-two-block I/O request size, the I/O request size would be halved again. So we now need sixteen contiguous pages. There are sixteen contiguous pages left in the buffer, so MSCP reserves those sixteen pages and services the I/O request, this time in four separate I/O requests to the disk (64/16=4). From a performance standpoint, this is a more serious problem than the fragmented request rate.

3. **Buffer Wait Rate** — A buffer wait is the strongest indicator that the MSCP buffer area is badly fragmented and its size needs to be increased. MSCP computes a minimum fragment size. If it cannot find enough contiguous space in the MSCP buffer to accommodate this minimum size, it will not attempt to service the I/O request until more space in the buffer is freed, that is, until other I/O requests have been serviced. Smaller fragment sizes mean more physical I/O to the disk, more bus arbitration, or more overhead to satisfy a single logical I/O request.

Controlling MSCP

Almost all functions of the MSCP server are controlled by SYSGEN parameters. The MSCP SYSGEN parameters and their definitions follow:

MSCP_BUFFER — Specifies the number of pages to be allocated to the MSCP server's local buffer area. This buffer area is the space used by the server to transfer data between the client system and local disks.

MSCP_CREDITS — Specifies the number of outstanding I/O requests that can be active from one client system.

MSCP_SERVE_ALL — Controls the serving of disks during a system boot. Valid values are:

0   Do not serve any disk. This is the default value.

1   Serve all available disks.

2   Serve only locally attached (non-HSC) disks.

If the MSCP_LOAD system parameter is zero, MSCP_SERVE_ALL is ignored.

MSCP_LOAD — Controls the loading of the MSCP server during a system boot. Valid values are:

0   Do not load the MSCP server. This is the default value.

1   Load the MSCP server and serve disks as specified by the SYSGEN parameter MSCP_SERVE_ALL.

MSCP LOAD BALANCING

With OpenVMS V5.5-2 there are two ways to load-balance your MSCP-served disks. If the MSCP_SERVE_ALL parameter is set to 1, the server will monitor MSCP traffic for load balancing. The MSCP_LOAD parameter is used to specify the load capacity of the server. If MSCP_LOAD is set to 1, the load capacity is set to the default value of the server's CPU. If MSCP_LOAD is set to a value greater than 1, the server's load capacity is set to the value of MSCP_LOAD. Prior to OpenVMS VAX V6.0, there is no dynamic load balancing. The load balancing occurs only when a disk is mounted or a failover occurs.

When a system attempts to mount a disk that is MSCP-served and there is more than one server for that disk, the serving system is selected on the basis of the system with the largest load availability rating.

All systems that serve MSCP disks maintain a load availability rating that is calculated as shown in Equation 2-3.

$$Load\ Availability = LOAD\ CAPACITY - \frac{\sum_{i=1}^{20} OP\_COUNT}{20}$$

Equation 2-3. MSCP Load Availability

The load capacity for a system depends on the system type. Table 2-5 lists current load capacity ratings for some CPUs. The program in Appendix J can be used to determine the load availability, load capacity, and operation counts.

Default Load Capacity	OpenVMS CPU Types
45	VAXstation 3100, MicroVAX 3100
70	VAX 11/780
100	VAX 11/785, VAX 86xx
130	MicroVAX 3300, MicroVAX 3400
165	MicroVAX 3500/3600/3800/3900
	VAX 4000-xxx
340	VAX 6000-xxx, VAX 9000-xxx
340	All AXP Systems

Table 2-5. MSCP Server Load Capacity

MSCP DYNAMIC LOAD BALANCING

With the upgrade to OpenVMS VAX V6.0, MSCP dynamic load balancing is implemented to efficiently balance the I/O load among serving systems in the cluster. Dynamic load balancing can result in better I/O performance, better workload balance within the cluster, and faster I/O response.

Dynamic load balancing is checked every 5 seconds. If the server activity is determined to be excessive, the I/O load for MSCP is automatically shifted to other servers in the VMScluster. Server activity is considered excessive when the "load available" value is less than or equal to 10. To determine "load availability" for your system, run the program in Appendix J and check the line "Load Available is."

Each MSCP server checks its load availability every 5 seconds. If load availability is less than or equal to 10, the server initiates dynamic load balancing. Dynamic load balancing works like this:

1. The overloaded server selects the disk with the highest read/write-operations-per-second rate that has not been involved in load balancing in the last 30 seconds.

2. A load balance request is sent to all MSCP nodes with MSCP_SERVE_ALL set to 1.

3. If all of the following on the receiving node are true:

28

- load availability is greater than 10,

- the addition of the load for the new device is less than load availability - 10,

- the node can serve the new device,

then the receiving node tells the requesting node that this system is willing to acquire the serving of the device.

4. The first node to respond with a "willing to acquire" to the overloaded node is selected as the new serving node, and the overloaded node "fails" the disk serving over to that node.

File System Analysis

A MAJOR FACTOR IN OVERALL SYSTEM PERFORMANCE IS THE EFFECTIVE USE OF THE DISK I/O resources. One of the most-used measures of disk I/O performance is average response time. Average response time is the elapsed time between when the program issues the $QIO and the data requested is available to the program. The time required to perform a disk seek is the major factor in average response time. Faster seeks are one major key to faster file performance.

Notice that only 8 percent of the average response time is based on the CPU (see Table 3-1). This is why buying a faster CPU for a disk I/O-bound system has little or no effect.

Component	Cost	Based On
I/O Setup	4%	CPU Speed
Controller Latency	2%	Controller
Seek Time	58%	Disk
Rotation Latency	20%	Disk
Transfer Time	12%	Controller/Disk
I/O Post Processing	4%	CPU Speed

Table 3-1. I/O Costs on Typical Disk Transfer

CHECKING FOR PROBLEMS

To check for problems on your system, issue the DCL command MONITOR IO and observe the direct input/output (DIO) and buffered input/output (BIO) rates. If your system is not performing any direct or buffered I/O, you do not have a file system problem. Otherwise, there may be a problem, so read on.

Figure 3-1 shows the sample output of the DCL command MONITOR IO. The row labeled "Direct I/O Rate" is used to determine the level at which your system is accessing the file system.

```
┌─────────────────────────────────────────────────────────────────────┐
│ ▭          ▓▓▓▓▓▓▓▓▓▓▓  OpenVMS Performance  ▓▓▓▓▓▓▓▓▓▓▓      ◄ ▭ │
├─────────────────────────────────────────────────────────────────────┤
│  File   Edit   Commands   Options   Print                      Help  │
├─────────────────────────────────────────────────────────────────────┤
│                      OpenVMS Monitor Utility                     ▲   │
│                      I/O SYSTEM STATISTICS                           │
│                        on node XXXXXX                                │
│                          SUMMARY                                     │
│                                                                      │
│                            CUR       AVE       MIN       MAX         │
│                                                                      │
│     Direct I/O Rate        22.22     26.89      8.59    208.30       │
│     Buffered I/O Rate      30.86     34.54      7.50    122.48       │
│     Mailbox Write Rate      0.00      0.91      0.00     41.78       │
│     Split Transfer Rate     1.08      1.70      0.00     19.67       │
│     Log Name Translation Rate 125.77 133.35    30.31   2142.99       │
│     File Open Rate          6.79      7.81      1.53     34.74       │
│                                                                      │
│     Page Fault Rate        60.49     57.31     26.91    160.06       │
│     Page Read Rate          0.00      8.48      0.00     54.74       │
│     Page Read I/O Rate      0.00      2.79      0.00     15.59       │
│     Page Write Rate         0.00      0.59      0.00    144.49       │
│     Page Write I/O Rate     0.00      0.01      0.00      2.49       │
│     Inswap Rate             0.15      0.01      0.00      0.46       │
│     Free List Size       1816.00   3121.66    222.00   6497.00   ▮   │
│     Modified List Size   2372.00   2716.09   2209.00   3825.00       │
├─────────────────────────────────────────────────────────────────────┤
│  PLAYBACK                     SUMMARIZING                        ▼   │
└─────────────────────────────────────────────────────────────────────┘
```

Figure 3-1. I/O System Statistics

GETTING STARTED

To get a feel for the current performance of your file system, you will need to generate a chart of the average response time for each disk. To collect the data for this chart, use MONITOR DISK to collect disk I/O operation rates and disk I/O queue lengths for all systems using these disks.

Figure 3-2 shows the output of the DCL command MONITOR DISK /ITEM= OPERATION_RATE. The data you need for generating your chart is found in the AVE column.

Output from the DCL command MONITOR DISK/ITEM=QUEUE_LENGTH is shown in Figure 3-3. The data you need for generating your chart is found in the AVE column. For a disk that is accessible from more than one node in a cluster environment, you will need to collect monitor data for all nodes that mount the disk. With this data, generate a combined summary report and use the values found in the ROW SUM column. Figures 3-2 and 3-3 reflect a single-node environment for purposes of simplification.

```
┌────────────────────────────────────────────────────────────────────┐
│ ▬                      OpenVMS Performance                    ▬  ▭   │
├────────────────────────────────────────────────────────────────────┤
│  File   Edit   Commands   Options   Print                      Help  │
├────────────────────────────────────────────────────────────────────┤
│                      OpenVMS Monitor Utility                      ▲  │
│                       DISK I/O STATISTICS                            │
│                        on node XXXXXX                                │
│                           SUMMARY                                    │
│                                                                      │
│ I/O Operation Rate                     CUR      AVE      MIN     MAX  │
│                                                                      │
│ ASCAXP$DKA0:        SYSAXP            47.68    50.68    23.04   99.84 │
│ ASCAXP$DKA100:      SMSDSK             0.00     0.45     0.00   10.57 │
│ ASCAXP$DKA200:      DSK000             0.00     0.00     0.00    0.00 │
│ ASCAXP$DKB100:      DSK001             0.00     0.00     0.00    0.00 │
│ ASCAXP$DKB200:      DSK002             0.00     0.09     0.00    8.73 │
│ ASCAXP$DKB300:      DSK003             0.61     9.04     0.00  165.36 │
│ ASCAXP$DKC100:      DSK004            15.74    15.58     0.00   51.61 │
│ ASCAXP$DKC200:      DSK005             7.87    11.98     3.96  140.86 │
│ ASCAXP$DKC300:      DSK006             0.00     0.00     0.00    0.00 │
│ ASCAXP$DKD100:      DSK007             0.00     0.00     0.00    0.00 │
│ ASCAXP$DKE100:      AXPFTDFEB931       0.00     0.00     0.00    0.00 │
│ ASC387$DKA300:      SYS387     (R)     0.00     0.00     0.00    0.00 │
│ ASC360$DKA300:      SYS360     (R)     0.00     0.00     0.00    0.00 │
│ ASC311$DKA300:      SYS311     (R)     0.00     0.00     0.00    0.00 │
│ ASC383$DKA300:      SYS383     (R)     0.00     0.00     0.00    0.00 │
│                                                                      │
│  PLAYBACK                     SUMMARIZING                          ▼  │
└────────────────────────────────────────────────────────────────────┘
```

Figure 3-2. I/O Operation Rate

```
┌────────────────────────────────────────────────────────────────────┐
│ ▬                      OpenVMS Performance                    ▬  ▭   │
├────────────────────────────────────────────────────────────────────┤
│  File   Edit   Commands   Options   Print                      Help  │
├────────────────────────────────────────────────────────────────────┤
│                      OpenVMS Monitor Utility                      ▲  │
│                       DISK I/O STATISTICS                            │
│                        on node XXXXXX                                │
│                           SUMMARY                                    │
│                                                                      │
│ I/O Request Queue Length              CUR     AVE     MIN     MAX    │
│                                                                      │
│ ASCAXP$DKA0:        SYSAXP           1.23    1.74    0.00    8.94    │
│ ASCAXP$DKA100:      SMSDSK           0.00    0.00    0.00    0.58    │
│ ASCAXP$DKA200:      DSK000           0.00    0.00    0.00    0.00    │
│ ASCAXP$DKB100:      DSK001           0.00    0.00    0.00    0.00    │
│ ASCAXP$DKB200:      DSK002           0.00    0.00    0.00    0.31    │
│ ASCAXP$DKB300:      DSK003           0.00    0.08    0.00    0.78    │
│ ASCAXP$DKC100:      DSK004           0.77    0.33    0.00    1.88    │
│ ASCAXP$DKC200:      DSK005           0.61    0.24    0.00    1.42    │
│ ASCAXP$DKC300:      DSK006           0.00    0.00    0.00    0.00    │
│ ASCAXP$DKD100:      DSK007           0.00    0.00    0.00    0.00    │
│ ASCAXP$DKE100:      AXPFTDFEB931     0.00    0.00    0.00    0.00    │
│ ASC387$DKA300:      SYS387     (R)   0.00    0.00    0.00    0.00    │
│ ASC360$DKA300:      SYS360     (R)   0.00    0.00    0.00    0.00    │
│ ASC311$DKA300:      SYS311     (R)   0.00    0.00    0.00    0.00    │
│ ASC383$DKA300:      SYS383     (R)   0.00    0.00    0.00    0.00    │
│                                                                   ▼  │
└────────────────────────────────────────────────────────────────────┘
```

Figure 3-3. I/O Request Queue

Calculate the average response time using the formula in Equation 3-1, which comes from John D. Little's "A Proof for the Queuing Formula: L=AW," *Operations Research*, 1961. This formula is derived from Little's Law, which states that the waiting time in the system is equal to number of customers divided by average arrival rate over the long run.

$$Average\ Response\ Time = 1000.0\ X\ \frac{\sum_{i=1}^{\#\ Mount\ Count} I/O\ Request\ Queue\ Length}{\sum_{i=1}^{\#\ Mount\ Count} I/O\ Operation\ Rate}$$

Equation 3-1. Average Response Time

A value between 25 to 40 milliseconds is average. As you can see from the data in Table 3-2, there is a problem with DSK024 and DSK112, and there is a possible problem with DSK036. Your time should be spent determining the cause of the load on these disks.

Disk	Queue	I/O	Response Time
DSK024	0.71	11.65	60.94
DSK035	0.07	1.85	37.84
DSK109	0.26	6.83	38.07
DSK112	1.60	20.11	79.56
DSK029	0.51	15.01	33.98
DSK036	0.16	3.32	48.19

Table 3-2. Average Response Time

The average response time measurement is useful because it indicates the perceived delay independent of the cause of the delay. Disks that have the largest average response times are the ones to work on first.

TYPES OF DISK PROBLEMS
Disk problems come in four basic classes:

1. Seek-intensive.

2. Data-transfer-intensive.

3. Overhead-intensive.

4. Controller blockage.

34

Disks that exhibit high operation rates are usually seek-intensive, and data-transfer-intensive disks have lower operation rates. Both types cause a high average response time. These are not absolute rules, however. Controller blockage can cause seek-intensive problems to look just like data-transfer-intensive problems. Knowledge of your system is essential for any performance work.

Using the program in Appendix K, we can get values for I/O rates and queue lengths for several disks over a long period of time. From this raw data we can create a table , such as the one shown in Table 3-3. Since tabular data is not always easy to understand, we can convert this data into the plot shown in Figure 3-4.

Queue Depth	I/O Rate	Average Access	Queue Depth	I/O Rate	Average Access	Queue Depth	I/O Rate	Average Access
0.10	2.30	43.48	0.50	12.10	41.32	1.00	16.50	60.61
0.10	20.70	4.83	0.50	22.40	22.32	1.10	31.00	35.48
0.10	5.10	19.61	0.50	15.40	32.47	1.10	26.90	40.89
0.10	9.80	10.20	0.60	24.50	24.49	1.10	28.40	38.73
0.20	3.10	64.52	0.60	16.40	36.59	1.10	77.10	14.27
0.20	10.20	19.61	0.60	18.20	32.97	1.30	25.30	51.38
0.20	7.80	25.64	0.70	24.00	29.17	1.30	18.60	69.89
0.20	15.00	13.33	0.70	20.90	33.49	1.40	12.60	111.11
0.30	31.10	9.65	0.70	21.50	32.56	1.40	24.10	58.09
0.30	15.60	19.23	0.70	23.50	29.79	1.40	60.70	23.06
0.30	20.40	14.71	0.90	38.20	23.56	1.40	54.40	25.74
0.30	29.60	10.14	0.90	24.10	37.34	1.50	24.70	60.73
0.40	15.00	26.67	0.90	20.70	43.48	1.50	28.80	52.08
0.40	16.80	23.81	0.90	17.50	51.43	1.70	43.70	38.90
0.40	11.80	33.90	1.00	42.40	23.58	2.20	43.60	50.46
0.40	19.40	20.62	1.00	24.80	40.32	2.30	45.20	50.88
0.50	5.50	90.91	1.00	29.80	33.56	2.30	60.10	38.27

Table 3-3. Access Data

The chart in Figure 3-4 clearly shows which disks to spend time on with further investigations. Those disks with low I/O rates and excessive queues (plot points below the shaded triangle) are usually a result of one of the following problems:

- Data-transfer-intensive.

- Overhead-intensive.

- Controller blockage.

Those disks that have high I/O rates and excessive queues (plot points above the shaded triangle) are usually a result of the following problem:

- Seek-intensive.

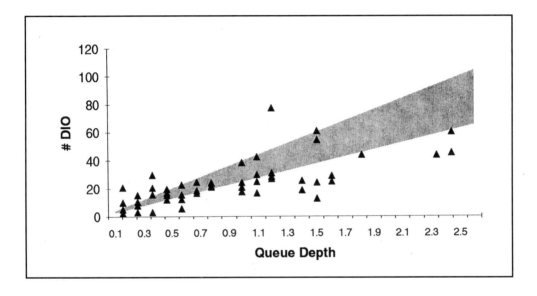

Figure 3-4. Disk Response

Hopefully, most of your data points will fall within the 25- to 40-millisecond range (plot points within the shaded triangle).

Using the program in Appendix K, we can collect data from two disks that are connected to the same SCSI controller. If we examine the data for each disk in Table 3-4, we can see the blockage. You will see that when there is a queue on disk1, the response time for disk2 greatly increases.

Disk1			Disk2		
I/O Rate	Queue	Average Response Time	I/O Rate	Queue	Average Response Time
206	10	48.54	47	3	63.83
223	4	17.94	22	2	90.91
211	10	47.40	40	1	25.00
355	12	33.80	82	5	60.98
170	2	11.76	47	2	42.55

Table 3-4. Controller Blockage

FRAGMENTATION

Often, a major cause of seek-intensive disk problems is fragmentation. A file is said to be fragmented if there are two or more file header mapping pointers. Fragmentation is severe if there are so many file header mapping pointers that more than one file header is needed to store all the mapping pointers.

There are several ways to determine whether a file is fragmented. I will start with a very general method and work my way toward more specific methods.

MONITOR UTILITY

There are two basic monitor commands that will show whether you have disk fragmentation: MONITOR FCP and MONITOR IO.

MONITOR FCP

This command shows disk read, write, and erase rates. If the sum of the XQP rates is a significant percentage of the overall I/O operation rate, you need to attempt to make improvements to reduce XQP disk I/Os from one of three sources: fragmentation, cache misses, and erase operations.

Window turns are a direct result of disk fragmentation. In Figure 3-5, a nonzero window turn rate indicates fragmentation.

```
┌─────────────────────────────────────────────────────────────────────────┐
│ ─     ▓▓▓▓▓▓▓▓▓▓▓▓ OpenVMS Performance ▓▓▓▓▓▓▓▓▓▓▓▓      ▫ ▫ │
├─────────────────────────────────────────────────────────────────────────┤
│  File   Edit   Commands   Options   Print                      Help      │
├─────────────────────────────────────────────────────────────────────────┤
│                      OpenVMS Monitor Utility                          ▲  │
│                     FILE PRIMITIVE STATISTICS                            │
│                         on node XXXXXX                                   │
│                           SUMMARY                                        │
│                                                                          │
│                          CUR      AVE      MIN      MAX                   │
│                                                                          │
│       FCP Call Rate      30.70    30.96    7.35     99.20                 │
│       Allocation Rate     0.00     0.31    0.00      4.25                 │
│       Create Rate         0.00     0.11    0.00      0.94                 │
│                                                                          │
│       Disk Read Rate      0.00     0.29    0.00     17.29                 │
│       Disk Write Rate     0.00     0.48    0.00      4.09                 │
│       Volume Lock Wait Rate 0.00   0.00    0.00      0.30                 │
│                                                                          │
│       CPU Tick Rate       2.77     2.14    0.31      5.97                 │
│       File Sys Page Fault Rate 0.00 0.00   0.00      0.00                 │
│       Window Turn Rate    0.00     0.29    0.00      4.09                 │
│                                                                          │
│       File Lookup Rate   23.91    22.01    4.61     66.66              ■  │
│       File Open Rate      6.79     7.81    1.53     34.74                 │
│       Erase Rate          0.00     0.00    0.00      0.15                 │
│                                                                          │
│  PLAYBACK                SUMMARIZING                                   ▼  │
└─────────────────────────────────────────────────────────────────────────┘
```

Figure 3-5. File Primitive Statistics

The ratio of window turn rate to overall I/O operation rate indicates the level of fragmentation. To measure the severity of disk fragmentation, use Equation 3-2.

$$DFSeverity\_rate = 100.0 * \frac{WindowTurn\ Rate}{Direct\ I/O\ Rate}$$

Equation 3-2. Disk Fragmentation Severity

This equation is not very exact, but several refinements will be presented as we go along.

MONITOR IO

This command gives the rates of direct I/Os and buffered I/Os and also gives the numbers for split I/Os. A large split transfer rate from Figure 3-1 indicates fragmentation, since split I/Os usually are caused by fragmentation.

Equation 3-3 yields the split I/O severity rate. If you find the value from Equation 3-3 to be more than 25 percent, you need to investigate further.

$$SIOSeverity\_rate = 100.0 * \frac{Split\ I/O\ Rate}{Direct\ I/O\ Rate}$$

Equation 3-3. Split I/O Severity

Split I/Os can be caused by factors other than fragmentation. This split I/O severity value is only an indication of possible fragmentation. It is possible to have a very high split I/O severity value without any fragmentation, but you cannot have a very low split I/O severity value if fragmentation is a problem.

PMS DATABASE

The second way to determine the extent of file fragmentation on your system is to use the PMS database. You can access this database with the OpenVMS ANALYZE/SYSTEM command or by writing a program, in the language of your choice, that references the PMS$ symbols. Appendix A contains a program that shows PMS information about window turns and split I/Os. The output from that program is shown in Figure 3-6.

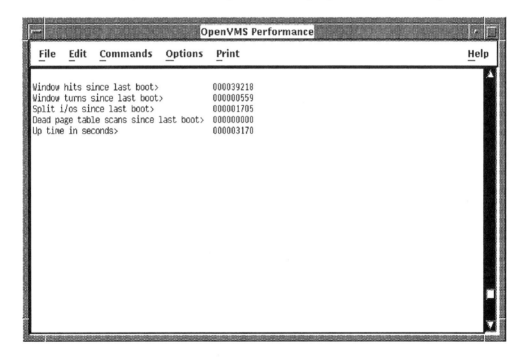

Figure 3-6. PMS Output Listing

By using the PMS database, you can calculate a very good value for how bad a fragmentation problem you have. Since the values used in the PMS versions of the equations are actual counts, they are much more accurate than the "rate" values from the MONITOR reports.

All data in the PMS database is local to your node and is a cumulative value since the time the node was booted.

Using PMS data, we can calculate the values found in Equation 3-4. However, since these values are calculated from counts that could cover large time frames, we need to collect only those counts that occur during the time in which we wish to do our analysis.

$$DFSeverity\_rate = 100.0 * \frac{Window\ Turn\ Count}{Direct\ I/O\ Count}$$

$$SIOSeverity\_rate = 100.0 * \frac{Split\ I/O\ Count}{Direct\ I/O\ Count}$$

Equation 3-4. PMS Severity Calculations

This can be done easily by getting the appropriate PMS values at the beginning of the analysis time and at the end of the analysis time. We then use the difference in the counts for our analysis. Using the program in Appendix K, we can collect data points for the delta change in the values over an extended period of time at regular intervals. The program in Appendix K collects the PMS values on 10-second intervals. If we plot these values, we can do an even better analysis.

With the plot in Figure 3-7, we can determine whether there are problems with window turns and/or split I/Os and can determine whether the problem is ongoing or occurs only during specific times. If there is a problem and it is not continuous, there is need to investigate further. It may well be that a certain process, program, or user is causing the fragmentation problems. Using image accounting data, we can determine which programs were run during the period of high window turn and/or split I/O activity.

FILE HEADER DUMP

You can determine the fragmentation of a specific file using the VMS DUMP command. To dump out a file header and look at the file fragmentation level, enter the DCL command:

```
DUMP/HEADER/BLOCK=COUNT=0 file.ext
```

Appendix B shows the output from this command. The map area shows the mapping of file logical blocks to disk blocks. Under the map area section is a listing of each fragment of the file. Listed for each fragment are the count of blocks in the fragment and the starting virtual disk block location. If there is more than one retrieval pointer, the file has some fragmentation. If there are more pointers than the value of SYSGEN parameter ACP_WINDOW, there is a real problem.

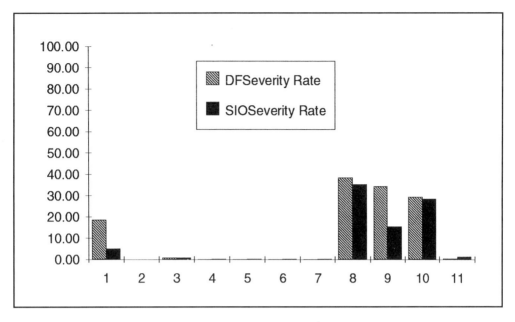

Figure 3-7. PMS Severity Plots

FINDING ALL FRAGMENTED FILES

You must be able to determine all files on a disk that are fragmented. From your DECUS Local Users Group you can obtain a copy of the VMS Symposia tapes at little or no cost. There is a utility called INDEX on the tape that you may want to use to determine which files on a disk are fragmented. The command:

```
$ INDEX /DISPLAY=( EXTENTS, HEADERS) /EXTENTS= 'F$GETSYI("ACP_WINDOWS")'
```

will display all files with more than SYSGEN ACP_WINDOWS file mapping pointers (see Figure 3-8). These files are potentially performance bottlenecks.

Other files that are potential bottlenecks are files with extension headers. These files can be found with the command:

```
$ INDEX /DISPLAY=( EXTENTS, HEADERS) /HEADERS=1
```

If the files located from either of these commands are in active use, you may want to reduce the fragmentation level by making a new copy of the file with the command:

```
$COPY/CONTIGUOUS FILE.EXE;n FILE.EXT;n+1
```

If the copy fails, you will need to defragment your disk to reduce the number of extents in the file and to make more contiguous space available.

41

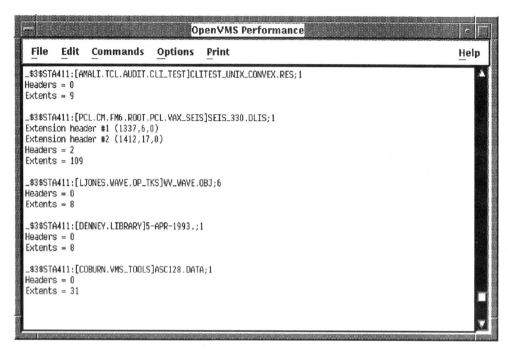

Figure 3-8. INDEX Output Listing

FRAGMENTATION COST

The following example illustrates the high cost of fragmentation. First, create two files where one is contiguous and the other is fragmented and each is 1,000 blocks in size. The fragmented file is structured as shown in Table 3-5.

Fragment Count	Number of Blocks
1 Fragment	462 Blocks
1 Fragment	366 Blocks
3 Fragments	4 Blocks
80 Fragments	2 Blocks

Table 3-5. Fragmentation Index

Use a simple program to issue 2,000 QIOs, each of which reads in three blocks. The logical block to read is determined by a random number. The result is displayed in Table 3-6.

	Fragmented	Contiguous
Window Hits	2305.0	2000.0
Window Turns	1222.0	0.0
Split I/Os	302.0	0.0
DIOs	2000.0	2000.0
CPU Time	14.1	6.7
Elapsed Time	76.0	59.0

Table 3-6. Cost of Fragmentation

In this simple example there was an increased CPU time of approximately 100 percent and an increased elapsed time of approximately 30 percent. While this is only a test program, it does show that fragmentation overhead can be very high. In most real programs you will be doing things other than I/Os, but the cost of fragmentation will still exist. The difference between fragmented versus contiguous files for both "CPU Time" and "Elapsed Time" will decrease as the percentage of time spent doing I/O decreases.

DATA TRANSFER PROBLEMS

Another concern for file system performance is data transfers. Note, however, that Digital states that in a typical time-sharing environment, 90 percent of I/O transfers are smaller than sixteen blocks. If you have a time-sharing environment and are running MSCP-served disk, you can get a feel for the average I/O transfer size from the command that generated Figure 3-11 (see the Detecting MSCP Problems section of this chapter). In a software development environment where our basic tasks are editing, compiling, linking, and running with the debugger, the vast majority of I/Os are less than thirty-two blocks in size.

Since data transfer problems are limited, I will not spend considerable time trying to detect and tune for that set of problems.

DETECTING DATA TRANSFER PROBLEMS

Two basic monitor commands indicate disk transfer problems:

MONITOR DISK — Shows the I/O operation rates and the I/O request queue length.

MONITOR IO — Gives the rates of direct I/Os and buffered I/Os and the numbers for split I/Os.

A low operation rate combined with a high request queue length is a good indicator of disk transfer problems. A low direct I/O rate and a large split I/O rate indicates a data transfer problem.

ACCOUNTING UTILITY

Accounting data can be useful in understanding resource use. If you keep image-level accounting data, you can obtain a more detailed understanding. However, be aware that image-level accounting involves a huge amount of overhead in disk space, CPU time, and disk bandwidth. In many cases you will find that it is useful to know what was running during the time a performance event occurred. With image accounting data you can get a much better-detailed view of which programs your system was running during the period of interest.

To determine which images are heavy I/O users, generate an accounting summary report using the command:

```
$ ACCOUNTING/ TYPE=IMAGE /OUT=file.list /SUMMARY=IMAGE -
/REPORT=(PROCESSOR, ELAPSED, DIRECT_IO, PAGE_READ, RECORDS )
```

Note the following points:

- Processor time indicates the highest consumer of CPU.

- Direct I/O identifies which images are the consumers of the file system. This data can be used to determine the highest percentage users of I/O for CPU and elapsed time.

- The heaviest hard page faulters (a hard page fault requires a disk I/O) are noted by page reads.

- There is one record for each image activation. By installing the most-used images and their related sections, you can sometimes reduce overall hard page faulting.

Figure 3-9 shows sample output that you can use to locate programs that are using a large number of direct I/Os.

Another report that will be of major interest is the report that shows what programs were running during a given period of time. Using this report you can often determine which programs were causing your system to slow down. The following DCL command will produce a list of images running during a selected time interval:

```
$ ACCOUNTING/ TYPE=IMAGE /SINCE=Time1 / BEFORE=Time2 /OUT=file.list
```

```
┌──────────────────────── OpenVMS Performance ──────────────────────────┐
│ File   Edit   Commands   Options   Print                       Help   │
├───────────────────────────────────────────────────────────────────────┤
│ From:                VMS Accounting Report                            │
│              Time          Time        I/O   Reads    Records         │
│ Image name   Processor     Elapsed     Direct Page IO  Total          │
│ ─────────────────────────────────────────────────────────────────────│
│ DECC$COMPIL  0 00:04:59.77  0 00:32:13.48  11011  2559   66           │
│ SEARCH       0 00:00:28.18  0 00:01:08.43   4739    38    6           │
│ LINK         0 00:00:08.54  0 00:05:48.63   4254   332   27           │
│ UTOOL        0 00:00:03.32  0 00:00:06.40     26    19    1           │
│ BUILD_PROCE  0 00:00:03.20  0 00:06:41.30    604   134    5           │
│ BUILD_DG_C   0 00:00:02.49  0 00:00:55.09    359   529   23           │
│ EXPAND_FILE  0 00:00:02.15  0 00:00:44.53    263   352   16           │
│ BUILD_UPDAT  0 00:00:01.51  0 00:00:58.60    343    46    2           │
│ ACC          0 00:00:01.42  0 00:00:29.77    109   193   16           │
│ LIBRARIAN    0 00:00:01.23  0 00:00:44.85    610    61    5           │
│ BUILD_DG_LN  0 00:00:01.14  0 00:00:35.45    212   368   16           │
│ BUILD_DEPEN  0 00:00:01.00  0 00:00:08.08    203    59    2           │
│ CHTOOL       0 00:00:00.80  0 00:00:02.50     32    19    1           │
│ MONITOR_TV   0 00:00:00.69  0 00:05:04.70    109   194    3           │
│ BUILD_DG_FO  0 00:00:00.65  0 00:00:21.68    109   230   10           │
│ BUILD_EXPAN  0 00:00:00.60  0 00:00:28.49     93   259   12           │
│ BUILD_DELET  0 00:00:00.52  0 00:00:08.43     50    24    1           │
│ EDT_TV       0 00:00:00.48  0 00:01:38.29     42   102    2           │
│ DELETE       0 00:00:00.48  0 00:00:22.02    126   166   27           │
│ TYPE         0 00:00:00.45  0 00:00:27.45     19    60    9           │
└───────────────────────────────────────────────────────────────────────┘
```

Figure 3-9. OpenVMS VAX Accounting Program

FILE SYSTEM OVERHEAD

The last major area covered is the file system (XQP) I/O activity. The output from MONITOR FCP lists the overhead associated with file management, and MONITOR FILE_SYSTEM_CACHE lists the breakout of the components of the overhead.

There are two basic monitor commands that you can use for detecting XQP overhead problems:

MONITOR FCP — Shows disk read, write, and erase rates. If the sum of the XQP rate is a significant percentage of the overall I/O operation rate, you need to attempt to make improvements to reduce XQP disk I/Os from one of three sources: cache misses, erase operations, and fragmentation.

MONITOR FILES_SYSTEM_CACHE — Shows a breakout for all the XQP overheads. A low cache hit rate combined with a high attempt rate indicates a problem with cache sizing.

FILE PRIMITIVE STATISTICS

Use the output from MONITOR FCP to determine the rate of I/O operations issued by the XQP for file overhead management. The percentage of I/Os attributed to file overhead management is determined by Equation 3-5.

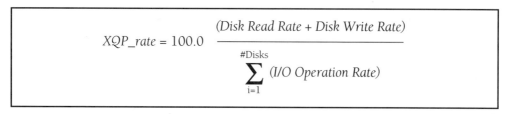

$$XQP\_rate = 100.0 \ \frac{(Disk\ Read\ Rate + Disk\ Write\ Rate)}{\displaystyle\sum_{i=1}^{\#Disks} (I/O\ Operation\ Rate)}$$

Equation 3-5. XQP_Rate

The value of XQP_Rate will help you determine how much effort to put into tuning the file caches. XQP_Rate is the percentage of I/O operations being used to support the file system.

Once again, we can get a better value by using the data from the PMS database. From the data collected by the Monitor program in Appendix K and by changing Equation 3-5 to use incremental counts instead of rates, we can plot the overhead for running the file system.

Figure 3-10 shows the plot for a well-tuned system. For most systems, the overhead for running the file system should be less than 10 percent. If your system is using more than 10 percent of all I/Os to support running the file system, you have a problem with excessive overhead. How to tune to adjust for excessive file system overhead is detailed in Chapter 4.

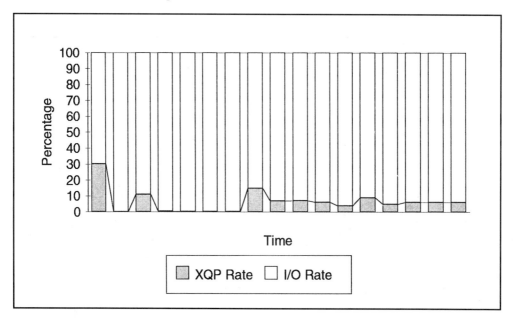

Figure 3-10. File Overhead

FILE_SYSTEM_CACHES

Check the MONITOR FILE_SYSTEM_CACHE output display for the level of activity (attempt rate) and hit percentage for each of the caches (see Figure 3-11).

```
┌─────────────────────────────────────────────────────────────────────┐
│                      OpenVMS Performance                              │
├─────────────────────────────────────────────────────────────────────┤
│  File   Edit   Commands   Options   Print                     Help    │
├─────────────────────────────────────────────────────────────────────┤
│                      OpenVMS Monitor Utility                          │
│                  FILE SYSTEM CACHING STATISTICS                       │
│                        on node XXXXXX                                 │
│                          SUMMARY                                      │
│                                                                       │
│                            CUR      AVE      MIN      MAX              │
│                                                                       │
│      Dir FCB   (Hit %)     100.00   99.99    98.00    100.00          │
│                (Attempt Rate)  23.76  22.06    4.61    66.98          │
│      Dir Data  (Hit %)     100.00   99.35    90.00    100.00          │
│                (Attempt Rate)  23.76  23.35    4.61    81.60          │
│      File Hdr  (Hit %)     100.00   97.86    57.00    100.00          │
│                (Attempt Rate)   6.79   8.50    1.83    35.69          │
│      File ID   (Hit %)       0.00   95.28    0.00    100.00          │
│                (Attempt Rate)   0.00   0.06    0.00     0.47          │
│                                                                       │
│      Extent    (Hit %)       0.00  100.00    0.00    100.00          │
│                (Attempt Rate)   0.00   0.33    0.00     4.25          │
│      Quota     (Hit %)       0.00    0.00    0.00     0.00          │
│                (Attempt Rate)   0.00   0.00    0.00     0.00          │
│      Bitmap    (Hit %)       0.00    0.00    0.00     0.00          │
│                (Attempt Rate)   0.00   0.00    0.00     0.00          │
│                                                                       │
│  PLAYBACK                  SUMMARIZING                                │
└─────────────────────────────────────────────────────────────────────┘
```

Figure 3-11. File Caching

Every "cache miss" requires one or more disk I/O requests. Since it is critical to performance to maintain "good" disk caching, a system with no caching is almost unusable.

For this reason you must know how to determine the effectiveness of the caches (see Equation 3-6).

$$XQP\_Index = (100.0 - Hit\ \%) * Attempt\ Rate * 60.0$$

Equation 3-6. XQP_Index

Using the data collected from MONITOR FILE_SYSTEM_CACHE, compute a value for XQP_Index using the formula in Equation 3-6. This will generate a table of values similar to Table 3-7. The values in the table show the number of I/Os per minute occurring as a result of cache misses. These values define the upper bounds on the number of I/Os that can be saved if you were able to make caches as large as you liked.

Item	Index
Dir FCB	13.236
DIR Data	910.65
File HDR	1091.4
File ID	16.992
Extent	0.0
Quota	0.0
Bitmap	0.0

Table 3-7. Cache Index of Help

The data in Table 3-7 will be used in Chapter 4 to help determine how to size your caches correctly.

Warning: When a process requests additional free space, it is possible to cause the extent caches on all nodes to be flushed. If all the remaining space in the storage bitmap has been assigned to the local extent cache and there is still not enough space available to fill the user request, the cache is flushed clusterwide. As a result, all cluster extent cache entries are returned to the storage bitmap. The file system then searches the bitmap to determine whether the remaining space is sufficient for the request. To detect this problem, watch for:

- The extent cache with a large access rate and a low hit rate.

- The bitmap cache with a large access rate and a high hit rate.

As you increase the size of the cache, your system will slow down, and the hit rate will not increase for the extent cache. In this case, decreasing the size of the cache will increase the hit rate, but only slightly.

MSCP SERVER

The MSCP disk server's purpose is to allow locally connected disks to appear on other VMScluster nodes as local devices. Thus, if you are not running VMSclusters, there is no need to perform the analysis described in this section.

DETECTING MSCP PROBLEMS

There is one monitor command that shows indications of MCSP problems:

MONITOR MSCP — Shows I/O rates, types, and sizes. Also shown is a composite overview of the MSCP buffer usage. A nonzero extra fragment rate, fragmented request rate, or buffer wait rate is an indication that an MSCP buffer problem is present.

Figure 3-12 shows MSCP server statistics. While MONITOR MSCP provides information about current usage, a better way to determine long-term usage is via the SHOW DEVICE command or via a program that accesses the MSCP performance data structure.

```
┌─────────────────────────── OpenVMS Performance ───────────────────────────┐
│                                                                            │
│  File   Edit   Commands   Options   Print                          Help    │
│ ┌────────────────────────────────────────────────────────────────────┐    │
│ │                      OpenVMS Monitor Utility                       ▲ │    │
│ │                      MSCP SERVER STATISTICS                          │    │
│ │                        on node XXXXXX                                │    │
│ │                          SUMMARY                                     │    │
│ │                                                                      │    │
│ │                          CUR      AVE      MIN      MAX              │    │
│ │                                                                      │    │
│ │  Server I/O Request Rate  47.99   53.87    22.43   140.58            │    │
│ │  Read Request Rate        42.90   48.31    19.58   134.76            │    │
│ │  Write Request Rate        5.09    5.55     1.58     7.14            │    │
│ │                                                                      │    │
│ │  Extra Fragment Rate       0.30    2.46     0.00     7.29            │    │
│ │  Fragmented Request Rate   0.30    2.46     0.00     7.29            │    │
│ │  Buffer Wait Rate          0.00    0.00     0.00     0.00            │    │
│ │                                                                      │    │
│ │  Request Size Rates     1 10.33    9.05     1.42    41.78            │    │
│ │  (Blocks)             2-3  3.24    5.21     0.94    11.70            │    │
│ │                       4-7  5.09   10.91     0.90    96.47            │    │
│ │                      8-15  4.62    3.29     0.95     6.72            │    │
│ │                     16-31 22.68   18.07     5.68    32.38          ■ │    │
│ │                     32-63  0.30    1.47     0.00     4.87            │    │
│ │                       64+  1.69    5.84     0.14    16.56          ▼ │    │
│ │ PLAYBACK                SUMMARIZING                                  │    │
│ └────────────────────────────────────────────────────────────────────┘    │
└────────────────────────────────────────────────────────────────────────────┘
```

Figure 3-12. MSCP Server Statistics

SHOW DEVICE

Figure 3-13 is the output from the command $ SHOW DEVICE/SERVED/ALL. From this output we can detect several problems. If queued requests are present for either devices or hosts, the settings for MSCP_BUFFER were insufficient to serve all requests. Each queue request indicates that the requesting systems experienced a long access time for that I/O request to complete.

From the resources area, we can see the current settings for MSCP_BUFFER and the current free blocks and in-use blocks. Also present are the number of I/Os (I/O packets) currently being handled. A major performance indicator is the buffer wait area. Buffer waits are caused when the requesting system issues more I/O requests at the same time than allowed by the settings of MSCP_CREDITS.

```
┌──────────────────────────────────────────────────────────────────────────────┐
│ ═                          OpenVMS Performance                         ┌ □    │
├──────────────────────────────────────────────────────────────────────────────┤
│  File   Edit   Commands   Options   Print                           Help      │
├──────────────────────────────────────────────────────────────────────────────┤
│        MSCP-Served Devices on ASCAXP 28-APR-1993 12:55:10.80              ▲   │
│                                                                                │
│                                          Queue Requests                        │
│ Device:             Status     Total Size    Current    Max      Hosts         │
│    DKA0             Online       2050860          0       16         8         │
│    DKA100           Online       2050860          0        3         8         │
│    DKA200           Online       2050860          0        3         8         │
│    DKB100           Online       3907911          0        3         8         │
│    DKB200           Online       3907911          0        3         8         │
│    DKB300           Online       3907911          0        3         8         │
│    DKC100           Online       3907911          0        3         8         │
│    DKC200           Online       3907911          0        3         8         │
│    DKC300           Online       3907911          0        3         8         │
│    DKD100           Online       3907911          0        2         8         │
│    DKE100           Online        401384          0       12         8         │
│    DKE400           Avail              0          0        0         0         │
│                                                                                │
│                                          Queue Requests                        │
│ Host:               Time of Connection      Current    Max     Devices         │
│    ASC591       26-APR-1993 16:30:56.98         0       11        11           │
│    ASC383       26-APR-1993 16:30:57.79         0       11        11           │
│    ASC386       26-APR-1993 16:30:57.86         0       11        11           │
│    ASC385       26-APR-1993 16:30:58.23         0       11        11           │
│    ASC387       26-APR-1993 16:30:58.44         0       11        11           │
│    ASC311       26-APR-1993 16:30:58.68         0       11        11           │
│    ASC384       26-APR-1993 16:30:59.07         0       11        11           │
│    ASC360       27-APR-1993 10:29:37.30         0        7        11           │
│                                                                                │
│ Resources:         Total       Free      In Use                                │
│    Buffer Area:     ***         ***         0                                  │
│    I/O Packets:      0           0                                             │
│                                                                                │
│                    Current    Maximum                                          │
│    Buffer Wait:      0           0                                             │
│                                                                                │
│ Request Count:                                                                 │
│      0-7:    394983       32-39:     7479       88-103:     9548               │
│      8-15:    22163       40-55:     5431      104-127:    18536               │
│     16-23:    33252       56-71:     4675                                      │
│     24-31:     4346       72-87:     3714                                      │
│                                                                                │
│ Operations Count:                                                              │
│    ABORT            0    ERASE          0   READ           494317              │
│    ACCESS           0    FLUSH          0   REPLACE             0              │
│    AVAILABLE       15    GET COM STS    0   SET CTL CHR       22               │
│    CMP CTL DAT      0    GET UNT STS 64128   SET UNT CHR      253              │
│    CMP HST DAT      0    ONLINE       103   WRITE           9810               │
│    Total       568648                                                      ▼   │
└──────────────────────────────────────────────────────────────────────────────┘
```

Figure 3-13. Show Device/Served

Request count shows the number of MSCP I/O requests by block size. Figure 3-14 displays the data from which the request count section of Figure 3-13 is derived.

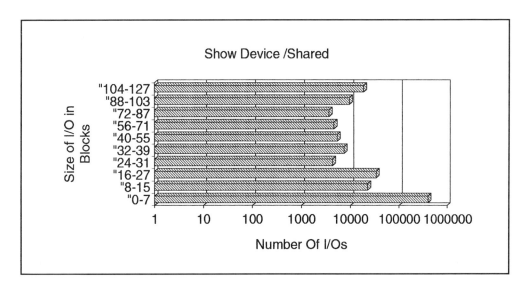

Figure 3-14. Plot of Show Device

MSCP BUFFER ANALYSIS

MSCP I/O fragmentation and buffer waits can be caused by several conditions. Using the data from the program described in Appendix K, I will show you how to determine the cause of these problems.

I/O OVERLOAD

If you plot the total number of MSCP I/Os versus the sum of all I/Os that incurred extra overhead (fragmented I/O, extra fragment, and buffer waits), you will be able to see the correlation between these items. Overhead I/Os are the extra I/Os created by tuning conditions but not necessary to perform the MSCP I/O under ideal conditions.

The MSCP I/O load should not have any significant impact on the ratio of overhead I/Os to total I/Os. If during periods of heavy I/O load you get a large ratio of overhead I/Os to total I/Os, and if during periods of low overall I/O rates there is a much smaller ratio of overhead I/Os to total I/Os, then I/O overload may have occurred.

Figure 3-15 shows the plot used for this analysis. From this plot we can see that there is a problem with overhead I/Os. If the overhead I/Os are not being caused by I/Os so large that they induce automatic overhead (see the next section), then the problem is I/O overload. Chapter 4 shows how to tune for this problem.

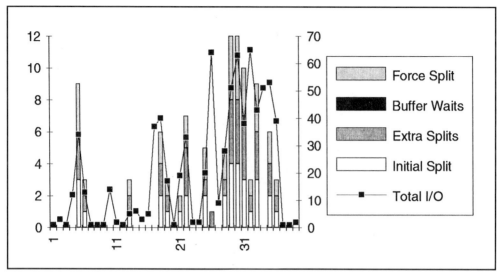

Figure 3-15. MSCP I/O Versus Overhead I/Os

LARGE I/O

Since MSCP must split all I/Os that are over 127 blocks in size, overhead I/Os will occur for these I/Os regardless of how you tune your system. Since these large I/Os give almost the same appearance as an overloaded system, we must find a way to distinguish between them. You can tune for an overloaded system, but you cannot tune for the actual operation of the system. I/Os greater than 127 blocks via MSCP always incur overhead I/Os. Thus, we will refer to I/Os that are larger than 127 blocks as *forced splits*.

If you plot large I/Os versus overhead I/Os and you get a high correlation, the problem is caused by large I/O sizes via MSCP. The Large I/Os section in Chapter 4 deals with this situation. Note that the action to take for large I/Os is not the same as the action required for an overloaded system.

EXCESSIVE OVERHEAD

If you incorrectly set up MSCP, you can incur large I/O overhead in the running of MSCP. To determine the overhead for running MSCP, plot total I/Os versus the sum of all reads and writes. In most cases you should see that 75 to 85 percent of I/Os are reads or writes.

While from the plot in Figure 3-14 we see there is a problem with I/O overload, we can present the data in a more understandable manner in Figure 3-16 to check for excessive I/O overhead.

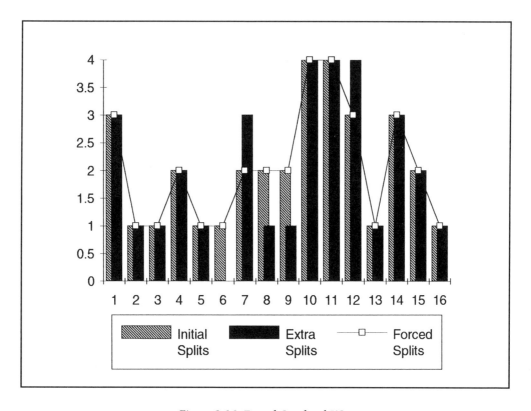

Figure 3-16. Forced Overhead I/Os

If the data from the plot in Figure 3-17 shows an overhead value that is greater than:

- 5 to 15 percent for systems with MSCP_SERVE_ALL set to 2,
- 15 to 30 percent for systems with MSCP_SERVE_ALL set to 1,

then check Chapter 4 for the correct tuning steps.

In addition, we could plot total MSCP operations by type over a period of time (compute average values for pie chart plot) to check for excessive overhead in running MSCP. Figure 3-18 shows how the breakdown should look after you have correctly tuned your MSCP parameters.

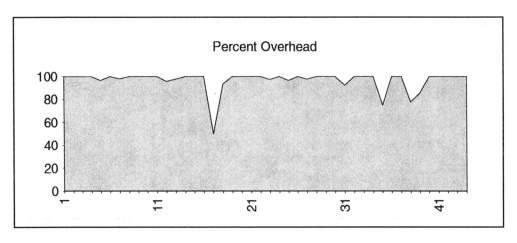

Figure 3-17. MSCP Overhead

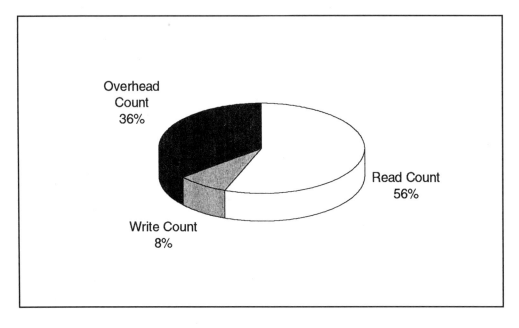

Figure 3-18. Tuned MSCP

MSCP WRAP-UP

Once you have tuned your system for MSCP performance, you should be able to get a plot much like the one in Figure 3-19. Read and write should account for 80 to 90 percent of I/Os. If running on an AXP processor, and if page/swap files or executable images are being served, then there will be some percentage of forced splits.

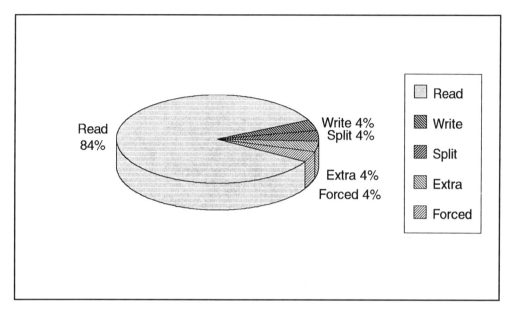

Figure 3-19. Tuned MSCP

File System Tuning

Y OUR ANALYSIS PHASE WILL HAVE DETERMINED WHETHER OR NOT THE DISK PROBLEM is due to direct I/O. Direct I/O problems will show up because of the very long delay between the time the I/O is issued and its completion. The fastest way to discover direct I/O problems is to detect that there is a queue of waiting I/Os for a particular disk (MONITOR DISK/ITEM=QUEUE). Since direct I/Os use direct memory access and have little CPU overhead, performance cannot be greatly improved with a faster CPU. These I/O queues are caused by one of the following:

- A slow device unable to keep up with demand.
- Overall demand exceeding capacity, resulting in some queued requests.
- Unbalanced loading of available capacity.

Several basic solutions are available to you:

- Acquire faster hardware.
- Acquire more bandwidth.
- Use available memory to reduce direct I/Os.
- Structure your workload to match your file system.

IMPROVING I/O PERFORMANCE

To improve the performance of your file system, there are several things you can do:

- Balance disk access.
- Balance controller access.
- Place "hot" files for rapid access.
- Expand available capacity by acquiring more and/or faster controllers/disks.
- Optimize the file system.

In the following sections we will cover each of these items. Also, using the data collected in Chapter 3, we will determine the "correct" tuning response to each of the problems we found.

BASIC CHECKS

Before making any major changes, you should perform some basic checks. The items discussed in the following sections can have a major impact on performance, but they are easily corrected.

HIGH-WATER MARKING

By default, high-water marking is enabled for all volumes. This is unnecessary overhead for many sites. High-water marking is used to ensure that a user cannot access data from allocated disk blocks that were not written by the user. With high-water marking on, allocated but not yet written disk data blocks are overwritten with a known pattern before the user is allowed to access the data. This prevents the user from accessing data from a deleted file.

DEFEATING FRAGMENTATION

By default, the OpenVMS file system does not make any attempt to create files in a manner to minimize fragmentation. There are, however, several options available to maximize the performance of your file system.

- Use the contiguous best try (CBT) option when creating and extending files.

- If you know that a file will grow to a very large size, create the file with a reasonable initial size. If you know that a database file is usually 100 to 140K blocks in size, then create with an initial size of 100K and extend in chunks of 10K.

- Convert all files that have high usage rates to contiguous files. If you are developing software, then the commonly included files (for VAX C, SYS$SHARE:*.H) should all be converted to contiguous files.

- Where possible, use disk striping.

- If memory is available, increase the value of ACP_WINDOW.

DEFAULT RMS VALUES

If possible, use your "inside knowledge" of your system to make OpenVMS work better. By default, RMS uses the following algorithm to extend a file:

If RMS_EXTENT is not 0, then extend by RMS_EXTENT BLOCKS; otherwise, extend by 2*RMS_DFMBC.

Thus, if you use the default SYSGEN RMS values (the default value for RMS_EXTENT is zero and for RMS_DFMBC is sixteen blocks), you will use a default extension size of thirty-two blocks. If your basic file system uses mostly files from forty to eighty blocks, this is not a good value. Your files, by default, are truncated on close. This means that the file of size forty used/sixty-four allocated will return twenty-four blocks of space when the file is closed with truncation. However, twenty-four blocks will not be usable in a contiguous fashion. If all the files on your system are forty blocks in length, then at some time you will have fragmented files. When the twenty-four-block fragment returned above is used, there will be no way to use it in a contiguous manner.

For simplicity, let's assume you have a disk with 640 blocks. Then, if we assume two users, we have the following:

For each user, create a file, extend to forty blocks used, close with truncate. For the first five files for each use, the files will be contiguous. There are now 240 free blocks, meaning that we can now create six more forty-block files. None of these files will be contiguous. If we did the same set of actions but set RMS_EXTENT to 40, then we would create sixteen contiguous files.

DIRECTORIES VERSUS LIBRARIAN

Do not use the file system as a librarian. If you do, you will create many problems, including:

- Huge directories.
- Long file searches.
- Frequent opens/closes.
- Frequent allocates/deallocates.

Directories are lists of file names and other information (see Chapter 2). The lookup time for a file, however, is nonlinear in relation to the overall size of the directory files. Also, RMS will not cache directories larger than 128 blocks. Frequent directory updates severely reduce the effectiveness of all directory caches.

Use of the supplied librarians will solve many of these problems. If the supplied librarians do not suit your needs, all library functions are available as system calls (LBR$).

The best case is sixty-two files per directory block; the worst case is six files per directory block. For the equivalent library only 100 blocks of data storage space is needed — a block for the file header and a single directory entry. As you can see, the disk savings are large for using libraries.

To minimize the number of I/Os needed to get directory data into memory, set ACP_MAXREAD to be the size of the average active directory file on your system.

DECOMPRESS SYSTEM LIBRARIES

One of the options available during OpenVMS installation or upgrade is to decompress system libraries. By default libraries are supplied in a compressed form. Object libraries take about 25 percent more disk space when decompressed; the help libraries, 50 percent more space. If you do not decompress the system libraries, there are two major performance hits:

- The CPU must dynamically decompress them each time you access an entry in the library.

- The internal hashing function to look up library entries is not usable for the library in a compressed state. Thus, if your libraries are compressed, the system must read in all library records, decompress them, and then search for the requested entry. This linear search incurs huge I/O and CPU overhead, especially when searching for an item at the end of large libraries.

The only reason for not decompressing system libraries is an extreme shortage of disk space.

INSUFFICIENT POOL

There is a real pitfall in the Mount utility. If the amount of pool available is insufficient to allocate the requested XQP caches, then OpenVMS mounts the disks with the following cache sizes:

- Bitmap = 2.

- Header = 6.

- Directory = 4.

- Directory index = 2.

To make matters worse, no error message is issued. You must look at the output of a SHOW DEVICE command to see the damage caused.

KNOW YOUR HARDWARE

When making performance decisions, you need to take into account the hardware you are using or planning to use.

PERFORMANCE FOR HSC CONTROLLERS

While there have always been performance considerations in regard to configuring devices on the HSC, until the release of the RA90/RA70 series of disks these considerations were not very critical, because the speed of the available devices did not stress the bandwidth of the HSC. For RA90/RA70 and newer disks, configuration is important for optimal performance.

Figure 4-1 shows the output from the HSC that shows which disks are on which controllers. If you have more than one controller, balance controllers so that the sum of the direct I/O rates for the disks on a controller is about the same for each controller.

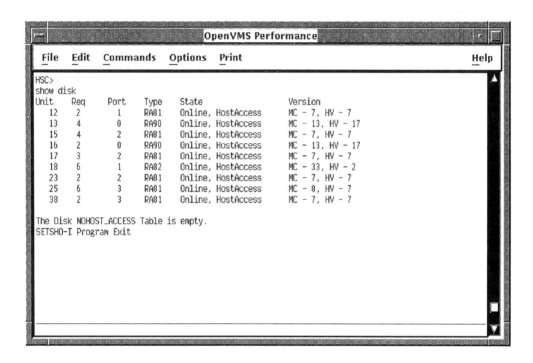

```
HSC>
show disk
Unit    Req     Port    Type    State                   Version
  12      2       1      RA81    Online, HostAccess      MC - 7,  HV - 7
  13      4       0      RA90    Online, HostAccess      MC - 13, HV - 17
  15      4       2      RA81    Online, HostAccess      MC - 7,  HV - 7
  16      2       0      RA90    Online, HostAccess      MC - 13, HV - 17
  17      3       2      RA81    Online, HostAccess      MC - 7,  HV - 7
  18      6       1      RA82    Online, HostAccess      MC - 33, HV - 2
  23      2       2      RA81    Online, HostAccess      MC - 7,  HV - 7
  25      6       3      RA81    Online, HostAccess      MC - 8,  HV - 7
  38      2       3      RA81    Online, HostAccess      MC - 7,  HV - 7

The Disk NOHOST_ACCESS Table is empty.
SETSHO-I Program Exit
```

Figure 4-1. Balancing HSC Controllers

There are some general rules to keep in mind when configuring a device on an HSC:

- Only one device on a requestor can transfer data at a time.

- Shadow set members require separate requestors.

- Requestors have priority.

- Device speeds are important and must be taken into account when setting up the devices on the requestors.

While a requestor can serve more than one device, only one device can transfer data at any one time. While one device is transferring data, other devices can be seeking. For most cases this is not a problem. For files that experience large transfers, there can be loss of performance if all disk ports on a requestor are in active use. Activities that can cause problems include:

- Paging and swapping disks.

- Disks that support large amounts of image activation.

- Applications that use large byte counts.

One of the most important performance considerations for HSC controllers is to place shadow set members on separate requestors. When the HSC selects which drive to read from on a shadow set, the first check made is for members on the same requestor. If all members are on the same requestor, the HSC just uses the primary member, and no read optimization is done. This means that the same drive is used on all reads, and all possible speed advantages for shadow set reads are negated. On writes, only one drive can be written to at one time; thus, all writes, instead of occurring in parallel, now occur sequentially.

Each requestor card in an HSC has a priority. The highest priority channel cards must contain the highest peak transfer disks. If this is not done, the HSC will adjust for possible data loss/data overrun problems and run at the peak transfer speed of the slowest device on the highest priority requestor. If you have an RA70 device on the highest priority requestor and RA92s on all other ports, you will have a serious performance impact due to the "incorrect" placement of devices on requestors.

MSCP BALANCING

Figure 4-2 shows how to determine which disks are being served by which nodes. In this case, device 3STA402: is served by node ASCVX3, and device 3STA411: is served by node ASCVX5. You should try to balance your MSCP-served disks, because this is also a possible I/O bottleneck.

SCSI INTERFACES

Another good example of "Know Your Hardware" is the performance limitation of SCSI disk devices. Returning to the Fragmentation Cost section in Chapter 3, we can rerun the test, but this time compare SCSI disks and local RA-type disks.

As Figure 4-3 shows, if you have SCSI disks, you gain no real advantage by using large transfers to contiguous disk files. This is due to the restriction of a maximum transfer size of thirty-one blocks for a SCSI disk from a VAX. Thus, the 120-block transfer was converted into three thirty-one-block transfers and one twenty-seven-

```
┌─────────────────────────────────────────────────────────────────┐
│ ─                          OpenVMS Performance                  ◄ ▢│
├─────────────────────────────────────────────────────────────────┤
│  File   Edit   Commands   Options   Print                    Help │
│                                                                   │
│  Device               Device     Error   Volume      Free  Trans Mnt│
│  Name                 Status     Count    Label     Blocks Count Cnt│
│  $3$STA402:  (ASCVX3)  Mounted      0    DSK402    1468832    1  47 │
│  $3$STA403:  (ASCVX3)  Mounted      0    DSK403    2479968    1  47 │
│  $3$STA404:  (ASCVX3)  Mounted      0    DSK404    1116536    1  47 │
│  $3$STA411:  (ASCVX5)  Mounted      0    DSK411     525648   23  47 │
│  $3$STA412:  (ASCVX5)  Mounted      0    DSK412     629264    1  47 │
│  $3$STA413:  (ASCVX6)  Mounted      0    DSK413     715176    1  47 │
│  $3$STA414:  (ASCVX5)  Mounted      0    DSK414    1831728    1  47 │
│  $3$STA415:  (ASCVX5)  Mounted      0    DSK415    1406016    1  47 │
│                                                                   │
└─────────────────────────────────────────────────────────────────┘
```

Figure 4-2. MSCP Balancing

block transfer. If you were using SCSI devices in a VAXcluster, the default transfer size for paging I/Os was thirty-two blocks. This is possibly the worst choice for a transfer size. This restriction was removed in VMS V5.3.

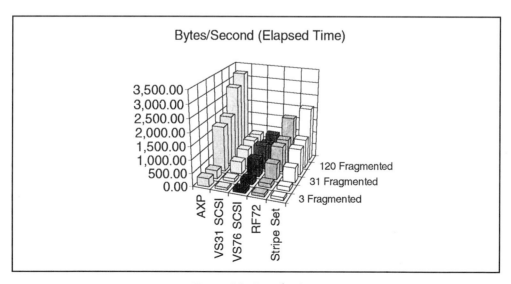

Figure 4-3. Transfer Size

DISK PORT SWITCHES

VMScluster software supports alternate paths to a disk. To determine all possible paths, the software issues a topology command to each disk drive every few minutes. This command causes the following to occur:

- All I/Os to the disk are suspended.

- The disk disconnects from the controller to which it is connected.

- The disk attempts to switch to the alternate port's controller.

- The alternate controller sees the disk and notifies OpenVMS of the alternate path.

- The disk then connects to the original controller.

- I/Os to the disk resume.

In this manner, OpenVMS builds and maintains a map of all possible alternate paths to the disk to be used in the event that the current path fails. When all is well, this entire process takes only a few tens of milliseconds. If there is no alternate port or if the alternate port switch is disabled, then the entire process still takes only a few tens of milliseconds.

However, if the alternate port is enabled but no controller is connected, the disk must wait until the connection times out before reporting that the alternate path is not available. This time out takes on the order of several seconds, over 1,000 times as long as normal! The cure is quite simple; if you do not have a controller port to which to connect the disk port, then disable the port switch on the disk.

OFFLOADING DISK ACTIVITY

One of the easiest and fastest ways to improve performance for your file system is to offload the disk activity by balancing the disk load. In most cases the system overloads the system disk. The next section shows you how to reduce the demand on the system disk. You will want to do this if your analysis from Chapter 3 determined that the system disk was a problem.

SYSTEM FILES

At almost all sites, the system disk has the largest I/O load. A simple and easy way to offload I/O from the system disk is to move a few of the most-used files from the system disk. The following are some of the files you might want to move:

- SYSUAF.DAT.

- NETPROXY.DAT.

- RIGHTSLIST.DAT.

- VMSMAIL_PROFILE.DATA.

- ERRLOG.SYS.

- OPERATOR.LOG.

To move these files, you need to set up special logical names. There are two ground rules for this:

1. The logical names must be defined before the files are accessed.

2. The logical names must be system executive logical names.

To have the logical names defined at the correct time in the boot procedures, add the define statements to the file SYS$MANAGER:SYLOGICALS.COM. Also make sure you mount the alternate disks needed.

Be sure to offload the system disk load to a disk or disks that have load usage. There is no requirement to put any of these files on the same disk. If possible, use as many disks as you need to balance the load.

If you move SYSUAF.DAT to another disk and that disk crashes, your system will not have a valid authorization file. To plan for this possibility, it is a good idea to create an alternate copy of the authorization file on another disk. The OpenVMS manual explains how to use this alternate authorization file. It is also wise to test these procedures before the real event occurs.

Here are some example commands:

```
$ DEFINE/SYSTEM/EXEC SYSUAF DISK$:[DIR]SYSUAF.DAT

$ DEFINE/SYSTEM/EXEC NETPROXY DISK$:[DIR]NETPROXY.DAT

$ DEFINE/SYSTEM/EXEC RIGHTSLIST DISK$:[DIR]RIGHTSLIST.DAT

$ DEFINE/SYSTEM/EXEC VMSMAIL_PROFILE DISK$:[DIR]VMSMAIL_PROFILE.DATA

$ DEFINE/SYSTEM/EXEC SYS$ERRORLOG DISK$:[DIR]ERRLOG.SYS
```

The state of the operator on OPA0: and the state of the operator log file can be controlled by defining logical names. By default, the operator states are as follows:

1. For all systems except workstations in a VMScluster:

   - OPA0: is enabled for all classes.

   - The log file SYS$MANAGER:OPERATOR.LOG is opened for all classes.

2. For workstations in a VMScluster:

- OPA0: is not enabled. OPA0: will also be SET TERMINAL /PERMANENT /NOBROADCAST.

- No log file is opened.

To override the default enabled classes, define the following SYSTEM logical names:

- OPC$OPA0_ENABLE — If defined to be true, OPA0: is enabled as an operator. If defined to be false, OPA0: is not enabled as an operator.

- OPC$OPA0_CLASSES — This logical defines the operator classes to be enabled on OPA0:. The logical can be a search list of the allowed classes, a list of classes, or a combination of the two. For example:

```
$ DEFINE /SYSTEM OPC$OPA0_CLASSES CENTRAL,DISKS,TAPE
$ DEFINE /SYSTEM OPC$OPA0_CLASSES "CENTRAL,DISKS,TAPE"
$ DEFINE /SYSTEM OPC$OPA0_CLASSES "CENTRAL,DISKS",TAPE
```

OPC$OPA0_CLASSES can be defined even if OPC$OPA0_ENABLE is not defined. In that case, the classes are used for any operators that are enabled, but the default is used to determine whether or not to enable the operator.

- OPC$LOGFILE_ENABLE — If defined to be true, an operator log file is opened. If defined to be false, no log file is opened.

- OPC$LOGFILE_CLASSES — This logical defines the operator classes to be enabled for the log file. The logical can be a search list of the allowed classes, a list separated by commas, or a combination of the two.

OPC$LOGFILE_CLASSES can be defined even if OPC$LOGFILE_ENABLE is not defined.

- OPC$LOGFILE_NAME — This logical supplies information for use with the default name SYS$MANAGER:OPERATOR.LOG to define the name of the log file. If the log file is directed to a disk other than the system disk, commands to mount that disk should be included in the command procedure SYLOGICALS.COM. This log file name will be used whenever a log file is recreated.

Only OPC$LOGFILE_NAME is used for more than the initial startup of OPCOM. For example, issuing the command REPLY/LOG will open a new file with the specified name and with all classes enabled. OPC$LOGFILE_ENABLE and OPC$LOGFILE_CLASSES are ignored.

The list of all operator classes is CENTRAL, PRINTER, TAPES, DISKS, DEVICES, CARDS, NETWORK, CLUSTER, SECURITY, LICENSE, OPER1, OPER2, OPER3, OPER4, OPER5, OPER6, OPER7, OPER8, OPER9, OPER10, OPER11, and OPER12.

ACCOUNTS

Make sure not to allow any user disk areas on the system disk. You can also move the default DECnet account to a disk other than the system disk. Check out all third-party software to force installs on disks other than the system disk.

QUEUES

If you have a lot of queue activity, it is fairly easy to move the job controller database to another disk. If you are using a pre-VMS V5.5 version, then use DCL to define the job controller database:

```
$ start/queue/manager disk$:[dir]jbcsysque.dat
```

QUEUE MANAGER

As of VMS V5.5, the job controller database is not a massive user of disk. However, if you decide to move the database, the procedure for doing so has changed dramatically. The file JBCSYSQUE.DAT is no longer used! It has been replaced by the following files:

QMAN$MASTER.DAT, which contains:

- The queue and journal file location.

- Forms and characteristic definitions.

- Names of all known queues.

SYS$QUEUE_MANAGER.QMAN$QUEUES, which contains:

- Information supplied by the INITIALIZE/QUEUE command.

- Information supplied by the START/QUEUE command.

- Information supplied by the SET QUEUE command.

SYS$QUEUE_MANAGER.QMAN$JOURNAL, which contains:

- Information for failover and recovery.

To move these files from their default area of SYS$SYSTEM, follow these steps:

1. Mount the disk where the files are located before the CONFIG phase of startup.

2. Define the logical QMAN$MASTER as follows before the CONFIG phase of startup:

- DEFINE/SYSTEM/EXEC QMAN$MASTER

  DISK$:[DIR]QMAN$MASTER.DAT

- QMAN$MASTER must be the same on all cluster nodes that wish to use queue services.

HARDWARE

Disk offloading also involves controllers. If you have multiple controllers, make sure the total I/O load is balanced among them. A controller can do only one READ/WRITE at a time; it is easy to cause file system problems by having unbalanced controllers.

TRADE MEMORY FOR DISK

The other main option for improving disk performance is to trade off CPU cycles and/or memory to gain substantial increases in disk response.

GLOBAL BUFFERS

Files can be set up to use global buffers. Read-only data can be cached, but writes will not be cached and will cause the cache to be flushed. The major drawback to global buffers is their very negative impact on the memory manager when a global buffer is deleted. Global buffers are deleted when the last channel is closed.

WINDOW TURNS

If your analysis determined that you have an excessive number of window turns, there are two basic solutions:

1. Defragment your file system.

2. Increase the value for ACP_WINDOW.

You need 14 bytes of nonpaged pool for each entry extent that is allowed. When you increase ACP_WINDOW, you increase for all processes on the system. The real increased memory usage is determine by Equation 4-1.

$$Pool\_Used = 14 * ACP\_WINDOWS * CHANNELCNT * MAXPROCESSCNT$$

Equation 4-1. Window Pool Usage

CACHES

To achieve acceptable performance, it is critical to maintain extensive caches of components of the file system. On a well-tuned system, caching removes 70 to 80 percent of all disk I/Os that the file system would otherwise incur in performing file management functions.

All caches except the directory FCB cache are kept in paged pool. This means that a low-usage attempt rate on a memory-short system can convert a disk I/O into a hard page fault — a poor trade-off.

CACHE TUNING

Using the data from the Monitor utility, you can determine how to tune the file system caches correctly. Remember that AUTOGEN is still very conservative in setting up cache sizes. Watch out for:

- Making excessive system faults.

- Inducing file system faults.

- Increasing fragmentation.

Using the data from Table 3-7 in Chapter 3, you can determine which SYSGEN parameter to change and by how much.

Tune for File_Id, extent, and quota caching using the mount command qualifiers (see Table 4-1). You do this because these quotas need to vary from disk to disk, and SYSGEN parameters supply a value of all disks.

Item	SYSGEN Parameter	Value
Dir FCB	ACP_DINDXCACHE	1 Page
Dir Data	ACP_DIRCACHE	1 Page
File HDR	ACP_HDRCACHE	1 Page
File ID	ACP_FIDCACHE	4 Bytes/Slots/Volume
Extent	ACP_EXTCACHE	8 Bytes/Extent/Volume
	ACP_EXTLIMIT	% Free Space *100
Quota	ACP_QUOCACHE	28 Bytes/Slot/Volume
Bitmap	ACP_MAPCACHE	1 Page

Table 4-1. Cache Tuning

Allocate memory to the remaining quota using the index values from Table 3-7 to determine the best return per page of memory used. Since the remaining cache entries are sized by increasing the corresponding SYSGEN value by one, this will increase the size by one page. The value in Table 3-7 shows the relative possible returns for increasing the cache size. The larger the value, the more I/Os saved as the size of the cache is increased.

USING A NEW CACHE VERSION

To use any new SYSGEN ACP values, you must stop and restart the XQP. To stop the XQP, you must dismount all volumes mounted by it. In most systems, however, all disks, including the system disk, are mounted using the same XQP, so a system reboot is needed to make the change take effect.

SECONDARY XQPS

In almost all cases it is better to have a single XQP and its associated caches. However, if you have devices with major differences in performance characteristics (for example, RA81 disk drives on a KDA-50 controller and an ESE-20 on a KDM-70 controller), it may be advantageous to create a secondary XQP and cache. Another reason for creating multiple caches is to prevent excessive activity on other devices from flushing the caches used by the static device. To mount a device and create a different cache for it, use the command:

```
$ MOUNT/PROCESSOR=UNIQUE DUA1:
```

This will create a unique XQP cache for device DUA1. Assuming that DUA0 is the system disk and thus is using the primary cache, to mount a device to use the primary cache use the command:

```
$ MOUNT/PROCESSOR=SAME:DUA0: DUA2:
```

EXTENT CACHE FLUSHING

When a process requests additional free space, it is possible to cause the extent caches on all nodes to be flushed. If all the remaining space in the storage bitmap has been assigned to the local extent cache and there is still not enough space available to fill the user request, the cache is flushed clusterwide. As a result, all cluster extent cache entries are returned to the storage bitmap. The file system then searches the bitmap to determine whether the remaining space is sufficient for the request.

If you detect excessive extent cache flushing on your cluster, you will need to either disable extent caching on the affected disks or reduce the value for ACP_EXTCACHE to a value that will allow all active nodes to maintain their caches without flushing.

Size the extent caches such that the sum of the ACP_EXTCACHE values for all systems actively using a volume is less than 80 percent of the available volume free space. If you are setting the size of the extent cache via the MOUNT command, use that value instead of the SYSGEN value for ACP_EXTCACHE.

MSCP

There are opportunities to improve MSCP performance if the extra fragment rate, fragmented request rate, or buffer wait rate is nonzero. However, as we found out in Chapter 3, MSCP performance can be negatively affected by several causes. In the next sections I will discuss how to tune for the problems uncovered by our analysis.

I/O OVERLOAD

In most cases, you can solve the problem of I/O overload by increasing the size of the buffer used by MSCP. By increasing the size of the SYSGEN parameter, MSCP_BUFFER, MSCP will be able to handle more I/O requests without having to either put the requesting system in a buffer wait state or split the I/O into multiple smaller I/O requests.

Warning: If MSCP is trying to handle I/O to a disk that has a nonzero queue due to other activity, then as the average response time for the disk increases, more buffer space will be needed by MSCP to handle a constant MSCP I/O load. If the I/O via MSCP must stay in the MSCP buffer for several thousand milliseconds waiting on its turn to be written to or read from disk, then effectively the overall size of the MSCP decreases. If this is the case, increasing the size of the MSCP buffer will help, but the real solution is to tune to correct the large disk queues.

LARGE I/OS

Because of a typographical error in SYS$UPDATE:AUTOGEN.COM, PFCDEFAULT will be set to 128, and this will cause severe problems with using MSCP. For more information, see the MSCP and PFCDEFAULT section in Chapter 7.

If you attempt an I/O that is larger than 127 blocks via MSCP, MSCP will split these I/Os into chunks of a maximum 127 blocks each. If PFCDEFAULT is set to 128 pagelets, then two MSCP I/Os occur, one for 127 pagelets and one for 1 pagelet. This effectively doubles your I/O load even if there is no further MSCP fragmenting on the server side.

For a description of pagelets, see the AXP Versus VAX Memory Management section of Chapter 6.

To tune for large I/Os, you need to track down all system parameters that control I/O packet size. These include:

- ACP_MAXREAD.

- MPW_WRTCLUSTER.

- PFCDEFAULT.

- Various RMS parameters.

- SWPALLOCINC.

Ensure that the maximum size that any of these parameters allow is less than 128 blocks/pagelets. For OpenVMS AXP pay special attention to how the internal values of these parameters are affected by rounding. Some parameters are rounded down and some are rounded up.

Once you have removed all large I/Os caused by system parameters, you will need to track down which programs, if any, are issuing large I/Os. Where possible, you will need to change these programs to issue I/Os that are less than the 127-block maximum enforced by the file system.

Keep all the above changes in mind if and when the restriction of a maximum 127-block transfer is lifted from the file system. Given that Digital has discussed future RISC-based AXP systems with a page size of 128 pagelets, it is a good bet that this restriction will be lifted in the near future. It is highly unlikely that the company will release a system that will require, at a minimum, two I/Os per page fault.

EXCESSIVE OVERHEAD

If your systems are having problems with excessive overhead, the first thing to check is the setting of the system parameter MSCP_SERVE_ALL.

Locally attached disks are disks that can only be accessed by a single system. For example, disks connected to a SCSI controller are only available to a single system. Dual-pathed disks such as DSSI disks can be directly used by more than one system at a time.

If all the disks being served are locally attached, setting MSCP_SERVE_ALL to 1 will cause excessive overhead. Once every 20 seconds, MSCP will talk to all cluster nodes to inform them of the current paths to all disks that are being served from a system with MSCP_SERVE_ALL set to 1. The fact that the paths cannot change will not decrease the overhead. The current path for the locally attached disk will not change, but since MSCP_SERVER_ALL is set to 1, the system will inform all other systems of the current path selection once every 20 seconds.

In almost all other cases, the excessive overhead is caused by problems with cluster stability. Rebooting a node that serves disks via MSCP causes a very large number of MSCP overhead messages to be exchanged between all nodes.

How to Build a Better Disk

D EFRAGMENTING OPENVMS VAX DISKS IS AN INCREASINGLY POPULAR CONCERN IN the OpenVMS world. Defragmentation is generally understood to mean making files contiguous and consolidating free space into as few contiguous chunks as possible. Historically, defragmentation has been accomplished by performing a complete disk backup, reinitializing the disk, and then restoring the files using the VMS Backup utility.

DEFRAGMENTATION VERSUS OPTIMIZATION

However, defragmentation is simply a special subset of the larger problem of optimizing your entire disk structure. It is now possible to defragment more quickly and efficiently with commercial products than with the "out-to-tape" method. It is also possible to build an optimal disk, one much better than that created by mere defragmentation.

WHY OPTIMIZE YOUR DISK?

There are only two good reasons to optimize your disk structure. The first is to make your system run faster. The second is to create large amounts of contiguous free space so that applications needing large contiguous blocks of free space will run. Although abundant, such applications are in the minority.

There are no other valid reasons for optimizing your disk structure. The technical details such as fewer split I/Os, faster file space allocation, and shorter average seek distance are important only in that they make your system run faster. Consolidated free space is simply a speed issue unless your application absolutely needs it.

KEY OPTIMIZATION ISSUES

The two main issues regarding disk optimization are safety and the quality of optimization. Safety is the overriding concern when optimizing a disk. If you cannot optimize your disk safely, you should not optimize it. The overhead of rebuilding a disk even once dwarfs the benefits of running slightly faster for extended time periods.

Quality is the other key issue. In particular, consider how much faster the system runs when the disk is optimized and how long the increased performance lasts. Does the overhead of optimizing the disk outweigh the benefits of the otherwise increased performance? For environments with contiguous free space requirements, consider how long the free space remains contiguous.

SAFETY

Statistics show that if you run your system long enough, it will crash and some data will be lost. If you are extremely unlucky, you may lose an entire disk structure, or worse. That is why your system manager backs up the system regularly (we hope).

Reading and especially writing to disks is also dangerous. You never know when you might have a head crash. Anything reading or writing to your disk can potentially destroy the disk structure. Disk optimization does a lot of reading and writing, presenting the danger of hardware failure.

Having contemplated the worst, understand that most systems are reliable, particularly if they are well-maintained. Maintenance is vital. If you are logging errors on your disk, be sure to fix the problem. If not, it will most likely get worse. If you have a problem, running a program that copies most of the files on your disk will most likely aggravate it.

If you are not having problems (that is, if the mean time between failures is large), then you are unlikely to experience a problem during the 5 to 10 minutes it usually takes for a regular disk optimization run.

The chance of a hardware failure occurring during any given run is minute. Anything else you might do during a hardware failure might also hurt your disk, so the real risk is running your system at all.

ERROR CHECKING IN COMMERCIAL DEFRAGMENTERS

Commercial disk defragmenters incorporate various levels of error checking. One of the more common strategies is to use the OpenVMS read- and write-checking features, which work about as well as you might expect. A properly written optimizer would stop the copy process if an error were detected, at least for the offending file. Depending on the nature of the error, it might be wise to shut down the entire optimization process. If the error were just a read error on a bad block, the problem would probably be local and would not recur when copying other files. But what if it is some sort of controller error? In that case, other errors are likely to occur at random. Since certain types of errors are unrecoverable, as I will show, you will really want to avoid them.

Although data checking can tell you that your I/O has gone bad, it cannot guarantee safety. When a file is moved on the disk (you cannot optimize a disk unless files are moved), the mapping pointers in the index file (INDEXF.SYS) must be updated to point to the new locations.

Some defragmenting programs write into the index file directly, whereas others make standard OpenVMS calls that let OpenVMS update the pointers. In either case, if hardware problems cause the pointers to be written incorrectly with no hope of recovery, your disk structure has been damaged, perhaps beyond repair. All you can do is get out the backup tapes.

The standard OpenVMS functions of creating, extending, truncating, and deleting files are all risky. Even disk optimizers that use nothing but the standard OpenVMS file system calls documented in the OpenVMS manuals to perform their operations involve some risk.

ERRORS CAUSED BY BAD DISK STRUCTURE

Even if your hardware works properly, there is still potential for damage to the system, even when performing only standard OpenVMS file I/O. If the disk structure is not perfect (that is, if there are multiply allocated blocks, blocks incorrectly marked free, or end-of-file pointer/mapping pointer mismatches), then extending or truncating files can cause the contents of otherwise good files to become corrupted. On such disks, just copying files with the COPY command or editing them with EDT is dangerous. If one of the new files to become corrupted happens to be the index file or the bitmap file, the entire disk structure can be lost.

To avoid this, it is imperative that you run ANALYZE/DISK_STRUCTURE periodically. Once again, since a disk optimizer is likely to copy many of the files on your system, it is even more important that you start with a sound disk structure. If possible, run ANALYZE/DISK_STRUCTURE or an equivalent check for multiply allocated blocks or blocks incorrectly marked free before running any disk defragmenter. If there are problems, fix them, or at least do not run the defragmenter.

QUALITY OF OPTIMIZATION

There are several popular models for a defragmented disk: Backup, Reverse Backup, and Optimized. Although all the disks modeled are initially defragmented, not all are optimal. Before considering the popular models, I will make some analogies and describe some distinctions among some of the files on a disk.

For this discussion, I will ignore the exact disk geometry and consider it to be a long line of blocks. Each block's position in the line corresponds to its logical block number on the disk. Logical blocks with low numbers are near the beginning of the line, and those with high numbers are near the end of the line. This analogy holds well for all conceptual propositions offered in this book, especially considering that seek distance is roughly proportional to the difference between any two block numbers. References to a disk's beginning, middle, and end mean low, middle, and high logical block numbers respectively.

DEFINITIONS OF FILE TYPES

I will define some file types so that I can distinguish among them and position them accordingly.

Index File — On a typical disk the bulk of the index file is positioned at the center of the disk. For the example disk (see Figures 5-1, 5-2, and 5-3), the index file takes up 5 percent of the disk, 1 percent at the beginning and 4 percent starting at the exact middle.

Directory Files — These files tend not to move frequently on a typical disk. The directory files take up 5 percent of the example disk.

Warehouse Files — Files seldom accessed during normal timesharing are warehouse files. In this example they constitute 25 percent of the disk.

Volatile Files — Files that are very likely to be deleted soon are volatile files. These files make up 20 percent of the example disk.

Ordinary Files — Files likely to be accessed but unlikely to be deleted are considered ordinary files. These files make up 25 percent of the example disk.

Free Space — The remaining 20 percent of the example disk is free space.

COMPARING THE THREE MODELS

In the following sections, each model is considered first in its initial ideal state. Files are then created and deleted as users normally would by copying or editing files, that is, copying a file by creating a new version and then deleting the old.

New space must be allocated before old space is freed. The new space is allocated according to the rule that it will be allocated in the space with the lowest block number, where it can be allocated contiguously. This is not exactly the way OpenVMS always allocates space, but it illustrates problems encountered by many disk structures.

BACKUP MODEL

The Backup model is so named because it is approximately what you would expect to find after backing up to tape and then restoring a disk's contents with VMS Backup. That is, all files are contiguous and squeezed down toward the beginning of the disk, leaving the free space consolidated at the end of the disk. The bulk of the index file is at the center of the disk. Other files, including directory files, are located randomly with respect to the different file types shown in the models.

Upon creating new files and deleting volatile files, space is freed in small pieces all over the disk, which fragments free space. It also requires accesses to all portions of the bitmap, which makes it cache less efficiently and requires more disk accesses. Newly created files are created mostly near the end of the disk, an unfortunate location, since you will very likely access them.

Figure 5-1 shows how the Backup model deteriorates. The top line shows the disk in its model's ideal state. All files are contiguous, and all free space is contiguous at the back of the disk. To get to the state shown in the second line, arbitrary copying is started at the left-hand side of the disk (the low-numbered logical block side), and every other volatile file is copied.

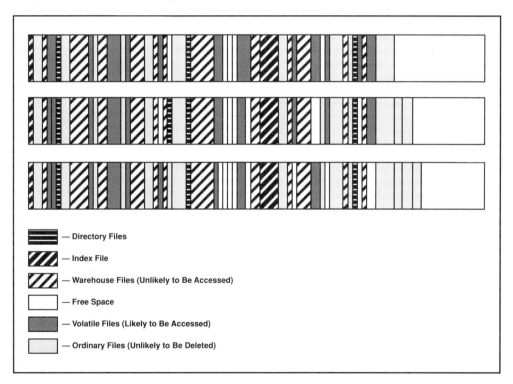

Figure 5-1. Backup Model

The rule for copying is that new space must be allocated before old space is freed. The new space was allocated contiguously to as low a block number as possible.

While this is not exactly what would happen on a multiuser OpenVMS system, it adequately demonstrates what causes the refragmentation.

To arrive at the state shown in the third line, the process again begins at the left-hand side of the disk and copies all the volatile files that were not copied in the first pass, in the same manner as the first pass. After this amount of activity, the free space is already fragmented into six pieces, five of which are small.

When free space becomes fragmented, newly created or extended files tend to become more fragmented. The size of the largest free space chunk has shrunk by one-third. There will probably be heavy disk activity from the beginning of the disk to the 87 percent point, and even farther if any large file is created.

Therefore, in addition to quick refragmentation, it is clear that the average seek distance is high, because there is no locality among frequently accessed files. One silly variation on the Backup model has the "enhancement" that files are placed as near as possible to their corresponding directory file — so-called juxtapositioning. The supposed rationale for juxtapositioning is that before you access a file, you do a directory access to look it up. But it almost never happens this way. The typical sequence is that a directory access is performed, and the next access is to the index file. Only if the proper block in the index file is cached and the directory files are not cached does juxtapositioning offer any benefit. A system would have to be strangely mistuned for this to occur more than rarely. It is better to position the directory files near the index file.

Juxtapositioning's main effect is to guarantee scattered directory files all over the disk, helping to maximize their average distance from the index file. The files for each account will also be in separate areas on the disk. If you have multiple users in multiple accounts (typical on all but single-user systems), juxtapositioning guarantees maximum average seek distance from file to file. Fortunately for juxtapositioning users, it is generally no worse than random positioning.

REVERSE BACKUP MODEL

The Reverse Backup model is exactly like the Backup model except that files are kept at the back of the disk with the supposed advantage of keeping free space at the start of the disk. The popularity of this model is a triumph of marketing effort over logical thought. The rationale for putting free space at a disk's beginning is the mistaken notion that OpenVMS starts searching for free space at a disk's beginning and hence finds it faster.

Except for the most sadly mistuned systems, OpenVMS seldom starts searching for free space at a disk's beginning. Even if this were so, the search overhead is negligible compared with the overhead suffered from adverse effects of this strategy.

For the sake of argument, assume that OpenVMS does allocate space as close to the start of a disk as possible. Figure 5-2 shows the results of the Reverse Backup model. The top line reflects the model's ideal state. All files are contiguous, and the free space is consolidated at the front of the disk. The first piece of the index file is always at the start of the disk and can never be moved. Fortunately, its existence there is inconsequential when considering performance.

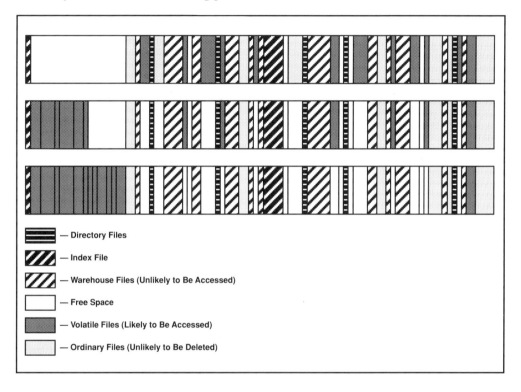

Figure 5-2. Reverse Backup Model

Line two captures one pass just like the Backup model, starting at the left-hand side of the disk and performing a copy of every other volatile file. This method of disk space allocation uses the exact rule that proponents of the Reverse Backup model claim OpenVMS follows to position files. That is, new space is allocated as close as possible to the start of the disk.

The state in the third line reflects a second pass that copies all of the volatile files not copied in the first pass. Look at what happens. New files are created at the beginning of the disk as far away as possible from the rest of the data on the disk, some of which will presumably be accessed. There is no better way to guarantee a greater average seek distance (that is, slowest access times) on the disk than to put the new files at the beginning of the disk.

Furthermore, when the files were deleted, little holes appeared in the high end of the disk where the files used to be. These holes will not be filled until all of the contiguous free space at the beginning of the disk is used. Thus, this strategy also guarantees the quickest possible refragmentation of the free space on the disk.

After these two passes, free space has been fragmented into twelve chunks, each of which is relatively small. The largest contiguous chunk is only 3 percent of the disk's size. Heavily accessed files are scattered over the entire disk, causing maximum average seek distance for future activity. Because space allocations and deallocations occur all over the disk, maximum overhead occurs, updating the bitmap file and searching the caches. As necessity is the mother of invention, and vice versa, quick deterioration of the disk structure from this strategy accounts for the curious popularity of "continuous" defragmentation.

OPTIMIZED MODEL

In the Optimized model, all files are made contiguous and free space is consolidated into one chunk, but now files are positioned according to their expected use.

Directory files are placed as close as possible (with a least squares fit) to the index file. Typically, this means that they are placed at the low end of the large chunk of the index file positioned in the middle of the disk upon initialization. If first a directory file and then the index file are accessed, seek time is greatly reduced. It should be noted that in multiuser systems this is not necessarily common. However, this strategy is never worse than random placement.

Warehouse files, those not likely to be accessed, are placed at the end of the disk. As a result, the disk head is unlikely to ever seek to the back 25 percent of the disk. With this strategy alone, average seek distance is cut by 25 percent over random file placement. It is not difficult to recognize files that are unlikely to be accessed soon. By turning on volume retention dates, OpenVMS effectively keeps a date of last access for each file. (Do not confuse this with the date of last modification.) Files that have not been accessed recently are not likely to be accessed soon. If a file is not accessed for 6 months, you probably would not expect to access it tomorrow.

Free space is centered between the files that will actually be accessed. Because this free space is most likely to be used for new files, the new files — those very likely to be accessed — will be positioned near the center of the action. This helps reduce average seek distance even more.

Volatile files will be positioned to both sides of the free space, with those most likely to be deleted placed closest to the free space. Since this positions these files next to other volatile files or free space, when these files are deleted they tend to enlarge an existing chunk of free space rather than create a new small chunk.

All file creations and deletions occur in a small area on the disk containing a high percentage of free space, the ideal situation for avoiding refragmentation. Only a small portion of the bitmap need be cached or accessed, another performance savings.

It is easy to recognize files that will be deleted soon. They are the files created most recently. To convince yourself that this is so, consider the converse: If a file has existed on the disk for a long time, why would you expect it to be deleted soon? There are some cyclical systems in which files have a constant life span, say 30 days, but such systems are in the minority. Surprisingly, this model still works much better than random placement on such systems.

Ordinary files are placed in the remaining space, with those likely to be accessed most often placed closest to the center of the disk that is used, that is, around the free space area.

Figure 5-3 illustrates the Optimized model. The top line shows the model's ideal state. The second line reflects deletion of one-half of the volatile files. Since the files most likely to be deleted were placed closest to the free space, they were deleted first. Reallocation occurs according to the same rules that apply to the other models.

The third line shows the copying of the volatile files not copied in the first pass. At this point, the disk still looks very good, so let's try two more passes.

The fourth line shows the copying of every other volatile file, just as in the first two models, since you are no longer likely to know which volatile files are most likely to be copied or deleted.

The fifth line reflects copying all the volatile files not copied in the previous pass. This disk is still in better shape than the resultant disks from either of the other models. Repeat this process many times, and the disk structure does not significantly deteriorate.

After two passes, free space is in two chunks. The largest chunk is still 95 percent of its original size. The most heavily used files are concentrated in roughly the disk's first half, and the head never seeks to the back 25 percent of the disk.

After four passes, free space is in three chunks. The largest chunk is still three-fourths of its original size. The most heavily used files are still concentrated in roughly the first half of the disk, and the head still never seeks to the back 25 percent of the disk. After four passes this model is still clearly better than the Backup and Reverse Backup models in their ideal states.

Even after four passes, the heaviest file activity is contained in a relatively small area of the disk containing a high percentage of free space. Average seek time has been greatly reduced, and bitmap and extent caching demands are reduced. Most important, the file creations and deletions remain in a small area on the disk. The structure cannot degrade until the nature of the files changes. Files that previously were unlikely to be deleted or even accessed must be deleted to upset this stability.

The optimized model clearly remains far more efficient than the other models.

OTHER CONSIDERATIONS

Other considerations you should take into account when determining the relative merits of disk defragmentation include open files, heavy disk activity, and the effect of the defragmentation process on other users.

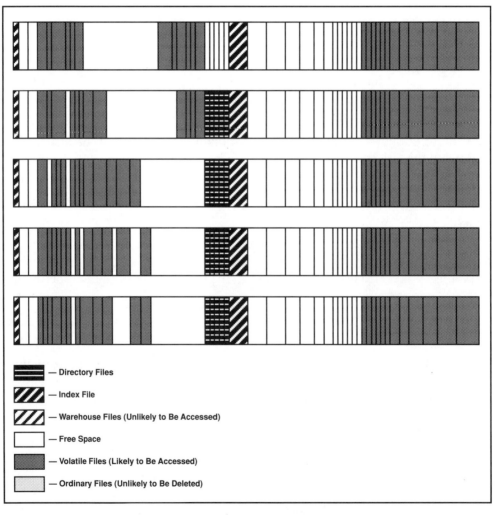

— Directory Files

— Index File

— Warehouse Files (Unlikely to Be Accessed)

— Free Space

— Volatile Files (Likely to Be Accessed)

— Ordinary Files (Unlikely to Be Deleted)

Figure 5-3. Optimized Model

OPEN FILES

Currently, there is no commercially available disk defragmenter that can move a file kept continually open by another process. I do not believe that there will ever be a product that will copy a file held open with write access by another process. As long as there are other users accessing the disk being optimized, there will be files that cannot be moved. These files cannot be made contiguous, nor can they be moved to their optimum locations. They may fragment the rest of the disk so badly that other files cannot be made contiguous or even moved. Even though the disk optimizer doesn't interfere with other user activity, user activity interferes with the disk optimization process, and optimization quality suffers.

HEAVY DISK ACTIVITY

During periods of heavy disk activity, the ANALYZE/DISK_STRUCTURE command may report erroneous errors in the disk structure. During such periods it is difficult to know if the errors reported are the result of normal OpenVMS caching and heavy activity or if there is truly a problem with the disk structure. Absolute reliability requires taking the resulting error messages seriously, unless you have another way of determining the true status of the disk structure.

EFFECT ON OTHER USERS

Another problem arises when trying to run a disk defragmenter during periods of heavy usage. The disk defragmenter slows the system. Even if a defragmenter is run at low priority on a disk that is not being used by another user, it will significantly slow the rest of the system. There are several reasons for this:

- Disk I/O transfers slow the bus.

- CPU demands eventually take a toll. Even though the system may not be making CPU demands when the I/Os are queued, they will finish some time later, and the device handler will interrupt whatever process is running at whatever priority when the I/O completes.

- The defragmenter process uses main memory. Systems short on memory cause other processes to page and swap more than they would otherwise.

- Priorities shift. No matter how low the priority is set on the defragmenting process, OpenVMS occasionally boosts its priority high enough that it will receive some CPU time.

- There may be heavy access competition. On disks being accessed by other users, the large I/O transfers to and from the disk being optimized will compete heavily with other users, causing them to be much more disk-bound than usual.

These reasons show that a disk optimizer is optimally run during periods of minimal user access to the disk.

FILE SYSTEM PERFORMANCE CHECKLIST

To give your system its optimal file system performance:

1. Choose the time of minimum activity on the disk to be optimized. Doing a regular image backup means kicking users off the system anyway. An ideal time for disk optimization is when this backup is finished.

2. Check your device status to verify that you are not currently logging device errors on the devices to be used. Use the SHOW DEVICE command and check the error counts.

3. Determine whether the disk targeted for optimization has a problem that needs to be solved by using the ANALYZE/DISK_STRUCTURE command. If there are any multiply allocated blocks, repair the problem before proceeding. Repairing multiply allocated blocks will require manual intervention; at least one file must be deleted.

4. Structure your disk as described in the Optimized model, and you will enjoy a well-optimized disk that stays optimized for a long time.

Basic System Tuning

MEMORY MANAGEMENT

OpenVMS is based on a virtual memory system. This chapter explains the main features of the memory management subsystem and some of the data structures it uses and manipulates. Also discussed are other data structures that have a major impact on memory management.

The main components of the memory management subsystem are the page fault handler and the swapper. The three major data structures discussed in this chapter are the page frame number (PFN) database, process page tables, and system page tables.

For a virtual memory system to perform efficiently, applications need to have good code and data locality. That is, the code should avoid frequent large leaps, and references to data should tend to stay in one area of memory for reasonable amounts of time. A good example of an application that works very efficiently in a virtual memory environment is the compilers. Compilers execute in phases; when in a phase there is almost no access to code in any other phase.

AXP VERSUS VAX MEMORY MANAGEMENT

OpenVMS was designed to implement a process-local page replacement algorithm. Thus, a process pages against itself for the most part. This helps to minimize the probability of page fault thrashing and makes for more predictable performance for a real-time process. One drawback to this method is that a heavily faulting process can cause the contents of the free and modified page lists to cycle rapidly, thus indirectly affecting other processes.

OpenVMS does not keep a set of reference bits in the page table entry (PTE) to help identify the least recently referenced pages. Instead, OpenVMS uses the order of the working set list entries to determine the least recently referenced page. The working set list is a ring buffer, with a pointer to the entry most recently added to the working set. This allows OpenVMS to determine which page to remove from a process's working set with almost no overhead. The page selected is the page following the most recently added, that is, the oldest.

While this algorithm is easy to implement and has almost no overhead, the page selected is not optimal and can cause even more page faults. To minimize the impact of this algorithm, OpenVMS creates secondary page caches so that a page faulted out of a process's working set can be faulted back in with little or no overhead. Between these two features, OpenVMS gets most of the benefits of a least-recently used algorithm without the overhead. What is required is that the working set sizes, the amount and method by which they increase and decrease, and the secondary page caches must be set correctly to obtain optimal performance.

OpenVMS AXP memory management is based on OpenVMS VAX memory management. In OpenVMS AXP a virtual address is represented as a 64-bit unsigned integer, while in OpenVMS VAX a virtual address is represented as a 32-bit unsigned integer.

One of the goals of OpenVMS AXP was to make true the contention that "VMS is VMS is VMS." However, the architectural differences introduced by the AXP processor required a change in the basic definition of the size of a page.

Because OpenVMS is a virtual memory system, the size of a page is of basic concern. Page size dependencies are distributed throughout the OpenVMS operating system code. While only a few areas show through to the system management or programmer interface level, these areas are critical to effective performance management.

For OpenVMS to effectively use the speed of the AXP chip, the basic page size had to be increased. For the initial release, the page size was increased from 512 bytes to 8,192 bytes. To support even faster chip designs, support is included for 16,384 bytes, 32,768 bytes, or 65,536 bytes per page. To correctly use page size, the user must now query OpenVMS for the size of a page in bytes for the current platform. To determine the size of a page, include the code fragment in Figure 6-1. Page size is also available to the Command Language Interpreter (CLI) via use of the F$GETSYI lexical function.

```
struct ItemList
{
  unsigned short jpilen, jpicode;
  int *jpibufadr,*jpiretadr;
} jpi_list[2];
#include <syidef.h>
#ifndef SYI$_PAGE_SIZE
#define SYI$_PAGE_SIZE 4452
#endif
.......
  jpi_list[0].jpilen   = sizeof( PageSize);
  jpi_list[0].jpicode  = SYS$_PAGE_SIZE ;
  jpi_list[0].jpibufadr = (int * )&(PageSize);
  jpi_list[0].jpiretadr = (int *)&ReturnLength;
  jpi_list[1].jpilen   = 0;
  jpi_list[1].jpicode  = 0;
/*
  Call SYS$GETSYIW to get the page size.
*/
  status = SYS$GETSYIW(0, 0, 0, &jpi_list, (struct IOSB *) &iosb, 0, 0);
```

Figure 6-1. Determining Page Size

To reduce the confusion caused by changing the size of a page, the new term *pagelet* has been introduced. A pagelet is defined as 512 bytes of memory. Thus, an AXP page is 16 pagelets in size, and a VAX page is 1 pagelet in size.

The old VAX/VMS page is now equivalent to the new pagelet. Figure 6-2 shows the relationship between AXP "pages" and VAX "pages."

MEMORY USAGE

OpenVMS memory can be categorized into four major groups:

1. OpenVMS nonpageable memory.

2. System working set.

3. Secondary page caches.

4. Process working sets.

Figure 6-3 shows how to get a quick but good estimate of each of these memory types. The last line of the SHOW MEMORY command shows the number of pages permanently allocated to OpenVMS.

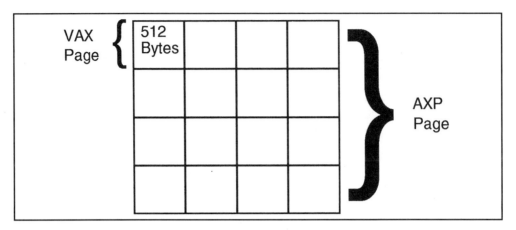

Figure 6-2. VAX Versus AXP Page

```
┌─────────────────────────────────────────────────────────────────────┐
│ ─                          OpenVMS Performance                    □ □ │
├───────────────────────────────────────────────────────────────────────┤
│  File   Edit   Commands   Options   Print                        Help │
│                                                                       │
│          System Memory Resources on 28-APR-1993 13:21:15.30           │
│                                                                       │
│ Physical Memory Usage (pages):    Total     Free     In Use   Modified│
│   Main Memory (128.00Mb)          16384     6531      8005      1848  │
│                                                                       │
│ Granularity Hint Regions (pages): Total     Free     In Use   Released│
│   Code region                      512        0       469        43  │
│   Data region (User Read)          128        5        67        56  │
│   Data region (Exec Read)          720        0       720         0  │
│                                                                       │
│ Slot Usage (slots):               Total     Free    Resident  Swapped │
│   Process Entry Slots              256       206       47         3  │
│   Balance Set Slots                254       206       45         3  │
│                                                                       │
│ Dynamic Memory Usage (bytes):     Total     Free     In Use    Largest│
│   Nonpaged Dynamic Memory        7553024   611776   6941248    23424 │
│   Paged Dynamic Memory           5021696  3280464   1741232  3272320 │
│                                                                       │
│ Paging File Usage (blocks):                Free  Reservable    Total  │
│   DISK$SYSAXP:[SYS0.SYSEXE]SWAPFILE.SYS    32128    32128     38272   │
│   DISK$SYSAXP:[SYS0.SYSEXE]PAGEFILE.SYS   262032   186688    270080   │
│   (Page file name not available)          292336   206256    299904   │
│                                                                       │
│ Of the physical pages in use, 2531 pages are permanently allocated to VMS. │
│                                                                       │
│ The Virtual I/O Cache is DISABLED on this node.                       │
│ $ write sys$output "''f$getsyi("SYSMWCNT")' ''f$getsyi("FREELIM")' ''f$getsyi("MPW_LOLIMIT")' " │
│ 8840 200 120                                                          │
│                                                                       │
└───────────────────────────────────────────────────────────────────────┘
```

Figure 6-3. Show Memory

The DCL command:

```
$ write sys$output " "f$getsyi("SYSMWCNT")' ...
```

will show the size of the system working set, the minimum free list size, and the minimum modified list size.

The line in Figure 6-3 labeled Main Memory shows the current size of the free list and modified list. The sum of these two numbers is the current size of the secondary page cache.

You can determine the amount of memory available to be used by processes on the system by using Equation 6-1.

$$System\_Usage = Nonpaged + SYSMWCNT + FREELIM +$$
$$MPW\_LOWLIM + XQP$$
$$XQP \cong 140 \ pagelets$$
$$Available\_Process\_memory = Total\_Physical\_Memory - System\_Usage$$
$$Total\_Physical\_Memory =$$
$$MIN(PHYSICALPAGES, Actual\_memory) \ (VAX)$$
$$MIN(PHYSICAL\_MEMORY, Actual\_memory) \ (AXP)$$

Equation 6-1. Memory Allocations

OPENVMS NONPAGEABLE MEMORY

The loadable system images code and the device drivers code make up the majority of the nonpageable memory that is code. On OpenVMS AXP, images installed as resident also reside in the area. The size of this code area varies little among the various OpenVMS platforms. The real variables are the number and type of device drivers loaded.

The largest part of nonpageable memory that is data consists of the nonpaged pool, lookaside lists, and the PFN database. OpenVMS keeps track of physical memory through the PFN database. The size of the nonpaged data areas is determined largely by the following SYSGEN parameters:

- COUNT and COUNTV for SRP, IRP, and LRP lookaside lists. These SYSGEN parameters and the associated lookaside lists were dropped with the release of OpenVMS VAX V6.0 and OpenVMS AXP V1.0. They were replaced by an adaptive pool management scheme. However, previous versions of VMS depended heavily on the correct sizing of these structures.

- NPAGEDYN and NPAGEVIR, which specify the number of bytes to allocate for the initial size of nonpaged pool and the maximum size in bytes to which the nonpaged pool may be extended.

- PHYSICALPAGES for OpenVMS VAX and PHYSICAL_MEMORY for OpenVMS AXP are used to specify the amount of physical memory on a system. This is often used to test the removal of physical memory without actually having to remove the memory boards. If this parameter is set to a value less than the actual physical memory in the system, the system only allows the user access to the reduced set of physical memory. For example, if your system has 32 MB of memory and you set PHYSICAL_MEMORY to 24 MB, the SHOW MEMORY command will only show that your system has 24 MB of memory.

- VIRTUALPAGECNT, which specifies the total number of pages that can be mapped for a process. These pages are the sum of P0 and P1 space. There is no determination of which space (P0 or P1) has what percentage of the virtual page count.

- BALSETCNT, which limits the number of memory-resident processes on the system.

ADAPTIVE POOL MANAGEMENT

To provide better and more efficient methods of pool management, adaptive pool management was introduced with OpenVMS VAX V6.0 and OpenVMS AXP. Adaptive pool management eliminates the four separate virtual regions of system space for nonpaged pool — the three lookaside lists, SRP, IRP and LRP, and the general nonpaged pool. There is now one large virtual region, which contains eighty lookaside lists and a general pool area.

These eighty lookaside lists are created initially as empty lists of sizes 1 to 5,120 bytes in increments of 64 bytes. When an allocation for a given list's size fails because the list is empty, allocation occurs from the general pool. When the memory is deallocated, it is added to the lookaside list for the specific size. Thus, the lookaside lists populate over time to the size needed by the current average workload on the system.

This feature of dynamic lookaside lists plus a reclamation policy for returning excess entries from the lists to the general pool provides a reduction in overall pool memory requirements and less frequent cases of pool allocation failure. The increase from three to eighty lookaside lists greatly increased the hit rate for the faster allocation from lookaside lists.

A "packet" of memory can be in one of the following states:

- Allocated.

- Free and part of the general pool.

- Free and attached to the "correct" lookaside list.

To keep the lookaside list from growing too large as a result of peaks in system usage, there is a first-level recovery algorithm. Every 30 seconds, each of the lookaside lists is examined. If there are at least two entries on the list, one entry is removed to a scratch list. Thus, a maximum of eighty packets containing at most 207,361 bytes of memory are on the scratch list at the end of the search. All entries on the scratch list are then returned to the general pool. Thus, over time a large list that is no longer in active use will be returned to the general pool, and the memory will become available for reuse in other lists.

Before pool expansion takes place, a last attempt is made to recover memory from the lookaside lists. All lists are examined, and if there is an entry on the list, then one entry is moved to the scratch list. All entries on the scratch list are then returned to the general pool.

In addition, adaptive pool management maintains usage statistics and increases the detection of pool corruption. The SYSGEN parameter POOLCHECK now provides boot-time selection of pool code statistics and corruption detection:

- If POOLCHECK is zero, then the nonstatistics, nonchecking version of adaptive pool management is loaded.

- If POOLCHECK is nonzero, then the full pool checking and monitoring version is loaded.

If you load the full checking version, then two new ANALYZE/SYSTEM commands are available (see Appendix H for example output):

- SHOW POOL/RING_BUFFER displays the most recent 256 pool allocation and deallocation requests.

- SHOW POOL/STATISTICS displays the statistics for each lookaside list.

With the addition of adaptive pool management, the MONITOR POOL command is no longer supported. In addition, the following SYSGEN parameters are no longer used:

- SRPCOUNT, SRPCOUNTV, SRPMIN, and SRPSIZE.

- IRPCOUNT and IRPCOUNTV.

- LRPCOUNT, LRPCOUNTV, LRPSIZE, and LRPMIN.

System Working Set

The system working set count (SYSMWCNT) is the number of pages for the working set containing the currently resident pages of pageable system space. Since system pages are the same for all processes, there is little locality associated with the use of system space. Thus, system page faulting can easily become a bottleneck. SYSMWCNT is used to control system faulting. The limiting factor for setting SYSMWCNT is that pages allocated to the system via SYSMWNCT are permanently allocated to the system and therefore are no longer available for process working sets, even if they are not in use by the system. Unlike other working set lists, the system working set list does not increase or decrease in response to the system page fault rate.

A change to any of the SYSGEN parameters VAXCLUSTER, GBLPAGES, and PAGEDYN can change the calculated value of SYSMWCNT.

To ensure that your system will reboot after changing any of the above, always make these changes via the AUTOGEN procedures. Make the necessary changes in your system's MODPARAMS.DAT file and run AUTOGEN to change the system values and to reboot your system.

Secondary Page Caches

The secondary page caches are made up of the modified and free lists. These caches minimize the impact of the OpenVMS page replacement algorithm. The Free List and Modified List sections of this chapter discuss this category in more detail.

The minimum size of memory used by the secondary page caches can be calculated using Equation 6-2.

$$FREELIM + MPW\_LOLIMIT + ZERO\_LIST\_HI \leq Secondary\_Page\_Caches$$
$$Secondary\_Page\_Caches \leq (Size\ of\ Free\ List) + (Size\ of\ Modified\ List)$$
$$+ (Size\ of\ Zero\ List)$$

Equation 6-2. Size of Secondary Caches

OpenVMS AXP introduces a new page list called the zero page list. The Free List, Modified Page List, and Zero Page List sections in this chapter cover secondary page caches in more detail.

Process Working Sets

The final memory category is process working sets. You normally will want the majority of physical memory available for this category. The Working Set List and Working Set sections of this chapter discuss this category in more detail.

PAGING

OpenVMS keeps track of virtual memory mapping through the use of process and system page tables. Page tables consist of page table entries (PTE), which map a page of virtual space to its physical memory location or its backing storage location. The location on mass storage from which a virtual page is read is called its backing store. A common example of backing store is a set of locks in an executable image.

There are four types of virtual memory:

S1 Space — Originally defined as $C0000000_{16}$ through $FFFFFFF_{16}$ and reserved to Digital, the architecture has since changed, and these virtual addresses are now part of S0 space.

S0 Space — Virtual addresses in the range of 80000000_{16} through $FFFFFFF_{16}$ are S0 (system) space. For OpenVMS AXP, the virtual addresses are $FFFFFFF\ 80000000_{16}$ through $FFFFFFF\ FFFFFFF_{16}$. During system initialization, all available system space is mapped. The maximum size of system space is fixed. Translation from system space to physical memory must always be possible.

P1 Space — Virtual addresses in the range of 40000000_{16} through $7FFFFFFF_{16}$ are P1 space. P1 space contains the process stack and process permanent control information maintained by the executive. It also contains the process address space used by RMS and DCL. These virtual addresses are the same for OpenVMS AXP.

P0 Space — Virtual addresses in the range of 00000000_{16} through $3FFFFFFF_{16}$ are P0 space. P0 space maps the image currently in use by the process. These virtual addresses are the same for OpenVMS AXP.

PAGE FAULTS

Page faults occur when a reference is made to a virtual address whose PTE valid bit is clear, that is, a page that is not valid. There is no "loader" for images. Images are activated by allowing their pages to fault. The first time you access a page that is not a global page, it will not be valid. Consequently, there must always be page faults in OpenVMS.

HARD FAULTS

Hard faults are page faults that result in disk reads to bring the appropriate pages into memory. Because images are activated from disk images, there must always be some hard faults unless all executable pages are global pages that have already been faulted in by another process.

PFCDEFAULT

The PFCDEFAULT SYSGEN parameter determines the default number of pages read from disk when a hard fault occurs. For OpenVMS AXP systems this parameter is expressed in pagelets and is rounded up to the next page size. If the system faulted in just the one faulting page from disk whenever a hard fault occurred, then a huge number of hard faults would be required for image activation. Therefore, the system tries to fault in several pages at once, but not more than PFCDEFAULT pages (except in special cases). PFCDEFAULT is set at login. Login copies PFCDEFAULT from the SYSGEN-loaded value SGN$GW_DFPFC to the process header (offset PHD$B_DFPFC).

PFCDEFAULT can be overridden, but this seldom happens. It can be set dynamically for each process and can be linked into images by the LINKER with the CLUSTER =nnn link option, where nnn will be used as the PFCDEFAULT for the specified cluster. A large PFCDEFAULT speeds image activation, since it takes fewer hard faults to give a process the pages it needs to execute. A small PFCDEFAULT saves CPU time, since the smaller size takes less work to map into the process's working set, and it is much less likely to bring in unneeded pages with the smaller size.

SOFT FAULTS

Soft faults are page faults to pages whose contents are already in physical memory, but the page is not a part of the current process's working set. If the contents of the page have never been modified, the fault will bring in a page from the free list. If the contents of the page have been modified, the fault will bring in a page from either the modified or the free list.

Demand-zero faults are faults that would otherwise be hard faults. But in this case the page contents are known to be zero. They are a part of normal image activation and are unavoidable. There are no system parameters on OpenVMS that directly affect the number of demand-zero page faults.

To speed up demand-zero faulting on the AXP, where pages are much bigger and thus a demand-zero page fault takes much longer, a new demand-zero faulting mechanism has been implemented. A list is kept of pages containing all zeros. When the system is not busy, a page on the free list that has no ties to a virtual page (that is, a page whose contents have been deleted) is selected, its contents are zeroed, and it is placed on the zero list. To maintain a reasonable balance, a new SYSGEN parameter has been added: ZERO_LIST_HI, which is the maximum number of pages zeroed and put on the zeroed page list.

Global valid faults are page faults resolved by valid pages in the systemwide global page tables that were already mapped to another process.

Free list faults are pages that were read from the free list as a result of page faults. This can be caused by a process soft-faulting back in pages that were removed from its working set. It can also be caused by access to global pages that are not currently mapped in any process's working set. On a single-user system you will see a large number of free list faults for installed images that are frequently used. If you IN-STALL the DEC C compiler as shared images, the code pages of the compiler will be put on the free list when you exit from the compiler. If you then reinvoke the compiler, you will see a large number of free list faults as these valid global pages are removed from the free list and added back into your process without any I/Os being done by the page fault handler.

FREE LIST

The free list is not necessarily wasted memory. It probably contains pages that can be soft-faulted back into processes. Pages are called free because they are available for immediate use by any process without the need to copy their contents elsewhere.

The free list may contain:

- Unmodified pages that are otherwise valid in some active process's address space.

- Unmodified global pages that are not valid in any active process's address space.

- Modified pages whose contents have been written to disk and are otherwise valid in some active process's address space.

- Modified or unmodified pages associated with an inactive process.

Figure 6-4 shows the layout of the free list.

FREELIM AND FREEGOAL

FREELIM is the minimum size of the free list. When the free list becomes smaller than FREELIM, the swapper takes steps to make it at least FREEGOAL pages in size. For more information see the Swapper Steps section of this chapter. FREELIM and FREEGOAL are typically set too low by AUTOGEN for OpenVMS VAX systems.

GROWLIM AND BORROWLIM

Automatic Working Set Adjustment (AWSA) will not increase a process's working list size unless there are at least BORROWLIM pages on the free list.

Actual pages are not allocated to a process unless there are at least GROWLIM pages on the free list. Pages are allocated to a process as the result of a page fault.

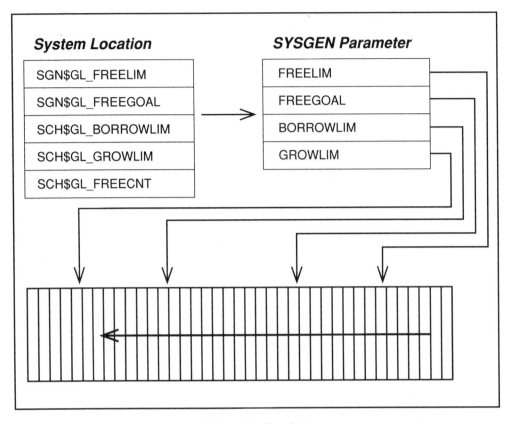

Figure 6-4. Free List

MODIFIED LIST

The modified page list contains pages that cannot be reused unless they are written to disk (backing store) or faulted back into the owning process. The modified list may contain pages modified by processes that were subsequently removed from the process's working set. These pages still have valid contents; they can be added back to the owning process with minimum overhead. Figure 6-5 shows the layout of the modified list.

After pages on the modified list are written to backing store, they are placed on the free list. These pages can still be faulted back into the owning process, without needing any I/Os to be performed. Thus, if your process faults a page back in from the modified list, no I/Os are needed. If your process faults a page back in from the free list that was placed on the free list from the modified list after its contents were written to backing store, one I/O will have been done. If your process faults a page back in from backing store, two I/Os will have been done: one I/O to place into backing store and one I/O to fetch from backing store.

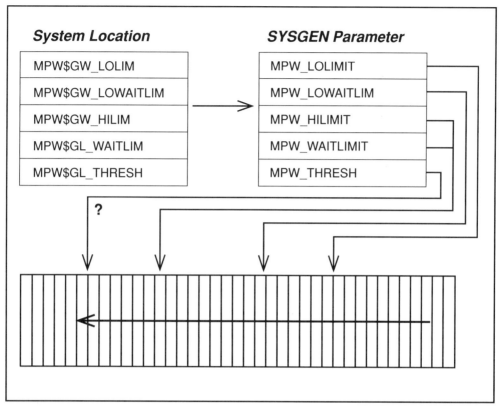

Figure 6-5. Modified List

MPW_HILIMIT AND MPW_LOLIMIT

If the modified list is larger than MPW_HILIMIT, the swapper can reduce it to MPW_LOLIMIT. OpenVMS frequently flushes the modified page list. Pages flushed from the modified page list are added to the end of the free page list after a copy of the page contents is written to backing storage. These pages still have valid contents; they can be added back to the owning process with minimum overhead. However, once they have been written to backing store, one half of the I/O overhead has already occurred.

Writing the modified list can be one of the major performance slowdowns on a system. In many cases it is not easy to detect the cause of this problem. Chapter 7 covers this problem in detail.

OTHER MODIFIED LIST PARAMETERS

The following SYSGEN parameters also control or depend on the size of the modified list:

1. The modified page writer busy wait limit, MPW_WAITLIMIT, indicates when to put a process into resource wait. If a process is generating a modified page entry and the size of the modified list is greater than MPW_WAITLIMIT, then the process is put into the MPWBUSY resource wait mode.

2. The modified page writer threshold, MPW_THRESH, is the lower limit threshold, which stops the use of the modified page list as the primary source to recover memory. For more information, see the Swapper Steps section in this chapter.

3. The modified page list low-wait limit, MPW_LOWAITLIMIT, is the threshold at which processes in the miscellaneous wait state MPWBUSY are allowed to resume.

   Prior to VMS V5.0, processes were not removed from the MPWBUSY wait state until the size of the modified page list was reduced to MPW_LOLIMIT. MPW_LOWAITLIMIT increases system performance for fast processors with large memories by reducing the amount of time processes spend in the MPWBUSY wait state.

4. MPW_IOLIMIT defines the number of outstanding I/Os to the modified page writer. Prior to VMS V5.0, the modified page writer never had more than one I/O outstanding. With VMS V5.0, the modified page writer can have up to 127 I/Os outstanding. The default is four.

   Each I/O requires a permanent nonpaged pool allocation, as calculated in Equation 6-3. With the default MPW_WRTCLUSTER of 96, for example, the required allocation per I/O is 752 bytes.

I/O Request Packet + (6 * *MPW_WRTCUSTER*)

Equation 6-3. MPW_IOLIMIT Memory Requirements

5. MPW_WRTCLUSTER specifies the number of page file pages (better expressed as number of disk blocks) written per I/O from the modified page list. The modified page writer attempts to write from the modified page list as a single contiguous I/O transfer to disk in sizes of MPW_WRTCLUSTER pages. Larger I/Os consume more CPU but are much more efficient in the overall use of CPU time.

   MPW_WRTCLUSTER is rounded down to the next closest multiple of 8 and cannot exceed 512. However, since the maximum size of any disk transfer is 127 blocks, the effective maximum value for MPW_WRTCLUSTER is 127 for VAX and 120 for AXP, until the 127-block maximum transfer to a disk is lifted.

ZERO PAGE LIST

Introduced with OpenVMS AXP, the zero page list is used to redistribute the overhead for demand-zero pages. Pages on AXP are substantially larger than on the VAX. Thus, the time to create a demand-zero page is also substantially longer and takes more CPU resources. The zero page list was created to use otherwise idle (wasted) cycles to zero pages of memory. The new system parameter ZERO_LIST_HI limits the number of pages on this list. Pages are zeroed and added to the zero page list when the following conditions exist:

- The system is idle.

- Sufficient memory is available.

- The number of pages on the zero page list is less than ZERO_LIST_HI.

This allows the system to use otherwise idle time to decrease the CPU time needed to supply demand-zero pages.

DEAD PAGE TABLE SCANS

When a process working set is full and needs to page-fault another page into its working set, OpenVMS must select a page to be removed from the working set to make room for the new page. The system scans the process working set list looking for a page to remove. If the selected page is a process page table page (a page of memory containing only page table pointer entries), the system checks whether any of the entries point to pages currently in the working set. If none of the entries points to any pages in the working set, this page is considered a dead page table page. The system global symbol PMS$GL_DPTSCN is incremented in the PMS area to track how many dead page table scans occur.

Prior to VMS V5.2, the system scanned the modified page list looking for any of the pages pointed to by the dead page table page. If any of these pages were on the modified page list, the entire modified page list was written, or flushed, from memory to the appropriate backing store (either the page file or a section file).

In versions of OpenVMS later than VMS V5.2, the entire list is no longer flushed. The system scans the modified page list looking for any of the pages to which the dead page table points. If any of these pages are on the modified page list, they are moved to the "high" end of the modified page list. The system then selectively purges the modified page list. The steps of scanning and flushing are continued until all required pages have been written to backing store. A maximum of 128 pages will be moved to the head of the modified list per scan.

WORKING SET LIST AND WORKING SET

The working set is the set of virtual pages mapped into your process context. Figure 6-6 shows the layout of a process's working set. The working set list does not reflect the number of pages in your working set. It defines the limits of the maximum number of pages in your working set. The actual number of pages in your working set is defined in the process control block (PCB) at offsets PCB$W_GPGCNT (global pages) and PCB$W_PPGCNT (process local pages). The working set list always contains at least enough entries to map the sum of process local and global pages.

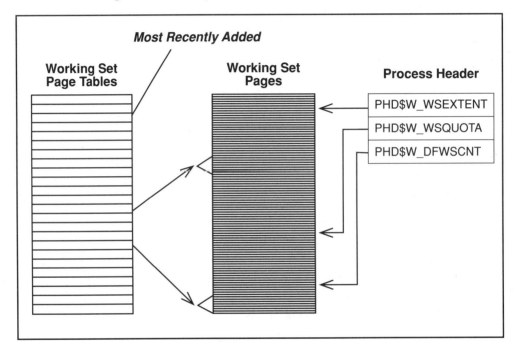

Figure 6-6. Working Set

Working set sizes are controlled by process quotas set by one of the following:

- AUTHORIZE.

- PQL parameters.

- System PQL list.

WSDEFAULT, WSQUOTA, AND WSEXTENT

The working set default, WSDEFAULT, is the initial size of the working set list. The list size is shrunk to WSDEFAULT upon image exit.

The working set quota, WSQUOTA, is the maximum working set size when the free list is less than BORROWLIM. Working sets can be expanded up to working set extent (WSEXTENT) only when the free list is above GROWLIM. Working set list sizes grow in increments of WSINC and shrink in decrements of WSDEC.

WSDEFAULT, WSQUOTA, and WSEXTENT are per-process parameters. They are set as follows:

1. Use the values passed to the SYS$CREPRC call. If no value is passed for any item, use the corresponding values of PQL_DWSDEFAULT, PQL_WSQUOTA, and PQL_DWSEXTENT.

2. The values just calculated are compared with the associated PQL_M parameters:

- If the current value for WSDEFAULT is less than PQL_MWSDEFAULT, the value for WSDEFAULT is set to PQL_MWSDEFAULT.

- If the current value for WSQUOTA is less than PQL_MWSQUOTA, the value for WSQUOTA is set to PQL_MWSQUOTA.

- If the current value for WSEXTENT is less than PQL_MWSEXTENT, the value for WSEXTENT is set to PQL_MWSEXTENT.

WSMAX

WSMAX (SGN$GL_MAXWSCNT) is the systemwide maximum working set size. Some systemwide data structures are based on WSMAX. Therefore, to change WSMAX, you must reboot your system. WSDEFAULT, WSQUOTA, and WSEXTENT are effectively limited by WSMAX.

AWSA

AWSA is the basic OpenVMS mechanism used to increase or decrease the memory allocated to processes. AWSA is queued as AST at the end of QUANTUM by the QUANTUM-end processing routine. The AWSA AST occurs at the start of the next QUANTUM. This means that for a process that does not consume much CPU resources and thus rarely reaches QUANTUM end, AWSA has little or no effect on the working set size.

IOTA is used to help I/O-bound processes reach quantum end. At the completion of each I/O, the remaining QUANTUM of a process is decremented by IOTA. This helps a process to reach end of quantum much faster and thus have its working set adjusted.

WORKING SET INCREMENT

The increment function is based on AWSTIME, PFRATH, and WSINC using the following rule: If at least AWSTIME of CPU time has been used by the process since the last increment, and if the process has been faulting at the rate of PFRATH faults per 10 seconds or more and the working set list is more than 75 percent full, then increment the working set list size by WSINC pages. Do not raise the working set list above WSQUOTA unless the free list is at least BORROWLIM pages in size. And do not raise it above WSEXTENT.

WORKING SET DECREMENT

The decrement function is based on AWSTIME, PFRATL, and WSDEC using the following rules:

- If PFRATL is nonzero, then if at least AWSTIME of CPU time has been used by the process since the last change and if the process has been faulting at less than PFRATL faults per 10 seconds, then decrement the working set by WSDEC pages. However, do not lower the working set so that there are fewer than AWSMIN private pages in it. Only private pages are considered, since removing a global page from one working set will not usually generate a free page to be added to the secondary caches.

- If PFRATL is zero, the process has had a priority boost in the last thirty-two quantum intervals, the size of the free list is less than BORROWLIM, and the working set list is greater than WSQUOTA, then decrement the working set list by the current working set list minus WSQUOTA or WSDEC, whichever is smaller.

Because of the side effects of having PFRATL nonzero, many people recommend that PFRATL always be set to zero. PFRATL is zero by default. To get a nonzero PFRATL, you must change the value. AUTOGEN will not set PFRATL to a nonzero value.

Given the usual values for AWSTIME (approximately one-fifth of a second), PFRATL and PFRATH must be changed often to affect the algorithm. For example, PFRATL values from 1 to 50 would all have the same effect, and processes that have had one fault or more would be exempted from decrementing.

PUTTING IT ALL TOGETHER

Because it is critical to understand how paging works, I will present a simple example of the way pages move around in your working set. I will use the default values supplied by OpenVMS for system/authorize parameters.

Image Startup — At image startup (that is, $ run executable_image.exe), your process will have a working set list entry count of WSDEFAULT (150 pages). But for the image, the total number of pages in memory is zero. The system will start executing your image.

First Fault — The first address you attempt to access will not be valid. In this case you will hard-fault to the file executable_image.exe. The system will hard-fault in PFCDEFAULT (32 pages) from the file executable_image.exe (assuming it is contiguous). Your process now has a total of thirty-two valid pages. Execution continues.

When WSDEFAULT Is Reached — After four hard faults, your process has 128 pages in its working set. On the fifth hard fault, a decision point is reached, since you have not met the conditions for a working set increment. In most cases you will not yet have used up your QUANTUM (20), 0.20 CPU seconds. Thus, you have only twenty-two working set entries remaining for pages (150 minus 128). This means that you must move ten pages (thirty-two minus twenty-two) from your working set to either the free or the modified list. This will put your valid pages at 150, the same as the working set entry count. From now until the time you get a working set increment, your process must move a page out of the working set for each page that is brought in. This is a time during which many processes have a very high fault rate. Execution continues.

Working Set Increment — To get a working set increment of WSINC (150 pages), your process must reach QUANTUM end and have had at least two faults since the last QUANTUM end (PFRATH 120 faults per 10 seconds). When this occurs, your working set list entry count is increased by WSINC to either WSQUOTA (256 pages) or 300 pages, depending on whether the current size of the free list is greater than GROWLIM (sixty-three pages). You will still have only 150 pages in your working set. But now on the next fault, hard or soft, your process can add a physical page to the working set without moving a page out of the working set. Execution continues.

Reaching WSQUOTA — Once the total number of physical pages in your working set is equal to WSQUOTA (256 pages), the way page faults are handled changes again. If there are more than GROWLIM pages on the free list, your working set list entry count can be increased by WSINC, but the value cannot exceed WSEXTENT (512 pages). You get lucky, and your working set list count is increased to 406 pages (256 plus 150 pages). You may or may not be able to get more pages into your working set. Execution continues.

Using WSEXTENT — Your program continues to page-fault. Only if there are more than BORROWLIM pages (300) on the free list when your program reaches QUANTUM end can your program use the available working set list count and add pages to the working set without removing pages first. The next time the program gets a working set increment, the size of the working set list count will be set to WSEXTENT (512 pages). Once your program has used up this count and has 512 pages in the working set, your only option will be to remove pages from your working set before new pages can be added.

Conclusion — Since even the simplest program now needs hundreds if not thousands of pages in the working set, it is obvious that the default values for WSQUOTA and WSEXTENT are far too small.

SWAPPER STEPS

The three main jobs of the swapper are:

1. Maintain a minimum number of pages (FREELIM) on the free list.

2. Maintain a maximum bound on the modified list (MPW_HILIMIT).

3. Manage balance set slots (BALSETCNT).

The swapper's first action is to ensure that the current size of the free list is greater than FREELIM. To maintain the free list, the swapper takes the following four steps to get pages onto the free list:

1. If the modified list has more than MPW_THRESH pages, the swapper checks whether writing the modified list will recover enough pages. If writing the modified list back to MPW_LOLIMIT will recover enough pages to make the free list larger than FREEGOAL, the swapper trims the modified list back to MPW_LOLIMIT.

2. If there are Process Header Descriptors (PHD) of deleted or outswapped processes still around, the swapper reclaims them.

3. If the swapper still needs pages of the free list, the swapper shrinks processes, first to WSQUOTA and then to SWPOUTPGCNT.

4. If all else fails, the swapper swaps out entire processes.

The SYSGEN parameters SWPOUTPGCNT, LONGWAIT, and BALSETCNT affect the actions of the swapper. These parameters are discussed in the following sections.

SWPOUTPGCNT

SWPOUTPGCNT is the size to which processes are to be trimmed before total swapping occurs. Pages tend to be trimmed from inactive processes and put onto the free or modified list. This tends to replace likely candidates for soft-faulting by unlikely candidates. In addition, there is no check to ensure that global pages are not removed. The removal of global page entries usually will not recover pages.

When a process becomes active again, it may need to hard-fault pages back in from many locations instead of just being swapped back in from one location if the whole process were swapped out.

Thus, in many cases, if the swapper trims a process back to SWPOUTPGCNT, there are severe performance penalties when SWPOUTPGCNT is set to too low a value.

DORMANTWAIT

DORMANTWAIT specifies in seconds the amount of time that may elapse without a significant event before the system treats a low-priority computable process as a dormant process for scheduling purposes. After SUSP processes, dormant processes are the most likely candidates for memory reclamation by the swapper.

In VMS V5.0, PIXSCAN also affected inactive processes. Since a dormant process may be holding resources needed by other processes, PIXSCAN was used to give temporary priority boosts to these inactive processes so that the processes would run for a small amount of time and hopefully release the resources. Thus, while PIXSCAN was making the idle processes active, DORMANTWAIT was trying to trim or swap them out. Often, these two methods were in direct conflict.

VMS V5.2 changes the way DORMANTWAIT is used to delete inactive processes.

LONGWAIT

LONGWAIT is the time a process must be in Hibernate (HIB) or Logical Event Flag (LEF) wait state before the swapper considers it idle and therefore a prime candidate for outswapping. Logically, this parameter makes good sense. If a process has not been active recently, there is no reason to expect it to be active again soon.

BALSETCNT

BALSETCNT is the maximum number of processes that can reside in memory at a given time. The swapper will swap the remainder of the processes in and out as it deems necessary. BALSETCNT is useful for forcing outswaps of idle processes.

BALSETCNT is dangerous. If the BALSETCNT is too small, it causes very high swapper overhead and defeats the OpenVMS priority boost scheme. The reason is that whenever there is a process in the COMO queue (computable, outswapped), other processes are immediately lowered to their base priorities at end of QUANTUM.

NEW MEMORY RECOVERY MECHANISM

As of VMS V5.4-3 there are significant changes to the memory management. One major change was the implementation of proactive memory reclamation. Previously, memory was removed from a process only by QUANTUM-end processing, swapper trimming, or swapping out of a process.

A new SYSGEN parameter, MMG_CTLFLAGS, is used to enable memory recovery. This parameter sets two bit flags that turn on the two new memory recovery procedures:

- Bit 0 controls the use of the function that reclaims memory from periodically executing processes.

- Bit 1 controls the use of the function that reclaims memory from idle processes.

- Bits 2 through 7 currently are not used.

PERIODICALLY EXECUTING PROCESSES

Processes that wake, do minimal work, and go back to hibernation in a cyclical manner are referred to as periodically executing processes. "Watchdog" processes are a good example of these types of processes. If you are running DECwindows or Motif, there are many processes that fall into this category.

Because watchdog processes do have active CPU use, they are not selected as candidates for swapping. Since their CPU use is very limited, QUANTUM-end processing cannot handle reclaiming memory from their working sets. Swapper trimming will be able to reclaim memory from these processes, but as you will see later this is not a good way to recover memory in this case.

By setting bit 0 of MMG_CTLFLAGS, the swapper will implement the following procedure: If the size of the free list drops below 2*FREEGOAL, it attempts to recover memory from periodically executing processes. If the process has 30 seconds of elapsed time in which it used 0.3 seconds or less of CPU time (99 percent idle), then trim 25 percent of the process's working set pages.

To allow the periodic process to recover from this trimming quickly, the swapper does not change the working set size of the process. Only the memory pages are removed; the process can add pages back into its working set without reaching QUANTUM end and doing a working set increment. The same is not true if a process is trimmed by the swapper via the SWPOUTPGCNT mechanism.

IDLE PROCESSES

The swapper considers a process idle if it has been in either HIB or LEF state for more than LONGWAIT seconds. When memory becomes scarce and the size of the free list drops below FREEGOAL, these idle processes are candidates for swapping. If an idle process is selected for swapping, the following procedure is used:

- The working set pages of the process are removed to reduce the working set pages to SWPOUTPGCNT.

- The working set size is not changed. In a normal swap, the working set is also reduced to SWPOUTPGCNT.

SIDE EFFECTS

The setting of FREEGOAL has a crucial effect on proactive memory recovery. The larger the value for FREEGOAL, the more memory recovered via proactive memory recovery. Once you have upgraded to VMS V5.5, the system parameter FREEGOAL will change to a dynamic parameter. This allows for easy testing of the new memory reclamation parameters.

Because reclaimed memory could well be pages whose contents have been modified, you need to keep track of page and swapfile usage. Enabling proactive memory recovery could well create significant increases in page/swap file page usage.

PAGE AND SWAP FILES

Page and swap files are used to save the contents of pages and process working sets. Only page files are used to save the contents of modified pages that are not currently in physical memory. Both the page and swap files are used to save the working sets of processes that are not in the balance set. The incorrect sizing of page or swap files can have a major impact on the working of the memory system.

Page and swap files are treated as special files by OpenVMS. To create page and swap files, use the following commands respectively:

```
SYSGEN Create dsk:[dir]pagefile.sys/size=10000
SYSGEN Create dsk:[dir]swapfile.sys/size=1000
```

Never under any circumstances create a page or swap file other than with SYSGEN or AUTOGEN. If the page file/swap file you create has an extension header, it cannot be used as a page/swap file. When the system next boots, this page/swap file with an extension header will not be installed as a page/swap file. This hidden loss of a page/ swap file can cause major performance problems, and it will not be obvious what has happened.

The size of page, swap, and dump files can be affected by SYSGEN. SYSGEN uses special symbols in the MODPARAMS.DAT file to modify the size of page, swap, and dump files. You set system file sizes explicitly by specifying the keywords PAGEFILE, SWAPFILE, and DUMPFILE, followed by an equal sign and the size of the file in blocks. A value of 0 for any of these keywords instructs AUTOGEN not to modify the size of the corresponding file. Secondary page and swap files can be manipulated as well. To do so, use the keyword {PAGE/SWAP}FILEn_{NAME/SIZE}. Use the following keywords to set the size of pagefile1 to 10,000 and to use the name DSK001:[page_file]page_file.sys:

```
PAGEFILE1_NAME="DSK001:[page_file]page_file.sys"
PAGEFILE1_SIZE=10000
```

QUANTUM

QUANTUM is a SYSGEN parameter. Although not a memory management parameter, QUANTUM is important for interactive response time. QUANTUM is the amount of CPU time given to a CPU-bound process when it is scheduled before it is superseded by another process of the same priority. QUANTUM is measured in 1/100ths of a second. QUANTUM values are stored at the global location SCH$GW_QUAN and are negative. For example, a QUANTUM value of 10 would be stored as -10 at SCH$GW_QUAN and would be a QUANTUM of one-tenth of a second.

The OpenVMS priority boost works approximately as follows: When certain events happen in a process, such as disk or terminal I/O completion, the process's run priority (as opposed to the base priority) is raised by an amount that varies depending on the event. For example, when terminal I/O completes, the process's priority is raised by four. This is normally desirable, because it favors interactive processes over CPU-bound processes. Each time a process is rescheduled by the scheduler, the scheduler lowers its run priority by one until the run priority is back down to the base priority.

The OpenVMS priority boost is a simple but effective way to help interactive processes get the CPU when needed and to help eliminate throughput bottlenecks on I/O devices in general.

Memory System Analysis

T HE KEY TO MEMORY PERFORMANCE IS TO MINIMIZE BALANCED PAGING. THIS IS DONE by maintaining working sets of appropriate sizes and managing the secondary caches.

A key measurement of responsiveness for memory tuning is the amount of time needed for a process to acquire its share of memory. This is indirectly measured by page faulting and swapping. Since these activities slow the faulting process as well as all other processes, one goal of memory tuning is to minimize faulting and swapping rates.

PAGE FAULTING

MONITOR PAGE provides a good overall indication of how the memory management system is working (see Figure 7-1). If you have little or no page fault rate, page read I/O rate, and no swapping, you do not have a memory tuning problem and should work on other tuning problems.

Rates listed in Figure 7-1 are measured in per-second intervals and are defined as follows:

Page Fault Rate — The overall page fault rate for all working sets.

Page Read Rate — The rate of pages read from disk as a result of a page read I/O.

Page Read I/O Rate — The rate of read I/O operations from disk as a result of page faults. This is your system's hard fault rate.

Page Write Rate — The rate at which pages were written to the page files.

Page Write I/O Rate — The rate of write I/O operations to the page files.

Free List Fault Rate — The rate at which pages were read from the free list as a result of page faults.

Modified List Fault Rate — The rate at which pages were read from the modified list as a result of page faults.

Demand-Zero Fault Rate — The rate at which zero-filled pages were generated as a result of page faults.

Global Valid Fault Rate — The rate at which page faults were resolved by valid pages in the systemwide global page tables.

Wrt in Progress Fault Rate — The rate of page reads that mapped to a page that was in the process of being written to disk.

System Fault Rate — The rate of page faults in system space (S0).

Free List Size — The number of pages on the free list.

Modified List Size — The number of pages on the modified list.

```
┌─────────────────────────────────────────────────────────────────────┐
│  ─                        OpenVMS Performance                    ⌐  □ │
├─────────────────────────────────────────────────────────────────────┤
│   File   Edit   Commands   Options   Print                    Help    │
├─────────────────────────────────────────────────────────────────────┤
│                     OpenVMS Monitor Utility                        ▲  │
│                  PAGE MANAGEMENT STATISTICS                           │
│                      on node XXXXXX                                   │
│                         SUMMARY                                       │
│                                                                       │
│                          CUR        AVE       MIN        MAX          │
│                                                                       │
│    Page Fault Rate      60.49      57.31     26.91     160.06         │
│    Page Read Rate        0.00       8.48      0.00      54.74         │
│    Page Read I/O Rate    0.00       2.79      0.00      15.59         │
│    Page Write Rate       0.00       0.59      0.00     144.49         │
│    Page Write I/O Rate   0.00       0.01      0.00       2.49         │
│                                                                       │
│    Free List Fault Rate       6.01    5.17    0.00     33.85          │
│    Modified List Fault Rate  15.89    5.46    0.00     66.77          │
│    Demand Zero Fault Rate    33.48   37.59   13.71     65.88          │
│    Global Valid Fault Rate    5.09    6.22    0.00     37.30          │
│    Wrt In Progress Fault Rate 0.00    0.00    0.00      0.00          │
│    System Fault Rate          0.00    0.00    0.00      0.00          │
│                                                                       │
│    Free List Size       1816.00   3121.66   222.00    6497.00      ■  │
│    Modified List Size   2372.00   2716.09  2209.00    3825.00         │
│                                                                       │
│   PLAYBACK                   SUMMARIZING                           ▼  │
└─────────────────────────────────────────────────────────────────────┘
```

Figure 7-1. Page Fault Monitoring

RULES OF THUMB

There are no correct values for memory statistics. But there are some rules of thumb to help you determine the correct values for your system. Equation 7-1 lists some rules you can use to start your analysis of the memory system. Using the data collected from the MONITOR PAGE command, you can make some quick checks to see where you need to start your analysis.

$$(1) \longrightarrow \frac{Page\ Write\ Rate}{Page\ Write\ I/O\ Rate} \cong MPW\_WRTCLUSTER$$

$$(2) \longrightarrow 5.0 \le \frac{Page\ Read\ Rate}{Page\ Read\ I/O\ Rate} \le 15.0$$

$$(3) \longrightarrow Page\ Write\ I/O\ Rate \le 0.5 * VUP$$

$$(4) \longrightarrow System\ Fault\ Rate \le 1.0$$

$$(5) \longrightarrow Demand\ Zero\ Fault\ Rate \le Page\ Fault\ Rate * 0.5$$

$$(6) \longrightarrow Page\ Read\ I/O\ Rate \le 0.10 * Page\ Fault\ Rate$$

$$(7) \longrightarrow Demand\ Zero\ Fault\ Rate < ZERO\_LIST\_HI$$

$$(8) \longrightarrow 30.0 \le \frac{Page\ Fault\ Rate - Demand\text{-}Zero\ Fault\ Rate}{Page\ Read\ I/O\ Rate} \le 70.0$$

Equation 7-1. Page Fault Rules

If rule (1) is not true, check whether:

- Your page file is too small (see the Page File section of this chapter).

- Your page file is fragmented (see the Page File Fragmentation section of this chapter).

- There is any significant mapped file activity (see the Mapped Files section of this chapter).

- The system parameters that set up the secondary page caches are not in synchronization with how the rest of your system is set up to run (see the Modified List Writing Problems section of this chapter).

If rule (2) is not true, check whether:

- There is a low hard fault rate. If so, there is little need to worry.

- There is a high hard fault rate (see the Modified List section of this chapter).

- Programs are using vast amounts of virtual memory badly (see the Image Accounting section of this chapter).

Warning: The value of page read I/O rate does not necessarily reflect the number of I/Os needed to read in pages. Page read I/Os are counted only once by the performance subsystem, while in truth, if the page read I/O is split into multiple I/Os by the file system, only the extra split I/Os will be recorded. Split I/Os that occur for page faults greatly increase the I/O load needed to support paging, and they are not recorded as page read I/Os.

If rule (3) is not true, check for:

- Dead page table scans (see the Dead Page Table Scans section of Chapter 6).

- Incorrect sizing of the modified list (see the Modified List section of this chapter).

- Incorrect sizing of the working sets (see the Working Set Sizing section of this chapter).

- Programs using vast amounts of memory (see the Image Accounting section of this chapter).

- Global section use (see the Installed Images section of this chapter).

If rule (4) is not true, check for:

- SYSGEN SYSMWCNT being set too small (see the System Working Set section of this chapter).

If rule (5) is not true, check for:

- Excessive image activations (see the Excessive Image Activations section of this chapter).

- Heavy use of DCL (see the Excessive Image Activations section of this chapter).

If rule (6) is not true, check for:

- Incorrect sizing of the modified and/or free list (see the Secondary Page Cache section of this chapter).

If rule (7) is not true, check for:

- The zero list is too small. This equation applies only to OpenVMS AXP. Averaged over long periods of time during which the system is busy, the system should be able to get most if not all demand-zero pages from the zero list (see the Secondary Page Cache section of this chapter). Do not include periods of time during which idle time is the majority of the CPU usage.

If rule (8) is not true, check for:

- One or both of the secondary caches is sized incorrectly. Follow the procedures in the Secondary Page Cache section of this chapter to determine which cache is incorrectly sized.

SECONDARY PAGE CACHE

The second worst memory tuning error occurs when the secondary page cache (modified list or free list) is too small. The main purpose of the secondary cache is to reduce hard faulting. You cannot affect demand-zero faults (caused by image activation) by modifying the secondary page cache.

In trying to reduce hard faulting by increasing the size of the secondary page caches, you need to be aware of several pitfalls and how to detect and avoid them. Some of these pitfalls occur only for certain types of system usage.

FREE LIST

If you attempt to make the free list too large or too small, you will cause overall system performance to decrease. Since the total amount of memory available for the system is a constant, making the free list larger requires that some other use of memory must decrease.

Unless you have made changes to system parameters to affect the use of memory other than increasing the size of the free list, by default the extra memory for the free list will come from the working sets of the processes.

MONITOR STATES (see Figure 7-2) will show a large number of processes in one or more of the following states if the free list is sized incorrectly:

```
┌──────────────────────────────────────────────────────────────────────┐
│ ═                        OpenVMS Performance                      ◢  □ │
├──────────────────────────────────────────────────────────────────────┤
│  File   Edit   Commands   Options   Print                       Help   │
├──────────────────────────────────────────────────────────────────────┤
│                      OpenVMS Monitor Utility                        ▲  │
│                         PROCESS STATES                                 │
│                         on node XXXXXX                                 │
│                            SUMMARY                                     │
│                                                                        │
│                         CUR      AVE      MIN      MAX                  │
│                                                                        │
│    Collided Page Wait          0.00     0.00     0.00     0.00         │
│    Mutex & Misc Resource Wait  0.00     0.04     0.00     1.00         │
│    Common Event Flag Wait      0.00     0.00     0.00     0.00         │
│    Page Fault Wait             0.00     0.16     0.00     3.00         │
│    Local Event Flag Wait      19.00    18.89    16.00    23.00         │
│    Local Evt Flg (Outswapped) 12.00    10.90     8.00    13.00         │
│                                                                        │
│    Hibernate                  18.00    17.94    12.00    20.00         │
│    Hibernate (Outswapped)      5.00     5.04     3.00    11.00         │
│    Suspended                   0.00     0.00     0.00     0.00         │
│    Suspended (Outswapped)      0.00     0.00     0.00     0.00         │
│    Free Page Wait              0.00     0.00     0.00     0.00         │
│    Compute                     9.00     8.24     5.00    11.00      ■   │
│    Compute (Outswapped)        0.00     0.00     0.00     1.00         │
│    Current Process             1.00     1.00     1.00     1.00         │
├──────────────────────────────────────────────────────────────────────┤
│  PLAYBACK                  SUMMARIZING                             ▼  │
└──────────────────────────────────────────────────────────────────────┘
```

Figure 7-2. State Monitoring

Free Page Wait — Indicates that there is not enough physical memory available on the free list to satisfy a page fault.

Collided Page Wait — Indicates the occurrence of a page fault for a page already being read from disk.

Page Fault Wait — Indicates that a page fault that requires a read to resolve is in progress.

It is difficult to distinguish between an undersized and oversized free list from the system reactions. You will need to first check the values for FREELIM and FREEGOAL. If FREEGOAL is less than 10 percent of total memory, check for the free list's being too small. Otherwise, check for the free list's being too large.

FREE LIST TOO SMALL

Free page wait states are always an indicator that the free list has been reduced in size below FREELIM and that the system is attempting to expand the free list to contain at least FREEGOAL pages (see Equation 7-2).

$$(1) \rightarrow FREEGOAL \geq Size\ of\ Free\ List \geq FREELIM$$

$$(2) \rightarrow Page\ Fault\ Wate\ State \geq 0.10 * Compute\ State$$

$$(3) \rightarrow Free\ List\ Fault\ Rate \geq Page\ Fault\ Rate * 0.10$$

Equation 7-2. Free List Too Small

This could also be an indicator that the free list system parameters have been set to invalid or unrealistic values. Collided page wait and page fault wait can be caused by an undersized free or modified list. However, the same tuning action needed due to free page wait states will also handle collided page wait and page fault wait if they are being caused by an undersized free list.

Next, using the data collected, determine whether the size of the free list is averaging between FREELIM and FREEGOAL. If the data from MONITOR PAGE shows that Equation 7-2 (1) is true:

- This indicates insufficient memory to maintain the requested size for FREEGOAL. Unfortunately, your list could also be too large and cause the same symptoms.

If Equation 7-2 (2) is true:

- Excessive numbers of processes are waiting for memory to become available. If FREELIM is set to a small value, this is an indicator that the free list is too small to help resolve hard faults in an effective manner.

If Equation 7-2 (3) is true:

- Either the free list system parameters have been set to invalid or unrealistically low values or your system is out of memory. If the free list is not being used to satisfy page faults, in most cases the size of the free list, and thus the amount of time a page is on the free list, is too small.

Warning: If you are analyzing a single-user system and there is frequent usage of installed images, you want Equation 7-2 (3) to be true. In many cases you will see 80 to 90 percent of all page faults as free list faults under these conditions (see the Soft Faults section of Chapter 6).

Chapter 8 shows how to size your free list correctly.

FREE LIST TOO LARGE

Several symptoms appear when the free list is sized too large. Typically, overall faulting, especially hard faulting, will decrease when the free list is sized correctly.

If from Figure 3-1 you see a large inswap rate and from Figure 7-2 you see that many processes are entering one of the outswapped states and then in a short time period are leaving the outswapped state, you may have done the following:

- Proactive memory reclamation is enabled and the value for FREEGOAL is set too high. This will cause the swapper to swap out processes in the attempt to recover memory needed to keep the free list at or above FREEGOAL. With proactive memory reclamation enabled, the swapper will swap out jobs much more frequently than if proactive memory reclamation were turned off. If you have set MPW_THRESH such that the swapper uses the modified list to grow the free list, then you will see an increase in both the number of page write I/Os and page write rate.

If you have periods where Equation 7-1 (6) is true, followed by periods with a large number of processes in free page wait state, then you could have done the following:

- The difference between FREELIM and FREEGOAL is greater than ten to twenty times the value of MPW_WRTCLUSTER. Thus, once your free list falls below FREELIM, it takes considerable system time and resources to free up enough pages to get the size of the free list above FREEGOAL. While the swapper is working to get pages for the free list, the rest of the processes attempting to access the free list go into free page wait states.

If from Figure 7-1 you see that the free list fault rate accounts for 10 percent or more of the total page fault rate:

- If the page faults are not being caused by referencing of installed images that were just used (see the Soft Faults section of Chapter 6) and if you also have a very large page fault rate, the problem is caused by an oversized free list and undersized working sets.

- If the overall fault rate is not a problem and Equation 7-1 (6) is not true, this is a minor problem, but if Equation 7-1 (6) is true, you need to make the free list smaller.

For OpenVMS VAX all demand-zero page faults are satisfied directly from the free list, and for OpenVMS AXP all demand-zero page faults are satisfied indirectly from the free list via the zero list.

MODIFIED LIST

If MONITOR PAGE shows that Equation 7-1 (2) or (6) is not true, ensure that the modified list is correctly sized. In many cases the modified list is sized too small by AUTOGEN. You will want to size the modified list such that the majority of modified pages removed from your process are either faulted back in from the modified list or are never faulted back into the working set.

Remember that the total amount of memory available for the system is a constant. Thus, making the modified list larger requires that some other use of memory decrease.

Beware: There are as many problems caused by an oversized modified list as there are caused by an undersized modified list.

MODIFIED LIST TOO SMALL

If you observe many processes oscillating between modified page write busy and computable states, this is an indicator that you have set the size for the modified list too small. If you observe heavy page faulting, large numbers of hard faults and little or no modified list faults, this is another indicator of an undersized modified list. If in either of the cases above you also determine that there are large amounts of memory on the free list, then you need to review the parameter settings for the modified list.

MODIFIED LIST TOO LARGE

If you observe many processes in the free page wait state and you have a large modified list, this indicates that the modified list may be oversized. The upper bounds on the modified list (MPW_HILIMIT) should not exceed 15 percent of the total memory on the system, unless special conditions warrant.

When a program purges a data page that is no longer needed, if the data page was modified (by definition, all demand-zero pages are modified on creation), then the data page must traverse the entire modified list before it gets to the free list and becomes a candidate for reuse by another program. Thus, an oversized modified list effectively removes a page of memory from active use by the amount of time it takes for the data page to traverse the excessive size of the modified list.

MODIFIED LIST WRITING PROBLEMS

Yet another performance problem occurs when the writing of the modified list causes the entire system to hang for several seconds. If you are experiencing this random pause behavior, you could be suffering from excessive modified page writing.

Analyze your system to determine whether the following set of conditions exists:

- The majority of programs that are adding pages to the modified list are being serviced by the same set of page files.

- The value from Equation 7-3, where PageSize is 1 for OpenVMS VAX and 16 for OpenVMS AXP, is greater than 30 to 40.

$$\frac{(MPW\_HILIMIT - MPW\_LOLIMIT) * PageSize}{MPW\_WRTCLUSTER}$$

Equation 7-3. Excessive Modified Page Writing

The I/Os generated by writing the modified list are using all available disk bandwidth. If Equation 7-3 gives a value of 80, this means that it will take 80 disk I/Os, at a minimum, to write the modified list back to its low limit. On a typical machine, this will take about 2 to 3 seconds (25 to 40 I/Os per second per disk controller).

Another way excessive modified page writing can occur is if all parts of Equation 7-4 are true. The swapper is able to use the modified list to keep the free list at the correct size. Recall from Chapter 6 that the first swapper step is to attempt to recover memory from the modified list to keep the free list at the required size.

$$MPW\_THRESH < ModifiedList\ Size$$

$$(FREEGOAL - FREELIM) < (ModifiedList\ Size - MPW\_LOLIMIT)$$

$$\frac{(FREEGOAL - FREELIM) * PageSize}{MPW\_WRTCLUSTER} \geq 30$$

Equation 7-4. Excessive Modified Page Recovery

If you use AUTOGEN to size your modified list, then for a 128-MB AXP system Equation 7-4 will generate the following values (assume free list size of 8,000 pages):

$$1268 < 8000 \; (TRUE)$$

$$(1024 - 200) < (8000 - 120)$$

$$824 < 7880 \; (TRUE)$$

$$\frac{(1024 - 200) * 16}{64} \geq 30$$

$$206 \geq 30 \; (TRUE)$$

Special Memory Problems

Using the default SYSGEN setting and default calculated AUTOGEN settings will cause problems in some cases. In the next sections I will discuss how and why these settings cause problems.

Free List and Modified List

For OpenVMS AXP the following default parameters apply:

- FREELIM = 32.

- FREEGOAL = 200.

Thus, when the size of the free list goes below thirty-two pages, the swapper will take the necessary action to free at least 168 pages to put on the free list, the minimum required to reach FREEGOAL. In most cases the majority of pages that get put on the free list have been modified. But for AXP, the size of a page is 8,192 bytes. Thus, the system will need to free up 1,376,256 bytes (8,192 bytes/page * 168 pages or 2,688 pagelets). If the pages come from the modified list, the system will require a minimum of 21 (2,688 * 127) I/Os to satisfy the requirement of making the free list at least as large as FREEGOAL. (For most systems, 127 pagelets is the maximum size for a single disk transfer.) A reasonable average value would be 40 to 50 I/Os. Assuming that you can write these I/Os to two page files on two controllers, you will experience a system delay of about 0.5 seconds while these I/Os complete. With OpenVMS VAX this is not a problem due to the small page size.

If you have a 128-MB system, AUTOGEN will calculate the following:

- FREELIM = 200.

- FREEGOAL = 1024.

For AXP this calculates to 824 pages, 6.75 MB, and this could require 103 I/Os of 127 blocks. Assuming 25 I/Os per second and four page files, this will result in a delay of at least 2 seconds. But on most systems this delay will be at least two to ten times as long!

If you are running on a workstation with only one page file, this could easily take 10 to 20 seconds! Using OpenVMS VAX, this delay would be only 1 to 2 seconds.

This is one reason large OpenVMS AXP clusters experience periodic delays.

MSCP AND PFCDEFAULT

If you are running an AXP system in a cluster and are using default values:

- MSCP_BUFFER = 128
- PFCDEFAULT = 128

then you have a major problem with the performance of your cluster. Using the data from the output of Appendix J, Figure J-1, for starters, we see that there is a very large percentage of I/Os forced to split due to size.

The problem is caused by how the system works. A PFCDEFAULT of 128 will attempt to get 128 pagelets when the I/O is issued for the page read I/O. But since MSCP allows a maximum transfer of only 127 blocks, this I/O is converted to two MSCP transfers, one for 127 blocks one for one block. In the best case the serving node will have all buffer space available. This means that the 127-block request will be split into two transfers, one for sixty-four blocks and one for sixty-three blocks. In the worst case the sixty-four- and sixty-three-block transfers will each be split eight times into eight-block transfers, the minimum size.

Thus, in the best case your one read I/O translates into three I/Os on the serving system. In the worst case your single I/O request translates into 17 I/Os on the serving system. In a cluster with three or more remote members, with a reasonable hard fault rate from the clients, 10 to 20 per second translates into a massive I/O load on the serving node for the disk (30 to 60 I/Os per second per node up to 170 to 340 I/Os per second per node). There is no way for the server to handle such a load; thus, the average response time for I/Os on the clients will greatly increase, and the overall performance of the AXP will drop back to, and in some cases below, the overall performance of a VMScluster.

Using Monitor, determine the average I/O rate to all MSCP-served disks. Calculate the total I/O rate for all disks served by each server. You will use this data in Chapter 8 when you tune for MSCP.

MODIFIED LIST FLUSHING

The modified list is flushed for four events. One of these events is when you run SYS$SYSTEM:OPCCRASH, but since this is only run immediately before a system shutdown, it is not usually a performance consideration.

Dead Page Table Scans — You can examine the dead page table scan count with the System Dump Analyzer (SDA), using the following commands:

```
$ ANALYZE/SYSTEM
SDA> EVALUATE @PMS$GL_DPTSCN
Hex = 0000041F Decimal = 1055 BUG$_UNXSIGNAL+00007
```

There is no good number of dead page table scans on an OpenVMS system, and the number varies with each system. Appendix A displays the count of dead page table scans since system boot. The primary cause for dead page table scans is working sets that are too small. This can occur if WSQUOTA is set to a small value. For most uses this small value is about 150 to 200 pages. Setting SWPOUTPGCNT to a value of 150 to 200 pages can also cause this problem.

Global Section Deletion — When the last user of a writable global section exits, the system must ensure that all pages of the global section currently on the modified list are written back to the global section before the section file is closed. The same procedure used for dead page table scans is used to ensure that all modified global section pages have been written back to the file.

Process Header Outswap — The process header is now swapped out with the main body of the process. For the process header to be swapped out, all pages in the process must be removed from the modified list. This is one of the reasons the process header is not swapped with the main body of the process. Delaying the swapout of the header allows more time for the process's modified pages to be removed from the modified list. The same procedure that is used for dead page table scans is used to ensure that all modified global section pages have been written back to the file.

WORKING SET SIZING

One of the worst tuning problems is caused by poor choices for the WSDEFAULT, WSQUOTA, and WSEXTENT values. Denying a process the memory it needs will cause the entire system to perform poorly. Giving a process small values for WSDEFAULT, WSQUOTA, and WSEXTENT will not stop the process from faulting but rather will make it fault more often. While this will slow the process, it will also have a negative impact on the entire system. You have two choices:

1. Give the process a larger working set to reduce its overall fault rate.

2. Lower the process's priority so that it runs less often and give the process a larger working set.

Only if it is not possible to give the process a working set that reduces faulting to a reasonable level should you force a process to run in a working set that makes the process have excessive faulting.

IMAGE ACCOUNTING

Using the report generated by the accounting command in the Accounting Utility section of Chapter 3, you can begin to determine which processes have poor working set parameters.

If Equation 7-5 is true, check for a problem with working set sizes using the image accounting data as follows:

- If the maximum working set size is less than WSEXTENT, then the secondary caches are too large (the process is not allowed to grow to WSEXTENT) or the system is short on memory.

- If the maximum working set is equal to WSEXTENT, then the problem is that either WSEXTENT or WSMAX is too small.

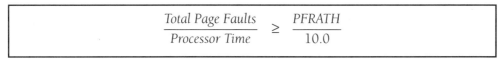

$$\frac{Total\ Page\ Faults}{Processor\ Time} \geq \frac{PFRATH}{10.0}$$

Equation 7-5. PFRATH Check

$GETJPI USAGE

Using either F$GETJPI from DCL or SYS$GETJPI from your favorite language, you can locate processes that have an excessive number of page faults, regardless of the images they are currently executing. Make sure that the users of these processes are using OpenVMS effectively. Excessive image activation or poorly designed programs are just two of the reasons for very large numbers of page faults.

Figure 7-3 was generated with the code in Appendix C, Page Monitor. The column labeled "PAGES" includes both process private and global pages. Look for processes that have a value of "PAGES" that is larger than "WSQUOTA" and contain relatively few "GPRCNT" (global) pages. These are the processes you will need to investigate further. The weak point for this program is that the "PAGEFLTS" (total page faults) is a cumulative figure since the job was started (that is, the user logged in, spawned, and so on). By making multiple runs and comparing the values for "PAGEFLTS," you can determine whether these processes are sized incorrectly. If the entry for "Image

Name" changes at a rapid pace, there might be a problem with excessive image activations.

Image Name		WSQUOTA	WSEXTENT	PAGEFLTS	PPGCNT	GPGCNT	PAGES	WSLIST
COBURN 28e00082		4096	18432	213305	410	97	507	1024
MAIL 28e00083	[SYSEXE]DECW$MAIL.EXE;3	4096	18432	598507	2479	1760	4239	4663
VUE$COBURN_3 28e00095	[SYSEXE]DECW$BOOKREADER.EXE;3	4096	18432	12149	2702	1394	4096	5120
VUE$COBURN_4 28e00088	[SYSEXE]DECW$CARDFILER.EXE;3	4096	18432	5569	1752	975	2727	2727
BATCH_385 28e00110	[SYS26.SYSCOMMON.][SYSEXE]LSEDIT.EXE	4096	18432	16876	1903	1233	3136	4470
DECW$SESSION 28e00055	[SYSEXE]DECW$SESSION.EXE	4096	18432	14312	3904	2370	6274	8272
BATCH_613 28e000d6	[SYS26.SYSCOMMON.][SYSEXE]LSEDIT.EXE	4096	18432	142758	1963	1560	3523	4039
_FTA7: 28e000a1	PROCESS_SCAN.EXE;1	4096	18432	165262	731	302	1033	1536
VUE$COBURN_5 28e0032a		4096	18432	48057	399	76	475	1024
VUE$COBURN_6 28e0032b	[SYSEXE]DECW$PRINTSCREEN.EXE;2	4096	18432	77924	881	274	1155	1667
_FTA12: 28e00331	[SYS26.SYSCOMMON.][SYSEXE]RTPAD.EXE	4096	18432	11225	343	142	485	1024
BATCH_983 28e00278	[SYS26.SYSCOMMON.][SYSEXE]LSEDIT.EXE	4096	18432	119699	2930	1166	4096	4096
CALENDAR 28e000fb	[SYSEXE]DECW$CALENDAR.EXE;3	4096	18432	80220	517	321	838	1338
DECW$MWM 28e0007d	[SYS26.SYSCOMMON.][SYSEXE]DECW$MWM.EXE;	4096	18432	64195	926	609	1535	2501
DECW$TE_007f 28e0007f	[SYSEXE]DECW$TERMINAL.EXE	4096	18432	611518	1278	643	1921	2319

Figure 7-3. Process Working Set Information

SWAPPING

If working sets are set too large, swapping can be induced. You can determine whether a few processes are configured to use too much memory using several methods.

When MONITOR I/O has a nonzero inswap rate, you have swapping and must investigate further (see Figure 3-1 in Chapter 3). If you have large amounts of null time or many processes in the compute (outswapped) state (see Figure 7-2), there is a problem with swapping.

To check for processes with very large working sets running at low priority, use the DCL command:

```
$ SHOW System
```

or use the DCL program listed in Appendix C. The output from the command file in Appendix C is shown in Figure 7-4.

Page faults are cumulative since process creation, not just for the current image. For AXP, "Quota" and "Extent" are expressed in pagelets while "Pages(p)," "Pages(G)," and "Pages(T)" are expressed in CPU-specific page sizes.

Another way to determine whether swapping is getting out of hand is to look for processes that have experienced second-level trimming. A system with several processes

```
┌──────────────────────────────────────────────────────────────────────┐
│ ▬                           OpenVMS Performance                  ◠ ▢   │
├──────────────────────────────────────────────────────────────────────┤
│  File   Edit   Commands   Options   Print                      Help    │
├──────────────────────────────────────────────────────────────────────┤
```

		VMS Tuning (AXP)					
Username	Image	Faults	Quota	Extent	Pages(p)	Pages(G)	Pages(T)
COBURN		6598	24000	60000	1488	592	2080
COBURN	RTPAD	3195	24000	60000	1776	624	2400
COBURN_P		1456	24000	60000	1424	352	1776
COBURN_P	DECW$TERMI	699	24000	60000	6912	4368	11280
COBURN_P	RTPAD	1047	24000	60000	1792	496	2288
COBURN_P		2762	24000	60000	1424	384	1808
COBURN	NETSERVER	289	24000	60000	1792	672	2464

		VMS Tuning (VAX)					
Username	Image	Faults	Quota	Extent	Pages(p)	Pages(G)	Pages(T)
COBURN		129386	4096	18432	460	135	595
COBURN	DECW$MAIL	501613	4096	18432	498	371	869
COBURN	DECW$BOOKR	10985	4096	18432	3419	2272	5691
COBURN	DECW$CARDF	5569	4096	18432	1842	1056	2898
COBURN	LSEDIT	11004	4096	18432	3949	3272	7221
COBURN	DECW$SESSI	13788	4096	18432	3441	2365	5806
COBURN	LSEDIT	116389	4096	18432	3805	1249	5054
COBURN	RTPAD	145733	4096	18432	434	131	565
COBURN		6353	4096	18432	317	148	465
COBURN	DECW$TERMI	525301	4096	18432	1881	937	2818

```
$ ▮
```

Figure 7-4. DCL Page Monitor

with current working set sizes equal to the value of SWPOUTPGCNT indicates that second-level trimming is occurring and that OpenVMS thinks there is or has been a severe memory shortage. If any of the processes in Figure 7-3 have a "WSLIST" value at or near SWPOUTPGCNT, in most cases swapper trimming has occurred.

If inswapping is occurring, there are no free balance set slots (SHOW MEMORY/ SLOTS), and there is a lot of free memory, you must correct for tuning-induced swapping by increasing the system parameters MAXPROCESSCNT and BALSETCNT.

WORKING SET OSCILLATION

If you have made large errors in assigning values to working set sizes, you will have major performance problems. You will have oscillations on your system if the values for working set quota and working set extent are out of range.

To detect this problem, you must monitor for processes that have very large drops in the working set size during the normal running of an image. This occurs if the system has allowed the process to run with a large working set extent and it runs out of memory. The system will take back all pages between working set quota and working set extent. If this occurs on a regular basis, you must reduce the working set extent or increase the working set quota for the process. In Figure 7-5 you can see that at time 20 there was a purge of about 1,600 pages from the process's working set. Not only will the program suffer, but the addition of 1,600 pages to the secondary cache will effectively remove all other valid pages. Thus, all other processes on the system will experience higher hard fault rates!

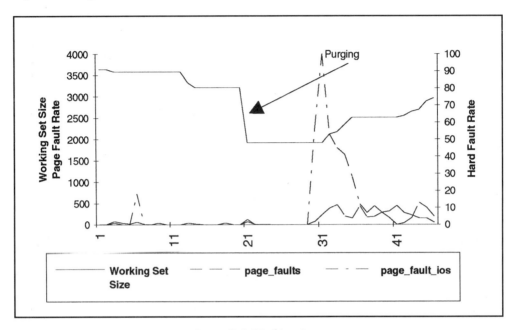

Figure 7-5. Working Sets

If you overcommit the amount of memory assigned to working set quotas, you will notice processes with working set pages equal to the value of SWPOUTPAGCNT. If you have set the values for the working set default and working set quota too small, you will find that performance for the DCL procedure is poor, and image activation will take a very long time. Check this by running the debugger.

If your settings for the working set quota and working set extent are too conservative, you will notice a very high overall fault rate and a very large free or modified list. Using the program in Appendix K, you can locate programs that have undersized working sets. To check for undersized working sets, do the following:

- Start the monitor program (from Appendix K).

- Run the program you want to check for undersized working sets.

- Stop the monitor program.

- Using the Process dump program from Appendix K, dump out the data for the program you were testing.

- Plot working set size divided by working set quota and working set size divided by working set extent over time.

- Plot page faults by type over time.

From the working set plot (see Figure 7-6) you will see that the value for working set size divided by working set quota is greater than 1 and that the value for working set size divided by working set extent is usually 1.

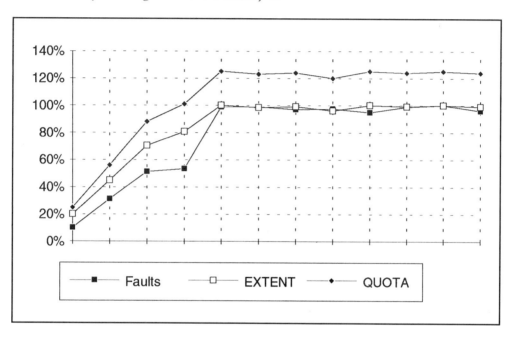

Figure 7-6. Working Set Too Small

PAGE FILE FRAGMENTATION AND SIZING

If you ever see the following commands on your system console, you have a page file fragmentation problem:

```
%SYSTEM-W-PAGEFRAG, page file badly fragmented, system continuing
%SYSTEM-W-PAGECRIT, page file space critical, system trying to continue
```

For OpenVMS AXP, and with the release of OpenVMS VAX V6.0, these messages have changed to:

```
%SYSTEM-W-PAGEFRAG, page file filling up; please create more space
%SYSTEM-W-PAGECRIT, page file nearly full; system trying to continue
```

Since you cannot always monitor your system console and it is possible for the page file to become severely fragmented and fail to print the above message, you need to use an alternative method of determining whether the above messages have been sent.

Use the SDA procedure or the program listed in Appendix D to check that the page files are not severely fragmented. If the current allocation size is less than the requested allocation size and 50 percent or more of the page file is free, you have a fragmentation problem. You can also use SDA to determine the largest users of page file space and to check whether their page files are excessively fragmented.

In the case of page file fragmentation, I am referring to the fragmentation of the internal structures of the page file, not the underlying disk structures that make up the page file. A page file can be severely fragmented internally, even if the file structure on disk itself is contiguous.

If the output from Figure 7-7 indicates that there is less than 50 percent of free space in the page file and the current allocation is less than the requested allocation, your page files need to be extended. Note the following:

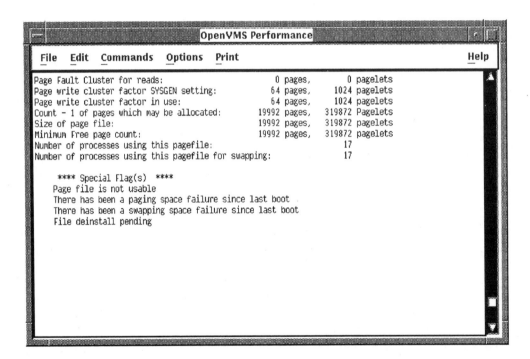

Figure 7-7. Page File Reporter

- The value for "Page write factor SYSGEN setting" comes from the SYSGEN parameter PFCDEFAULT.

- "Minimum free page count" is the low-water mark for this pagefile.

- Special Flags are:

  1. "Page file not usable."

  2. "There has been a paging space failure since last boot."

  3. "There has been a swapping space failure since last boot."

  4. "File deinstall pending."

Another good indicator that your page file is too small is processes in the RWMPB or RWMPE state. If Figure 7-2 shows processes in the Mutex & Misc. Resource Wait category, check for processes in either of these states by using a DCL SHOW SYSTEM command. The Page File Fragmentation section of Chapter 8 discusses how to solve this problem.

MAPPED FILES

For some applications, users map large data structures into virtual memory via mapped files. This makes the data appear as a very large memory structure, while the underlying structure is mapped to a disk section file.

In most cases this mapping results in a very high hard fault rate for the process, because there is no real locality of data. Since no one portion of memory is used more than any other portion, the memory management system will not be able to effectively manage this situation.

Another side effect of this type of usage is that the sequential use of a very large memory area tends to generate a tremendous amount of memory movement through the process. This is what accounts for the high fault rate of the process. The side effect is that the average amount of time a page spends on either the free or modified list will be greatly reduced. Thus, all other processes on the system will generate a much higher hard fault rate.

You can detect this type of problem from several clues:

- A process with a very large hard fault rate.

- A process with a very large working set size.

- A value from Equation 7-1 (2) that is far outside the expected values.

- A writable section installed by the user. This is detected with the Install utility.

Note that not all usage of mapped files is incorrect.

AWSA IS INEFFECTIVE

If the values of WSINC and WSDEC are nonzero, then AWSA is in use. As of VMS V5.0, working set decrement occurs even if PFRATL is zero. Setting PFRATL to zero only changes the manner in which the working set is adjusted.

As of VMS V5.0, there is a new selective working set decrement algorithm for QUANTUM-end processing. If all of the following are true, the system will reduce the working set size by WSDEC but will not reduce the working set below WSQUOTA:

- PFRATL = 0.

- WSDEC ! = 0.

- The size of the free list is less than BORROWLIM.

- The process has received a priority boost in the last thirty-two QUANTUM intervals.

Because of this feature, you need to set WSDEC to a large value if PFRATL is zero. The new selective working set decrement algorithm will affect a process only after a long time, so if you do a working set decrement, make sure it is a large one.

Warning: Watch for WSINC set to zero, forcing all processes to run at WSDEFAULT sizes.

INSTALLED IMAGES

Memory sharing allows multiple processes to use the same pages of physical memory. This sharing of memory is accomplished through installed images. You cannot share memory just because an image is shareable. The image must be installed as a shared image for sharing to occur. You only gain the benefit of saving physical pages from shared images when the number of simultaneous users of a shared page is two or more.

The Install utility creates a known file entry (KFE) for each image. These KFEs are grouped into known file directories (KFD), one for each unique device and directory combination.

Although the directory DISK:[000000.sys0] is the same as DISK:[sys0] for the file system, they are not the same for the KFD lookup algorithm. This can cause major problems. The command that starts the image must exactly match the device and directory specifications used when the image was installed. For example:

```
$ Install dua0:[sys]image.exe/share
$ run node$dua0:[sys]image.exe
```

The above run command will not make use of the image installed via the Install command. To determine whether you have this problem, check your installed image usage by entering the DCL command:

```
$ show device/file devicename
```

You will get a display like the one shown in Figure 7-8. The entry with the eight zeros indicates an installed image, and the same image with a user or users is a sure sign of install problems. Check your command procedures to locate this problem.

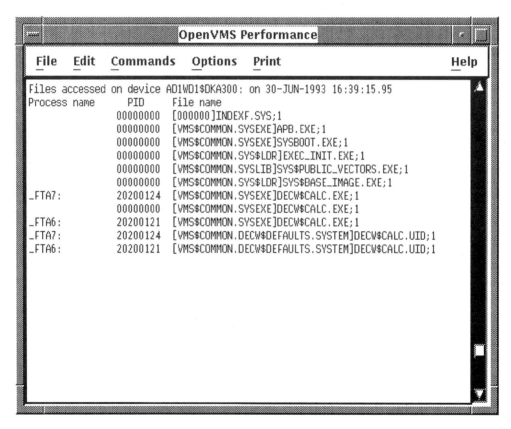

Figure 7-8. Install Name Problem

These memory savings require a certain amount of overhead. The overhead consists of the global page table entries and global section table entries required to map the code. There are 4 bytes of system memory overhead per global page and 32 bytes of system memory per global section descriptor. The SYSGEN parameter GBLPAGES defines the size of the global page table, and GBLSECTIONS defines the size of the global section tables.

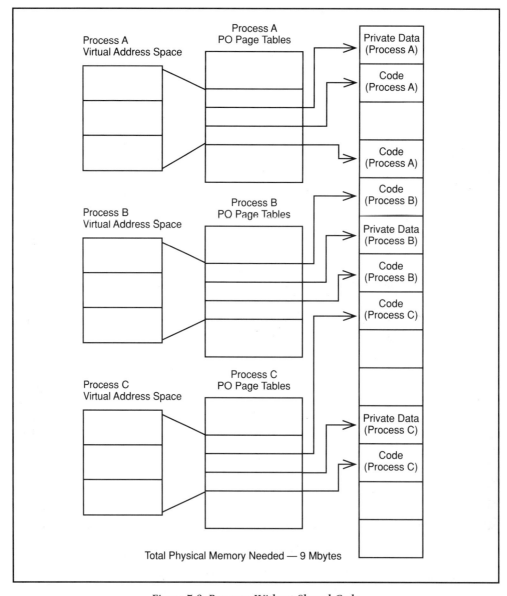

Figure 7-9. Program Without Shared Code

Figure 7-9 shows a program without shared code, and Figure 7-10 shows a program with shared code.

With just three users, we were able to save 4 MB of physical memory. The overhead to map the 3 MB of shared code can be calculated using Equation 7-6.

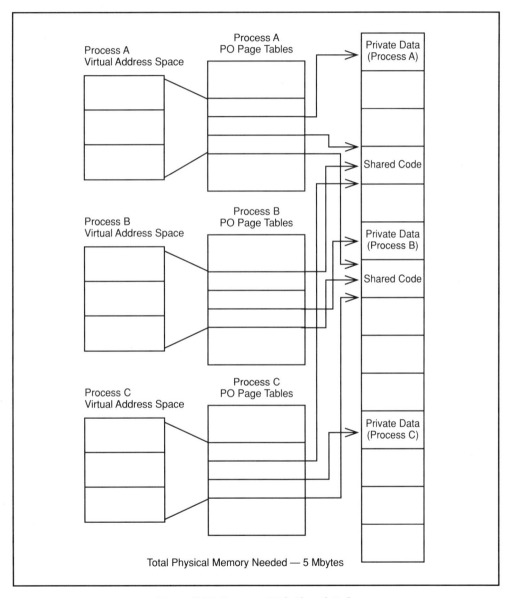

Figure 7-10. Program With Shared Code

133

$$\frac{32 * 32 + ((1024*2)*3)*4}{512} \cong 50\ Pagelets$$

Equation 7-6. Overhead to Map Shared Code

An evaluation of Equation 7-6 for our example gives:

$$\frac{\#GBLSECTIONS * 32 + \#GBLPAGES*4}{512} = Overhead\ Pages$$

Therefore, we consumed about forty-nine pages of physical memory to save almost 5,860 pages of memory. This is a better than 100/1 ratio — a very good trade-off.

Warning: A process always needs the same or larger working sets when using shared memory. Physical, not virtual, memory is saved. Do not make working sets smaller when using shared code; make them bigger.

SELECTING IMAGES

To determine which images to install, determine which are used most often. Refer to the Accounting Utility section in Chapter 3. Figures 3-8 and 3-9, which show a list of the images sorted by most references, are a good starting point. Another method is to use the following DCL commands:

```
$ SHOW DEVICE/FILE/NOSYSTEM DUAO: /output=Files.list
$ SORT/KEY = (POS:27, SIZE:60) Files.list Files.sorted
$ TYP Files.sorted
```

Image files or libraries that occur many times in the output are initial candidates for installation as shareable images.

EXCESSIVE IMAGE ACTIVATIONS

A fast indicator of excessive image activation is when demand-zero page faults exceed 50 percent of total page faults. Another fast check is to check the output from MONITOR MODES for a large percentage of time spent in SUPERVISOR mode. This indicates a large amount of DCL usage, which causes large numbers of image activations. Otherwise, enable the image-level accounting to determine which images are being activated most often and who uses those images.

USE OF LOGICAL NAMES

By default, AUTOGEN sets your system parameters to generate logical name hash tables of 128 entries. On almost all systems this is too small a value for the system logical name hash table, and in most cases it is too small for the process logical name hash table.

You can determine the correct size by using MONITOR IO. This provides the log name translation rate, which is the number of attempted logical name translations. The larger this number, the more important it is to size the hash tables correctly. You can also use the program in Appendix E. Using this program, you can determine the fill rate of the hash table, the average queue length of a hash entry, and the worst sixteen queues (see also Figure 7-11). The average queue length should be between 1 and 1.750, and there should be about 50 percent free entries in the hash.

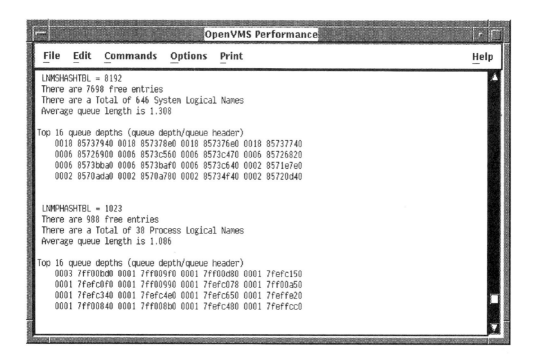

Figure 7-11. Dump Logical Names

Using the output in Figure 7-11, not only can you determine how to size the logical name hash tables, but you can also use this information to determine whether your logical names are "correct." Using the second program in Appendix E, you can dump out the logical names that are hashed to the entries with the most items. If there are hash entries with significantly more entries than the other hash locations, you can dump out the logical names that hash to that entry. You can then use this data to reduce the number of logical names or change selected names to reduce the length of the hash entries.

135

Warning: There will always be at least three logical names that hash to the same location for all processes, SYS$INPUT, SYS$OUTPUT, and SYS$ERROR. There is nothing you can do to change this, so ignore the very long hash queues for these entries.

SYSTEM POOL SPACE

Two basic memory areas are reserved for the system:

- The system working set and the associated paged pool area.

- The nonpaged pool area.

OpenVMS uses these areas for storing the code and data structures it uses to implement user processes. Because there is little locality associated with the pageable areas, even small faulting rates indicate serious problems.

PAGED DYNAMIC POOL

Paged pool is used to store the following:

- All logical names tables except for the process logical name tables.

- Global section descriptors.

- Install data structures.

- Some RMS data structures.

- Some mount device data structures.

- Process-specific usage.

In almost all cases AUTOGEN will correctly calculate the size needed for paged pool. The system parameter PAGEDYN will need to be increased in most cases when new software is installed on the system. Using the output in Figure 7-12, you should see that the value for "Free Space (bytes)" is greater than or equal to 128,000. If this is not true, check out the tuning requirements in Chapter 8.

SYSTEM WORKING SET

System working set size is controlled by the SYSGEN parameter SYSMWCNT. This parameter specifies how many paged pool pages are currently valid at any one time. All pages allocated to the system by SYSMWCNT, whether used or not, are permanently allocated to the system and are not available for process working sets. Do not set SYSMWCNT to a large arbitrary value. A nonzero value for system page faults is an indication that SYSMWCNT is too small. However, a zero value indicates either a very correct setting or that the system working set is set too large.

ADAPTIVE POOL MANAGEMENT

Once you have upgraded your system to at least OpenVMS VAX V6.0 or OpenVMS AXP V1.5, the next section on Nonpaged Pool does not apply to your system, and you can safely skip it.

```
┌─────────────────────────────────────────────────────────────────────────┐
│                          OpenVMS Performance                              │
├───────────────────────────────────────────────────────────────────────┤
│  File   Edit   Commands   Options   Print                          Help   │
├───────────────────────────────────────────────────────────────────────┤
│           System Memory Resources on 28-APR-1993 13:12:01.88              │
│                                                                           │
│ Small Packet (SRP) Lookaside List         Packets       Bytes      Pages  │
│     Current Total Size                        3000      384000       750   │
│     Initial Size (SRPCOUNT)                   3000      384000       750   │
│     Maximum Size (SRPCOUNTV)                 30000     3840000      7500   │
│     Free Space                                1314      168192            │
│     Space in Use                              1686      215808            │
│     Packet Size/Upper Bound (SRPSIZE)                      128            │
│     Lower Bound on Allocation                               32            │
│                                                                           │
│ I/O Request Packet (IRP) Lookaside List    Packets       Bytes      Pages │
│     Current Total Size                        2000      352000       688   │
│     Initial Size (IRPCOUNT)                   2000      352000       688   │
│     Maximum Size (IRPCOUNTV)                 20000     3520000      6875   │
│     Free Space                                 736      129536            │
│     Space in Use                              1264      222464            │
│     Packet Size/Upper Bound (fixed)                        176            │
│     Lower Bound on Allocation                              129            │
│                                                                           │
│ Large Packet (LRP) Lookaside List          Packets       Bytes      Pages │
│     Current Total Size                         110      204160       399   │
│     Initial Size (LRPCOUNT)                    110      204160       399   │
│     Maximum Size (LRPCOUNTV)                   550     1020800      1994   │
│     Free Space                                  86      159616            │
│     Space in Use                                24       44544            │
│     Packet Size/Upper Bound (LRPSIZE + 352)               1856            │
│     Lower Bound on Allocation                             1088            │
│                                                                           │
│ Nonpaged Dynamic Memory                                                   │
│     Current Size (bytes)       2499584  Current Total Size (pages)  4882   │
│     Initial Size (NPAGEDYN)    2499584  Initial Size (pages)        4882   │
│     Maximum Size (NPAGEVIR)    9999872  Maximum Size (pages)       19531   │
│     Free Space (bytes)          978624  Space in Use (bytes)     1520960   │
│     Size of Largest Block       897616  Size of Smallest Block       16    │
│     Number of Free Blocks          248  Free Blocks LEQU 32 Bytes    63    │
│                                                                           │
│ Paged Dynamic Memory                                                      │
│     Current Size (PAGEDYN)      982016  Current Total Size (pages) 1918    │
│     Free Space (bytes)          503120  Space in Use (bytes)     478896    │
│     Size of Largest Block       499664  Size of Smallest Block       16    │
│     Number of Free Blocks           98  Free Blocks LEQU 32 Bytes    76    │
│                                                                           │
│                                                                           │
└───────────────────────────────────────────────────────────────────────┘
```

Figure 7-12. Show Memory Expansion

NONPAGED POOL

Nonpaged pool is used for storing device drivers and data structures. The initial size is set by the SYSGEN parameter NPAGEDYN.

If more space is required, the system expands nonpaged pool by permanently allocating memory from the free list. These pages cannot be returned to use by processes until the system is rebooted. There is an overhead of about 4 percent to expand nonpaged pool. You must trade off this overhead cost with the cost of the permanent allocation of nonpaged pool.

It is possible to determine that pool expansion has occurred. Using the output listed in Figure 7-12, if the initial size is less than the maximum size for any of the lookaside lists or if the initial size is less than the current size for nonpaged dynamic memory, then pool expansion has occurred.

If pool expansion is occurring and you do not know where the pool is being used, use the ANALYZE/SYSTEM command. Appendix F shows the output of ANALYZE/SYSTEM. Using this command, you can get as detailed as you want in tracking down pool usage.

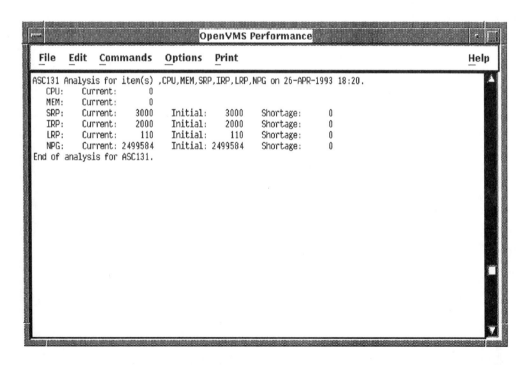

```
OpenVMS Performance

 File   Edit   Commands   Options   Print                                Help

ASC131 Analysis for item(s) ,CPU,MEM,SRP,IRP,LRP,NPG on 26-APR-1993 18:20.
   CPU:     Current:       0
   MEM:     Current:       0
   SRP:     Current:    3000   Initial:    3000   Shortage:   0
   IRP:     Current:    2000   Initial:    2000   Shortage:   0
   LRP:     Current:     110   Initial:     110   Shortage:   0
   NPG:     Current: 2499584   Initial: 2499584   Shortage:   0
End of analysis for ASC131.
```

Figure 7-13. Check Memory for Expansion

138

As an alternative, you can use the program listed in Appendix I if you are running OpenVMS VAX prior to version 6.0. Since you can use the program on a periodic basis, it is not only a good way to check for memory expansion, but it also will help keep track of the time of the expansion.

Use the program in Appendix I to generate a summary of memory usage (see Figure 7-13). When your system reports a shortage within the first day after a system reboot, you have undersized the pool areas. If the shortage occurs more than 24 hours after system startup, check the SDA to determine where the pool is being used (see Appendix F). Do not try to tune for hardware failures or unusual system usage!

Memory System Tuning

T HIS CHAPTER EXPLAINS HOW TO CORRECT THE PROBLEM UNCOVERED BY THE ANALYSIS
in Chapter 7.

REDUCING PAGE FAULTS

In Chapter 7 we discussed how to determine how many and what type of page faults
are occurring on your system. In this section we will take a brief look at each type of
fault and the appropriate tuning action for the fault type. The following is a quick-
and-dirty list of ways to tune for the different types of page faults on your system:

Page Read Rate and Page Read I/O Rate — The rate of read I/O operations from a
disk or disks as a result of page faults, and the hard fault rate for your system. If you
have a value outside the range given in Equation 7-1 (2) and if your value is less than
the lower value:

- Have the programmer check and correct for poor code and/or data locality.

- Ensure that the free list and/or the modified list is not too small (see the
  Secondary Page Cache section of this chapter).

For OpenVMS AXP the actual maximum size is 15 due to the page size and the
maximum transfer size for the file system.

If your value is greater than the upper value:

- It is not a big problem if the page read I/O rate is low.

- You could be overdriving your system if the page read I/O rate is high.

This could also be due to a large program using mapped files. If this is true you
should see few if any demand-zero pages.

Page Write Rate and Page Write I/O Rate — The rate at which pages were written
to the page file or files, and the rate of write I/O operations to the page files. If
Equation 7-1 (1) is not true, and by using the SDA procedure or the program listed
in Appendix I you determine that the page files are severely fragmented, increasing

the size of the page files will help. Also, if you used SDA to determine the largest user of page file space, ensure that if his or her usage is causing excessive fragmentation you notify the user so that the program can be corrected.

Free List Fault Rate — The rate at which pages were read from the free list as a result of page faults. Remember that the processes generating these faults could be accessing global pages from the free list. If this is the case there is nothing you can or should do from a tuning perspective. However, if the virtual size of the program is constant and the faults are not from global shared pages, then the working set size for the process is too small.

Modified List Fault Rate — The rate at which pages were read from the modified list as a result of page faults. Make sure that the processes generating these faults have correct working set sizes. This is a minor problem.

Demand-Zero Fault Rate — There is nothing you can do from the system level to reduce the overall rate of this type of page fault. Only by making changes to the programs causing these faults can you affect the demand-zero fault rate.

Global Valid Fault Rate — The rate at which page faults were resolved by valid pages in the systemwide global page tables. Since a high global valid rate is a possible indicator of incorrectly sized working sets, correlate this data with other work to determine whether the working set sizes for the user need to be changed.

System Fault Rate — The rate of page faults in system space (S0). If this rate does not satisfy Equation 7-1 (4), increase the SYSGEN parameter SYSMWCNT until this equation is satisfied.

SYSTEM POOL SPACE

Since the basic memory areas reserved for the system are used by all processes, we will tune for these areas first. Once we have tuned for the system areas, we can proceed to tuning other parts of the memory system. Because there is little locality associated with these areas, even small faulting rates are indicators of serious problems.

PAGED DYNAMIC POOL

Using the output in Figure 7-12, you should see that the value for "Free Space (bytes)" is greater than or equal to 128,000. If this is not true, you need to add the following line to the file SYS$SYSTEM:MODPARAMS.DAT:

```
ADD_PAGEDYN=nnnnn
```

where nnnnn is the amount needed to bring the value for "Free Space (bytes)" up to a minimum value of 128,000.

SYSTEM WORKING SET

SYSMWCNT should be set to reduce the number of system page faults to fewer than one per second. Initially size the initial value of SYSMWCNT as the sum of the following:

- One page for paged executive data.

- The number of pageable image sections of loadable executive images. Since not all loadable images are required, this value depends on your system. If unsure, use a value of 512.

- The number of paged pool pagelets derived by Equation 8-1.

- The number of global page table pagelets derived by Equation 8-1.

$$PagedPoolPagelets = \frac{PAGEDYN}{512}$$

$$GlobalPageTablePages = \frac{GBLPAGES + 127}{128}$$

Equation 8-1. SYSMWCNT Sizing

If you use AUTOGEN, it will correctly calculate a very good initial size for SYSMWCNT.

What we would like to do is set SYSMWCNT such that the number of system page faults is zero. However, you cannot detect whether you are at the correct size or whether you have oversized SYSMWCNT if the number of system faults is zero. To take care of this, we tune such that the number of system faults is close to but not zero. Once this is done, you can proceed to the next section.

To tune, you need to add the following line to the file SYS$SYSTEM:MODPARAMS.DAT:

```
MIN_SYSMWCNT=nnnnn
```

ADAPTIVE POOL MANAGEMENT

Once you have upgraded your system to at least OpenVMS VAX V6.0 or OpenVMS AXP V1.5, the next section on Nonpaged Pool does not apply to your system, and you can safely skip it.

NONPAGED POOL

If from your analysis in Chapter 7 you determined that pool expansion has occurred, you need to make the following changes. From Figure 7-13, "Check Memory for

Expansion," use the value from the "Shortage:" field(s) and add the following lines to your MODPARAMS.DAT file if the shortage number is greater than zero:

- Small request packet (SRP) List — SRPCOUNT, SRPCOUNTV

  ADD_SRPCOUNT = srp_shortage

- I/O request packet (IRP) List — IRPCOUNT, IRPCOUNTV

  ADD_IRPCOUNT = irp_shortage

- Large request packet (LRP) List — LRPCOUNT, LRPCOUNTV

  ADD_LRPCOUNT = lrp_shortage

- Nonpaged dynamic memory — NPAGEDYN, NPAGEVIR

  ADD_NPAGEDYN = npg_shortage

Ensure that you are tuning for "normal" operating conditions. Pool expansion is also a side effect of several hardware problems. It is not unusual for pool expansion to occur. What you want to check for is pool expansion that occurs due to normal activity. If you use the program listed in Appendix H, you can easily determine on a daily basis when pool expansion is occurring. This type of problem is why AUTOGEN is limited in its ability to provide feedback.

A good start is to set the lookaside list COUNT value to about 1.1 times the largest amount used during normal operations. Paged and nonpaged pool should be set so that about 128 KB always remains.

SECONDARY PAGE CACHE

Keep in mind that the "correct" sizing for the secondary page cache depends heavily on the working set sizes of the active processes and the paging characteristics of those processes. Also, you will want to have tuned the size of the system working set before trying to tune the size of the secondary caches.

For single-user workstations you will want to take special note if you are using installed images. As discussed in Chapter 7, installed images have a major effect on the way in which we analyze and tune for sizing the secondary caches.

The secondary page cache is controlled by setting the SYSGEN parameters FREELIM and FREEGOAL for the free list and MPW_HILIMIT and MPW_LOLIMIT for the modified list. Since the objective is to balance the hard/soft fault ratio, keep in mind that a larger free or modified list tends to reduce hard faults while increasing soft faults. Also remember that a larger modified list decreases the number of modified list writes, increases the number of soft faults, and decreases the number of hard faults.

INITIAL SIZING

Initially set up the free list as shown in Equation 8-2.

$$FREELIM = 10\% \ of \ PhysicalMemory$$
$$FREEGOAL = FREELIM + 3 * MPW\_WRTCLUSTER$$
$$BORROWLIM = FREEGOAL + 4 * MPW\_WRTCLUSTER$$
$$GROWLIM = BORROWLIM + 4 * MPW\_WRTCLUSTER$$

Equation 8-2. Initial Free List Sizing

Initially set up the modified list as shown in Equation 8-3.

$$MPW\_HILIMIT = 10\% \ of \ PhysicalMemory$$
$$MPW\_WAITLIMIT = MPW\_HILIMIT$$
$$MPW\_LOWAITLIMIT = MPW\_HILIMIT - 3 * MPW\_WRTCLUSTER$$
$$MPW\_LOLIMIT = MPW\_HILIMIT - 6 * MPW\_WRTCLUSTER$$
$$MPW\_THRESH = MPW\_HILIMIT + 10 * MPW\_WRTCLUSTER$$

Equation 8-3. Initial Modified List Sizing

For FREELIM and MPW_HILIMIT round up to the next even multiple of MPW_WRTCLUSTER.

Set the initial value of MPW_IOLIMIT as follows:

- Two for getting started.

- Add one for each disk used to support a page/swap file.

- Add one for each disk used to support an installed image or writable global section.

FREE LIST TUNING

After setting the initial values for the free list, recollect the paging data as shown in Chapter 7. Using this data, we will now detail the tuning steps needed, using the results of your analysis to correctly size the free list.

BUY MORE MEMORY

If your analysis determines that Equation 7-2 (1) is true, your system does not have enough memory. The first and best action to take is to acquire more memory. However, if you are unable to acquire more memory, then take the step listed below for a system with a free list that is too small.

FREE LIST TOO SMALL

If your analysis from Chapter 7 determines that your free list is too small, you will need to increase the size of the free list. Increment the various parameters that affect the free list size according to the following:

- If Equation 7-2 (2) is true, you have too many processes trying to execute at the same time, working set sizes for the processes are too large, or the parameters that size the free list are set too low.

- If you have not already done so, turn on proactive memory recovery (see the New Memory Recovery Mechanism section of Chapter 6) by adding the following line to your MODPARAMS file:

```
MMG_CTLFLAGS = 3
```

Next, check for too many processes. Major clues that too many processes are active include CPU queues, high kernel mode time, high interrupt mode time, and active in and out swapping of processes. If you have too many processes active, you need to buy more memory or reduce the process load.

Next, check for excessive working set sizes (see the Incorrect Working Set Sizes of Chapter 8). If you make corrections to working set sizes, reanalyze and retune.

Next, attempt to increase the size of the free list. Increase the size of the free list as follows:

$$ADD\_FREELIM = MPW\_WRTCLUSTER + \frac{((BALSETCNT *2) + MPW\_WRTCLUSTER -1)}{MPW\_WRTCLUSTER}$$

Add this entry to MODPARAMS.DAT after the entry added by the initial settings from Equation 8-2 "Initial Free List Sizing." This will ensure that all the entries are updated. We are increasing the size of the free list by at least two clusters from the modified list. This will be a slow, iterative process, but it is much safer than trying to update in large increases.

Also make these changes if Equation 7-2 (3) is true.

Free List Too Large

If your analysis determines that your free list is too large, you will need to take one or more of the following tuning steps:

- If proactive memory reclamation is enabled, reduce the size of FREEGOAL. Ensure that FREEGOAL is always at least as large as FREELIM + MPW_WRTCLUSTER. If you have been setting the size for FREEGOAL via Equation 8-2, you will need to add the following line to MODPARAMS.DAT:

```
ADD_FREELIM = - 2 * MPW_WRTCLUSTER
```

Otherwise, add the following line:

```
ADD_FREEGOAL = - 2 * MPW_WRTCLUSTER
```

- If Equation 7-1 (6) is true, the difference between FREEGOAL and FREELIM is excessive. Change the parameters in MODPARAMS.DAT such that the following is true:

```
FREELIM + 10 * MPW_WRTCLUSTER < FREEGOAL (AXP)
FREELIM + 20 * MPW_WRTCLUSTER < FREEGOAL (VAX)
```

- For all other cases you will just need to decrease the overall size of the free page cache. Add the following line to MODPARAMS.DAT:

```
ADD_FREEGOAL = - MPW_WRTCLUSTER
```

You could get the same results by modifying or deleting existing entries in MODPARAMS.DAT, but by always adding extra lines you can keep a historical track of changes and when they were made. This will be useful if you find out that you are increasing then later decreasing the same set of parameters. If this happens, decrement the amount by which you increase/decrease for each change. Below is an extract from a MODPARAMS file that gives an example of how things might look on an active system:

```
FREELIM = (32 * 1000 *2) / 10 ! For VAX 10% of 32 MB of memory
FREEGOAL = FREELIM + 3 * MPW_WRTCLUSTER ! Initial setup
BORROWLIM = FREEGOAL + 4 * MPW_WRTCLUSTER ! Initial setup
GROWLIM = BORROWLIM + 4 * MPW_WRTCLUSTER ! Initial setup
MMG_CTLFLAGS = 3 ! Enable proactive memory recovery
ADD_FREELIM= MPW_WRTCLUSTER + ( (( BALSETCNT*2)+MPW_WRTCLUSTER-1)
   /MPW_WRTCLUSTER) ! Increase free list 6-92 jwc
```

```
ADD_FREELIM= MPW_WRTCLUSTER + ( (( BALSET*2)+MPW_WRTCLUSTER-1)
  /MPW_WRTCLUSTER) ! Increase free list 7-92 jwc
ADD_FREELIM= MPW_WRTCLUSTER + ( (( BALSET*2)+MPW_WRTCLUSTER-1)
  /MPW_WRTCLUSTER) ! Increase free list 7-92 jwc
ADD_FREELIM= - 2 * MPW_WRTCLUSTER ! Decrease free list 6-92 jwc
```

MODIFIED LIST TUNING

After setting the initial values for the modified list, recollect the paging data as shown in Chapter 7. Using this data, we will now detail the tuning steps needed, using the results of your analysis to correctly size the modified list.

MODIFIED LIST TOO SMALL

If your analysis determines that the modified list is too small, start the process of increasing the size of the modified list:

- If you have been setting the size for MPW_HILIMIT via Equation 8-3, you will need to add the following line to MODPARAMS.DAT:

  ```
  ADD_MPW_HILIMIT = 2 * MPW_WRTCLUSTER
  ```

  Otherwise, add the following lines:

  ```
  ADD_MPW_HILIMIT = 2 * MPW_WRTCLUSTER
  ADD_MPW_LOLIMIT = 2 * MPW_WRTCLUSTER
  ```

- Ensure that you have multiple page files, if possible. Also ensure that the value for MPW_IOLIMIT is set correctly.

- If possible, use a locally attached disk for all pagefiles. If the pagefile is located on an MSCP-served disk, excessive network traffic will make your analysis appear as if the modified list is too small even if it is sized correctly or even, in some cases, if it is too large!

MODIFIED LIST TOO LARGE

If your analysis determines that the modified list is too large, start the process of decreasing the size of the modified list:

- If you have been setting the size for MPW_HILIMIT via Equation 8-3, you will need to add the following line to MODPARAMS.DAT:

```
ADD_MPW_HILIMIT = - MPW_WRTCLUSTER
```

Otherwise, add the following lines:

```
ADD_MPW_HILIMIT = - MPW_WRTCLUSTER
ADD_MPW_LOLIMIT = - MPW_WRTCLUSTER
```

Be sure to recheck your analysis after making changes. Do not continue to decrease the size of the modified list if decreasing the size does not decrease the number of processes in free page wait state. Also, remember that decreasing the size of an oversized modified list should not significantly increase the hard fault rate. In most cases it should decrease the overall hard fault rate. If the hard fault rate increases significantly after reducing the size of the modified list, remove the change that decreased the size of the modified list and look for other solutions.

SPECIAL MEMORY PROBLEMS

If you used AUTOGEN to size your secondary page cache, there is a very real possibility of this problem. Closely check each of the following items to cure problems of system pauses/hangs for large memory systems.

MODIFIED LIST WRITING PROBLEMS

If the value for Equation 7-3 "Excessive Modified Page Writing" gives a value greater than 30, you need to make changes such that the writing of your modified page list does not cause the entire system to experience random pauses that are several seconds in length:

- If MPW_WRTCLUSTER is not set to 64 or 112 for OpenVMS AXP, change to one of these two values. Change to 64 if CPU time is scarce. Otherwise, use a value of 112.

- For OpenVMS VAX, set MPW_WRTCLUSTER to 64 for systems that have little or no free CPU cycles or have pagefiles on MSCP-served disks. For all other systems, set to 120.

If all parts of Equation 7-4 "Excessive Modified Page Recovery" are true, immediate action is needed to stop system pauses and, in severe cases, system hangs:

- Ensure that FREEGOAL and FREELIM are sized correctly in relationship to each other:

```
FREELIM + 10 * MPW_WRTCLUSTER < FREEGOAL (AXP)
FREELIM + 20 * MPW_WRTCLUSTER < FREEGOAL (VAX)
```

- If you do not want the modified list to be used to recover pages for the free list, set MPW_THRESH to be greater than MPW_HILIMIT.

- Ensure that MPW_LOLIMIT is set correctly relative to MPW_HILIMIT.

- If MPW_WRTCLUSTER = 64 or 112 for OpenVMS AXP, change to one of these two values. Change to 64 if CPU time is scarce. Otherwise, use a value of 112.

- For OpenVMS VAX set MPW_WRTCLUSTER to 64 for systems that have little or no free CPU cycles or have pagefiles on MSCP served disks. For all other systems, set to 120.

MSCP AND PFCDEFAULT

The default values for MSCP_BUFFER are too small. If your pagefile is located on a disk that is being MSCP-served to your system, set MSCP_BUFFER on the serving system as follows. Using the MSCP I/O rate determined in Chapter 7, calculate the value for MSCP_BUFFER from Equation 8-4.

$$MSCP\_BUFFER = \sum_{i=1}^{\#system\ served} MAX(PFCDEFAULT, MPW\_WRTCLUSTER) * MSCP\ I/O\ Rate$$

Equation 8-4. MSCP_BUFFER Sizing

If you have trouble determining a good value for MSCP I/O rate, use the value for MSCP_CREDIT from the serving system.

Also, set PFCDEFAULT to valid values:

- For OpenVMS VAX, limit PFCDEFAULT to a maximum value of 120.

- For OpenVMS AXP, limit PFCDEFAULT to a maximum value of 112. This converts to an internal value of seven pages. When OpenVMS AXP supports larger page sizes and if the file system still limits I/Os to a maximum of 127 blocks, then the value of PFCDEFAULT (internal value in pages converted to pagelets) must not exceed 127 pagelets!

MODIFIED LIST FLUSHING

If you are experiencing excessive dead page table scans, you need to take the following actions:

- Ensure that SWPOUTPGCNT is set to a minimum value of 512 pages.

- Ensure that the total number of page table pages, when a process is at its WSEXTENT, is less than 25 percent of WSQUOTA size:

$$WSQUOTA \geq \frac{WSEXTENT}{Entries\ Per\ Page} * 0.25$$

Entries Per Page ==128 *for OpenVMS VAX*
Entries Per Page ==1024 *for OpenVMS AXP*

This is usually a problem only on OpenVMS VAX systems.

Also ensure that the above equations hold true for SWPOUTPGCNT versus WSQUOTA.

- The second item that usually causes dead page table scans is deleting writable global sections. The only way to solve excessive deletes of writable global sections is to have the users/producers of the program change the way in which the program is used.

WORKING SET SIZING

If your analysis determines that certain users had incorrect working set sizes for the programs they were executing, you have several basic solutions:

- Modify the programs to use less memory.

- Modify the system authorization file to allow the user a larger WSQUOTA and/ or WSEXTENT. An alternative is to create a special queue with very large working set limits to run specific programs. The purpose of the queue is to control on which system and during what time the program is run.

- If the program is running in detached mode, check the working set qualifiers on the run command and make sure the PQL parameters are set to the appropriate values. For most cases the default PQL_* parameters are set to excessively small values. For OpenVMS AXP these parameters have been defaulted to much more reasonable values.

- If all else fails, lower the priority of the process. A process running in an undersized working set will negatively affect all users on the system!

CALCULATING WORKING SET SIZES

This section discusses the commonly manipulated SYSGEN and AUTHORIZE parameters that control memory management and shows how and what to set in order to size your process working sets correctly. Some of the worst crimes against OpenVMS memory management are committed by the poor choices of values commonly found for WSQUOTA, WSDEFAULT, and WSEXTENT.

When tuning, there seems to be an irresistible tendency to set process quotas low for most users. Unfortunately, this approach succeeds. The processes are kept small and use a lot of CPU time and I/O overhead to process the extra hard and soft faults generated. While those users will experience a slow system, so will every other user competing for the extra resources used by the processes with low quotas. Worse, because the processes are faulting a lot, they tend to flush the free and modified lists, which causes other processes on the system to suffer hard faults when they might otherwise be able to obtain the pages via soft faults.

A reasonable use of WSDEFAULT, WSQUOTA, and WSEXTENT is to set them to moderate values to hold down total system demand for memory. Controlling total memory demand via PFRATL, PFRATH, WSDEC, and WSINC allocates memory much more equitably (that is, based on need), but as we shall see, they cannot be set well statically for a wide range of loads.

Setting WSDEFAULT, WSQUOTA, and WSEXTENT high works well on a system with abundant memory, but if memory gets tight, individual processes can take up too much memory. If you must set the values statically, then:

- The value for WSDEFAULT should be set so that a process can handle several hard faults at image activation. Thus, WSDEFAULT should be at least four to five times the value for PFCDEFAULT.

- WSQUOTA should be set to allow all processes on the system to run in a reasonable manner. The sum of WSQUOTA for all active processes should not exceed the available memory. The sizes for WSQUOTA should be such that all active processes can reside in memory without requiring active inswapping of processes.

- WSEXTENT should allow the processes with heaviest faulting to increase their working sets when the system is lightly loaded. WSEXTENT should be such that most processes can run with little or no page faulting during the majority of the execution time for the program.

WSDEFAULT

If a process has a WSDEFAULT that is less than about five times PFCDEFAULT, you will have the following problems:

- Immediately upon image activation you will have a hard fault to page in the image you are running if the image is not currently valid as global pages. In almost all cases you will have two to five more hard faults to finish paging in the initialization portion of your image.

- If WSDEFAULT is less than five times PFCDEFAULT, your process will have to remove pages it just hard-faulted in to make room for the pages requested by the fourth hard fault. Since it will take at least PFRATH hard and soft faults to get a WSINC increment of your working set list, and you only get a WSINC after the end of quantum, the process will have a hard time acquiring a reasonable working set size. If this is happening, you will notice that image activations required a lot of hard and soft faults. In addition, most image activation will be very slow.

Increasing WSDEFAULT will have a major impact on the speed of DCL procedures, since most DCL is restricted by the speed of image activations.

WSQUOTA

WSQUOTA is the amount of memory you have committed to a process. It is important that you do not commit more memory than you have on your system. A simple and effective approach is to ensure that the sum of the working set quotas of all active processes is less than the amount of memory available (see Equation 6-1 in Chapter 6). Remember that the portion of the working set quotas that consists of global pages should be counted only once per system, not once per process.

For most processes, when WSQUOTA is set correctly the process will be able to execute for extended periods of time with very low fault rates — fewer than ten faults per second — and most of those faults should be soft faults.

WSEXTENT

Since working set extents are used to give more memory to a process under lightly loaded conditions, you need to be generous when assigning the value to WSEXTENT.

For most processes, when WSEXTENT is set correctly the process will be able to execute for extended periods of times with extremely low fault rates — fewer than one fault per second — and most of those faults should be demand-zero faults.

PFRATL AND WSDEC

PFRATL, AWSTIME, and WSDEC are used in conjunction with the AWSA routine to take memory away from processes that are faulting very little. Specifically, if during the last AWSTIME a process has been faulting at a rate of less than PFRATL faults per 10 seconds, its working set size will be decremented by WSDEC pages.

Setting the PFRATL parameter presents a dilemma. If PFRATL is set to zero, disabling working set decrement (the AUTOGEN default), then working sets will be hundreds of pages too large, because pages are not removed from the working set until the working set entries are needed (process at or above WSQUOTA). A large amount of startup code or data that is accessed only once can remain in the working set for a long time.

On the other hand, if PFRATL is greater than zero, then processes that might run for a long time without generating a page fault will be forced to fault frequently by the automatic working set decrement. If memory is tight, set PFRATL to nonzero and set WSDEC to a value that is a relative prime to WSINC (fifty-seven pages). In a memory-tight system, most processes are faulting anyway, so the little extra faulting caused by a nonzero PFRATL will not hurt.

If memory is not tight, leave PFRATL at zero and use other means to recover memory. With a zero PFRATL, remember to set WSDEC to a large value (512 pages) to help implement the new AWSA algorithm as described in the New Memory Recovery Mechanism section of Chapter 6.

The best solution is to implement a simple tuner to dynamically set the "correct" value for PFRATL depending on current memory conditions. (See the PFRATL and WSDEC section of Chapter 9.)

PFRATH AND WSINC

PFRATH, AWSTIME, and WSINC are analogous to PFRATL and WSDEC, except that they are used to increase, not decrease, working set size. Setting the PFRATH and WSINC parameters presents a dilemma similar to the one found with PFRATL and WSDEC, only not as severe. If PFRATH is set low and WSINC is set high, working sets will tend to expand rapidly, once again holding large amounts of startup code in the working set (that is, in main memory), when it may never be used again.

On the other hand, if PFRATH is set high and WSINC is set low, processes will fault heavily, especially during image activation and at other times when their working sets need to expand rapidly. For most systems set PFRATH to a value of 100 and set WSINC to a value of 256.

PFCDEFAULT

The default value of 64 for non-Local-Area-VAXcluster nodes is a reasonable value. If PFCDEFAULT is set higher, some processes will be able to fault into memory more quickly, but there is a small CPU penalty. There is a greater CPU penalty if soft faulting increases because of low values for WSDEFAULT, WSQUOTA, and WSEXTENT. A lower PFCDEFAULT value saves a small amount of CPU time but can slow image activation and increase hard faults.

On a system with high process quotas and memory and CPU time to spare (null time consistently greater than zero), setting PFCDEFAULT up to 120 can provide a performance improvement. Unfortunately, most systems do not always have memory and CPU time to spare. Therefore, with static tuning, you will generally be forced to compromise and set PFCDEFAULT to 64.

Warning: Remember that for OpenVMS AXP the default value will be set to 128 due to an AUTOGEN bug. This bug should be fixed in OpenVMS AXP V2.0.

CONTROLLING SWAPPING

The basic rule for swapping is that a little is good and a lot is bad. More specifically, swapping out idle processes frees memory at a very low cost. Rolling active processes in and out on a regular basis is costly. It would be better to cut their working set sizes a little and page a little.

When tuning statically, one way to force idle processes to be swapped out is to set the SYSGEN parameter BALSETCNT to a value less than the number of processes expected to be active at any given time. BALSETCNT is the maximum number of processes that can be memory-resident at any time. The swapper's first choice is to swap out obviously idle processes, so this works very well until the swapper needs to swap out active processes. When this happens, the swapper uses a lot of resources to shuffle processes in and out. It is difficult to set BALSETCNT well for all system loads.

Set BALSETCNT such that during normal operations there are no inswaps of processes that have been outswapped in the last 300 seconds. If this cannot be done, lower the value of WSQUOTA for all processes until there are no inswaps of processes that have been outswapped in the last 300 seconds.

PAGE FILE FRAGMENTATION

The only real solution for a fragmented page file is to increase the size of the page file or to create more page files. Any time the output of the program in Appendix D shows that there has been a page/swap space failure since last boot, you need to determine why there was a failure. In most cases, the page/swap file is too small. If you have a page file that you want to make larger, use the following DCL commands:

```
$ MCR SYSGEN
SYSGEN> CREATE SYS$SYSTEM:PAGEFILE.SYS/SIZE=100000
```

These commands will try to extend the size of the current page file. Note that a page file cannot have extension headers. Thus, there is an upper limit to the number of times a page file can be extended.

To create a new version of an existing file or to create a new page file, use the following DCL commands:

```
$ MCR SYSGEN
SYSGEN> CREATE -
SYSGEN> SYS$SYSTEM:PAGEFILE.SYS/SIZE=100000/CONTIG
```

To use the new, larger file, you must reboot your system. To allow use of new page files without having to reboot your system, set the following system parameters:

- PAGFILCNT = 2 + number of currently active page files.
- SWPFILCNT = 2 + number of currently active swap files.

The overhead for the four unused slots is minimal, and it will save having to reboot your system in many cases. If the disk drive that contains a page file fails, you can create a temporary page file on another disk and keep running until the disk is repaired and ready to be put back into operation.

INSTALLED IMAGES

The way to control memory sharing is to use the Install utility to install shareable read/write global sections. Notice that when you are trying to use a shared image, linking an image in shared mode does not make the image shared. You must use INSTALL and install the image with the /SHARED qualifier for memory sharing to occur. The /OPEN qualifier causes the directory information for the file to be loaded into memory. This saves the disk I/Os needed for file lookup when the image is accessed. The cost of installing an image with the /OPEN qualifier is approximately one page of dynamic memory.

The /HEADER_RESIDENT qualifier loads the file header into dynamic memory. This allows for faster loading of the image by reducing I/O overhead. The cost of this qualifier depends on the size of the file header; for images with only one fragment, the cost is less than one page of paged dynamic memory.

Warning: Every program that uses any part of an installed image must map the entire image into its virtual space. Adding additional installed libraries could require increasing the value of VIRTUALPAGECNT for your system.

The /SHARED qualifier implicitly declares the /OPEN qualifier. Installing the image with the /SHARED qualifier requires both global pages, GBLPAGES, one per virtual page in the image section, and an extra two pages for the section rounded to the next even value. For every image section, one global section descriptor (GBLSECTIONS) is also needed.

When you install a shared image, be sure you are installing the correct parts! Figure 8-1 shows the two main parts for the Language Sensitive Editor (LSEDIT). There are only six pages of shareable memory in the image itself (SYS$SYSTEM:LSEDIT.EXE).

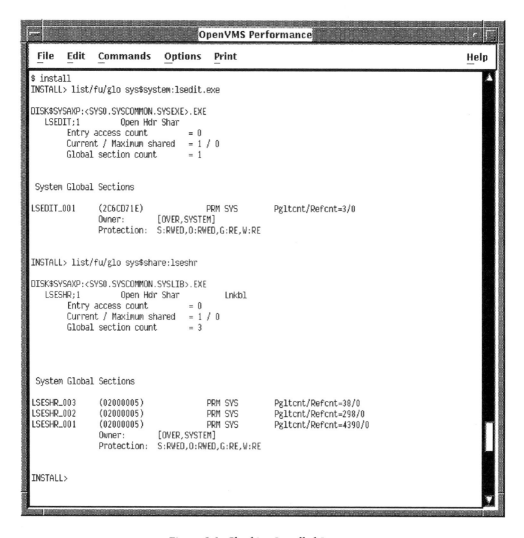

Figure 8-1. Checking Installed Images

The image that needs to be installed is the shareable library, SYS$SHARE:LSESHR.EXE. LSEDIT links against and uses LSESHR, which has 1,163 pages of shareable memory.

For most Digital products, this scheme (SYS$SYSTEM:XXX.EXE, SYS$SHARE:XXXSHR.EXE) is now used, so you want to install XXXSHR for product XXX to make use of shared memory.

EXCESSIVE IMAGE ACTIVATION

An easy way to help solve the problem of excessive image activation is to change frequently run DCL programs into OpenVMS images. Another method is to change users' habits so that they use commands that minimize the number of images activated. Correct use of DECwindows and/or Motif will go a long way in helping reduce the number of image activations required.

Using the image accounting data collected in your analysis, determine which are the most-used images. You should then consider installing these images. While this will not directly reduce the number of image activations, it will reduce the load on the system caused by the image activations.

Be careful of DCL loops. The great bulk of DCL commands are implemented as image activations.

USE OF LOGICAL NAMES

If you are having a problem with logical name translations, increase either the SYSGEN parameter LNMPHASHTBL for process-level logical names or LNMSIIASIITBL for all other logical names until the output from the program in Appendix F is within the bounds specified in the Use of Logical Names section of Chapter 7.

On a heavily used system, the logical name translation rate will be in the hundreds per second. To ensure high performance, make logical name lookups as fast as possible. A small overall queue length on the hash tables will greatly speed up logical name lookups for both success and failure, both of which are critical.

SYSGEN DEFAULTS

Appendix G is a listing of the MODPARAMS.DAT file we use as a starting point for our VAX workstations running DECwindows and OpenVMS V6.0. Also included are examples of how to make changes to the MODPARAMS.DAT file.

Static Versus Dynamic Tuning

W HEN I REFER TO TUNING MEMORY MANAGEMENT, I AM REFERRING TO THE manipulation of SYSGEN and AUTHORIZE parameters so that memory is allocated to the processes on the system in such a way that the total memory management overhead is minimized. Generally speaking, this means that processes that need large amounts of memory to avoid high fault rates get large amounts of memory, and processes that will fault very little with even small working sets will be allocated only a small amount of memory when memory is scarce.

Static tuning is the traditional method of watching the system run with whatever tools are available, for example, MONITOR. With static tuning, you collect statistics for a while, reset some SYSGEN parameters, and see how the system runs. If your system still does not run well, you repeat the process. If it runs well, you do not touch it. Static tuning is held by some to be a black art practiced well only by highly paid specialists.

Dynamic tuning is done every few seconds under the control of a process on the system. Dynamic tuning has many advantages over static tuning. Although it may be possible to statically tune a system optimally for an exact given load, changes in the load will leave the system tuned less than optimally. Because the load varies on most real-world systems, dynamic tuning has a greater potential to tune well for a wide mix of loads.

In practice, statically tuned systems start out with compromised SYSGEN parameters, because they cannot be changed as the load changes, and it is important to avoid a number of bad cases. In this chapter I discuss the commonly manipulated SYSGEN and AUTHORIZE parameters that control memory management and demonstrate the opportunities that exist when tuning dynamically.

PFRATL AND WSDEC

PFRATL and WSDEC (global symbols SCH$GL_PFRATL and SCH$GL_WSDEC) are used in conjunction with the AWSA routine to take memory away from processes that are faulting very little. With dynamic tuning, PFRATL can be set depending on the size of the free list. If the free list is large, there is no need to decrement working set sizes, so PFRATL can be set to zero. If the free list is low, PFRATL can be set greater than zero so that processes will be decremented. (The free page count is stored at global symbol SCH$GL_FREECNT.) The program in Figure 9-1 illustrates how easily this can be done.

```
        .TITLE  DYN_1
; Just a quickie program to set PFRATL based on the size of the free list.
; Copyright (C) 1989; William R. Davy.
; Copyright (C) 1991; James W. Coburn.
; Copyright (C) 1992; Professional Press Books.
; Copyright (C) 1993; Cardinal Business Media.
; This program may be copied for noncommercial purposes. Use of this program
; for any other purpose without the express written consent of the publisher
; is prohibited.
        MAX_PFRATL=200      ;Don't move pfratl above this value
        TARGET_SIZE=2000   ;Target Size For Free List
        .PSECT    DYN_1,EXE,NOWRT,QUAD
        .ENTRY    DYN_1,^M<>
        $CMKRNL_S IDLE       ;Change Mode To Kernel And Idle There
; Start here and Hibernate until next scheduled wakeup.
        .ENTRY    IDLE,^M<>
10$:    $HIBER_S  ;Hibernate Until Next Wakeup
        CMPL      SCH$GL_FREECNT,#TARGET_SIZE ;Is Free List At Least 2000
Pages?
        BLEQU     50$       ;No, Set Pfratl There
; Fall through when there is plenty of space on the free list.
        CLRL      SCH$GL_PFRATL  ;Set Pfratl = 0
        BRB       10$          ;And Go Back And Wait
; Branch here when free list is low.
50$:    AOBLEQ    #MAX_PFRATL,SCH$GL_PFRATL,10$ ;Bump Pfratl And Then Go Wait
        DECL      SCH$GL_PFRATL  ;Max Pfratl Here Can Only Be 200
        BRB       10$          ;Go Wait Again
        .END      DYN_1
```

Figure 9-1. Simple Dynamic Tuner

The Dynamic Tuner program can be assembled and linked with the following command file:

```
$ MACRO DYN_1
$ LINK DYN_1,SYS$SYSTEM:SYS.STB/SEL
```

If the user has DETACH, CMKRNL, and SETPRI privileges, the program can be run with a wakeup interval of 2 seconds with the following command:

160

```
$ RUN DYN_1 /DETACHED /INTERVAL="0 00::02" /PRIORITY=17
/PROCESS_NAME=DYN_1
```

The process has an interesting feature: It appears to use no CPU time. It runs off the system clock and will probably be the highest-priority process in the system. Therefore, when the clock ticks (the tick that wakes up DYN_1), DYN_1 will not be seen to be running and consequently will not be charged for that tick. DYN_1 starts and finishes its work so fast (in less than the length of time between clock ticks) that it will be done long before the clock ticks again. Therefore, OpenVMS will never see DYN-1 as the current process. Thus, DYN-1 will never be charged CPU time.

Figure 9-2 shows the equivalent program in C.

PFRATH AND WSINC

PFRATH and WSINC (global symbols SCH$GL_PFRATH and SCH$GL_WSINC) are similar to PFRATL and WSDEC except that they are used to increase rather than decrease the working set size.

With dynamic tuning you can repeatedly look at the size of the free list. If it is large, set PFRATH low and WSINC high so that images will expand their working sets rapidly when needed. If OpenVMS has the memory to spare, use it. If the free list is small, raise PFRATH and lower WSINC so that processes do not expand so rapidly.

Appendix H lists a program that shows how to dynamically tune PFRATL and WSINC.

GROWLIM AND BORROWLIM

GROWLIM (global symbol SGN$GL_GROWLIM) and BORROWLIM (global symbol SGN$GL_BORROWLIM), in addition to FREELIM (global symbol SCH$GL_FREELIM) and FREEGOAL (global symbol SCH$GL_FREEGOAL), are used in conjunction with WSEXTENT to control a process's ability to grow larger than its normal working set quota. The goal is to obtain a reasonable balance between hard and soft faults. What is reasonable is difficult to determine statically. Certain hard faults (the first fault for any page in an image) and certain soft faults (demand-zero faults) are unavoidable. Of those left, you want to minimize the value calculated by using Equation 9-1.

$$\text{Hard Page Faults} * 50 + \text{Soft Page Faults}$$

Equation 9-1. Balance Faults

With dynamic tuning you can keep count of the relevant faults by looking into image headers and guessing that the first few hard faults are unavoidable image activation

```
/* Just a quickie program to set PFRATL based on the size of the
** free list.
** Copyright (C) 1993; James W. Coburn.
** Copyright (C) 1993; Cardinal Business Media.
**
** This program may be copied for noncommercial purposes. Use of this
program
** for any other purpose without the express written consent of the
publisher
** is prohibited.
*/
#define MAX_PFRATL 200     /* Don't move pfratlabove this value */
#define TARGET_SIZE 2000   /* Target Size For Free List */
main()
{
  int IdleWork();
  sys$cmexec ( IdleWork, 0);
}
/*
** Kernel Code for doing all work.
*/
int IdleWork()
{
  for(;; )
  {
/*
** Loop Forever.
*/
    sys$hyber(); /* Hibernate until next scheduled wakeup. */
    if( SCH$GL_FREECNT >= TARGET_SIZE ) /* At lease TARGET_SIZE pages on
    free list */
    {
      SCH$GL_PFRATL = 0;
    }
    else /* Not enough page on free list */
    {
      if( SCH$GL_PFRATL < MAX_PFRATL )
      {
        SCH$GL_PFRATL++;
      }
    }
  }
}
```

Figure 9-2. Simple Dynamic Tuner (C Version)

faults. You can also throw out the demand-zero faults, because they are counted separately in the Performance Management Subsystem (PMS) statistics.

By comparing hard to soft faults in what is left, you can determine whether the free list is grossly large or small. Because you are tuning dynamically, you can adjust GROWLIM and BORROWLIM accordingly to help control the size of the free list.

CONTROLLING SWAPPING

Remember that the basic rule for swapping is that a little swapping is good, and a lot is bad. Dynamic tuning takes a different approach to controlling swapping. Set BALSETCNT to a value that is at least as large as the maximum number of processes that will ever be concurrently active. This way, the swapper will never needlessly force processes to thrash in and out.

The way to force idle processes out without causing thrashing is to control PFRATL and WSDEC so that the free page list can drop below FREELIM for short periods of time before turning on PFRATL. The swapper will then swap out the idle processes. If the system performs a significant number of swap ins, then there is too much swapping, and PFRATL and WSDEC should be raised to keep the free list larger than FREELIM.

WSDEFAULT, WSQUOTA, AND WSEXTENT

Some of the worst crimes against OpenVMS memory management are committed by the poor choices of values commonly found for WSDEFAULT, WSQUOTA, and WSEXTENT (offsets PHD$L_DFWSCNT, PHD$L_WSQUOTA, and PHD$L_WSEXTENT in the process header). These per-process parameters (set via AUTHORIZE) are, respectively, the working set size to which a process is shrunk upon image exit, the maximum working set size a process is allowed when the free list has fewer than GROWLIM pages, and the maximum working set size allowed for the process when the free list has more than GROWLIM pages.

With dynamic tuning, the problem becomes trivially easy. Set WSDEFAULT, WSQUOTA, and WSEXTENT high. You can control total memory demands (as shown earlier) by manipulating PFRATL, PFRATH, WSDEC, and WSINC, which do a much better job of allocating memory.

PFCDEFAULT

Dynamic tuning gives you the freedom to do the best job at all times with PFCDEFAULT. If null time has been consistently nonzero recently, it probably will stay that way for the next short interval. Therefore, you can afford the CPU time that is lost if PFCDEFAULT is raised to 120 for OpenVMS VAX and to 112 for OpenVMS AXP. Furthermore, if the process quotas are set high and the free list is moderately large, there is no reason not to raise PFCDEFAULT. Should CPU time or the free list become short, PFCDEFAULT can be lowered to 64. Doing this, you can easily have the best of all worlds.

The above discussion of PFCDEFAULT has oversimplified what needs to be done. PFCDEFAULT is actually copied into the process header when the process is created. Changing PFCDEFAULT only affects processes that are created after the change. Therefore, in order to get immediate benefits, you must change the field PHD$B_DFPFC (for OpenVMS AXP, use PHD$L_DFPFC) in all of the process headers.

DEFICIENCIES IN AWSA

When a process with an adjustable working set reaches end-of-QUANTUM, OpenVMS does its calculations with PFRATL, PFRATH, and so on, and determines whether that process's working set should be adjusted. If so, it queues an AST to the process, which calls $ADJWSL, thus adjusting the working set limits.

The weakness inherent in this algorithm is that jobs that do not reach end-of-QUANTUM are never adjusted. In particular, idle jobs are never decremented. VMS V5.0 addresses this deficiency somewhat by decrementing processes that have been idle for DORMANTWAIT seconds by WSDEC pages.

Dynamic tuning processes can do much better. You can correctly argue that the AWSA algorithm should be based on elapsed time rather than CPU time. That is, the fault rate that is compared to PFRATL and PFRATH should be the rate of faults per second of elapsed time rather than faults per second of CPU time.

Because all of the information needed to calculate fault rates is contained in the process headers, there is no reason a dynamic process could not perform an AWSA algorithm based on elapsed time rather than CPU time. When the dynamic process determines that a process should be decremented, it could queue its own AST to the process, the same way OpenVMS does. This feature, in conjunction with OpenVMS' AWSA, is an effective way to keep low-priority jobs from creating large amounts of memory management overhead.

QUANTUM

There are two major tradeoffs to consider when setting QUANTUM. First, there is CPU overhead associated with end-of-QUANTUM processing. Fortunately, on most VAXs CPU overhead is not high, even when QUANTUM is set to 2, its minimum value. There is a small amount of CPU time to be saved if you set QUANTUM high. If you set QUANTUM low, image activation tends to speed up greatly, as you will see in the following example.

Consider a system that has ten CPU-bound processes running at normal priority on a VAX with QUANTUM set to 20 (the SYSGEN default value). Each time one of those processes is scheduled, it can keep the CPU for one-fifth (20/100ths) of a second. After a process runs, it will be 1.8 seconds until it gets the CPU again.

Assume an image is to be activated by an interactive user who needs a fairly large number of hard faults before anything useful is done for the user. Forgetting about the image's initial priority boost, what you will see is:

- The process will generate a hard fault and have to wait for the disk I/O to complete. Time equals approximately one-twentieth of a second.

- The process becomes computable at the default priority. It must wait 2 seconds for the CPU-bound processes ahead of it in the queue to receive their quanta. Time equals approximately 2 seconds.

- The process gets access to the CPU and immediately faults again. Go back to the first step. If the process has to hard-fault ten times, you can expect it to take over 20 seconds for activation.

What would happen if that QUANTUM were 2 instead of 20? In this case, the middle step takes only 0.2 seconds, and activation is completed in closer to 2 seconds. You can see that a small QUANTUM can pay large dividends in interactive response.

The second trade-off in setting QUANTUM is that reaching end-of-QUANTUM sooner means that the OpenVMS priority boost is decremented sooner. Setting QUANTUM at 2 instead of 20 effectively defeats 90 percent of the OpenVMS priority boost.

Dynamic tuning presents several opportunities for improvement. If only a few processes are receiving CPU time, or if there is a lot of null CPU time, QUANTUM can be raised without significantly hurting response time, thus saving some end-of-QUANTUM processing CPU time. If there are many processes and no null CPU time, set QUANTUM low to help response time. The program in Figure 9-3 illustrates how you can dynamically alter QUANTUM on the basis of CPU usage.

```
        .TITLE QUANTUM_ADJUST
; A sample program to adjust QUANTUM based on system usage.
; Copyright (C) 1989; William R. Davy.
; Copyright (C) 1991; James W. Coburn.
; Copyright (C) 1992; Professional Press Books.
; Copyright (C) 1993; Cardinal Business Media.
; This program may be copied for non-commercial purposes. Use of this
; program for any other purpose without the express written consent
; of the publisher is prohibited.
        .PSECT QUANTUM,EXE,NOWRT
        .ENTRY QUANTUM,^M<>
        $CMKRNL_S IDLE      ;CHANGE MODE TO KERNEL
        .ENTRY IDLE,^M<>    ;HERE TO IDLE (WAIT TO AWAKE)
10$: $HIBER_S              ;HIBERNATE UNTIL AWAKENED
     BITL     #^X0FFFFFFF,@#SCH$GL_COMQS
;LOOK FOR COMPUTABLE JOBS>= DEFPRI
     BNEQ     50$      ;HAVE ONE OR MORE
; HERE IF CPU NOT BUSY WITH NORMAL-TO-HIGH PRIORITY JOBS NOW
     MNEGW    #2,@#SCH$GW_QUAN   ;SET QUANTUM LOW (2)
     BRB 10$   ;AND WAIT TILL NEXT INTERVAL
; HERE IF CPU IS BUSY WITH NORMAL-TO-HIGH PRIORITY JOBS
50$: MNEGW    #5,@#SCH$GW_QUAN   ;SET QUANTUM HIGH (5)
     BRB 10$
     .END QUANTUM
```

Figure 9-3. QUANTUM Adjuster

The QUANTUM Adjuster program can be assembled and linked with the following commands:

```
$ MACRO QUANTUM
$ LINK QUANTUM,SYS$SYSTEM:SYS.STB/SEL
```

If the user has DETACH, CMKRNL, and SETPRI privileges, the program can be run with a wakeup interval of 2 seconds with the following command:

```
$ RUN QUANTUM/DETACHED/INTERVAL="0-0::02" /PRIORITY=17/PROC=QUANTUM
```

ALPHABETIZING YOUR ASTS

One of the major features of OpenVMS is that no process can directly access the process memory space of any other process. Only memory that is mapped in system space is directly accessible to all processes. Thus, if you want to execute code in the context of another process, the only feasible method is to have the code and the associated data reside in system space.

In the bag of tricks for all VAX system programmers is the ubiquitous AST routine. Many of our favorite programs use ASTs to execute their code in the context of another process. For most programmers, this was the only method used to extend the available system procedures to access and/or control another process.

Using OpenVMS VAX, you can copy position-independent code (PIC) from one address range to another, usually in system address space, and then execute the code. If you compile this code for OpenVMS AXP, the code that was copied to system space will not execute correctly. There are two reasons for this:

1. The compiled code may not be in the same order as the source code. For OpenVMS AXP, MACRO-32 is compiled, not assembled. This compilation will in many cases change the order in which code is executed.

2. Code now requires a linkage section to make external references. This linkage section is not located in the same PSECT as the code itself. In addition, the linkage section contains absolute addresses fixed up by the linker and the image activator.

If you want to copy code to another address range for execution, you will need to fix up the linkage section to resolve all address fixups. To do this, your code will have to include many features of both the linker and the image activator.

With the introduction of VMS V5.0, an alternative to using ASTs became available. User executive images allow users to enhance and replace their existing AST routines used to execute code in the context of other processes.

Appendix M contains complete source code for all the routines referenced in these sections.

THREE STRIKES AND YOU'RE IN

To review this process of queuing an AST to another process, I will give a quick example of how to adjust the working set of any process on the system.

The basic algorithm is as follows:

- Create the AST routine.

- Create the loader routine.

- Create the driver routine.

AST Routine

To create a simple example, the AST routine adjusts the current process's working set. If passed a parameter of zero, the working set is adjusted down by 256 pages. Otherwise, the working set is adjusted up by 256 pages.

Loader Routine

The loader routine is fairly common to all of us. It has appeared in various forms in several articles in *Digital Systems Journal* over the years. Its basic algorithm is:

- Allocate an area of pool large enough to contain the AST routine.

- Copy the AST routine into the allocated pool space.

- Store the AST routine's entry point at a systemwide known location. One of the SYSGEN USER* values is most often used.

At this point the AST routine is available and addressable to any process on the system.

Driver Routine

The driver program, in a simple form, takes as input the Internal Process Identification (IPID) of the process whose working set is to be adjusted and a flag that indicates whether to increase or decrease the working set. The driver queues a kernel-mode AST to the indicated process. When the AST executes, the process's working set will be adjusted.

EVOLUTION IN ACTION

Early versions of the VAX/VMS executive consisted of the system image (SYS.EXE) and the Record Management Service (RMS.EXE). Features that were configuration-dependent were supported in separate images, such as device drivers and the processor-dependent SYSLOAxxx.exe images. Because of the relatively monolithic design, making changes to the executive required making complex patches to the system image. In many cases these patches had to be modified with each new release of the system image. Since most of us did not or could not support the development and support of device drivers, the pool loading methodology became the primary method of "extending" the available system routines.

VMS V5.0

VMS V5.0 further partitioned the executive to simplify making patches and to reduce the work required when the executive needed to be changed. This new, partitioned executive came to be known as the modular executive. One of the new features supplied by the modular executive was the loading of optional images as part of the system executive. One of the "documented" features of the SYSMAN utility showed how the user could produce and load a site-specific loadable executive image.

SUPPORT

While Digital "supports" only a limited use of user-written executive images, in reality there are almost unlimited ways to make use of this functionality. (Apart from replacements for the $ERAPAT and $MTACCESS system services, use of this mechanism is reserved to Digital.) I will show later how this affects you.

WHY SWITCH?

One of the problems with the pool-loaded routine is that all of the system addresses mapped by the routine are accessible only from kernel mode. This limits your ability to test the code and limits access to only those processes with CMKRNL. OpenVMS isn't gentle with routines that generate errors in kernel mode. Most errors will cause your system to crash. While you could bypass the system crash by adding kernel-mode exception handlers, this could lead to even worse problems. If you are modifying data structures and have acquired a spinlock, you cannot use conditional handlers.

However, because of the simplicity of the pool-loading scheme and because of the scarcity of documentation on how to produce user executive images (UEI), most of us have not made the switch from pool loading to UEI.

CONVERTING POOL LOADING TO UEIS

This section will cover the items needed to convert our program from a pool-loading algorithm to a UEI.

AST ROUTINE

The major change needed here is to add the necessary macros to allow the code and data to be mapped as part of the system executive. Example code is available in SYS$EXAMPLES:DOD*.* files.

LOADER ROUTINE

The loader routine is replaced by the addition of the EXEC$INIT_CODE psect to the AST routine. Example code is available in SYS$EXAMPLES: DOD*.* and SYS$EXAMPLES:HASH*.* files.

DRIVER ROUTINE

There are very few changes needed here. The best change is that the AST can now be run in other than kernel mode. Since the AST routine is now mapped into system space that is readable from any mode (before, it was readable only from kernel mode), you can run the AST in any mode you wish.

FINISHING TOUCHES

While the pool-loading code was a fairly simple link and run, the UEI requires a more complex link and special initialization via SYSMAN.

Figure 9-4 shows the link file needed to link and create the UEI when running on OpenVMS VAX.

```
$ LINK /NOSYSSHR/NOTRACEBACK -
       /SHARE=SYS$AST_ROUTINE -
       /MAP=SYS$AST_ROUTINE /FULL /CROSS -
       /SYMBOL=SYS$AST_ROUTINE -
       SYS$INPUT/OPTION
       AST_ROUTINE_UEI, -
       SYS$LIBRARY:STARLET/INCLUDE:(SYS$DOINIT),-
SYS$SYSTEM:SYS.STB/SELECTIVE
VECTOR_TABLE=SYS$SYSTEM:SYS.STB
COLLECT=NONPAGED_READONLY_PSECTS/ATTRIBUTES=RESIDENT,-
       EXEC$NONPAGED_CODE
COLLECT=NONPAGED_READWRITE_PSECTS/ATTRIBUTES=RESIDENT,-
       EXEC$NONPAGED_DATA
COLLECT=PAGED_READONLY_PSECTS,-
       EXEC$PAGED_CODE
COLLECT=PAGED_READWRITE_PSECTS,-
       EXEC$PAGED_DATA
COLLECT=INITIALIZATION_PSECTS/ATTRIBUTES=INITIALIZATION_CODE,-
       EXEC$INIT_CODE,-
       EXEC$INIT_000,-
       EXEC$INIT_001,-
       EXEC$INIT_002,-
       EXEC$INIT_PFNTBL_000,-
       EXEC$INIT_PFNTBL_001,-
       EXEC$INIT_PFNTBL_002,-
       EXEC$INIT_SSTBL_000,-
       EXEC$INIT_SSTBL_001,-
       EXEC$INIT_SSTBL_002
```

Figure 9-4. Link Commands for OpenVMS VAX

You will also have to add the UEI to your system. Figure 9-5 gives the command needed to add or remove the UEI from your system.

```
$!
$! Move your image in the system exec area.
$!
$ copy SYS$AST_ROUTINE.exe sys$COMMON:[SYS$LDR]/LOG
$ sysman :== mcr sysman
$ set noon
$!
$! remove the older version.
$! Ignore any errors about old versions not existing
$!
$ sysman sys_loadable remove _local_ SYS$AST_ROUTINE
$ set on
$ sysman sys_loadable add _local_ SYS$AST_ROUTINE -
/load_step = SYSINIT -
/severity = Warning -
/message = "Failure to load image specific file - AST_ROUTINE service"
$!
$! Update system database for loadable images.
$!
$ @sys$update:vms$system_images
$set noon
$exit
$quit:
$set noon
$write sys$output "SYS$AST_ROUTINE Failed to Load!!"
$exit
```

Figure 9-5. Install/Remove Commands for OpenVMS VAX and AXP

VMS IS VMS IS VMS

For a great many people, the port to OpenVMS on the AXP platform will require almost no work. Alas, one of the features of OpenVMS VAX that will not be available on OpenVMS AXP is position-independent code. Our old and trusted friend, pool loading, implicitly requires position-independent code. You cannot make the pool loading algorithm work on OpenVMS AXP.

To place code into system space, the easiest method available is to write a UEI. Just our luck, in the December 1989 issue of *Digital Systems Journal* is the article by Frank Dolatshahi titled "SQUEEZER: A Memory Economizer," which details how to produce an OpenVMS VAX UEI. Unfortunately, changes that Digital has made to UEIs require significant changes to the program to make the code work on OpenVMS AXP.

In the SQUEEZER program, the author used the loadable image data structures to locate the AST routine and its starting address. The program in Appendix M shows how to look up an image by name using the loadable image data structures. This program searches the loadable image data structures until the requested image is found and returns the starting virtual address for the image. For OpenVMS VAX this is the AST routine's starting address. Since AXP cannot generate position-independent code, you cannot locate the AST routine's starting address via these structures.

CONVERTING UEIS TO AXP

While it is not possible to convert the pool-loading algorithm from VAX to AXP, it is possible to convert the UEI from VAX to AXP with a little work.

CONVERTING THE AST ROUTINE

Since we can no longer get the address of the AST routine from the loadable image data structures, we must add an initialization routine to our executive image code. This code will be executed when the system loads the executive image at boot time.

CONVERTING THE LOADER ROUTINE

Since the UEI now contains an initialization routine that loads SYSGEN value USERD2 with the starting address of the AST routine, the loader routine is no longer needed.

CONVERTING THE DRIVER ROUTINE

To convert the driver routine, we need only to convert the .ENTRY macros to the AXP .CALL_ENTRY macros.

CONVERTING THE FINISHING TOUCHES

This is the hard part. As of yet there is no documentation available on how to link UEIs for the AXP platform. However, with much work and luck, the necessary link commands were found. Figures 9-6 and 9-7 show the link file needed to link and create the UEI.

```
$ LINK /ALPHA /USERLIB=PROC -
  /NATIVE ONLY /BPAGE=14 /SECTION /REPLACE /VMS_EXEC
/NODEMAND_ZERO-
  /NOTRACEBACK /SHARE=SYS$AST_ROUTINE /MAP /FULL /CROSS
/SYSEXE=SELECT -
  SYS$INPUT/OPTION
AST_ROUTINE_UEI_AXP.OBJ
PSECT_ATTR=$CODE$,PIC,USR,CON,REL,GBL,NOSHR,EXE,RD,NOWRT,NOVEC
PSECT_ATTR=$LINK$,PIC,USR,CON,REL,GBL,NOSHR,NOEXE,RD,WRT,NOVEC
PSECT_ATTR=$PLIT$,PIC,USR,CON,REL,GBL,NOSHR,NOEXE,RD,WRT,NOVEC
PSECT_ATTR=EXEC$INIT_LINKAGE,PIC,USR,CON,REL,GBL,NOSHR,EXE,RD,WRT,
NOVEC
PSECT_ATTR=EXEC$NONPAGED_LINKAGE,PIC,USR,CON,REL,GBL,NOSHR,NOEX
E,RD,WRT,NOV
EC
PSECT_ATTR=_AMAC$CODE,PIC,USR,CON,REL,GBL,NOSHR,EXE,RD,NOWRT,NO
VEC
PSECT_ATTR=_AMAC$LINKAGE,PIC,USR,CON,REL,GBL,NOSHR,NOEXE,RD,WRT,
NOVEC
PSECT_ATTR=EXEC$HI_USE_PAGEABLE_LINKAGE,PIC,USR,CON,REL,GBL,NOSH
R,NOEXE,RD,
WRT,NOVEC
PSECT_ATTR=EXEC$PAGED_LINKAGE,PIC,USR,CON,REL,GBL,NOSHR,NOEXE,RD
,WRT,NOVEC
!
```

Figure 9-6. Link Commands for OpenVMS AXP (Part 1)

If these commands change, you will need to redevelop them. To do this, you must:

- Determine whether the file HASH_PASSWORD_LNK.COM has been included in the example files for the AXP.

- Check the SYSMAN documentation.

- Check the system listings for system executive image map files.

- Check the map files in SYS$LOADABLE_IMAGES and SYS$SYSTEM.

- Determine whether *Digital Systems Journal* has loaded the new link files on the Internet and CompuServe's VAX Forum.

```
SYS$LIBRARY:STARLET/INCLUDE:(SYS$DOINIT)
SYS$LIBRARY:STARLET/lib
COLLECT=NONPAGED_READONLY_PSECTS/ATTRIBUTES=RESIDENT,-
    EXEC$NONPAGED_CODE,-
    _AMAC$CODE,-
    EXEC$HI_USE_PAGEABLE_CODE,-
    $CODE$
COLLECT=NONPAGED_READWRITE_PSECTS/ATTRIBUTES=RESIDENT,-
    _AMAC$LINKAGE,-
    EXEC$HI_USE_PAGEABLE_DATA,-
    EXEC$HI_USE_PAGEABLE_LINKAGE,-
    EXEC$NONPAGED_DATA,-
    EXEC$NONPAGED_LINKAGE,-
    $PLIT$,-
    $LINK$
COLLECT=PAGED_READONLY_PSECTS,-
    EXEC$PAGED_CODE
COLLECT=PAGED_READWRITE_PSECTS,-
    EXEC$PAGED_DATA,-
    EXEC$PAGED_LINKAGE
COLLECT=INITIALIZATION_PSECTS/ATTRIBUTES=INITIALIZATION_CODE,-
    EXEC$INIT_LINKAGE,-
    EXEC$INIT_CODE,-
    EXEC$INIT_000,-
    EXEC$INIT_001,-
    EXEC$INIT_002,-
    EXEC$INIT_SSTBL_000,-
    EXEC$INIT_SSTBL_001,-
    EXEC$INIT_SSTBL_002
SYS$LIBRARY:VMS$VOLATILE_PRIVATE_INTERFACES/lib
```

Figure 9-7. Link Commands for OpenVMS AXP (Part 2)

CONCLUSION

Not only can you set individual SYSGEN and AUTHORIZE parameters to near optimal values every few seconds when tuning dynamically, you can also set parameters more aggressively than you would ever dare when tuning statically because of the ability to quickly avoid the otherwise bad consequences of a large change in system load.

SYSGEN and Other Concerns

I N THIS CHAPTER WE WILL COVER VARIOUS TOPICS THAT EITHER DID NOT FIT INTO THE other chapters or are included at the request of seminar attendees or others who purchased the first edition of this book. Of crucial importance are the changes made to support the larger page size for OpenVMS AXP.

OPENVMS AXP VERSUS OPENVMS VAX

To adjust to the larger page size for OpenVMS AXP, we need to review the OpenVMS SYSGEN parameters that were measured in units of pages. For OpenVMS VAX, a page is used to represent:

- A disk block, that is, ten disk blocks expressed as ten pages.

- A byte count, that is, 2,048 bytes expressed as four pages.

- An absolute count, that is, ten working set list entries expressed as ten pages.

To clean up the ambiguities and confusion, for OpenVMS AXP the following changes were made:

- Some SYSGEN units were changed in name only.

- Some SYSGEN units were converted to CPU-specific values.

- Some SYSGEN units are now expressed as dual values (external and internal value).

ONLY THE NAMES HAVE CHANGED

While we need to know that the unit names have changed for some SYSGEN parameters, these changes have no effect on system performance. Table 10-1 shows the SYSGEN parameters whose units have changed in name only.

SYSGEN Parameter	OpenVMS VAX Units	OpenVMS AXP Units
ACP_DINDXCACHE	Pages	Blocks
ACP_DIRCACHE	Pages	Blocks
ACP_HDRCACHE	Pages	Blocks
ACP_MAPCACHE	Pages	Blocks
ACP_WORKSET	Pages	Pagelets
CLISYMTBL	Pages	Pagelets
CTLIMGLIM	Pages	Pagelets
CTLPAGES	Pages	Pagelets
ERLBUFFERPAGES	Pages	Pagelets
IMGIOCNT	Pages	Pagelets
MINWSCNT	Pages	Pure-Number
PIOPAGES	Pages	Pagelets
TBSKIPWSL	Pages	Pure-Number

Table 10-1. Name Changes

Since the only change made for OpenVMS AXP was in the units name, there is no real effect on performance. When making performance changes, you will not have to make any special changes for the OpenVMS AXP platforms. While you may need different values for the OpenVMS AXP platforms due to the greater speeds of OpenVMS AXP, no basic change is needed in determining the correct values. However, this is not the case with other changes that have been made to SYSGEN.

Also, the system parameter PHYSICALPAGES is not available in OpenVMS AXP. It has been replaced by the system parameter PHYSICAL_MEMORY.

CPU-SPECIFIC VALUES

For all SYSGEN parameters that changed from pages to CPU-specific pages, we will need to change the way in which we calculate their values. Currently, for these parameters, we make use of the fact that a page and 512 bytes are interchangeable. For the OpenVMS AXP systems, we need to take into account that a page is not 512 bytes. What we really need to do is take into account the actual CPU-specific size of a page when determining the correct setting for this class of SYSGEN parameters, since for future OpenVMS AXP platforms a page will not necessarily be 16 pagelets in size.

Table 10-2 shows the SYSGEN parameters that are now expressed as CPU-specific pages. For the initial release of OpenVMS AXP a page is 8,192 bytes. For OpenVMS VAX, a CPU-specific page is 512 bytes.

SYSGEN Parameter	Units
BORROWLIM	Pages
FREEGOAL	Pages
FREELIM	Pages
GROWLIM	Pages
GBLPAGFIL	Pages
MPW_HILIMIT	Pages
MPW_LOWLIMIT	Pages
MPW_LOWAITLIMIT	Pages
MPW_THRESH	Pages
MPW_WAITLIMIT	Pages
MPW_WRTCLUSTER	Pages
RSRVPAGCNT	Pages

Table 10-2. CPU-Specific Units

The change to CPU-specific units has a major impact on setting these SYSGEN parameters. You will need to take into account the fact that for OpenVMS AXP platforms, a page is not 512 bytes in length. All the algorithms we used previously to calculate these values will now have to change to take into account that while "VMS is VMS is VMS," a "page is not a page." In the chapters on memory management, take special note of the corrections that have been made to the old OpenVMS VAX-only formulas.

DUAL-VALUED PARAMETERS

The last set of SYSGEN parameters that we will identify are those that have dual values (see Table 10-3). These parameters are maintained in the SYSGEN data areas with both an external value (expressed in pagelets) and an internal value (expressed in CPU-specific pages). While the changes here do not have the impact the changes made in the CPU-Specific Values section have, it is still important that you realize these changes. In most cases, the values can be calculated for these parameters in the same way for both OpenVMS VAX and OpenVMS AXP systems.

SYSGEN Parameter	Externa Unitsl	Internal Units
PAGTBLPFC	Pagelets	Pages
PFCDEFAULT	Pagelets	Pages
SYSPFC	Pagelets	Pages
GBLPAGES	Pagelets	Pages
SYSMWCNT	Pagelets	Pages
WSMAX	Pagelets	Pages

Table 10-3. Dual Units

The real problem with the dual-valued parameters is the confusion and conflicts caused when using these parameters in calculations with parameters that use CPU-specific units. Another problem is that when dual-valued parameters are increased by less than a CPU page's worth of pagelets, the actual internal value used by the system does not change. Thus, if you increase the value of PFCDEFAULT from 128 pagelets to 136 pagelets, the internal value is still eight pages, so your change has no effect on system operation!

RISC VERSUS CISC

While the claim is that "VMS is VMS is VMS," there are key differences between OpenVMS VAX CISC and OpenVMS AXP RISC. You will need to keep these differences in mind when analyzing and tuning your system. In some cases these differences have a major impact on how things work. Therefore, your analysis and tuning strategy will also have to change.

The following list summarizes some of the major differences between OpenVMS AXP RISC and OpenVMS VAX CISC:

- While OpenVMS AXP RISC instructions are much faster than OpenVMS VAX CISC instructions, they are also much simpler. A single OpenVMS VAX instruction to increment a memory location converts to at least three OpenVMS

AXP RISC instructions in the simplest case. In some cases (alignments effects) even more instructions would be needed.

- Some OpenVMS VAX CPUs use instruction pipelines for performance improvements. All OpenVMS AXP CPUs depend on extensive instruction and data pipelines for performance.

- For an OpenVMS VAX CISC instruction, condition codes are set as part of the execution of the instruction. For OpenVMS AXP RISC, explicit tests are required to determine a condition.

- While OpenVMS VAX instructions can directly manipulate memory, OpenVMS AXP can only load from or store to memory. Thus, to increment a memory location, OpenVMS AXP must load the value from memory, increment the value in a register, and then store the new value back to memory.

- While OpenVMS VAX can directly address byte data, the minimum OpenVMS AXP address is in longwords. To address byte or word data, OpenVMS AXP must load longword data and then mask out unneeded data. This makes it much harder for OpenVMS AXP to manipulate data in a byte or word context.

- On OpenVMS VAX there are only sixteen longword registers; for OpenVMS AXP there are thirty-two quadword integer registers and thirty-two quadword floating-point registers. For OpenVMS AXP, therefore, there is correspondingly much more work to save and restore the register context for process context changing. On the bright side, four times as much data can be stored and manipulated in registers. This makes the job of code optimization much easier for the compilers.

- OpenVMS AXP is 64-bit-based; OpenVMS VAX is only 32-bit-based.

- When on OpenVMS VAX, every page requires a translation buffer (TB) entry to reference it. For a large memory system, the management of TBs becomes a large problem. For OpenVMS AXP, the introduction of granularity hints allows multiple contiguous pages to be referenced by a single TB entry. The granularity hint is an OpenVMS AXP architecture capability that allows a value in the PTE to denote how many pages to map beyond the page referenced in the PTE; thus, a single TB entry can map a very large number of pages on OpenVMS AXP. One requirement of a granularity hint region is that all pages in the region have the same characteristics.

DEFAULT VALUES

To account for the fact that OpenVMS AXP images are larger and require more memory than the equivalent OpenVMS VAX images, several important SYSGEN parameter's default values have been changed (see Table 10-4).

Parameter	OpenVMS VAX Value	OpenVMS AXP Value
AWSMIN	50 pages	2,000 pagelets
BALSETCNT	16 slots	32 slots
BUGREBOOT	1 Boolean	0 Boolean
CLISYMTBL	250 pages	500 pagelets
GBLPAGES	10,000 pages	20,000 pagelets
GBLPAGFIL	1,024 pages	128 pages
LNMPHASHTBL	128 entries	512 entries
LNMSHASHTBL	128 entries	512 entries
MAXBUF	2,064 bytes	8,192 bytes
MPW_HILIMIT	500 pages	512 pages
MPW_LOLIMIT	32 pages	16 pages
MPW_LOWAITLIMIT	380 pages	448 pages
MPW_THRESH	200 pages	16 pages
MPW_WAITLIMIT	620 pages	576 pages
MPW_WRTCLUSTER	120 pages	64 pages
NPAGEDYN	430,080 bytes	360,000 bytes
PAGEDYN	210,004 bytes	190,000 bytes
PQL_DBIOLM	18 I/Os	32 I/Os
PQL_DBYTLM	8,192 bytes	65,536 bytes
PQL_DDIOLM	18 I/Os	32 I/Os
PQL_DFILLM	16 files	128 files
PQL_DPGFLQUOTA	8,192 pages	65,536 pages

PQL_MPGFLQUOTA	512 pages	2,048 pages
PQL_DPRCLM	8 processes	32 processes
PQL_DTQELM	8 timers	16 timers
PQL_DWSDEFAULT	100 pages	2,000 pagelets
PQL_MWSDEFAULT	60 pages	2,000 pagelets
PQL_DWSQUOTA	200 pages	4,000 pagelets
PQL_MWSQUOTA	60 pages	4,000 pagelets
PQL_DWSEXTENT	400 pages	12,000 pagelets
PQL_MWSEXTENT	60 pages	4,000 pagelets
PQL_DENQLM	30 locks	64 locks
SPTREQ	3,900 pages	2,500 pagelets
SWPOUTPAGCNT	288 pages	512 pagelets
SYSMWCNT	500 pages	2,000 pagelets
VIRTUALPAGECNT	9,219 pages	65,536 pagelets
WSMAX	1,024 pages	4,000 pagelets

Table 10-4. Default Value Changes

For GBLPAGEFIL, notice that 128 pages on OpenVMS AXP is equivalent to an OpenVMS VAX value of 2,048 pages. This 16:1 ratio applies to all OpenVMS VAX/OpenVMS AXP parameters sets in which the units are of the form page/page.

SYMMETRIC MULTIPROCESSING

Symmetric multiprocessing (SMP) is supported in both OpenVMS VAX and OpenVMS AXP. SMP is managed on OpenVMS AXP and OpenVMS VAX systems using a set of system parameters.

MULTIPROCESSING

This system parameter controls the loading of the system images that control synchronization. Table 10-5 summarizes the values and the associated functions for multiprocessing.

Value	Function
0	Load uniprocessing image. No multiprocessing will be performed even if multiple CPUs exist.
1	Load full-checking multiprocessing synchronization image if CPU type is capable of SMP and two or more CPUs are present on the system.
2	Always load full-checking multiprocessing synchronization image regardless of system configuration or CPU availability.
3	Load the streamlined multiprocessing synchronization image if CPU type is capable of SMP and two or more CPUs are present on the system.
4	On OpenVMS AXP, always load full-checking multiprocessing synchronization image regardless of system configuration or CPU availability.

Table 10-5. Controlling Multiprocessing

Loading the full checking multiprocessing synchronization image causes OpenVMS to:

- Perform additional software checks.

- Provide a full history of CPU information in the event of a crash.

- Store PC history in the spinlock structures.

The performance of a CPU running the full-checking image is much slower compared to a node running the streamlined images. However, it is much easier to determine the cause of a system crash related to SMP and spinlock on a system using the full-checking image. If you do not need the additional data supplied by the full-checking images, you can make a noticeable performance improvement by using the streamlined image. Note, however, that you trade off the ability to quickly find the cause of the system crash by using the streamlined image for performance.

OTHER SMP PARAMETERS

If you enable SMP, there are other system parameters that further control the behavior of an SMP system. These parameters provide the equivalent functions on both OpenVMS VAX and OpenVMS AXP.

SMP_CPUS

This system parameter specifies which set of secondary processors to boot into the SMP environment at boot time. This parameter is a 32-bit mask. If the bit is set for the corresponding CPU ID, that CPU is booted if it is available. By default, all available CPUs are booted. If you have a CPU but do not want it to be booted into the SMP environment, then set the bit that corresponds to the CPU ID to zero, and that CPU will not be booted the next time the system is started. For example, if you have a three-CPU machine (CPU IDs 0, 1, and 2), setting SMP_CPUS to 5 (...0101) will cause CPU IDs 0 and 2 to boot, but CPU ID 1 will not boot.

SMP_SANITY_CNT

This system parameter establishes the time-out interval for each CPU in a multiprocessing environment. In SMP the CPUs monitor each other, and if a CPU does not respond within SMP_SANITY_CNT number of 10-millisecond clock ticks, a CPUSANITY bug check is issued.

SMP_SPINWAIT

This parameter establishes the number of 10-microsecond intervals that a CPU will wait for access to a shared resource. This waiting is called spinwaiting. If a CPU times out waiting for access, a CPUSPINWAIT bug check is issued.

SMP_LNGSPINWAIT

Why use one parameter when two will do? Certain resources require a much longer time to gain access. SMP_LNGSPINWAIT establishes a timeout based on 10-microsecond intervals. If a CPU times out waiting for access to one of these resources, a CPUSPINWAIT bug check is also issued.

OTHER SYSTEM DETAILS

AUTOGEN

AUTOGEN now considers the current setting of a parameter to be a minimum value. AUTOGEN now increases allocations unless an exact or a maximum value is specified in the MODPARAMS.DAT file. In previous versions, if you specified an exact value (for example, MPW_HILIMIT 512), AUTOGEN could and often would calculate a smaller value. Since you had not used the MIN_ qualifier, the value would be reset to a smaller value. This often happened with the setting of global pages, and when it happened you would have to find the error, make the correction in MODPARAMS.DAT file, run AUTOGEN, and reboot your system one more time.

If you wish to share parameter files between OpenVMS VAX and OpenVMS AXP, you will need to "appropriate" the page size calculations from AUTOGEN. Appendix G shows how to determine page size on a platform basis. If you use these calculations, be sure to verify them for each update of OpenVMS.

SYSUAF PARAMETER CHANGES

For OpenVMS AXP, the Authorize utility and its associated parameters have not changed. However, the default values have been set to considerably higher values. Table 10-6 shows the changes between OpenVMS VAX V5.5 and OpenVMS AXP V1.5.

Limit/Quota	OpenVMS VAX Value	OpenVMS AXP Value	Description
ASTLM	24	250	Maximum number of asynchronous system traps (AST)
BIOLM	18	150	Maximum number of buffered I/Os that can be outstanding at one time
BYTLM	8,192	64,000	Maximum number of bytes of nonpaged memory that the process's job can consume
DIOLM	18	150	Maximum number of direct I/Os that can be outstanding at one time
ENQLM	100	2,000	Maximum number of locks that the process can have queued at one time
FILLM	20	100	Maximum number of open files a process can have
JTQUOTA	1,024	4,096	Byte quota used by the job logical name table
PRCLM	2	8	Maximum number of subprocesses
PGFLQUOTA	10,240	50,000	Maximum number of pagelets that the process can use in the page files
WSDEFAULT	150	2,000	Initial size of the working set list in pagelets
WSQUOTA	256	4,000	Maximum working set size when the free list is less than BORROWLIM
WSEXTENT	512	16,384	Maximum working set size when the free list is greater than GROWLIM

Table 10-6. SYSUAF Changes

While there is a broad range of applications that run using OpenVMS VAX, it is impossible to offer precise default values. However, in almost all cases the default values are too low. A much better starting point would be to use the OpenVMS AXP defaults for OpenVMS VAX defaults and two to four times the OpenVMS AXP values for the OpenVMS AXP defaults. The default OpenVMS VAX values are based on a 4-MB system!

Be careful when changing any of the SYSUAF process quotas that have values based on pagelets. While OpenVMS AXP accepts and displays these values in pagelets, internally these values are converted to pages. If the values you specify are not even multiples of the page size (16 for 8-KB pages), then the value in pagelets is rounded up to the next higher value in pages. Thus, on an OpenVMS AXP system with 8-KB pages, a value in the range of 4,097 to 4,114 pagelets specifies the same value of 257 pages. This means that when you make changes to SYSUAF process quotas, you should make them in increments of 16 pagelets if your OpenVMS AXP has an 8-KB page size. For OpenVMS AXP machines with large page sizes, use an increment that corresponds to the associated pagelet count for the page size.

IMAGE SIZE

Native OpenVMS AXP images are on the order of twice as large as the corresponding OpenVMS VAX images. Translated images can be more than twice the size of the original OpenVMS VAX images. Thus, images on OpenVMS AXP require more virtual memory. Consequently, you will need to increase the page file quota and the actual size of the page file for OpenVMS AXP.

By default, on OpenVMS AXP the system parameters that control virtual memory sizing and page file use have been increased by a factor of eight. The VIRTUALPAGECNT default value has been increased from 9,216 pagelets to 65,536 pagelets. The PQL_DPGFLQUOTA default value has been increased from 8,192 pagelets to 65,535 pagelets.

To obtain maximum performance from your OpenVMS AXP system, *buy more memory*. RISC requires more memory in almost all cases. Many optimization techniques for RISC code entail converting tight code loops into long sequences of code (loop unrolling). Undersizing memory for OpenVMS AXP causes even more problems than were caused for OpenVMS VAX.

SHAREABLE IMAGE IMPROVEMENTS

These enhancements are available only on OpenVMS AXP and have not been implemented for OpenVMS VAX.

You can improve the performance of images (main and shareable images) by using the new LINK qualifier /SECTION_BINDING=CODE and the new INSTALL qualifier /RESIDENT. On OpenVMS AXP, the code sections of an installed resident image can reside in huge pages called granularity hint regions (GHR). The OpenVMS AXP hardware can consider a set of pages as a single GHR. There needs to be only one PTE in the TB for the GHR. This results in a reduction in the TB miss rates. This will also reduce the overall amount of page faulting, since a single page fault will load the entire GHR.

OpenVMS AXP makes use of this feature in the system executive images. This results in an overall system performance improvement. For loadable executive images, the entire image can be loaded into a GHR.

The slicing feature allows OpenVMS to split the contents of images and sort the sections so that they can be placed with other sections that have the same page protection. Consequently, on OpenVMS AXP the TBs can be used more efficiently than if the images were loaded in the traditional manner.

Two new system parameters are available to control GHRs, ITB_ENTRIES and GH_RSRVPGCNT.

ITB_ENTRIES specifies the number of huge pages (GHRs) that are available for use by OpenVMS AXP. The default value is 1. This GHR is used by the system loader to load executive images. It can also be used by installed resident images. If slicing is disabled or another GHR is needed, ITB_ENTRIES must be set to the required value. Initially, OpenVMS AXP has a GHR of 4 MB (512 pages), and you can specify a maximum of four GHRs.

GH_RSRVPGCNT specifies the number of unused pages within a GHR to be retained after system startup. At the end of startup the system executive image executes and releases all but GH_RSRVPGCNT unused pages in the GHR if bit 2 in LOAD_SYS_IMAGES is set.

USE OF LOCKS

All locks are associated with a resource name. In most cases lock activity is based on the resource name. To effectively use locks, your system must be able to look up and find the associated resource block data for a lock. Locks are used heavily by the file system, the cluster system, and many other systems within OpenVMS.

By default, AUTOGEN sets your system parameters to generate resource name hash tables of 128 entries. On almost all systems this is too small a value for the system resource name hash table.

You can determine the correct size by using MONITOR LOCK. This provides the number of locks and resources on your system. The larger this number, the more important it is to size the hash tables correctly. You can also use the first program in Appendix L. Using this program, you can determine the fill rate of the hash table, the average queue length of a hash entry, and the worst sixteen queues (see also Figure 10-1). The average queue length should be between 1 and 1.750, and there should be about 50 percent free entries in the hash table.

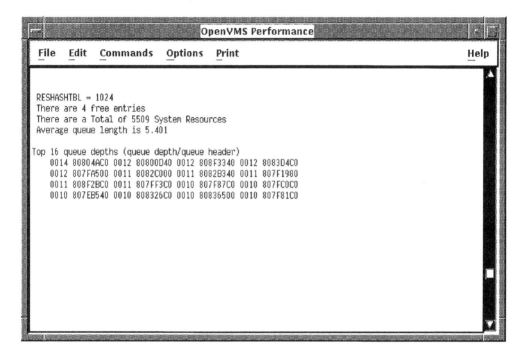

Figure 10-1. Dump Resource Names

Using the output in Figure 10-1, not only can you determine how to size the resource name hash tables, but you can also use this information to determine whether your resource names are "correct." Using the second program in Appendix L, you can dump out the resource names that are hashed to the entries with the most items. If there are hash entries with significantly more entries than the other hash locations, you can dump out the resource names that hash to that entry. You can then use this data to change selected names to reduce the length of the hash entries (see Figure 10.2).

CORRECT USE OF AUTOGEN

It is highly recommended that you use AUTOGEN to maintain your system parameters. To make system parameter changes, make the appropriate changes to the

MODPARAMS.DAT file. If you make the changes directly to the system by using SYSMAN or SYSGEN, there is a good chance that these changes will be lost the next time someone uses AUTOGEN to update your system parameters!

To ensure against loss, use the following procedure whenever you make changes to your system parameters:

- Get a listing of your currently active parameters:

```
$ run sys$system:sysman
SYSMAN> PARAMETERS USE ACTIVE
SYSMAN> PARAMETERS SHOW /ALL/ OUTPUT=PARAMS.OLD
SYSMAN> PARAMETERS SHOW /SPECIAL /OUTPUT=PARAMS.TMP
SYSMAN> EXIT
$ APPEND PARAMS.TMP PARAMS.OLD
$ DELETE PARAMS.TMP;
```

The file PARAMS.OLD now contains a listing of the parameter settings that the system is currently using.

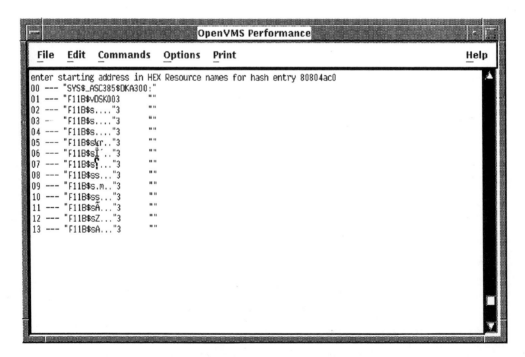

Figure 10-2. Dump Resource Names Entries

- Modify MODPARAMS.DAT by adding lines to the file. Each line added should have a comment that allows you to track the reason and time the change was made. It is much better to add a line to lower a value than to delete an existing line that increased the value in the first place. A detailed history of changes and dates is invaluable when problems occur.

- Run AUTOGEN via the command:

```
@SYS$UPDATE:AUTOGEN.COM SAVPARAMS SETPARAMS NOFEEDBACK
```

- Next, get a listing of your new parameters:

```
$ run sys$system:sysman
SYSMAN> PARAMETERS USE CURRENT
SYSMAN> PARAMETERS SHOW /ALL/ OUTPUT=PARAMS.NEW
SYSMAN> PARAMETERS SHOW /SPECIAL /OUTPUT=PARAMS.TMP
SYSMAN> EXIT
$ APPEND PARAMS.TMP PARAMS.NEW
$ DELETE PARAMS.TMP;
```

The file PARAMS.NEW now contains a listing of the parameter settings that the system will use if you reboot.

- Compare the new setting with the old to ensure that all changes that were made are accounted for by the changes you just made to MODPARAMS.DAT.

```
$ DIFFERENCES /PARALLEL /OUTPUT=PARAMS.CHANGES PARAMS.OLD
PARAMS.NEW
```

Now either print or type the file PARAMS.CHANGES in 132-column format.

Figure 10-3 shows a typical listing. If there are changes you cannot relate back to a change you made in the MODPARAMS file, investigate these items until you understand why the changes were made. In many cases there will be changes caused by someone making changes directly via SYSMAN or SYSGEN and not making the necessary changes to MODPARAMS.

Check the file SYS$SYSTEM:AGEN$PARAMETS.REPORT to check for misspellings and other possible problems.

While you can change a parameter via SYSMAN or SYSGEN by using just enough characters to make the parameter match (for example, NPAGED is sufficient to make changes to NPAGEDYN), you must spell out the entire parameter name when changing via MODPARAMS.

Warning: You cannot change the system startup file via the parameter STARTUP when using AUTOGEN. A bug in AUTOGEN generates an invalid SYSMAN command for this parameter, and it will not be changed. For most people the default file SYS$SYSTEM:STARTUP.COM. is always used.

SYSTEM STARTUP PERFORMANCE

In almost all cases when a system is shut down it is due to a system crash, not the orderly process of running system shutdown procedures. One significant side effect of system crashes is that the various XQP caches are not flushed back to the disks. When this happens, a small amount of disk space is marked as allocated when the space is actually free. While this is not a dangerous problem, it does waste disk space.

To recover this "lost" space, you must "rebuild" your disk drives. ACP_REBLDSYSD specifies whether the system disk should be rebuilt if it was improperly dismounted. Rebuilding will verify that no space is lost due to extent, file number, or diskquota caching. However, for large disks this rebuilding could take several minutes, and while the rebuild is in progress for the system disk, no other disk operations are allowed, thus adding several minutes to the boot time for your machine.

You will want to set ACP_REBLDSYSD to zero and rebuild the system disk after the system is back in production and is lightly loaded (late at night works for most

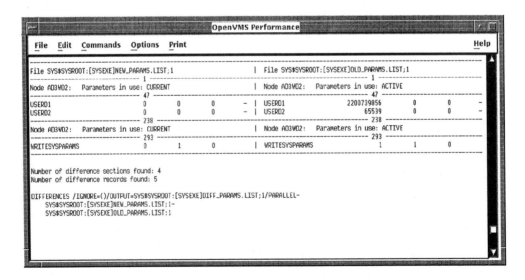

Figure 10-3. MODPARAMS Differences

users). This will speed up the system boot by several minutes. Also, to further decrease the time needed to boot your system, all disks that are mounted during the bootup should use the /NOREBUILD qualifier with their mount commands. These other disks can also be rebuilt at a later time when response is not so critical.

For a system with a large number of large disk drives, making these simple changes could have a dramatic effect on system boot times.

PMS Dump Program

EWDATADEF.H

```
#ifndef EWDATADEF_H
#define EWDATADEF_H
/*
** To update this for future releases of OpenVMS:
** Get library copy - lib/ext=$EWDATADEF sys$share:lib.mlb
** Insure offsets match the offsets in this file.
*/
#pragma nostandard

#pragma member_alignment __save
#pragma nomember_alignment
/*+                                                      */
/* $EWDATADEF - Symbolic offsets within the exec-writable page */
/*                                                       */
#define EW$K_LENGTH 378
#define EW$C_LENGTH 378
struct EWDATADEF {
 variant_struct {
    char EW_PMS$GL_FCP [];              /* start of the FCP counters */
    char EW_PMS$GL_FCP2 [];             /* start of the FCP2 counters */
    unsigned int EW_PMS$AL_COUNT [10];  /* number of operations */
    unsigned int EW_PMS$AL_MCNT [10];   /* number of modifiers */
    unsigned int EW_PMS$AL_READ [10];   /* number of disk reads */
    unsigned int EW_PMS$AL_WRITE [10];  /* number of disk writes */
    unsigned int EW_PMS$AL_CACHE [10];  /* number of cache hits */
    unsigned int EW_PMS$AL_CPU [10];    /* accumulated cpu times */
    unsigned int EW_PMS$AL_PFA [10];    /* accumulated page faults */
    unsigned int EW_PMS$GL_TURN;        /* number of window turns */
    unsigned int EW_PMS$GL_DIRHIT;      /* count of directory LRU hits */
    unsigned int EW_PMS$GL_DIRMISS;     /* count of directory LRU misses */
    unsigned int EW_PMS$GL_QUOHIT;      /* count of quota cache hits */
    unsigned int EW_PMS$GL_QUOMISS;     /* count of quota cache misses */
```

```
    unsigned int EW_PMS$GL_FIDHIT;       /* count of file ID cache hits */
    unsigned int EW_PMS$GL_FIDMISS;      /* count of file ID cache misses */
    unsigned int EW_PMS$GL_EXTHIT;       /* count of extent cache hits */
    unsigned int EW_PMS$GL_EXTMISS;      /* count of extent cache misses */
    unsigned int EW_PMS$GL_FILHDR_HIT;   /* count of file header cache hits */
    unsigned int EW_PMS$GL_FILHDR_MISS;  /* count of file header cache misses */
    unsigned int EW_PMS$GL_DIRDATA_HIT;  /* count of directory data block hits
*/
/* count of directory data block misses */
    unsigned int EW_PMS$GL_DIRDATA_MISS;
/* count of storage bit map cache hits */
    unsigned int EW_PMS$GL_STORAGMAP_HIT;
/* count of storage bit map cache misses */
    unsigned int EW_PMS$GL_STORAGMAP_MISS;
    unsigned int EW_PMS$GL_OPEN;         /* number of currently open files */
    unsigned int EW_PMS$GL_OPENS;        /* total count of opens */
    unsigned int EW_PMS$GL_ERASEIO;      /* total count of erase QIO's issued */
    unsigned int EW_PMS$GL_VOLLCK;       /* count of XQP volume synch locks */
    unsigned int EW_PMS$GL_VOLWAIT;      /* # of times XQP had to wait for a */
                                         /* volume synch lock */
    unsigned int EW_PMS$GL_SYNCHLCK;     /* count of XQP directory and */
                                         /* file synch locks */
    unsigned int EW_PMS$GL_SYNCHWAIT;    /* # of times XQP had to wait for a */
                                         /* directory or file synch lock */
    unsigned int EW_PMS$GL_ACCLCK;       /* count of XQP access locks */
    unsigned int EW_PMS$GL_XQPCACHEWAIT; /* # of times XQP had to wait for */
                                         /* free space in a cache   */
    } EW$R_PMSEWDATA;
 variant_struct{
/* current global buffer quota remaining */
    unsigned short int EW_RMS$GW_GBLBUFQUO;
    } EW$R_RMSEWDATA;
 } ;

#pragma member_alignment __restore
#pragma standard

#endif
```

PMS_DUMP.C

```
/*
**++
**   FACILITY:  OpenVMS Tools
**
** Copyright (c) 1991 James W. Coburn
** Copyright (c) 1992 James W. Coburn
** Copyright (c) 1993 James W. Coburn
** Copyright (c) 1992 Professional Press Books
** Copyright (c) 1993 Cardinal Business Media
** This program may be copied for noncommercial purposes. Use of this
** program for any other purpose without the express written consent
** of the publisher is prohibited.
**
**   MODULE DESCRIPTION:
**
** This module implements a program that dumps out selected PMS
** database entries for performance analysis.
**
** AUTHORS:
**
** Jim Coburn
**
** CREATION DATE: May, 1991
**
** DESIGN ISSUES:
**
** N/A.
**
** MODIFICATION HISTORY:
**
** Updated 1993 for AXP release.
**—
*/

/*
**
** INCLUDE FILES
**
*/
#include "pfm/ewdatadef.h"

main()
```

```
{
  globalref struct EWDATADEF *EXE$AR_EWDATA;
  globalref int PMS$GL_HIT;
  globalref int PMS$GL_SPLIT;
  globalref int PMS$GW_BATCH;
  globalref int PMS$GW_INTJOBS;
  globalref int PMS$GL_DPTSCN;
  globalref int EXE$GL_ABSTIM;

  printf ("\f");
  printf( "Window hits since last boot>           %9.9d\n", PMS$GL_HIT );
  printf( "Window turns since last boot>          %9.9d\n",
    EXE$AR_EWDATA->EW_PMS$GL_TURN);
  printf( "Split i/os since last boot>            %9.9d\n", PMS$GL_SPLIT );
  printf( "Dead page table scans since last boot> %9.9d\n", PMS$GL_DPTSCN );

  printf( "Up time in seconds>                    %9.9d\n", EXE$GL_ABSTIM );

}
```

PMS_DUMP.OPT

```
pfm:pms_dump.obj
#ifdef VAX
sys$share:vaxcrtl/lib
sys$system:sys.stb/sel
#endif
```

PMS_DUMP SAMPLE OUTPUT

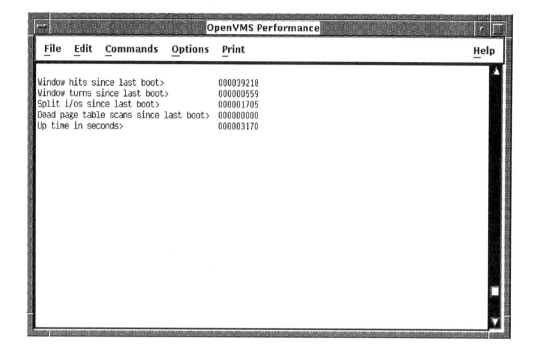

Output from Dump Command

DCL COMMAND

```
$ Dump /header /block=(count:0) SYS$ERRORLOG:errlog.sys
```

DUMP COMMAND SAMPLE OUTPUT

```
Dump of file SYS$SYSROOT:[SYSERR]ERRLOG.SYS;1 on 23-MAY-1993 20:38:03.55
File ID (21312,3,0) End of file block 1164 / Allocated 1164

        File Header

Header area
    Identification area offset:    40
    Map area offset:               100
    Access control area offset:    255
    Reserved area offset:          255
    Extension segment number:      0
    Structure level and version:   2, 1
    File identification:           (21312,3,0)
    Extension file identification: (634,13,0)
    VAX-11 RMS attributes
      Record type:                 Variable
      File organization:           Sequential
      Record attributes:           <none specified>
      Record size:                 304
      Highest block:               1164
      End of file block:           1164
      End of file byte:            292
      Bucket size:                 0
      Fixed control area size:     0
      Maximum record size:         0
      Default extension size:      0
      Global buffer count:         0
```

```
   Directory version limit:      0
 File characteristics:          <none specified>
 Map area words in use:         154
 Access mode:                   0
 File owner UIC:                [SYSTEM]
 File protection:               S:RWED, O:RWED, G:RE, W:
 Back link file identification: (16796,3,0)
 Journal control flags:         <none specified>
 Active recovery units:         None
 Highest block written:         1164

Identification area
 File name:                     ERRLOG.SYS;1
 Revision number:               50406
 Creation date:                 7-MAY-1992 13:14:30.88
 Revision date:                 23-MAY-1993 20:29:50.26
 Expiration date:               22-JUN-1993 20:29:50.26
 Backup date:                   20-MAY-1993 21:26:19.14

Map area
 Retrieval pointers
   Count:   4   LBN:    591948
   Count:   4   LBN:   1638652
   Count:   4   LBN:   2408620
   Count:   4   LBN:   1638608
   Count:   4   LBN:    445596
   Count:   4   LBN:   2419856
   Count:   4   LBN:    749572
   Count:   4   LBN:   1945448
   Count:   4   LBN:    461540
   Count:   4   LBN:    462680
   Count:   8   LBN:    462912
   Count:   4   LBN:    459008
   Count:   4   LBN:    459016
   Count:   4   LBN:    459200
   Count:   4   LBN:    432604
   Count:   4   LBN:   1474568
   Count:   4   LBN:   2408788
   Count:   4   LBN:    428912
   Count:   4   LBN:    429728
   Count:   8   LBN:    672516
   Count:   8   LBN:    732276
   Count:   4   LBN:    459036
```

```
Count:    4    LBN:     732300
Count:    4    LBN:     732288
Count:    4    LBN:     672492
Count:    4    LBN:     429716
Count:    4    LBN:    1980860
Count:    4    LBN:     214268
Count:    4    LBN:     214280
Count:    4    LBN:     177516
Count:    4    LBN:    1461632
Count:    4    LBN:     732320
Count:    4    LBN:    2181520
Count:    4    LBN:    2183908
Count:    8    LBN:     528504
Count:    4    LBN:     199808
Count:    4    LBN:    1454232
Count:    4    LBN:    2147440
Count:    4    LBN:    2147688
Count:    4    LBN:    2148236
Count:    4    LBN:     120200
Count:    4    LBN:     786432
Count:    4    LBN:     125272
Count:    4    LBN:    1867796
Count:    4    LBN:      71668
Count:    4    LBN:     437876
Count:    4    LBN:    1261688
Count:    4    LBN:    1261696
Count:    4    LBN:    1261568
Count:    4    LBN:    1261700
Count:    4    LBN:     207208
Count:    4    LBN:    1261936
Count:    4    LBN:    2253372
Count:    4    LBN:     433292
Count:    4    LBN:      83524
Count:    4    LBN:     213036
Count:    4    LBN:      90916
Count:    4    LBN:    1523576
Count:    4    LBN:      62224
Count:    4    LBN:    1097744
Count:    4    LBN:    1523616
Count:    8    LBN:    1558628
Count:    4    LBN:     213080
Count:    4    LBN:     100404
Count:    4    LBN:     100472
```

```
Count:    8   LBN:     524708
Count:    4   LBN:     524692
Count:   12   LBN:     524904
Count:    4   LBN:    2095092
Count:    4   LBN:    2657584
Count:    4   LBN:     130116
Count:    4   LBN:    1501668
Count:    8   LBN:     108176
Count:    4   LBN:     108188
Count:    4   LBN:     108196
Count:    4   LBN:     763384
Count:    4   LBN:    2022104

Checksum:              10107
```

Dump of file SYS$SYSROOT:[SYSERR]ERRLOG.SYS;1 on 23-MAY-1993 20:38:03.55
File ID (21312,3,0) End of file block 1164 / Allocated 1164

        File Header

Header area
    Identification area offset: 40
    Map area offset: 50
    Access control area offset: 255
    Reserved area offset: 255
    Extension segment number: 1
    Structure level and version: 2, 1
    File identification: (634,13,0)
    Extension file identification: (5555,30,0)
    VAX-11 RMS attributes
        Record type: Variable
        File organization: Sequential
        Record attributes: <none specified>
        Record size: 304
        Highest block: 344
        End of file block: 344
        End of file byte: 500
        Bucket size: 0
        Fixed control area size: 0
        Maximum record size: 0
        Default extension size: 0
        Global buffer count: 0
        Directory version limit: 0
```
```

```
     File characteristics:        <none specified>
     Map area words in use:       204
     Access mode:                 0
     File owner UIC:              [SYSTEM]
     File protection:            S:RWED, O:RWED, G:RE, W:
     Back link file identification: (21312,3,0)
     Journal control flags:       <none specified>
     Active recovery units:       None
     Highest block written:       344

Identification area
     File name:                   ERRLOG.SYS;1

Map area
   Retrieval pointers
      Count:    4   LBN:      82492
      Count:    4   LBN:    1914316
      Count:    4   LBN:     507984
      Count:    8   LBN:      81992
      Count:    4   LBN:      82008
      Count:    4   LBN:      68896
      Count:    4   LBN:      83480
      Count:    8   LBN:     527548
      Count:    4   LBN:     108184
      Count:    4   LBN:     108192
      Count:    4   LBN:      98576
      Count:    4   LBN:     474920
      Count:    4   LBN:     574420
      Count:    4   LBN:    2426756
      Count:    4   LBN:     732268
      Count:    4   LBN:     104252
      Count:    4   LBN:     104260
                *
                *
                *
                *
      Count:    8   LBN:    1563412
      Count:    4   LBN:    2321564
      Count:    4   LBN:     626616
      Count:    4   LBN:     333728
      Count:    4   LBN:      58516

Checksum:                        38837
```

Page Monitor

PAGE_MONITOR.COM

```
$ set NoOn
$ write sys$output -
"             VMS Tuning"
$ write sys$output -
" Username    Image  Faults  Quota  Extent Pages(p) Pages(G) Pages(T)"
$ context= ""
$ count = 0
$ total = 0
$loop:
$ if p1 .eqs. ""
 $ then
$       pid = f$pid( context )
$ else
$       PID = p1
$ endif
$       if pid .nes. ""
$       then
$               user_name= f$getjpi( "''pid'", "USERNAME" )
$               image = f$getjpi("''pid'", "IMAGNAME" )
$               image = f$parse(image,,, "name" )
$               quota = f$getjpi( "''pid'", "WSQUOTA")
$               extent = f$getjpi( "''pid'", "WSEXTENT")
$               faults= f$getjpi( "''pid'", "PAGEFLTS")
$               ppages= f$getjpi( "''pid'", "PPGCNT")
$               gpages= f$getjpi( "''pid'", "GPGCNT")
$               tpages = ppages+gpages
$               total = total+ tpages
$       else
$               exit 1
$       endif
$ string = f$fao( "!AS !10AS !10SL!5(9SL) ", -
        user_name, image, faults, quota, extent, ppages,gpages,tpages )
$ write sys$output string
$ if p1 .eqs. "" then goto loop
```

PAGE_MONITOR SAMPLE OUTPUT

```
┌─────────────────────────────────────────────────────────────────────────────┐
│ ─                          OpenVMS Performance                          ◄ □   │
├─────────────────────────────────────────────────────────────────────────────┤
│  File   Edit   Commands   Options   Print                          Help       │
├─────────────────────────────────────────────────────────────────────────────┤
```

Username	Image	Faults	Quota	Extent	Pages(p)	Pages(G)	Pages(T)
COBURN		6598	24000	60000	1488	592	2080
COBURN	RTPAD	3195	24000	60000	1776	624	2400
COBURN_P		1456	24000	60000	1424	352	1776
COBURN_P	DECW$TERMI	699	24000	60000	6912	4368	11280
COBURN_P	RTPAD	1047	24000	60000	1792	496	2288
COBURN_P		2762	24000	60000	1424	384	1808
COBURN	NETSERVER	289	24000	60000	1792	672	2464

VMS Tuning (AXP)

VMS Tuning (VAX)

Username	Image	Faults	Quota	Extent	Pages(p)	Pages(G)	Pages(T)
COBURN		129386	4096	18432	460	135	595
COBURN	DECW$MAIL	501613	4096	18432	498	371	869
COBURN	DECW$BOOKR	10985	4096	18432	3419	2272	5691
COBURN	DECW$CARDF	5569	4096	18432	1842	1056	2898
COBURN	LSEDIT	11004	4096	18432	3949	3272	7221
COBURN	DECW$SESSI	13788	4096	18432	3441	2365	5806
COBURN	LSEDIT	116389	4096	18432	3805	1249	5054
COBURN	RTPAD	145733	4096	18432	434	131	565
COBURN		6353	4096	18432	317	148	465
COBURN	DECW$TERMI	525301	4096	18432	1881	937	2818

```
$ █
```

PSCANDEF.H

```c
#ifndef PSCANDEF_H

#define PSCANDEF_H
/*
**To update this for future releases of OpenVMS:
** Get library copy — lib/ext=$PSCANDEF sys$share:lib.mlb
** Insure offsets match the offsets in this file.
*/

#define pscan$_BEGIN            0
#define pscan$_ACCOUNT          1
#define pscan$_AUTHPRI          2
#define pscan$_CURPRIV          3
#define pscan$_GRP              4
#define pscan$_HW_MODEL         5
#define pscan$_HW_NAME          6
#define pscan$_JOBPRCCNT        7
#define pscan$_JOBTYPE          8
```

```
#define pscan$_MASTER_PID          9
#define pscan$_MEM                 10
#define pscan$_MODE                11
#define pscan$_NODE_CSID           12
#define pscan$_NODENAME            13
#define pscan$_OWNER               14
#define pscan$_PRCCNT              15
#define pscan$_PRCNAM              16
#define pscan$_PRI                 17
#define pscan$_PRIB                18
#define pscan$_STATE               19
#define pscan$_STS                 20
#define pscan$_TERMINAL            21
#define pscan$_UIC                 22
#define pscan$_USERNAME            23
#define pscan$_GETJPI_BUFFER_SIZE  24
#define pscan$_END                 25
#define pscan$k_type               129
#define pscan$M_OR                 1
#define pscan$M_BIT_ALL            2
#define pscan$M_BIT_ANY            4
#define pscan$M_GEQ                8
#define pscan$M_GTR                16
#define pscan$M_LEQ                32
#define pscan$M_LSS                64
#define pscan$M_PREFIX_MATCH       128
#define pscan$M_WILDCARD           256
#define pscan$M_CASE_BLIND         512
#define pscan$M_EQL                1024
#define pscan$M_NEQ                2048
#define pscan$S_item_specific_flags 2
#define pscan$V_OR                 0
#define pscan$V_BIT_ALL            1
#define pscan$V_BIT_ANY            2
#define pscan$V_GEQ                3
#define pscan$V_GTR                4
#define pscan$V_LEQ                5
#define pscan$V_LSS                6
#define pscan$V_PREFIX_MATCH       7
#define pscan$V_WILDCARD           8
#define pscan$V_CASE_BLIND         9
#define pscan$V_EQL                10
#define pscan$V_NEQ                11

#endif
```

JPIDEF.H

```
#ifndef JPIDEF_H

#define JPIDEF_H
/*
** To update this for future releases of OpenVMS:
** Get library copy — lib/ext=$JPIDEF sys$share:lib.mlb
** Insure offsets match the offsets in this file.
*/

#define JPI$C_ADRTYPE                1
#define JPI$C_CTLTYPE                2
#define JPI$C_PCBTYPE                3
#define JPI$C_PHDTYPE                4
#define JPI$C_PCBFLDTYPE             5
#define JPI$C_PHDFLDTYPE             6
#define JPI$C_JIBTYPE                7
#define JPI$C_ARBTYPE                8
#define JPI$C_MAXSTRUC               6
#define JPI$C_LISTEND                0
#define JPI$_CHAIN                   -1
#define JPI$_GETJPI_CONTROL_FLAGS    -2
#define JPI$M_NO_TARGET_INSWAP       1
#define JPI$M_NO_TARGET_AST          2
#define JPI$M_IGNORE_TARGET_STATUS   4
#define JPI$S_JPICTLDEF              4
#define JPI$V_NO_TARGET_INSWAP       0
#define JPI$V_NO_TARGET_AST          1
#define JPI$V_IGNORE_TARGET_STATUS   2
#define JPI$K_OTHER                  0
#define JPI$K_NETWORK                1
#define JPI$K_BATCH                  2
#define JPI$K_INTERACTIVE            3
#define JPI$K_DETACHED               0
#define JPI$K_LOCAL                  3
#define JPI$K_DIALUP                 4
#define JPI$K_REMOTE                 5
#define JPI$_ASTACT                  768
#define JPI$_ASTEN                   769
#define JPI$_PRI                     770
#define JPI$_OWNER                   771
#define JPI$_UIC                     772
#define JPI$_STS                     773
```

```
#define JPI$_STATE              774
#define JPI$_MEM                775
#define JPI$_GRP                776
#define JPI$_PRIB               777
#define JPI$_APTCNT             778
#define JPI$_TMBU               779
#define JPI$_GPGCNT             780
#define JPI$_PPGCNT             781
#define JPI$_ASTCNT             782
#define JPI$_BIOCNT             783
#define JPI$_BIOLM              784
#define JPI$_BYTCNT             785
#define JPI$_DIOCNT             786
#define JPI$_DIOLM              787
#define JPI$_FILCNT             788
#define JPI$_TQCNT              789
#define JPI$_EFWM               790
#define JPI$_EFCS               791
#define JPI$_EFCU               792
#define JPI$_PID                793
#define JPI$_BYTLM              794
#define JPI$_PRCCNT             795
#define JPI$_PRCNAM             796
#define JPI$_TERMINAL           797
#define JPI$_JOBPRCCNT          798
#define JPI$_ENQCNT             799
#define JPI$_ENQLM              800
#define JPI$_SWPFILLOC          801
#define JPI$_MODE               802
#define JPI$_JOBTYPE            803
#define JPI$_PROC_INDEX         804
#define JPI$_MASTER_PID         805
#define JPI$_RIGHTSLIST         806
#define JPI$_CPU_ID             807
#define JPI$_STS2               808
#define JPI$_NODENAME           809
#define JPI$_NODE_CSID          810
#define JPI$_NODE_VERSION       811
#define JPI$_TT_PHYDEVNAM       812
#define JPI$_TT_ACCPORNAM       813
#define JPI$_LASTPCB            814
#define JPI$_CURPRIV            1024
#define JPI$_WSAUTH            1025
#define JPI$_WSQUOTA           1026
```

```
#define JPI$_DFWSCNT          1027
#define JPI$_FREP0VA          1028
#define JPI$_FREP1VA          1029
#define JPI$_DFPFC            1030
#define JPI$_CPUTIM           1031
#define JPI$_PRCLM            1032
#define JPI$_ASTLM            1033
#define JPI$_PAGEFLTS         1034
#define JPI$_DIRIO            1035
#define JPI$_BUFIO            1036
#define JPI$_CPULIM           1037
#define JPI$_PGFLQUOTA        1038
#define JPI$_FILLM            1039
#define JPI$_TQLM             1040
#define JPI$_WSSIZE           1041
#define JPI$_AUTHPRIV         1042
#define JPI$_IMAGPRIV         1043
#define JPI$_PAGFILCNT        1044
#define JPI$_FREPTECNT        1045
#define JPI$_WSEXTENT         1046
#define JPI$_WSAUTHEXT        1047
#define JPI$_AUTHPRI          1048
#define JPI$_PAGFILLOC        1049
#define JPI$_IMAGECOUNT       1050
#define JPI$_PHDFLAGS         1051
#define JPI$_LASTPHD          1052
#define JPI$_VIRTPEAK         512
#define JPI$_WSPEAK           513
#define JPI$_USERNAME         514
#define JPI$_ACCOUNT          515
#define JPI$_PROCPRIV         516
#define JPI$_VOLUMES          517
#define JPI$_LOGINTIM         518
#define JPI$_IMAGNAME         519
#define JPI$_SITESPEC         520
#define JPI$_MSGMASK          521
#define JPI$_CLINAME          522
#define JPI$_TABLENAME        523
#define JPI$_CREPRC_FLAGS     524
#define JPI$_UAF_FLAGS        525
#define JPI$_MAXDETACH        526
#define JPI$_MAXJOBS          527
#define JPI$_SHRFILLM         528
#define JPI$_LASTCTL          529
```

```
#define JPI$_EXCVEC                256
#define JPI$_FINALEXC              257
#define JPI$_LASTADR               258
#define JPI$_LASTPCBFLD            1280
#define JPI$_LASTPHDFLD            1536


#endif
```

PROCESS_SCAN

```
/*
**++
** FACILITY:  VMS_TOOLS
** Copyright (c) 1991 James W. Coburn
** Copyright (c) 1992 James W. Coburn
** Copyright (c) 1993 James W. Coburn
** Copyright (c) 1992 Professional Press Books.
** Copyright (c) 1993 Cardinal Business Media
** This program may be copied for noncommercial purposes. Use of this
** program for any other purpose without the express written consent
** of the publisher is prohibited.
**
** MODULE DESCRIPTION:
**
** This program dumps information about processes on the cluster.  You can
** either get working set or page file information.
**
** AUTHORS:
**
** Jim Coburn
**
** CREATION DATE:  January 3, 1991
**
** DESIGN ISSUES:
**
** TBS
**
**
** MODIFICATION HISTORY:
**
** Updated for OpenVMS VAX 6.0 and OpenVMS AXP 1.5
**-
```

```
*/


/*
**
** INCLUDE FILES
**
*/

#include <descrip.h>
#include <string.h>
#include <stdio.h>
#include <descrip.h>
#include <ssdef.h>
#include <starlet.h>
#include <libdtdef.h>
#include <lib$routines.h>
#include <stdlib.h>

#include <PRCSCAN/pscandef.h>
#include <PRCSCAN/jpidef.h>

#define TRUE 1
#define FALSE 0

main (int argc, char *argv[], char *envp[])
{
  static struct {              /*structure for $PROCESS_SCAN call*/
        short prclen, prccode;
        char *prcbufadr;
        int prcitmflags;
  } pscan_list[3];

  static struct {              /*structure for $GETJPIW call */
        short jpilen, jpicode;
        char *jpibufadr;
        char *jpiretadr;
  } jpi_list[20];

    static struct {            /*structure for IOSB */
        short cond, count;
        int other;
  } iosb;
```

```
      static int status, pidctx, pid,flag;
      static int prc_retlen,node_retlen,port_retlen,term_retlen;
      static int proc_l, image_l,wsq_l, wse_l, page_l, ppg_l, gpg_l;
      static int pid_l, trim_len, paget_l, trim_to;
      static int page_quota, page_count;

      static struct {
              char filler[3];
              unsigned char page_number;
      }page_location;

      static int wsquota, wsextent, pageflts, ppgcnt, gpgcnt, pages, page_tables;

      static char nodename[7];
      static char procname[16];
      static char imagename[255];
      static char trim_name[ 80 ];
      static $DESCRIPTOR( trim_name_desc, trim_name );
      static $DESCRIPTOR( imagename_desc, imagename );


      static struct dsc$descriptor dynstr = {0, DSC$K_DTYPE_T, DSC$K_CLASS_D, 0};
      int PagingInfo;

      set_up_output();

/*
    Build item list for $PROCESS_SCAN.
*/
    if (cli_present("PAGE_INFO") & 1)
          PagingInfo = 1;
    else
          PagingInfo = 0;

    if (cli_present("NODE") & 1)
    {
          status = cli_get_value("NODE",&dynstr);
    }

    pscan_list[0].prclen    = dynstr.dsc$w_length;
    pscan_list[0].prccode   = pscan$_NODENAME; /*return information
                                                   on a specified node*/
    pscan_list[0].prcbufadr = dynstr.dsc$a_pointer;
    if ( *(dynstr.dsc$a_pointer) == '*' )
```

213

```
                pscan_list[0].prcitmflags  =  pscan$M_WILDCARD;
    else
            pscan_list[0].prcitmflags  =  0;

  pscan_list[1].prclen    =  0;
  pscan_list[1].prccode    =  0;

/*
  Call $PROCESS_SCAN to set up the scan context.
*/

  if(((status = sys$process_scan(&pidctx,&pscan_list))&1)!=1)
          lib$stop(status);

/*
  Build a loop to look for all the specified processes and build an
  item list for $GETJPIW.
*/
  flag = TRUE;
  printf ("\n\n             Processes for Node %s\n", nodename );
  printf (" Process Name  PID");
  if( PagingInfo == 0 )
  {
          printf ("        Image Name     ");
          printf (" WSQUOTA WSEXTENT PAGEFLTS  PPGCNT  GPGCNT  PAGES
WSLIS
T\n");
  }
  else
  {
          printf ("              " );
          printf ("            Image Name        ");
          printf ("            " );
          printf (" Page Number   Pages in Use\n");
  }

  while(flag == TRUE)
  {
     jpi_list[0].jpilen     =  sizeof( procname );
     jpi_list[0].jpicode    =  JPI$_PRCNAM;
     jpi_list[0].jpibufadr  =  procname;
     jpi_list[0].jpiretadr  =  (char *) &proc_l;

     jpi_list[1].jpilen     =  sizeof(imagename);
```

```
jpi_list[1].jpicode     =   JPI$_IMAGNAME;
jpi_list[1].jpibufadr   =   imagename;
jpi_list[1].jpiretadr   =   (char *) &image_l;


jpi_list[2].jpilen      =   sizeof(nodename);
jpi_list[2].jpicode     =   JPI$_NODENAME; /*Node name*/
jpi_list[2].jpibufadr   =   nodename;
jpi_list[2].jpiretadr   =   (char *) &node_retlen;


jpi_list[3].jpilen      =   4;
jpi_list[3].jpicode     =   JPI$_PID;
jpi_list[3].jpibufadr   =   (char *) &pid;
jpi_list[3].jpiretadr   =   (char *) &pid_l;


    if( PagingInfo == 0 )
{
jpi_list[4].jpilen      =   4;
jpi_list[4].jpicode     =   JPI$_PAGEFLTS;
jpi_list[4].jpibufadr   =   (char *) &pageflts;
jpi_list[4].jpiretadr   =   (char *) &page_l;


jpi_list[5].jpilen      =   4;
jpi_list[5].jpicode     =   JPI$_WSQUOTA;
jpi_list[5].jpibufadr   =   (char *) &wsquota;
jpi_list[5].jpiretadr   =   (char *) &wsq_l;


jpi_list[6].jpilen      =   4;
jpi_list[6].jpicode     =   JPI$_WSEXTENT;
jpi_list[6].jpibufadr   =   (char *) &wsextent;
jpi_list[6].jpiretadr   =   (char *) &wse_l;


jpi_list[7].jpilen      =   4;
jpi_list[7].jpicode     =   JPI$_PPGCNT;
jpi_list[7].jpibufadr   =   (char *) &ppgcnt;
jpi_list[7].jpiretadr   =   (char *) &ppg_l;


jpi_list[8].jpilen      =   4;
jpi_list[8].jpicode     =   JPI$_GPGCNT;
jpi_list[8].jpibufadr   =   (char *) &gpgcnt;
jpi_list[8].jpiretadr   =   (char *) &gpg_l;


jpi_list[9].jpilen      =   4;
jpi_list[9].jpicode     =   JPI$_WSSIZE;
jpi_list[9].jpibufadr   =   (char *) &page_tables;
```

```
    jpi_list[9].jpiretadr  =  (char *) &paget_l;


  }
  else
  {
    jpi_list[4].jpilen    =  4;
    jpi_list[4].jpicode   =  JPI$_PAGFILCNT;
    jpi_list[4].jpibufadr =  (char *) &page_count;
    jpi_list[4].jpiretadr =  (char *) &page_l;

    jpi_list[5].jpilen    =  4;
    jpi_list[5].jpicode   =  JPI$_PAGFILLOC;
    jpi_list[5].jpibufadr =  (char *) &page_location;
    jpi_list[5].jpiretadr =  (char *) &wsq_l;

    jpi_list[6].jpilen    =  4;
    jpi_list[6].jpicode   =  JPI$_PGFLQUOTA;
    jpi_list[6].jpibufadr =  (char *) &page_quota;
    jpi_list[6].jpiretadr =  (char *) &wse_l;

    jpi_list[7].jpilen    =  0;
    jpi_list[7].jpicode   =  0;


  }
  jpi_list[10].jpilen   =  0;
  jpi_list[10].jpicode  =  0;

/*
  Call $GETJPIW to get the next process.
*/
      status = sys$getjpiw(0, &pidctx, 0, &jpi_list, &iosb,
             0, 0);

      if(status & 1) status = iosb.cond;
     if(status &1)
     {
       procname[proc_l]  = '\0';
       nodename[node_retlen]  = '\0';

       imagename[image_l]  = '\0';
       if( PagingInfo == 0 )
           trim_to = 40;
       else
           trim_to = 80;
```

```
        status = lib$trim_filespec (
            &imagename_desc,
            &trim_name_desc,
            &trim_to,
            &trim_len);
        trim_name[ trim_len] = '\Ø';

        pages = ppgcnt + gpgcnt;
        printf(" %15.15s",procname);
        printf(" %8.8x",pid);
        printf(" %*.*s", trim_to-1, trim_to-1, trim_name);
        if( PagingInfo == Ø )
        {
            printf(" %8d",wsquota);
            printf(" %8d",wsextent);
            printf(" %8d",pageflts);
            printf(" %8d",ppgcnt);
            printf(" %8d",gpgcnt);
            printf(" %8d",pages);
            printf(" %8d\n",page_tables);
        }
        else
        {
            printf(" %8d", page_location.page_number );
            if( page_quota > page_count )
            {
              printf("   %8d\n", page_quota - page_count );
              }
            else
            {
              printf("   Over Quota\n" );
            }
        }

    }
    else if(status == SS$_NOMOREPROC)
    {
      flag = FALSE;
    }
    else if(status == SS$_SUSPENDED)
    {
      flag = TRUE;
    }
    else lib$signal( status );
  }
}
```

SET_UP_OUTPUT.C

```
/*
**
** INCLUDE FILES
**
*/

#include <climsgdef.h>
#include <stdio.h>
#include <descrip.h>
#include <ssdef.h>
#include <dcdef.h>
#include <ssdef.h>
#include <stdio.h>

static struct dsc$descriptor command_line =
{0, DSC$K_DTYPE_T, DSC$K_CLASS_D, 0};
/*
**++
** FUNCTIONAL DESCRIPTION:
**
** Allows the user to redirect sys$output to a new file, or append to an
** existing file.
**
** FORMAL PARAMETERS:
**
** None
**
** RETURN VALUE:
**
** None
**
** SIDE EFFECTS:
**
** It is possible that sys$output has been redirected.
**
**—
*/

void set_up_output()
{

  int process_cld();
```

```
static struct dsc$descriptor dynstr = {0, DSC$K_DTYPE_T, DSC$K_CLASS_D, 0};
static $DESCRIPTOR(null,"\0");
static $DESCRIPTOR(command, "page_monitor ");
static struct dsc$descriptor full_command_line  =
      {0, DSC$K_DTYPE_T, DSC$K_CLASS_D, 0};

int status;
int func, index;

char *access[] = { "w", "a+" };

status = lib$get_foreign( &command_line );
str$append (&full_command_line, &command );
str$append (&full_command_line, &command_line);
status = cli$dcl_parse( &full_command_line, &process_cld, 0, 0, 0 );

/* we should see if they want output to go to a file or to SYS$OUTPUT */

if (cli_present("OUTPUT") & 1)
{
  status = cli_get_value("OUTPUT",&dynstr);
  if (status & 1)
  {
    if (cli_present("APPEND") & 1)
      index = 1;
    else
      index = 0;

    str$append(&dynstr,&null);
    freopen(dynstr.dsc$a_pointer, access[index],
         stdout,"rfm=var","rat=cr");
  }
}
}
```

PROCESS_CLD.CLD

```
module process_cld
define verb page_monitor
  qualifier OUTPUT
    value (default="Page_monitor.LIS",type=$outfile)
  qualifier APPEND
  qualifier PAGE_INFO
  qualifier NODE,default
    value (default=*)
```

CLI.C

```
#include <climsgdef.h>
#include <descrip.h>

int cli_get_value(s1,s2)
  char *s1;
  struct dsc$descriptor *s2;
{
  static struct dsc$descriptor s1_desc={0,DSC$K_DTYPE_T,DSC$K_CLASS_S,0};

  s1_desc.dsc$w_length = strlen(s1);
  s1_desc.dsc$a_pointer = s1;

  return(cli$get_value(&s1_desc,s2));
}

int cli_present(s1)
  char *s1;
{
  static struct dsc$descriptor s1_desc={0,DSC$K_DTYPE_T,DSC$K_CLASS_S,0};

  s1_desc.dsc$w_length = strlen(s1);
  s1_desc.dsc$a_pointer = s1;

  return(cli$present(&s1_desc));
}
```

PROCESS_SCAN.LNK_DEF

```
PRCSCAN:PROCESS_SCAN.obj
PRCSCAN:set_up_output.obj
PRCSCAN:process_cld.obj
DISK_SCAN:cli.obj
#ifdef VAX
sys$share:vaxcrtl/lib
#endif
```

PROCESS_SCAN SAMPLE OUTPUT

	Image Name	Page Number	Pages in Use
COBURN 28e00082		3	1200
MAIL 28e00083	3DIA155:[SYS26.SYSCOMMON.][SYSEXE]DECW$MAIL.EXE;3	3	20487
VUE$COBURN_3 28e00085	3DIA155:[SYS26.SYSCOMMON.][SYSEXE]DECW$BOOKREADER.EXE;3	3	5467
VUE$COBURN_4 28e00088	3DIA155:[SYS26.SYSCOMMON.][SYSEXE]DECW$CARDFILER.EXE;3	3	4653
BATCH_385 28e00110	3DIA155:[SYS26.SYSCOMMON.][SYSEXE]LSEDIT.EXE	3	7082
DECW$SESSION 28e00055	3DIA155:[SYS26.SYSCOMMON.][SYSEXE]DECW$SESSION.EXE	3	9917
BATCH_613 28e000d5	3DIA155:[SYS26.SYSCOMMON.][SYSEXE]LSEDIT.EXE	3	9659
_FTA7: 28e000a1	3STA411:[COBURN.VMS_TOOLS.PRCSCAN]PROCESS_SCAN.EXE;1	3	1659
VUE$COBURN_5 28e0032a		3	1194
VUE$COBURN_6 28e0032b	3DIA155:[SYS26.SYSCOMMON.][SYSEXE]DECW$PRINTSCREEN.EXE;2	3	4326
_FTA12: 28e00331	3DIA155:[SYS26.SYSCOMMON.][SYSEXE]RTPAD.EXE	3	1510
BATCH_983 28e00278	3DIA155:[SYS26.SYSCOMMON.][SYSEXE]LSEDIT.EXE	3	66176
CALENDAR 28e000fb	3DIA155:[SYS26.SYSCOMMON.][SYSEXE]DECW$CALENDAR.EXE;3	3	3526
DECW$MWM 28e0007d	3DIA155:[SYS26.SYSCOMMON.][SYSEXE]DECW$MWM.EXE;2	3	4951
DECW$TE_007F 28e0007f	3DIA155:[SYS26.SYSCOMMON.][SYSEXE]DECW$TERMINAL.EXE	3	9593

	Image Name	WSQUOTA	WSEXTENT	PAGEFLTS	PPGCNT	GPGCNT	PAGES	WSLIST
COBURN 28e00082		4096	18432	213305	410	97	507	1024
MAIL 28e00083	[SYSEXE]DECW$MAIL.EXE;3	4096	18432	598507	2479	1760	4239	4663
VUE$COBURN_3 28e00085	[SYSEXE]DECW$BOOKREADER.EXE;3	4096	18432	12149	2702	1394	4096	5120
VUE$COBURN_4 28e00088	[SYSEXE]DECW$CARDFILER.EXE;3	4096	18432	5569	1752	975	2727	2727
BATCH_385 28e00110	[SYS26.SYSCOMMON.][SYSEXE]LSEDIT.EXE	4096	18432	16876	1903	1233	3136	4470
DECW$SESSION 28e00055	[SYSEXE]DECW$SESSION.EXE	4096	18432	14312	3904	2370	6274	8272
BATCH_613 28e000d5	[SYS26.SYSCOMMON.][SYSEXE]LSEDIT.EXE	4096	18432	142758	1963	1560	3523	4039
_FTA7: 28e000a1	PROCESS_SCAN.EXE;1	4096	18432	165262	731	302	1033	1536
VUE$COBURN_5 28e0032a		4096	18432	48057	399	76	475	1024
VUE$COBURN_6 28e0032b	[SYSEXE]DECW$PRINTSCREEN.EXE;2	4096	18432	77924	881	274	1155	1667
_FTA12: 28e00331	[SYS26.SYSCOMMON.][SYSEXE]RTPAD.EXE	4096	18432	11225	343	142	485	1024
BATCH_983 28e00278	[SYS26.SYSCOMMON.][SYSEXE]LSEDIT.EXE	4096	18432	119699	2930	1166	4096	4096
CALENDAR 28e000fb	[SYSEXE]DECW$CALENDAR.EXE;3	4096	18432	80220	517	321	838	1338
DECW$MWM 28e0007d	[SYS26.SYSCOMMON.][SYSEXE]DECW$MWM.EXE;	4096	18432	64195	926	609	1535	2501
DECW$TE_007F 28e0007f	[SYSEXE]DECW$TERMINAL.EXE	4096	18432	611518	1278	643	1921	2319

Page File Utilization

PFLDEF.H

```
#ifndef PFLDEF_H

#define PFLDEF_H
/*
** To update this for future releases of OpenVMS:
** Get library copy — lib/ext=$PFLDEF sys$share:lib.mlb
** Insure offsets match the offsets in this file.
*/

#ifdef DEC_ARA
#pragma member_alignment __save
#pragma nomember_alignment
#endif
/*+                                                              */
/* PAGE FILE CONTROL BLOCK                                       */
/*-                                                              */
/*                                                               */
/* ***** L_VBN, L_WINDOW, and L_PFC must be the same offset values as the */
/* ***** equivalently named offsets in $SECDEF                   */
/*                                                               */
#define PFL$M_INITED 0x1
#define PFL$M_PAGFILFUL 0x2
#define PFL$M_SWPFILFUL 0x4
#define PFL$M_DINSPEN 0x10
#define PFL$M_STOPPER 0x80000000
struct PFLDEF {
  unsigned int PFL$L_BITMAP;        /*ADDRESS OF START OF BIT MAP */
/*BIT = 1 MEANS AVAILABLE */
  unsigned int PFL$L_STARTBYTE;     /*STARTING BYTE OFFSET TO SCAN */
  unsigned short int PFL$W_SIZE;    /*SIZE OF PAGE FILE CONTROL BLOCK */
  unsigned char PFL$B_TYPE;         /*PAGE FILE CONTROL BLOCK TYPE CODE */
#ifdef DEC_ARA
  unsigned char PFL$b_fill_3;
  unsigned int PFL$L_PFC;           /*PAGE FAULT CLUSTER FOR PAGE READS */
```

```
#else
  unsigned char PFL$B_PFC;          /*PAGE FAULT CLUSTER FOR PAGE READS */
#endif
  unsigned int PFL$L_WINDOW;        /*WINDOW ADDRESS */
  unsigned int PFL$L_VBN;           /*BASE VBN */
  unsigned int PFL$L_BITMAPSIZ;     /*SIZE IN BYTES OF PAGE FILE */
  unsigned int PFL$L_FREPAGCNT;     /*COUNT - 1 OF PAGES WHICH MAY BE
ALLOCATED*/
  unsigned int PFL$L_MINFREPAGCNT; /* Minimum free page count */
  unsigned int PFL$L_RSRVPAGCNT;    /* Count of pages which may be reserved */
/* without "overcommiting" the pagefile */
  unsigned int PFL$L_REFCNT;        /* No. of processes using this pagefile */
  unsigned int PFL$L_SWPREFCNT; /* No. of processes using file for swapping */
  unsigned int PFL$L_MAXVBN;        /*MASK APPLIED TO PTE WITH PAGING FILE   */
/* BACKING STORE ADDRESS */
#ifdef DEC_ARA
  unsigned int PFL$L_PGFLX;         /* Page file vector index */
  unsigned int PFL$L_ALLOCSIZ;      /*CURRENT ALLOCATION REQUEST SIZE */
/* (cannot exceed MPW PFC parameter) */
  variant_union {
    unsigned int PFL$L_FLAGS;       /*FLAGS FOR THIS PAGE FILE */
    variant_struct {
      unsigned PFL$V_INITED : 1;    /*THIS PAGE FILE IS USABLE */
      unsigned PFL$V_PAGFILFUL : 1; /*REQUEST FOR PAGING SPACE HAS FAILED */
      unsigned PFL$V_SWPFILFUL : 1; /*REQUEST FOR SWAPPING SPACE HAS FAILED
*/
      unsigned PFLDEF$$_FILL_2 : 1; /*SPARE */
      unsigned PFL$V_DINSPEN : 1;   /* File deinstall pending */
      unsigned PFLDEF$$_FILL_1 : 26; /*SPARE BITS FOR EXPANSION */
      unsigned PFL$V_STOPPER : 1; /*RESERVED FOR ALL TIME (MUST NEVER BE SET)
*/
    } PFL$R_FLAGS_BITS;
  } PFL$R_FLAGS_OVERLAY;
#else
  unsigned char PFL$B_PGFLX;        /* Page file vector index */
  unsigned char PFL$B_FILL_9;
  unsigned char PFL$B_ALLOCSIZ;     /*CURRENT ALLOCATION REQUEST SIZE */
/* (cannot exceed MPW PFC parameter) */
  variant_union {
    unsigned char PFL$B_FLAGS;      /*FLAGS FOR THIS PAGE FILE */
    variant_struct {
      unsigned PFL$V_INITED : 1;    /*THIS PAGE FILE IS USABLE */
      unsigned PFL$V_PAGFILFUL : 1; /*REQUEST FOR PAGING SPACE HAS FAILED */
```

```
      unsigned PFL$V_SWPFILFUL : 1;  /*REQUEST FOR SWAPPING SPACE HAS FAILED
*/
      unsigned PFLDEF$$_FILL_2 : 1;  /*SPARE */
      unsigned PFL$V_DINSPEN : 1;    /* File deinstall pending */
      unsigned PFLDEF$$_FILL_3 : 1;  /*SPARE */
      unsigned PFL$V_STOPPER : 1; /*RESERVED FOR ALL TIME (MUST NEVER BE SET)
*/
      } PFL$R_FLAGS_BITS;
    } PFL$R_FLAGS_OVERLAY;
#endif
  unsigned int PFL$L_BITMAPLOC;      /*BITMAP MUST FOLLOW FLAGS */
  } ;
#ifdef DEC_ARA
#pragma member_alignment __restore

#endif

#endif
```

PAGE_FILE.C

```
/*
**++
** FACILITY:  Page File Information
** Copyright (c) 1991 James W. Coburn
** Copyright (c) 1992 James W. Coburn
** Copyright (c) 1993 James W. Coburn
** Copyright (c) 1992 Professional Press Books.
** Copyright (c) 1993 Cardinal Business Media
** This program may be copied for noncommercial purposes. Use of this
** program for any other purpose without the express written consent
** of the publisher is prohibited.
**
** MODULE DESCRIPTION:
**
** This module allows the user to dump out various PageFile
** data structure entries.
**
** AUTHORS:
**
** Jim Coburn
**
** CREATION DATE:  Feb, 1993
```

```
**
** DESIGN ISSUES:
**
** Converted from old VAX Version to the new AXP and VAX 6.0.
**
** INCLUDED FILES:
**
** Standard header files: stdio, ssdef, starlet
** Generated header file pfldef.h, generated from CDROM listings
** file [lib.lis]pfldef.sdl
**
**
** MODIFICATION HISTORY:
**
** {@tbs@}...
**—
*/

#include <stdio.h>
#include <ssdef.h>
#Include <starlet.h>


#pragma nostandard
#include "PAGING:pfldef.h"

/*
** Define system locations we need access to that are not user readable.
*/
globalref struct PFLDEF **MMG$GL_PAGSWPVC;

/*
** Define system locations we need access to that are user readable.
*/
globalref const unsigned short SGN$GW_SWPFILES;
globalref const unsigned short SGN$GW_PAGFILCT;
globalref const unsigned short MPW$GW_MPWPFC;

#pragma standard

struct PFLDEF **MasterPointer, *LocalPointer, LocalCopy, *NullHolder;

/*
```

```
**  Prototypes.
*/
int GetHolder();
int IncrementHolder();
int CopyHolder();

main()
{
  int loop;
#ifdef DEC_ARA
#define PageSize 16
#else
#define PageSize 1
#endif
/*
** Get the Pointer ot the Page and Swap file vector list
*/

  MasterPointer = MMG$GL_PAGSWPVC;

/*
**Load NullHolder with shell entry.
*/
  sys$cmexec( GetHolder, 0);

/*
**Skip over shell entry and swap files.
*/

  sys$cmexec( IncrementHolder, 0);
  for( loop = 0; loop <= SGN$GW_SWPFILES; loop++)
  {
    sys$cmexec( IncrementHolder, 0);
  }

/* Process all Page File entries */

  for( loop = 0; loop < SGN$GW_PAGFILCT; loop++)
  {
/*
**  See if a Page File entry is valid.
*/
    if( LocalPointer != NullHolder )
    {
```

```
/*
** At one time this page file was mapped.
*/
      sys$cmexec( CopyHolder, 0);

#ifdef DEC_ARA
      printf("Page Fault Cluster for reads:     %8d pages, %8d pagelets\n",
         LocalCopy.PFL$L_PFC, (PageSize* LocalCopy.PFL$L_PFC) );
#else
      printf("Page Fault Cluster for reads:     %8d pages, %8d pagelets\n",
         LocalCopy.PFL$B_PFC, (PageSize* LocalCopy.PFL$B_PFC) );
#endif

      printf("Page write cluster factor SYSGEN setting:   %8d pages, %8d
pagelets\n",
         (int) MPW$GW_MPWPFC, (PageSize*(int) MPW$GW_MPWPFC) );
#ifdef DEC_ARA
      printf("Page write cluster factor in use: %8d pages, %8d pagelets\n",
         LocalCopy.PFL$L_ALLOCSIZ, (PageSize*LocalCopy.PFL$L_ALLOCSIZ) );
#else
      printf("Page write cluster factor in use: %8d pages, %8d pagelets\n",
         LocalCopy.PFL$B_ALLOCSIZ, (PageSize*LocalCopy.PFL$B_ALLOCSIZ) );
#endif

      printf("Count - 1 of pages which may be allocated: %8d pages, %8d
pagelets\n",
         LocalCopy.PFL$L_FREPAGCNT, (PageSize*LocalCopy.PFL$L_FREPAGCNT ));

      printf("Size of page file:                %8d pages, %8d pagelets\n",
         (LocalCopy.PFL$L_BITMAPSIZ*8), (PageSize*(LocalCopy.PFL$L_BITMAPSIZ*8
)) );

      printf("Minimum Free page count:          %8d pages, %8d pagelets\n",
         LocalCopy.PFL$L_MINFREPAGCNT, (PageSize* LocalCopy.PFL$L_MINFREPAGCNT
) );

      printf("Number of processes using this pagefile:        %8d\n",
         LocalCopy.PFL$L_REFCNT );
      printf("Number of processes using this pagefile for swapping: %8d\n",
         LocalCopy.PFL$L_REFCNT );

/*
**   Only print if some flag indicates something has happened.
*/
```

228

```
#ifdef DEC_ARA
  if( (LocalCopy.PFL$L_FLAGS & 0xFFFFFFFE) != 0 )
#else
  if( (LocalCopy.PFL$B_FLAGS & 0xFE) != 0 )
#endif
  {
printf("\n      **** Special Flag(s)  ****\n");
if( LocalCopy.PFL$V_INITED == 0 )
{
  printf("    Page file is not usable\n");
}
    if( LocalCopy.PFL$V_PAGFILFUL == 0 )
      {
        printf("  There has been a paging space failure since last boot \n");
        }
        if( LocalCopy.PFL$V_SWPFILFUL == 0 )
        {
          printf(" There has been a swapping space failure since last
boot\n");
        }
        if( LocalCopy.PFL$V_DINSPEN == 0 )
        {
          printf(" File deinstall pending\n");
        }
      }
      printf("\n\n");
    }
    sys$cmexec( IncrementHolder, 0);
  }
}
/*
**++
**   FUNCTIONAL DESCRIPTION:
**
** These routines get data that is protected as Executive Read.
** Ie. no direct user access.
**
**—
*/
int GetHolder()
{
  NullHolder = *MasterPointer;
}
```

```
int IncrementHolder()
{
  LocalPointer = *MasterPointer++;
}
int CopyHolder()
{
  LocalCopy = *LocalPointer;
}
```

PAGE_FILE SAMPLE OUTPUT

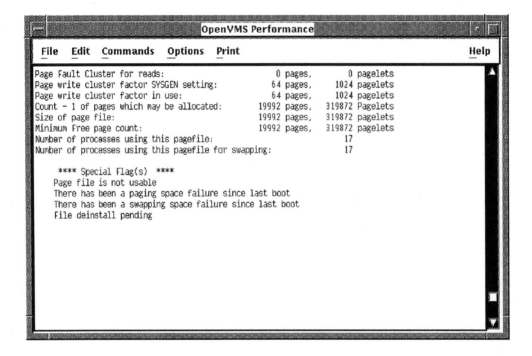

USING ANALYZE/SYSTEM

To get page file data via the ANALYZE utility, use the following commands:

- READ SYS$SYSTEM:SYSDEF (for VAX)

- READ SYS$LODADABLE_IMAGES:SYSDEF (for AXP)

- EVAL @SGN$GW_SWPFILCT

- EVAL @SGN$GW_PAGFILCT

- FORMAT <Address>

ANALYZE/SYSTEM SAMPLE OUTPUT

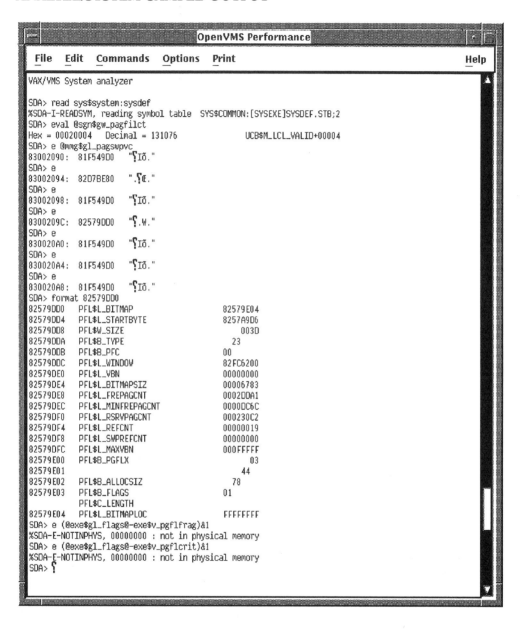

```
OpenVMS Performance

File    Edit    Commands    Options    Print                           Help

VAX/VMS System analyzer

SDA> read sys$system:sysdef
%SDA-I-READSYM, reading symbol table  SYS$COMMON:[SYSEXE]SYSDEF.STB;2
SDA> eval @sgn$gw_pagfilct
Hex = 00020004   Decimal = 131076              UCB$M_LCL_VALID+00004
SDA> e @mmg$gl_pagswpvc
83002090:  81F549D0    "¶Iõ."
SDA> e
83002094:  82D7BE80    ".¶Œ."
SDA> e
83002098:  81F549D0    "¶Iõ."
SDA> e
8300209C:  82579DD0    "¶.W."
SDA> e
830020A0:  81F549D0    "¶Iõ."
SDA> e
830020A4:  81F549D0    "¶Iõ."
SDA> e
830020A8:  81F549D0    "¶Iõ."
SDA> format 82579DD0
82579DD0    PFL$L_BITMAP            82579E04
82579DD4    PFL$L_STARTBYTE         8257A9D6
82579DD8    PFL$W_SIZE                  003D
82579DDA    PFL$B_TYPE                    23
82579DDB    PFL$B_PFC                     00
82579DDC    PFL$L_WINDOW            82FC6200
82579DE0    PFL$L_VBN               00000000
82579DE4    PFL$L_BITMAPSIZ         00006783
82579DE8    PFL$L_FREPAGCNT         0002DDA1
82579DEC    PFL$L_MINFREPAGCNT      0000DC6C
82579DF0    PFL$L_RSRVPAGCNT        000230C2
82579DF4    PFL$L_REFCNT            00000019
82579DF8    PFL$L_SWPREFCNT         00000000
82579DFC    PFL$L_MAXVBN            000FFFFF
82579E00    PFL$B_PGFLX                   03
82579E01                                  44
82579E02    PFL$B_ALLOCSIZ                78
82579E03    PFL$B_FLAGS                   01
            PFL$C_LENGTH
82579E04    PFL$L_BITMAPLOC         FFFFFFFF
SDA> e (@exe$gl_flags@-exe$v_pgflfrag)&1
%SDA-E-NOTINPHYS, 00000000 : not in physical memory
SDA> e (@exe$gl_flags@-exe$v_pgflcrit)&1
%SDA-E-NOTINPHYS, 00000000 : not in physical memory
SDA> ¶
```

Dump Logical Names

LNMSTRDEF.H

```
#ifndef LNMBSTRDEF
#define LNMBSTRDEF

#ifdef DEC_ARA
#pragma member_alignment __save
#pragma nomember_alignment
#pragma nostandard
#endif

#define LNMB$M_NO_ALIAS 0x1
#define LNMB$M_CONFINE 0x2
#define LNMB$M_CRELOG 0x4
#define LNMB$M_TABLE 0x8
#define LNMB$M_NODELETE 0x10
struct LNMBDEF {
    struct LNMBDEF *LNMB$L_FLINK;           /* Forward link in list
*/
    struct LNMBDEF *LNMB$L_BLINK;           /* Backward link in list
*/
    unsigned short int LNMB$W_SIZE;     /* Size of LNMB in bytes          */
    unsigned char LNMB$B_TYPE;          /* Structure type for LNMB        */
    char LNMB$B_PAD;                    /* Align to longword boundary     */
    unsigned int LNMB$L_ACMODE;         /* Owner access mode / integrity level
byte */
    unsigned int LNMB$L_TABLE;          /* Logical name table header address
*/
    unsigned int LNMB$L_LNMX;           /* Pointer to first LNMX          */
    variant_union  {
        unsigned int LNMB$L_FLAGS;      /* Name attributes                */
        variant_struct  {
            unsigned LNMB$V_NO_ALIAS : 1; /* Do not allow outer mode alias  */
            unsigned LNMB$V_CONFINE : 1; /* Do not copy into subprocess     */
            unsigned LNMB$V_CRELOG : 1; /* Created with old $CRELOG service */
```

```
            unsigned LNMB$V_TABLE : 1;  /* This is a table name          */
            unsigned LNMB$V_NODELETE : 1; /* Do not allow this table to be
deleted */
            unsigned LNMB$V_FILL_0 : 3;
            } LNMB$R_BITS;
        } LNMB$R_FLAG_BITS;
    unsigned int LNMB$L_NAMELEN;          /* Length of logical name string   */
    char LNMB$T_NAME[255];                    /* Name string
*/
/* Translation blocks follow name -                                       */
/* pointed to by LNMB$L_LNMX                                              */
    } ;
#define LNMX$M_CONCEALED 0x1
#define LNMX$M_TERMINAL 0x2
#define LNMX$C_HSHFCN -128              /* Hash function value           */
#define LNMX$C_BACKPTR -127            /* Backpointer translation       */
#define LNMX$C_TABLE -126             /* Logical name table header      */
#define LNMX$C_IGNORED_INDEX -125     /* Modified back pointer for process-
private names */
struct LNMXDEF {
    variant_union {
        unsigned int LNMX$L_FLAGS;      /* Translation attributes        */
        variant_struct {
            unsigned LNMX$V_CONCEALED : 1; /* Do not display result of
translation */
            unsigned LNMX$V_TERMINAL : 1; /* Do not retranslate result of
translation */
            unsigned LNMX$V_FILL_1 : 6;
            } LNMX$R_BITS;
        } LNMX$R_FLAG_BITS;
    int LNMX$L_INDEX;                   /* Translation index             */
    int LNMX$L_HASH;                    /* Hash code for logical names in
directories */
    unsigned int LNMX$L_NEXT;           /* Pointer to next lnmx          */
    unsigned int LNMX$L_PAD;            /* Padding to keep quadword alignment
*/
    unsigned int LNMX$L_XLEN;           /* Length of translation string  */
    char LNMX$T_XLATION;                /* Translation string            */
/* Additional translation blocks follow xlation -                        */
/* pointed to by LNMX$L_NEXT.                                             */
    } ;
#define LNMTH$M_SHAREABLE 0x1
#define LNMTH$M_DIRECTORY 0x2
#define LNMTH$M_GROUP 0x4
```

234

```
#define LNMTH$M_SYSTEM 0x8
#define LNMTH$K_LENGTH 40              /* Length of header              */
struct LNMTHDEF {
    variant_union {
        unsigned int LNMTH$L_FLAGS;    /* Logical name table flags      */
        variant_struct {
            unsigned LNMTH$V_SHAREABLE : 1; /* Logical name table is shareable
(S0 space) */
            unsigned LNMTH$V_DIRECTORY : 1; /* Logical name table is a
directory table */
            unsigned LNMTH$V_GROUP : 1; /* Logical name table is a group
logical name table */
            unsigned LNMTH$V_SYSTEM : 1; /* Logical name table is the system
logical name table */
            unsigned LNMTH$V_FILL_2 : 4;
            } LNMTH$R_BITS;
        } LNMTH$R_FLAG_BITS;
    unsigned int LNMTH$L_HASH;         /* Address of hash table         */
    unsigned int LNMTH$L_ORB;          /* Address of Object Rights Block */
    unsigned int LNMTH$L_NAME;         /* Address of containing LNMB block */
    unsigned int LNMTH$L_PARENT;       /* Address of parent table       */
    unsigned int LNMTH$L_CHILD;        /* Address of a child table      */
    unsigned int LNMTH$L_SIBLING;      /* Address of a sibling table    */
    unsigned int LNMTH$L_QTABLE;       /* Address of table holding quota */
    int LNMTH$L_BYTESLM;               /* Initial quota                 */
    int LNMTH$L_BYTES;                 /* Remaining quota               */
    } ;
#define LNMC$K_NUM_ENTRIES 25          /* Number of table header entries. */
#define LNMC$K_LENGTH 128              /* Length of header              */
struct LNMCDEF {
    unsigned int LNMC$L_FLINK;         /* Forward link in list          */
    unsigned int LNMC$L_BLINK;         /* Backward link in list         */
    unsigned short int LNMC$W_SIZE;    /* Size of LNMC in bytes         */
    unsigned char LNMC$B_TYPE;         /* Structure type for LNMC       */
    char LNMC$B_PAD;                   /* Align to longword boundary    */
    unsigned int LNMC$L_CACHEINDX;     /* Current entry number          */
    unsigned int LNMC$L_TBLADDR;       /* Logical name table name address */
    unsigned int LNMC$L_PROCDIRSEQ;    /* Process directory sequence number
*/
    unsigned int LNMC$L_SYSDIRSEQ;     /* System directory sequence number */
    int LNMC$L_ENTRY [25];             /* Logical name table header addresses
*/
    } ;
#define LNMHSH$C_BUCKET 12             /* Length of fixed part of LNMHSH */
```

```
#define LNMHSH$K_BUCKET 12              /* Length of fixed part of LNMHSH   */
struct LNMHSHDEF {
    unsigned int LNMHSH$L_MASK;         /* Mask for hash value          */
    int LNMHSH$L_FILL_1;                /* Spare longword               */
    unsigned short int LNMHSH$W_SIZE;   /* Size of LNMHSH in bytes      */
    unsigned char LNMHSH$B_TYPE;        /* Structure type for LNMHSH    */
    char LNMHSH$B_FILL_2;               /* Spare byte                   */
    struct LNMBDEF *lnmb[100000];       /* Roll your own */
    } ;


#ifdef DEC_ARA
#pragma member_alignment __restore
#pragma standard
#endif
```

DUMP_LNM.C

```
/*
**++
**   FACILITY:  VMS_TOOLS
**
**   MODULE DESCRIPTION:
**
**       Copyright (c) 1991 James W. Coburn
**       Copyright (c) 1992 James W. Coburn
**       Copyright (c) 1993 James W. Coburn
**       Copyright (c) 1992 Professional Press Books.
**       Copyright (c) 1993 Cardinal Business Media
**       This program may be copied for noncommercial purposes. Use of this
**       program for any other purpose without the express written consent
**       of the publisher is prohibited.
**
**       This program searches the LNM tables and lists the current size
**       average queue depth and the top 16 queue entries.
**
**       TEST on a single node cluster before running in a productions
**       environment.  This code uses kernel mode access and thus will
**       crash your system if there are coding bugs or if changes to
**       VMS introduce new bugs.
**
**       This code has been tested on:
**           OpenVMS AXP 1.5
**
**
```

```
**   AUTHORS:
**
**      Jim Coburn
**
**   CREATION DATE:  June 1993
**
**   DESIGN ISSUES:
**
**
**
**
**   MODIFICATION HISTORY:
**
**
**_
*/


/*
**
**   INCLUDE FILES
**
*/
#include <stdio.h>
#include <stddef.h>
#include <starlet.h>
#include <libdtdef.h>
#include <lib$routines.h>

#include <lnm/lnmstrdef.h>

#define MAXQUEUE 4*4

struct STATUS_BLOCK
{
    struct LNMHSHDEF *lnm_hash;
    int table_size;
    int free_entries;
    int total;
    float average_length;
    int max_length[MAXQUEUE];
    struct LNMBDEF *pointer[MAXQUEUE];
} status_block;
```

```
/* Pointer to hash table for all but process logicals */
globalref struct LNMHSHDEF **LNM$AL_HASHTBL;

/* Pointer to hash table for process logicals */
globalref struct LNMHSHDEF *CTL$GL_LNMHASH;

struct LNMHSHDEF *start;

/*
**   Macro routine to lock/unlock access to LNM tables.
*/
void lnmlock();
void lnmunlock();

/*
**   Prototypes
*/
int lnm_lookup( void );

main()
{
    int loop;


/*
**   Initialize our data area.
*/
    status_block.table_size = 0;
    status_block.free_entries = 0;
    status_block.total = 0;
    status_block.average_length = 0.0;

    for( loop = 0; loop < MAXQUEUE; loop++ )
    {
            status_block.max_length[loop] = 0;
            status_block.pointer[loop] = 0;
    }

/*
**   Get data in system hash table.
/*
    start = *LNM$AL_HASHTBL;
```

```
    sys$cmkrnl ( lnm_lookup, 0 );

/*
**   Print data in out data area.
*/
    print_it( "LNMSHASHTBL", "System" );

/*
**   Initialize our data area.
*/

    status_block.table_size = 0;
    status_block.free_entries = 0;
    status_block.total = 0;
    status_block.average_length = 0.0;

    for( loop = 0; loop < MAXQUEUE; loop++ )
    {
            status_block.max_length[loop] = 0;
            status_block.pointer[loop] = 0;
    }

/*
**   Get data in process hash table.
/*
    start = CTL$GL_LNMHASH;
    sys$cmkrnl ( lnm_lookup, 0 );

/*
**   Print data in out data area.
*/
    print_it( "LNMPHASHTBL", "Process" );

}

int lnm_lookup( void )
{
    struct LNMBDEF *pointer, *pointer2;
    int count, this_time, loop, loop1, loop2;
    int slot, update;

    lnmlock();
```

```
    status_block.lnm_hash = start;
    status_block.table_size = (status_block.lnm_hash->LNMHSH$W_SIZE)/4 - 4;


    for( count = 0; count < status_block.table_size; count++ )
    {
        pointer = status_block.lnm_hash->lnmb[count];
        pointer2 = status_block.lnm_hash->lnmb[count];
        for( this_time = 0; pointer != 0; pointer = pointer->LNMB$L_FLINK )
        {
            this_time++;
        }
        status_block.total += this_time;
        if( this_time == 0 )
                status_block.free_entries++;
        else
        {
            update = 0;

            for( loop = 0; loop < MAXQUEUE ; loop++ )
            {
                if( this_time > status_block.max_length[loop] )
                {
                    update = 1;
                    break;
                }
            }
            if( update == 1 )
            {
                slot = loop;

                for( loop1 = MAXQUEUE-1; loop1 > slot ; loop1-);
                {
                    status_block.max_length[loop1] =
status_block.max_length[loop1-1];
                    status_block.pointer[loop1] = status_block.pointer[loop1-
1];
                }
                status_block.max_length[slot] = this_time;
                status_block.pointer[slot] = pointer2;


            }
        }
```

```
        }

    lnmunlock();


}

print_it( type1, type2 )
char *type1, *type2;
{
        int loop, used;

        used = status_block.table_size - status_block.free_entries;
        used = used > 0 ? used : 1;
        status_block.average_length = ( (float) status_block.total / (float)
used );

        printf( "\n\n %s = %d\n", type1, status_block.table_size );
        printf( " There are %d free entries\n", status_block.free_entries);
        printf( " There are a Total of %d %s Logical Names\n",
            status_block.total, type2   );
        printf( " Average queue length is %3.3f\n", status_block.average_length
);

        printf( "\nTop %d queue depths (queue depth/queue header)\n", MAXQUEUE
);

        for( loop = 0; loop < MAXQUEUE; )
        {
            printf( "    %4.4d %08.8x %4.4d %08.8x %4.4d %08.8x %4.4d
%08.8x\n",
                status_block.max_length[ loop],
                status_block.pointer[ loop],
                status_block.max_length[ loop+1],
                status_block.pointer[ loop+1],
                status_block.max_length[ loop+2],
                status_block.pointer[ loop+2],
                status_block.max_length[ loop+3],
                status_block.pointer[ loop+3]);
            loop += 4;
        }


}
```

LOCKER.MAR

```
        .title lockers
;
;       Macro routines to lock and unlock the LNM database access
;
;       Use at your own risk.
;


        .ENTRY  lnmlock,^m<r2,r3,r4>

        movl    g^ctl$gl_pcb,r4
        jsb     g^lnm$lockw
        ret

        .ENTRY  lnmunlock,^m<r2,r3,r4>

        movl    g^ctl$gl_pcb,r4
        jsb     g^lnm$unlock
        ret


.end
```

DUMP_LNM.OPT

```
LNM:dump_lnm.obj
LNM:locker.obj
#ifdef VAX
sys$share:vaxcrtl.exe/share
sys$system:sys.stb/sel
#endif
```

DUMP_LNM SAMPLE OUTPUT

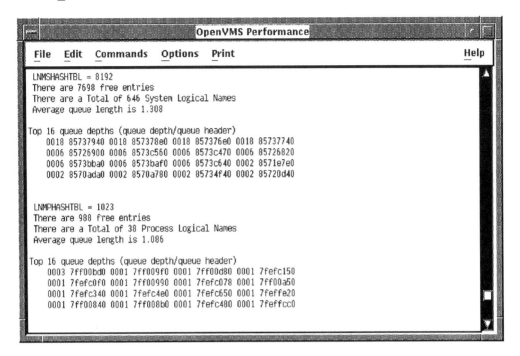

```
OpenVMS Performance
File   Edit   Commands   Options   Print                          Help

LNMSHASHTBL = 8192
There are 7698 free entries
There are a Total of 646 System Logical Names
Average queue length is 1.308

Top 16 queue depths (queue depth/queue header)
    0018 85737940 0018 857378e0 0018 857376e0 0018 85737740
    0006 85726900 0006 8573c560 0006 8573c470 0006 85726820
    0006 8573bba0 0006 8573baf0 0006 8573c640 0002 8571e7e0
    0002 8570ada0 0002 8570a780 0002 85734f40 0002 85720d40


LNMPHASHTBL = 1023
There are 988 free entries
There are a Total of 38 Process Logical Names
Average queue length is 1.086

Top 16 queue depths (queue depth/queue header)
    0003 7ff00bd0 0001 7ff009f0 0001 7ff00d80 0001 7fefc150
    0001 7fefc0f0 0001 7ff00990 0001 7fefc078 0001 7ff00a50
    0001 7fefc340 0001 7fefc4e0 0001 7fefc650 0001 7feffe20
    0001 7ff00840 0001 7ff008b0 0001 7fefc480 0001 7feffcc0
```

DUMP_LNM_NAMES

```
/*
**++
**   FACILITY:  VMS_TOOLS
**
**   MODULE DESCRIPTION:
**
**      Copyright (c) 1991 James W. Coburn
**      Copyright (c) 1992 James W. Coburn
**      Copyright (c) 1993 James W. Coburn
**      Copyright (c) 1992 Professional Press Books.
**      Copyright (c) 1993 Cardinal Business Media
**      This program may be copied for noncommercial purposes. Use of this
**      program for any other purpose without the express written consent
**      of the publisher is prohibited.
**
**      This program dumps out all names that hash to entered hash index.
**
**      TEST on a single node cluster before running in a productions
```

243

```
**      environment.  This code uses kernel mode access and thus will
**      crash your system if there are coding bugs or if changes to
**      VMS introduce new bugs.
**
**      This code has been tested on:
**          OpenVMS AXP 1.5
**
**
**  AUTHORS:
**
**      Jim Coburn
**
**  CREATION DATE:  June 1993
**
**  DESIGN ISSUES:
**
**
**
**
**  MODIFICATION HISTORY:
**
**
**—
*/


/*
**
**  INCLUDE FILES
**
*/
#include <stdio.h>
#include <stddef.h>
#include <starlet.h>
#include <libdtdef.h>
#include <lib$routines.h>
#include "LNM/lnmstrdef.h"

/*
**  Global Data
*/
static struct LNMBDEF *logical_name;
static char logical_name_local[256];
```

```
main()
{
        int lnm_lookup();
        unsigned int address;
        int loop;

        printf( "enter starting address in HEX ");
        scanf( "%x", &address);

        printf( "Logical names for hash entry %x\n", address );
        logical_name  = (struct LNMBDEF *) address;
        (void) sys$cmexec ( lnm_lookup, 0 );

        for( loop = 0; ;loop++ )
        {
            printf( "%2.2d - %s \n", loop,
                logical_name_local );
            if( logical_name != 0)
                (void) sys$cmexec( lnm_lookup, 0 );
            else
                break;
        }
}
/*
**   Must copy data from Exec read only to user readable space.
*/
int lnm_lookup()
{

    int i;
    for (i = 0; i < logical_name->LNMB$L_NAMELEN; i++)
    {
        logical_name_local[i] = logical_name->LNMB$T_NAME[i];
    }
    logical_name_local[logical_name->LNMB$L_NAMELEN] = '\0';
    logical_name = logical_name->LNMB$L_FLINK;

}
```

245

DUMP_LNM_NAMES SAMPLE OUTPUT

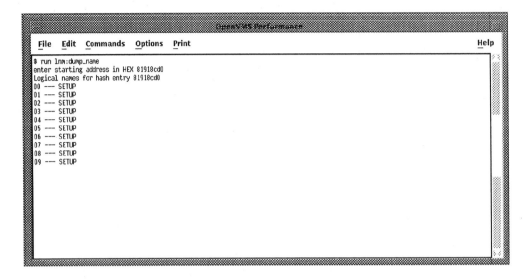

Show Memory

ANALYZE/SYSTEM

BEFORE OPENVMS VAX V6.0

```
SDA> show pool/summary

IRP lookaside list
LRP lookaside list
SRP lookaside list
Non-paged dynamic storage pool
Paged dynamic storage pool

Summary of IRP lookaside list

   69  UNKNOWN   =    12144  (5%)
    2  CRB       =      352  (0%)
   55  IRP       =     9680  (4%)
    1  WCB       =      176  (0%)
    5  NET       =      880  (0%)
   23  JIB       =     4048  (1%)
  754  RSB       =   132704  (64%)
    3  CDRP      =      528  (0%)
  237  IMSG      =    41712  (20%)
    1  SCS       =      176  (0%)
    2  LOADCODE  =     4224  (2%)

Total space used = 206624 out of 370480 total bytes, 163856 bytes left

Total space utilization = 55%
```

Summary of LRP lookaside list

```
 1   ADP       =    1856   (3%)
 1   ACB       =    1856   (3%)
 2   UCB       =     371   (6%)
 1   NET       =    1856   (3%)
 7   CXB       =   12992  (21%)
 1   DPT       =    1856   (3%)
 1   PFL       =    1856   (3%)
15   VCRP      =   27840  (46%)
 3   LAVC      =    5568   (9%)
```

Total space used = 59392 out of 204160 total bytes, 144768 bytes left

Total space utilization = 29%

Summary of SRP lookaside list

```
  10   UNKNOWN    =    1280   (0%)
  39   AQB        =    4992   (2%)
   1   CEB        =     128   (0%)
  41   CRB        =    5248   (2%)
  66   DDB        =    8448   (3%)
  44   IDB        =    5632   (2%)
  32   TQE        =    4096   (1%)
 294   WCB        =   37632  (15%)
  15   BUFIO      =    1920   (0%)
   2   NET        =     256   (0%)
   1   PTR        =     128   (0%)
   1   TWP        =     128   (0%)
   1   RBM        =     128   (0%)
   1   VCA        =     128   (0%)
   4   CDB        =     512   (0%)
1023   LKB        =  130944  (53%)
  94   CDRP       =   12032   (4%)
   7   CIMSG      =     896   (0%)
   2   RIGHTSLIS  =     256   (0%)
   1   CIA        =     128   (0%)
   2   ORB        =     256   (0%)
   1   DCB        =     128   (0%)
  13   SPL        =    1664   (0%)
 105   SCS        =   13440   (5%)
   2   INIT       =     256   (0%)
```

```
    1   CLASSDRV  =      128   (0%)
    3   CLU       =      384   (0%)
    1   DECW      =      128   (0%)
   89   DSRV      =    11392   (4%)
    4   NSA       =      512   (0%)
    1   CWPS      =      128   (0%)
    2   SHAD      =      256   (0%)
    5   VCC       =      640   (0%)
    1   ENS       =      128   (0%)
    1   DDTM      =      128   (0%)
    1   DECNET    =      128   (0%)
    1   QMAN      =      128   (0%)
```

Total space used = 244736 out of 384000 total bytes, 139264 bytes left

Total space utilization = 63%

Summary of non-paged pool contents

```
  272   UNKNOWN   =   284800   (12%)
  242   ADP       =    65792   (3%)
    5   CEB       =      880   (0%)
    2   CRB       =      336   (0%)
  422   FCB       =    87776   (4%)
    3   FRK       =     7024   (0%)
   24   PCB       =    10368   (0%)
    1   RVT       =     2592   (0%)
    2   TQE       =      128   (0%)
  202   UCB       =   110304   (5%)
   84   VCB       =    20160   (0%)
   46   WCB       =    15952   (0%)
  152   BUFIO     =    80896   (3%)
    1   MVL       =    20784   (0%)
   20   NET       =    10112   (0%)
   15   CXB       =    46272   (2%)
    4   NDB       =    24544   (1%)
   18   DPT       =   216496   (9%)
    1   JPB       =    50944   (2%)
    2   PFL       =    14560   (0%)
    1   PFLMAP    =    49280   (2%)
    1   PTR       =    14912   (0%)
    8   RBM       =    34704   (1%)
   65   VCA       =   169808   (7%)
```

```
    1  LKID      =     1104  (0%)
    2  RSHT      =    22848  (1%)
   77  CIDG      =    66528  (3%)
    1  CIMSG     =     6160  (0%)
    4  FLK       =    20384  (0%)
    1  CIA       =      224  (0%)
    1  PMB       =     1792  (0%)
  262  ORB       =    25152  (1%)
    2  UNC       =    50928  (2%)
    1  DCB       =    22048  (1%)
   49  VCRP      =    24848  (1%)
    1  SPL       =       80  (0%)
    6  ARB       =   215696  (9%)
    1  LCKCTX    =     2240  (0%)
    2  BOD       =    63328  (2%)
    3  FTRD      =     8768  (0%)
    1  DFLB      =    53248  (2%)
    3  RDPB      =    73984  (3%)
    1  RDDB      =     1280  (0%)
  326  SCS       =   118592  (5%)
    5  LOADCODE  =     1488  (0%)
    4  INIT      =    33488  (1%)
   14  CLASSDRV  =     6272  (0%)
   47  CLU       =    10432  (0%)
    1  DSRV      =      208  (0%)
   85  LAVC      =    21024  (0%)
    1  QMAN      =      528  (0%)
```

Total space used = 2192096 out of 2249728 total bytes, 57632 bytes left

Total space utilization = 97%

Summary of paged pool contents

```
   15  UNKNOWN   =    21904  (6%)
    1  PQB       =     2256  (0%)
  277  GSD       =    17616  (5%)
  175  KFE       =    12448  (3%)
   69  MTL       =     2208  (0%)
  132  KFRH      =    54192 (15%)
    1  RSHT      =     8208  (2%)
    2  ACL       =       64  (0%)
 1551  LNM       =   146240 (42%)
```

```
    2  FLK       =   22528  (6%)
   10  KFD       =     544  (0%)
    1  KFPB      =      16  (0%)
    2  PFB       =   23936  (6%)
    1  DCB       =   18432  (5%)
    2  FTRD      =    5632  (1%)
    1  DDTM_EVEN =    6912  (2%)
    1  PGD       =     208  (0%)
```

Total space used = 343344 out of 919040 total bytes, 575696 bytes left

Total space utilization = 37%

STARTING WITH OPENVMS VAX 6.0 AND OPENVMS AXP

```
SDA> show pool/summary
Nonpaged dynamic storage pool
Paged dynamic storage pool
```

Output is similar to that of pre-OpenVMS VAX V6.0, but the lookaside lists (IRP, LRP, and SRP) are no longer available.

ADAPTIVE POOL MANAGEMENT

```
$ ANA/SYSTEM

SDA> Show Pool/Ring
```

Non-Paged Pool History Ring-Buffer

(256 entries: Most recent first)

Packet Adr	Size	Type	Subtype	Caller's PC	Routine Called	Entry Adr
805AB800	384	IRP	65	80073A0C	EXE$DEANONPAGED	805B0F50
805AB800	384	IRP	65	80011308	EXE$ALONONPAGED	805B0F40
805AB800	360	IRP	65	80073A0C	EXE$DEANONPAGED	805B0F30
805AEA00	128	FRK	62	800114D0	EXE$ALONONPAGED	805B0F20
805AB800	384	IRP	65	80011308	EXE$ALONONPAGED	805B0F10
805AB800	384	IRP	65	80073A0C	EXE$DEANONPAGED	805B0F00
805AB800	384	IRP	65	80011308	EXE$ALONONPAGED	805B0EF0
805AB800	360	IRP	65	80073A0C	EXE$DEANONPAGED	805B0EE0
805AE5C0	128	FRK	62	800114D0	EXE$ALONONPAGED	805B0ED0
805AB800	384	IRP	65	80011308	EXE$ALONONPAGED	805B0EC0
805AB800	384	IRP	65	80073A0C	EXE$DEANONPAGED	805B0EB0

```
805AB800   384   IRP   65      80011308   EXE$ALONONPAGED   805B0EA0
805AB800   360   IRP   65      80073A0C   EXE$DEANONPAGED   805B0E90
805AC340   128   FRK   62      800114D0   EXE$ALONONPAGED   805B0E80
805AB800   384   IRP   65      80011308   EXE$ALONONPAGED   805B0E70
805AB800   384   IRP   65      80073A0C   EXE$DEANONPAGED   805B0E60
805AB800   384   IRP   65      80011308   EXE$ALONONPAGED   805B0E50
805AB800   360   IRP   65      80073A0C   EXE$DEANONPAGED   805B0E40
805B4A40   128   FRK   62      800114D0   EXE$ALONONPAGED   805B0E30
805AB800   384   IRP   65      80011308   EXE$ALONONPAGED   805B0E20
805AB800   384   IRP   65      80073A0C   EXE$DEANONPAGED   805B0E10
805AB800   384   IRP   65      80011308   EXE$ALONONPAGED   805B0E00
805AB800   360   IRP   65      80073A0C   EXE$DEANONPAGED   805B0DF0
805AEB00   128   FRK   62      800114D0   EXE$ALONONPAGED   805B0DE0
805AB800   384   IRP   65      80011308   EXE$ALONONPAGED   805B0DD0
805AB800   384   IRP   65      80073A0C   EXE$DEANONPAGED   805B0DC0
805AB800   384   IRP   65      80011308   EXE$ALONONPAGED   805B0DB0
805AB800   360   IRP   65      80073A0C   EXE$DEANONPAGED   805B0DA0
805AEA80   128   FRK   62      800114D0   EXE$ALONONPAGED   805B0D90
805AB800   384   IRP   65      80011308   EXE$ALONONPAGED   805B0D80
805AB800   384   IRP   65      80073A0C   EXE$DEANONPAGED   805B0D70
805AB800   384   IRP   65      80011308   EXE$ALONONPAGED   805B0D60


SDA> show pool/stat

Lookaside List Statistics
```

List Head Address	List Size	Alloc. Attempts	Alloc. Failures	Deallocs
8041B400	64	4222061	371	4221691
8041B408	128	1335	170	1171
8041B410	192	44635805	43834	
8041B418	256	4547	1147	3402
8041B420	320	2307	349	1959
8041B428	384	22878	1151	21729
8041B430	448	43	13	31
8041B438	512	9929	12	9918
8041B440	576	1465	25	1441
8041B448	640	25	14	11
8041B450	704	7	5	3
8041B458	768	10	8	3
8041B460	832	3	3	1
8041B468	896	2686	4	2683
8041B470	960	121	9	113

8041B478	1024	7	3	5
8041B480	1088	15	7	9
8041B488	1152	33	1	33
8041B490	1216	1	1	0
8041B498	1280	8	1	8
8041B4A0	1344	0	0	0
8041B4A8	1408	0	0	0
8041B4B0	1472	0	0	0
8041B4B8	1536	29	2	27
8041B4C0	1600	0	0	0
8041B4C8	1664	127	61	66
8041B4D0	1728	1	1	0
8041B4D8	1792	1	1	0
8041B4E0	1856	4663	1132	3537
8041B4E8	1920	0	0	0
8041B4F0	1984	1	1	0
8041B4F8	2048	1	0	2
8041B500	2112	3	3	0
8041B508	2176	0	0	0
8041B510	2240	0	0	0
8041B518	2304	1	1	1
8041B520	2368	0	0	0
8041B528	2432	1	1	0
8041B530	2496	0	0	0
8041B538	2560	0	0	0
8041B540	2624	1	1	0
8041B548	2688	0	0	0
8041B550	2752	1	1	0
8041B558	2816	0	0	0
8041B560	2880	1	1	0
8041B568	2944	0	0	0
8041B570	3008	0	0	0
8041B578	3072	39	15	23
8041B580	3136	0	0	0
8041B588	3200	0	0	0
8041B590	3264	0	0	0
8041B598	3328	0	0	0
8041B5A0	3392	0	0	0
8041B5A8	3456	0	0	0
8041B5B0	3520	0	0	0
8041B5B8	3584	0	0	0
8041B5C0	3648	0	0	0
8041B5C8	3712	0	0	0

8041B5D0	3776	0	0	0
8041B5D8	3840	0	0	0
8041B5E0	3904	1	1	0
8041B5E8	3968	0	0	0
8041B5F0	4032	0	0	0
8041B5F8	4096	0	0	0
8041B600	4160	0	0	0
8041B608	4224	0	0	0
8041B610	4288	0	0	0
8041B618	4352	0	0	0
8041B620	4416	0	0	0
8041B628	4480	0	0	0
8041B630	4544	0	0	0
8041B638	4608	0	0	0
8041B640	4672	0	0	0
8041B648	4736	0	0	0
8041B650	4800	0	0	0
8041B658	4864	0	0	0
8041B660	4928	0	0	0
8041B668	4992	0	0	0
8041B670	5056	0	0	0
8041B678	5120	0	0	0

SHOW MEMORY /POOL /FULL

BEFORE OPENVMS VAX V6.0

```
┌─────────────────────────────────────────────────────────────────┐
│ ─              OpenVMS Performance                         ◄ ─   │
├─────────────────────────────────────────────────────────────────┤
│  File   Edit  Commands  Options  Print                      Help │
├─────────────────────────────────────────────────────────────────┤
│          System Memory Resources on 28-APR-1993 13:12:01.88      ▲│
│                                                                   │
│ Small Packet (SRP) Lookaside List      Packets    Bytes    Pages │
│     Current Total Size                    3000    384000     750  │
│     Initial Size (SRPCOUNT)               3000    384000     750  │
│     Maximum Size (SRPCOUNTV)             30000   3840000    7500  │
│     Free Space                            1314    168192         │
│     Space in Use                          1686    215808         │
│     Packet Size/Upper Bound (SRPSIZE)              128           │
│     Lower Bound on Allocation                       32           │
│                                                                   │
│ I/O Request Packet (IRP) Lookaside List Packets    Bytes    Pages │
│     Current Total Size                    2000    352000     688  │
│     Initial Size (IRPCOUNT)               2000    352000     688  │
│     Maximum Size (IRPCOUNTV)             20000   3520000    6875  │
│     Free Space                             736    129536         │
│     Space in Use                          1264    222464         │
│     Packet Size/Upper Bound (fixed)                176           │
│     Lower Bound on Allocation                      129           │
│                                                                   │
│ Large Packet (LRP) Lookaside List      Packets    Bytes    Pages │
│     Current Total Size                     110    204160     399  │
│     Initial Size (LRPCOUNT)                110    204160     399  │
│     Maximum Size (LRPCOUNTV)               550   1020800    1994  │
│     Free Space                              86    159616         │
│     Space in Use                            24     44544         │
│     Packet Size/Upper Bound (LRPSIZE + 352)       1856           │
│     Lower Bound on Allocation                     1088           │
│                                                                   │
│ Nonpaged Dynamic Memory                                          │
│     Current Size (bytes)     2499584  Current Total Size (pages) 4882│
│     Initial Size (NPAGEDYN)  2499584  Initial Size (pages)      4882│
│     Maximum Size (NPAGEVIR)  9999872  Maximum Size (pages)     19531│
│     Free Space (bytes)        978624  Space in Use (bytes)   1520960│
│     Size of Largest Block     897616  Size of Smallest Block     16│
│     Number of Free Blocks        248  Free Blocks LEQU 32 Bytes  63│
│                                                                   │
│ Paged Dynamic Memory                                             │
│     Current Size (PAGEDYN)    982016  Current Total Size (pages) 1918│
│     Free Space (bytes)        503120  Space in Use (bytes)    478896│
│     Size of Largest Block     499664  Size of Smallest Block     16│
│     Number of Free Blocks         98  Free Blocks LEQU 32 Bytes  76│
│                                                                  ▼│
└─────────────────────────────────────────────────────────────────┘
```

STARTING WITH OPENVMS VAX V6.0 AND OPENVMS AXP

```
┌─────────────────────────────────────────────────────────────────────────┐
│                          OpenVMS Performance                              │
├─────────────────────────────────────────────────────────────────────────┤
│  File   Edit   Commands   Options   Print                         Help    │
├─────────────────────────────────────────────────────────────────────────┤
│          System Memory Resources on 26-APR-1993 18:15:45.57          ▲    │
│                                                                           │
│ Nonpaged Dynamic Memory      (Lists + Variable)                           │
│     Current Size (bytes)       6832128    Current Size (pagelets)   13344  │
│     Initial Size (NPAGEDYN)    5193728    Initial Size (pagelets)   10144  │
│     Maximum Size (NPAGEVIR)   20799488    Maximum Size (pagelets)   40624  │
│     Free Space (bytes)          140032    Space in Use (bytes)    6692096  │
│     Size of Largest Block         5696    Size of Smallest Block       64  │
│     Number of Free Blocks          545    Free Blocks LEQU 64 Bytes    178 │
│     Free Blocks on Lookasides      122    Lookaside Space (bytes)   49856  │
│                                                                           │
│ Paged Dynamic Memory                                                      │
│     Current Size (PAGEDYN)     5021696    Current Size (pagelets)    9808  │
│     Free Space (bytes)         3289824    Space in Use (bytes)    1731872  │
│     Size of Largest Block      3288128    Size of Smallest Block       16  │
│     Number of Free Blocks           48    Free Blocks LEQU 64 Bytes     46 │
│                                                                           │
│                                                                      ▼    │
└─────────────────────────────────────────────────────────────────────────┘
```

MODPARAMS File

SYS$SYSTEM:MODPARAMS.DAT

```
!
! Support Current OpenVMS VAX 6.0 and AXP 1.5
!
ARCH_TYPE = f$getsyi("ARCH_TYPE)
! if f$getsyi("ARCH_TYPE") .eq. 2 then AXP
! if f$getsyi("ARCH_TYPE") .eq. 1 then VAX
MEMSIZE = F$GETSYI("MEMSIZE")  ! Memory size in Pages
PAGESIZE=F$GETSYI("PAGE_SIZE") ! Page size in bytes
PAGELET_SIZE = 512
PLETS_PER_PAGE = PAGE_SIZE / PAGELET_SIZE
!
! one meg memory == 1048576 bytes)
!
MEGSOFMEMORY=(MEMSIZE*PLETS_PER_PAGE*PAGELET_SIZE)/(1048576)
!
!
! Common SystemParameters File
! MAKE NO CHANGES TO THIS FILE
!
agen$include_params sys$system:Init_modparams.dat
agen$include_params sys$system:mem_modparams.dat
agen$include_params sys$system:Node_modparams.dat
agen$include_params sys$system:Changes_modparams.dat
```

SYS$SYSTEM:MEM_MODPARAMS.DAT

```
! Setup the memory
!
! Swapper tuning done here!
!
If ARCH_TYPE .eq. 1 then SWPALLOCINC=120
If ARCH_TYPE .eq. 2 then SWPALLOCINC=64
```

```
!
MPW_WRTCLUSTER=SWPALLOCINC !These must be the same
!
MIN_FREELIM=MEMSIZE/10       !Start at 10% of memory
!Added after tuning work on 1/1/92
ADD_FREELIM = -2* MPW_WRTCLUSTER
ADD_FREELIM = -2* MPW_WRTCLUSTER
ADD_FREELIM = -2* MPW_WRTCLUSTER
ADD_FREELIM = -2* MPW_WRTCLUSTER


MIN_FREEGOAL=MIN_FREELIM+3*MPW_WRTCLUSTER
MIN_BORROWLIM=MIN_FREELIM+4*MPW_WRTCLUSTER
MIN_GROWLIM=MIN_BORROWLIM+4*MPW_WRTCLUSTER
!
! This is for the Modified Page Writer
!
MIN_MPW_HILIMIT=MEMSIZE/10 !Start at 10% of memory
ADD_MPW_HILIMIT = - MPW_WRTCLUSTER
ADD_MPW_HILIMIT = - MPW_WRTCLUSTER
ADD_MPW_HILIMIT = - MPW_WRTCLUSTER
ADD_MPW_HILIMIT = - MPW_WRTCLUSTER
ADD_MPW_HILIMIT = - MPW_WRTCLUSTER
!
MIN_MPW_WAITLIMIT=MIN_MPW_HILIMIT !Test must be the same
MIN_MPW_THRESH=MIN_MPW_HILIMIT+10*MPW_WRTCLUSTER
MIN_MPW_LOLIMIT=MIN_MPW_HILIMIT - 6*MPW_WRTCLUSTER
MIN_MPW_LOWAITLIMIT=MIN_MPW_HILIMIT - 3*MPW_WRTCLUSTER
MIN_MPW_IOLIMIT=2+2+1
!
MIN_PFCDEFAULT=64             !Using NI
!
if MEGSOFMEMORY.gt. 32 then min_NPAGEDYN=3500000
if MEGSOFMEMORY.lt. 32 then min_NPAGEDYN=2500000
if MEGSOFMEMORY.eq. 16 then MIN_NPAGEDYN=1500000
if MEGSOFMEMORY.lt. 16 then MIN_NPAGEDYN=1000000
!
MIN_NPAGEVIR=4*MIN_NPAGEDYN
! Working set section
MIN_PQL_MASTLM=500
MIN_PQL_DASTLM=500
MIN_PQL_MBIOLM=250
MIN_PQL_DBIOLM=250
MIN_PQL_MDIOLM=200
```

```
MIN_PQL_MDIOLM=100
MIN_PQL_MPRCLM=20
MIN_PQL_MFILLM=100
MIN_PQL_DBYTLM=100000
MIN_PQL_MBYTLM=300000
MIN_PQL_DWSEXTENT=4096
MIN_PQL_MWSEXTENT=MIN_WSMAX-1024   ! leave room for extra procsectcnt
MIN_PQL_MENQLM=650
MIN_PQL_DENQLM=200
MIN_PQL_MPGFLQUOTA=60000
MIN_PQL_DPGFLQUOTA=60000
MIN_PQL_MTQELM=60
!
MIN_SYSMWCNT=2*1024          !SYSTEM WORKING SET SIZE
if MEGSOFMEMORY.le. 16 then MIN_WSMAX=8192*2
if MEGSOFMEMORY.gt. 16 then MIN_WSMAX=8192*2+1024*2
!
```

SYS$SYSTEM:NODE_MODPARAMS.DAT

```
!
! SCSYSTEM = DECnet Node Address in the form
!   1024 * area + Nodenumber
! Thus node 4.513 would be
!   4*1024 + 512  => 4227
!
SCSSYSTEMID=4227
SCSNODE="ASC131   "
VAXCLUSTER=2
EXPECTED_VOTES=3
VOTES=0
DISK_QUORUM="
QDSKVOTES=1
QDSKINTERVAL=10
ALLOCLASS=0
LOCKDIRWT=0
NISCS_CONV_BOOT=0
NISCS_LOAD_PEA0=1
NISCS_PORT_SERV=0
!
!   This file is unique for each member of your cluster.
!
```

4

SYS$SYSTEM:INIT_MODPARAMS.DAT

```
ACP_REBLDSYSD=0
MIN_SCSCONNCNT=200
RECNXINTERVAL=40
DEADLOCK_WAIT=20
TMSCP_LOAD=0                !We do not wany MSCP Served Tapes
!
! Are you serving disks
!
MSCP_LOAD=1                 !Load the MSCP server and serve disks
MSCP_SERVE_ALL=2           !Serve only locally-attached (non-HSC) disks
!
! Do you do windows?
!
WINDOW_SYSTEM=1            !DECWindows
!
! Setup the cluster environment
!
RECNXINTERVAL=40          !Remote system reconnect polling interval
ALLOCLASS=0               !Allocation Class for your node
LOCKDIRWT=0               !Should be zero for all satellites
!
! We will set the files sizes by hand thank you.
!
PAGEFILE=0
SWAPFILE=0
DUMPFILE=0
!
! We want a spare Page/Swap file just in case.
!
PAGFILCNT=4
SWPFILCNT=4
!
! Turn off the dumps
!
DUMPBUG=0
!
! Now do the lookaside lists
!
!Next three lines removed with OpenVMS VAX 6.0 and OpenVMS AXP
!MIN_SRPCOUNT=3000
!MIN_IRPCOUNT=1200
!MIN_LRPCOUNT=75
```

260

```
!
MIN_NPAGEDYN=1500000          !For average memory systems
MIN_NPAGEVIR=3*MIN_NPAGEDYN
!
! How many process slots?
!
MIN_MAXPROCESSCNT=40               !40 FOR 16MB
MIN_BALSETCNT=MAXPROCESSCNT-2 !38 FOR 16MB
!


! Special Software wants these
!
MIN_CTLPAGES=400
MIN_CHANNELCNT=127
!
MIN_VIRTUALPAGECNT=100000
MIN_MAXBUF=4096
!
! These are modified quite often depending on products actually installed
!
MIN_GBLSECTIONS=300           !Heavy DECWindows Usage
MIN_GBLPAGES=30000            !Heavy DECWindows Usage
MIN_GBLPAGFIL=16384           !xxxxx
!
! This guy checks for sleepers, 20-300 seconds elapsed time.
!
LONGWAIT=20
!
! How many image sections in your link map?
! DON'T make too small or will cause massive Paging problems.
!
MIN_PROCSECTCNT=64
!
! These are the logical name table, resource and lock block tables
!
MIN_LNMSHASHTBL=2048
MIN_LNMPHASHTBL=512
MIN_LOCKIDTBL=4096
MIN_RESHASHTBL=2048
MIN_PIOPAGES=450

MIN_SWPOUTPGCNT=500           !DECWindows requires this value.
!
! Auto-working set adjustment section
```

```
!
MIN_PFRATL=1                   !Turn on aws adjustment

MIN_AWSMIN=512
MIN_WSDEC=57
MIN_PFRATH=10
MIN_WSINC=300
!
! Working set section
!
MIN_SYSMWCNT=2*1024            !SYSTEM WORKING SET SIZE
MIN_WSMAX=8192*2
!
! Process quotas
!
MIN_PQL_MASTLM=500
MIN_PQL_MBIOLM=100
MIN_PQL_MDIOLM=100
MIN_PQL_MPRCLM=8
MIN_PQL_MFILLM=60
MIN_PQL_MBYTLM=33000
MIN_PQL_MWSQUOTA=512
MIN_PQL_MWSDEFAULT=512
MIN_PQL_MWSEXTENT=MIN_WSMAX
MIN_PQL_MENQLM=650
MIN_PQL_MPGFLQUOTA=32768
MIN_PQL_MTQELM=60
!
! ACP parameter section
!
ACP_DATACHECK=0                !Trust your disk drives
ACP_DINDXCACHE=50
ACP_QUOCACHE=8
IF MSCP_SERVE .ne. 0 then ACP_DIRCACHE=128
IF MSCP_SERVE .eq. 0 then ACP_DIRCACHE=64
IF MSCP_SERVE .ne. 0 then ACP_HDRCACHE=128
IF MSCP_SERVE .eq. 0 then ACP_HDRCACHE=64
IF MSCP_SERVE .ne. 0 then ACP_MAPCACHE=64
IF MSCP_SERVE .eq. 0 then ACP_MAPCACHE=64!
! RMS tuning done here
!
MIN_RMS_DFNBC=32
MIN_RMS_DFMBFSDK=4             !Adjust for disk init/clus=
!
```

```
!
! Increase Mailbox quota
!
MIN_DEFMBXBUFQUO=2048*6
MIN_DEFMBXMXMSG=2046
!
!
POOLCHECK=0
!
! Increase Interrupt Stack
!
MIN_INTSTKPAGES=6
!
!
MAX_RJOBLIM=8
!
! Set Default Characteristics for All Terminals.
!
TTY_TIMEOUT=7200
TTY_DEFCHAR=402657952
TTY_DEFCHAR2=143490
TTY_SPEED=16

TTY_DEFPORT=1
TTY_DMASIZE=32
!
! Basic Security
!
LGI_BRK_LIM=3
LGI_BRK_TERM=0
LGI_BRK_TMO=300
LGI_RETRY_LIM=3
LGI_RETRY_TMO=30
LGI_BRK_DISUSER=1
!
  These are the logical name table, resource and lock block tables
!
MIN_LNMSHASHTBL=2048
MIN_LNMPHASHTBL=512
MIN_LOCKIDTBL=4096
MIN_RESHASHTBL=2048
!
QUANTUM=4
```

Simple Tuner

MEMORY.C

```
/*
**++
**   FACILITY:  Auto-Tuner
**
** Copyright (c) 1991 James W. Coburn
** Copyright (c) 1992 James W. Coburn
** Copyright (c) 1993 James W. Coburn
** Copyright (c) 1992 Professional Press Books.
** Copyright (c) 1993 Cardinal Business Media
** This program may be copied for noncommercial purposes. Use of this
** program for any other purpose without the express written consent
** of the publisher is prohibited.
**
** MODULE DESCRIPTION:
**
** This is a very simple dynamic tuner.  It adjusts WSDEC and WSINC
** depending on the size of the Free list. Currently we turn on
** AWSA if the size of the free list is below the size of GROWLIM.
**
**
** AUTHORS:
**
** Jim Coburn
**
** CREATION DATE:  January 16, 1991
```

```
**
** DESIGN ISSUES:
**
** This code executes in Kernel Mode, so don't make any mistakes.
** This is a simple work around the reason that most people don't
** use AWSA.
**
**
** MODIFICATION HISTORY:
**
** Updated for OpenVMS AXP 1993.
**—
*/


/*
**
**   INCLUDE FILES
**
*/

#include <descrip.h>
#include <string.h>
#include <stdio.h>
#include <rms.h>
#include <descrip.h>
#include <stdio.h>
#include <starlet.h>
#include <libdtdef.h>
#include <lib$routines.h>
#include <stdlib.h>


/*
```

```
**
**   Global References from SYS$SYSTEM:SYS.STB
**
*/

#pragma nostandard

globalref SCH$GL_PFRATL;
globalref SCH$GL_PFRATH;
globalref SCH$GL_GROWLIM;
globalref SCH$GL_FREECNT;
#ifdef DEC_ARA
   globalref SCH$GL_WSDEC_PAGES;
   globalref SCH$GL_WSINC_PAGES;
   globalref SCH$GL_WSDEC_PAGELETS;
   globalref SCH$GL_WSINC_PAGELETSS;
#else
   globalref SCH$GL_WSDEC;
   globalref SCH$GL_WSINC;
#endif
globalref short SCH$GW_QUAN;

#pragma nostandard

main()
{

   void auto_tune();
   auto_tune();
}

/*
**++
**   FUNCTIONAL DESCRIPTION:
```

267

```
**
** Set up a scheduled wakeup every 3 seconds to Auto Tune
** this system.
**
** FORMAL PARAMETERS:
**
** None.
**
** RETURN VALUE:
**
** None.
**
** SIDE EFFECTS:
**
** The values for WSDEC, WSDEC, PFRATL, PFRATH and QUANTUM
** area modified based on the current size of the free list.
**
** DESIGN:
**
** None
**
**
**
**-
*/
void auto_tune()
{
  int status;

  struct DATE_TIME
  {
      unsigned int item1, item2;
  };
```

```
  void turn_on_awsa();
  void turn_off_awsa();

/*
**  Auto tune every three seconds.
*/
  $DESCRIPTOR( delta_time, "0 00:00:03.00");

  struct DATE_TIME wake_up_time;

  sys$bintim( &delta_time, &wake_up_time );
  sys$schdwk( 0, 0, &wake_up_time, &wake_up_time );

  for(;;)
  {

      /*
      Wait for the next scheduled wakeup.
      */

      sys$hiber();

      /*
      If there is a "lot" of memory turn off working set adjust.
      */

      if( SCH$GL_FREECNT > SCH$GL_GROWLIM )
        status = sys$cmkrnl( turn_off_awsa, 0 );
      else
        status = sys$cmkrnl( turn_on_awsa, 0 );
  }
}
/*
**++
```

```
**   FUNCTIONAL DESCRIPTION:
**
** Stop Working Set Decrement (PFRATL == 0 )
** Make it easy to increment working set size (PFRATH == 10 )
** If doing memory recovery from "idle" process,
** do in large chunks (WSDEC == 257 )
** Give "lots" of memory when doing working set increment (WSINC ==
400 )
**
** FORMAL PARAMETERS:
**
** none.
**
** RETURN VALUE:
**
** None
**
** SIDE EFFECTS:
**
** Values of system parameters WSINC, WSDEC, PFRATL, and PFRATH are
changed.
**
** DESIGN:
**
** None
**—
*/

void turn_off_awsa()
{
#ifdef DEC_ARA
   SCH$GL_PFRATL = 0;
   SCH$GL_PFRATH = 8;
   SCH$GL_WSDEC_PAGES = 257;
```

```
    SCH$GL_WSINC_PAGES = 400;
    SCH$GL_WSDEC_PAGELETS = 257*16;
    SCH$GL_WSINC_PAGELETS = 400*16;
#else
    SCH$GL_PFRATL = 0;
    SCH$GL_PFRATH = 10;
    SCH$GL_WSDEC = 257;
    SCH$GL_WSINC = 400;
#endif
}


/*
**++
** FUNCTIONAL DESCRIPTION:
**
** Start Working Set Decrement (PFRATL == 1 )
** Make it harder to increment working set size (PFRATH == 50 )
** If doing memory recovery from "active" process,
** do in small chunks (WSDEC == 67 )
** Give "a little" memory when doing working set increment (WSINC ==
159)
**
** FORMAL PARAMETERS:
**
** none.
**
** RETURN VALUE:
**
** None
**
** SIDE EFFECTS:
**
** Values of system parameters WSINC, WSDEC, PFRATL, and PFRATH are
changed
```

```
.
**
** DESIGN:
**
** None
**
**
**
**—
*/

void turn_on_awsa()
{

#ifdef DEC_ARA
   SCII$GL_PΓRATL — 1;
   SCH$GL_PFRATH = 10;
   SCH$GL_WSDEC_PAGES = 257;
   SCH$GL_WSINC_PAGES = 400;
   SCH$GL_WSDEC_PAGELETS = 257*16;
   SCH$GL_WSINC_PAGELETS = 400*16;
#else
   SCH$GL_PFRATL = 1;
   SCH$GL_PFRATH = 50;
   SCH$GL_WSDEC = 67;
   SCH$GL_WSINC = 159;
#endif
}
```

MEMORY.OPT

```
TUNER:memory.obj
#ifdef VAX
sys$library:vaxcrtl/lib
sys$system:sys.stb/sel
#endif
```

Memory Checking

XRP.H

```
struct SYSTEM_PRIMITIVE_DATA
{
  unsigned int IOC_GQ_IRPIQ[2];
  unsigned int IOC_GL_IRPREM;
  unsigned int IOC_GL_IRPCNT;
  unsigned int IOC_GL_IRPMIN;
  unsigned int IOC_GL_XTRA1;
  unsigned int IOC_GQ_SRPIQ[2];
  unsigned int IOC_GL_SRPSIZE;
  unsigned int IOC_GL_SRPMIN;
  unsigned int IOC_GL_SRPSPLIT;
  unsigned int IOC_GL_SRPREM;
  unsigned int IOC_GL_SRPCNT;
  unsigned int IOC_GL_XTRA2;
  unsigned int IOC_GQ_LRPIQ[2];
  unsigned int IOC_GL_LRPSIZE;
  unsigned int IOC_GL_LRPMIN;
  unsigned int IOC_GL_LRPSPLIT;
  unsigned int IOC_GL_LRPREM;
  unsigned int IOC_GL_LRPCNT;
};

globalref struct SYSTEM_PRIMITIVE_DATA
  *EXE$AR_SYSTEM_PRIMITIVES_DATA;
```

CHECK_MEMORY.H

```
#ifndef CHECK_MEMORY_H
#define CHECK_MEMORY_H

struct FLAGS
{
#define check$c_COUNT  8

  variant_union
  {
      variant_struct
      {

#define check$k_cpu 0
#define check$k_mem 1
#define check$k_srp 2
#define check$k_irp 3
#define check$k_lrp 4
#define check$k_npg 5
#define check$k_pag 6
#define check$k_options 6

#define check$k_always 7

        unsigned check$v_cpu:1;
        unsigned check$v_mem:1;
        unsigned check$v_srp:1;
        unsigned check$v_irp:1;
        unsigned check$v_lrp:1;
        unsigned check$v_npg:1;
        unsigned check$v_pag:1;
        unsigned check$v_always:1;
      } check$r_flag_bits;
```

```
      unsigned int check$l_flags;
    }check$r_flag_overlay;

} check_mask;
char *label[check$c_COUNT] =
{"CPU", "MEM", "SRP", "IRP", "LRP", "NPG", "PAG", "ALW" };


#endif
```

CHECK_MEMORY.C

```
/*
**++
** FACILITY:  VMS_TOOLS
**
** Copyright (c) 1991 James W. Coburn
** Copyright (c) 1992 James W. Coburn
** Copyright (c) 1993 James W. Coburn
** Copyright (c) 1992 Professional Press Books.
** Copyright (c) 1993 Cardinal Business Media
** This program may be copied for noncommercial purposes. Use of this
** program for any other purpose without the express written consent
** of the publisher is prohibited.
**
** MODULE DESCRIPTION:
**
** This program checks pool usage and detects when the initial
** parameters are insufficient.
**
** This code has been tested on:
** OpenVMS VMS 5.5-2
**
**
** AUTHORS:
**
```

```
** Carl Braesicke (SWS ASC)
** Jim Coburn
**
** CREATION DATE:  June 1991
**
** DESIGN ISSUES:
**
**
**
**
** MODIFICATION HISTORY:
**
**
**—
*/


/*
**
** INCLUDE FILES
**
*/


#include <descrip.h>
#include <ctype.h>
#include <stdio.h>
#include <starlet.h>
#include <libdtdef.h>
#include <lib$routines.h>
#include <stdlib.h>
#include "memory:check_memory.h"


/*
```

```
**   Prototypes
*/


void print_trailer ( char *node_name );
void usage_error ( void );


main ( int argc, char *argv[] ) /* command line looks like: */
                /* $ check_memory -options */
                /* options: cmsilnpa =
cpu,mem,srp,irp,lrp,npg,pag,always */
{
  int i;
  char  *arg_flags;
  char  node_name[15];

/* turn all flags off initially */

  check_mask.check$l_flags = 0;

/* if only one arg, then default to full report */

  if ( argc <= 1 )
      check_mask.check$l_flags = (~(~0 << check$k_options ));
/* otherwise, there are two or more args, so parse them */
  else if ( argc > 2 ) /* too many args, confusion */
      usage_error ( );

  else
  {
      arg_flags = *++argv;   /* copy pointer */
      if ( arg_flags[0] != '-' || strlen ( arg_flags ) <= 1 )
      usage_error ( );    /* check for leading minus */
    else
    {
```

277

```
int arg_len;
arg_len = strlen ( arg_flags ) - 1;
for ( ; arg_len > 0; )
{
    switch ( _toupper( arg_flags[arg_len] ) )
    {
      case 'C':
          check_mask.check$v_cpu = 1;
          break;
      case 'M':
          check_mask.check$v_mem = 1;
          break;
      case 'S':
          check_mask.check$v_srp = 1;
          break;
      case 'I':
          check_mask.check$v_irp = 1;
          break;
      case 'L':
          check_mask.check$v_irp = 1;
          break;
      case 'N':
          check_mask.check$v_npg = 1;
          break;
      case 'P':
          check_mask.check$v_pag = 1;
          break;
      case 'A':
          check_mask.check$v_always = 1;
          break;
      default:
          usage_error ( );
          break;
```

```
            }           /* end case */
         arg_len--; /* consume argument a character at a time */
      }              /* end for */
    }                /* end else */
}                    /* end else */


/* if only flag on is ALWAYS, turn on rest */

  if ( check_mask.check$v_always == 1 &&
      ( (check_mask.check$l_flags & (~(~0 << check$k_options )) ) ) == 0
) )
        check_mask.check$l_flags |= (~(~0 << check$k_options ));

  get_node_name ( node_name );
  print_header ( node_name );
  print_memory_stats ();
  print_trailer ( node_name );
  define_memory_stats ();
}


print_header ( node_name )
char *node_name;
{
  char  date_time_s[18];
  int i;
  $DESCRIPTOR ( date_time, date_time_s );

  printf ( "%s", node_name );

  printf ( " Analysis for item(s) " );

  for ( i = 0 ; i < check$c_COUNT-2; i++ )
      if( ( check_mask.check$l_flags & (1 << i ) ) != 0 )
```

```
        printf ( ",%s", label[i] );
  printf ( " on " );
  lib$date_time ( &date_time );
  date_time_s[17] = '\0';
  printf ( "%s", date_time_s );
  printf ( ".\n" );
}


void print_trailer ( char *node_name )
{
  printf ( "End of analysis for " );
  printf ( "%s", node_name );
  printf ( ".\n" );
}


void usage_error ( void )
{
    printf ( "usage: check_memory [-cmsilnpa]\n" );
    exit ( 2 );
}
```

PRINT_MEMORY_STATS.C

```
/*
**
** INCLUDE FILES
**
*/


#include <descrip.h>
#include <ctype.h>
#include <stdio.h>
#include <starlet.h>
#include <libdtdef.h>
#include <lib$routines.h>
```

```
#include <stdlib.h>
#include <descrip.h>
#include "memory:check_memory.h"


#define INITIAL  0  /* offset to initial value */
#define CURRENT  1  /* offset to current value */
#define LINE_LEN 80

void print_memory_stats ( int flags[] )
{
  globalref  int  exe$gl_mchkerrs, exe$gl_memerrs;

  static $DESCRIPTOR( fao_format,
     "!7AS    Current:!8UL    Initial:!8UL    Shortage:!7UL" );
  static $DESCRIPTOR( fao_format_s,
        "!7AS    Current:!8UL" );
  static $DESCRIPTOR( cpu_s,  "   CPU:" );
  static $DESCRIPTOR( mem_s,  "   MEM:" );
  static $DESCRIPTOR( srp_s,  "   SRP:" );
  static $DESCRIPTOR( irp_s,  "   IRP:" );
  static $DESCRIPTOR( lrp_s,  "   LRP:" );
  static $DESCRIPTOR( npg_s,  "   NPG:" );

  int    srp[2], irp[2], lrp[2], npg[2]; /* holds current and initial
*/
  int    get_memory_stats ();
  short int i;
  int    report_line_len;

  char   report_line_buff[LINE_LEN];

  $DESCRIPTOR( report_line, report_line_buff );

  if ( check_mask.check$v_cpu )
```

281

```
      if ( exe$gl_mchkerrs != 0 || check_mask.check$v_always )
      {
        sys$fao ( &fao_format_s, &i, &report_line, &cpu_s,
            exe$gl_mchkerrs );
        report_line_buff[i] = '\0';
        printf ( "%s\n", report_line.dsc$a_pointer );
      }


  if ( check_mask.check$v_mem )
      if ( exe$gl_memerrs != 0 || check_mask.check$v_always )
      {
        sys$fao ( &fao_format_s, &i, &report_line, &mem_s,
            exe$gl_memerrs );
        report_line_buff[i] = '\0';
        printf ( "%s\n", report_line.dsc$a_pointer );
      }


  if ( check_mask.check$v_srp ||
      check_mask.check$v_irp ||
      check_mask.check$v_lrp ||
      check_mask.check$v_npg )
  {
    get_memory_stats ( srp, irp, lrp, npg );

      if ( check_mask.check$v_srp )
        if ( srp[CURRENT] != srp[INITIAL] || check_mask.check$v_always
)
        {
            sys$fao ( &fao_format, &i, &report_line, &srp_s,
              srp[CURRENT], srp[INITIAL], srp[CURRENT] - srp[INITIAL]
);
            report_line_buff[i] = '\0';
            printf ( "%s\n", report_line.dsc$a_pointer );
        }
```

```
    if ( check_mask.check$v_irp )
      if ( irp[CURRENT] != irp[INITIAL] || check_mask.check$v_always )
      {
          sys$fao ( &fao_format, &i, &report_line, &irp_s,
            irp[CURRENT], irp[INITIAL], irp[CURRENT] - irp[INITIAL]
);
          report_line_buff[i] = '\0';
          printf ( "%s\n", report_line.dsc$a_pointer );
      }


    if ( check_mask.check$v_lrp )
      if ( lrp[CURRENT] != lrp[INITIAL] || check_mask.check$v_always )
      {
          sys$fao ( &fao_format, &i, &report_line, &lrp_s,
            lrp[CURRENT], lrp[INITIAL], lrp[CURRENT] - lrp[INITIAL]
);
          report_line_buff[i] = '\0';
          printf ( "%s\n", report_line.dsc$a_pointer );
      }


    if ( check_mask.check$v_npg )
      if ( npg[CURRENT] != npg[INITIAL] || check_mask.check$v_always )
      {
          sys$fao ( &fao_format, &i, &report_line, &npg_s,
            npg[CURRENT], npg[INITIAL], npg[CURRENT] - npg[INITIAL]
);
          report_line_buff[i] = '\0';
          printf ( "%s\n", report_line.dsc$a_pointer );
      }


  }
}
```

GET_NODE_NAME.C

```
/*
**
** INCLUDE FILES
**
*/

#include <descrip.h>
#include <ctype.h>
#include <stdio.h>
#include <starlet.h>
#include <libdtdef.h>
#include <lib$routines.h>
#include <stdlib.h>

void get_node_name ( char *node_name )
{
    short    node_name_len;
    int      status;
    globalvalue    SYI$_NODENAME;

    struct
    {
        short buffer_length;
        short item_code;
        int   *node_name_adr;
        int   *node_name_len_adr;
        int   terminator_longword;
    } itmlst;

    itmlst.buffer_length = 15; /* return a node name of <= 15 chars */
    itmlst.item_code = SYI$_NODENAME;
    itmlst.node_name_adr = &node_name[0];
```

```
    itmlst.node_name_len_adr = &node_name_len;
    itmlst.terminator_longword = 0;


    status = sys$getsyiw ( 0, 0, 0, &itmlst, 0, 0, 0 );
    node_name[node_name_len] = '\0';


    return;
}
```

GET_MEMORY_STATS.C

```
#include <stdio.h>
#include <starlet.h>
#include <libdtdef.h>
#include <lib$routines.h>
#include <stdlib.h>
#include "memory:xrp.h"


void get_memory_stats ( int *srpcnt, int *irpcnt, int *lrpcnt, int
*npagedyn )
{
  int get_srpcnt_c ();
  int get_srpcnt_i ();
  int get_irpcnt_c ();
  int get_irpcnt_i ();
  int get_lrpcnt_c ();
  int get_lrpcnt_i ();
  int get_npaged_c ();
  int get_npaged_i ();


  *srpcnt++ = get_srpcnt_i ();
  *srpcnt = get_srpcnt_c ();
  *irpcnt++ = get_irpcnt_i ();
  *irpcnt = get_irpcnt_c ();
  *lrpcnt++ = get_lrpcnt_i ();
```

```
  *lrpcnt = get_lrpcnt_c ();
  *npagedyn++ = get_npaged_i ();
  *npagedyn = get_npaged_c ();

  return;
}

int get_srpcnt_i ( void )
{
  globalref int SGN$GL_SRPCNT;

  return SGN$GL_SRPCNT;
}

int get_srpcnt_c ( void )
{
  return EXE$AR_SYSTEM_PRIMITIVES_DATA->IOC_GL_SRPCNT;
}

int get_irpcnt_c ( void )
{
  return EXE$AR_SYSTEM_PRIMITIVES_DATA->IOC_GL_IRPCNT;
}

int get_irpcnt_i ( void )
{
  globalref int SGN$GL_IRPCNT;

  return SGN$GL_IRPCNT;
}

int get_lrpcnt_c ( void )
{
  return EXE$AR_SYSTEM_PRIMITIVES_DATA->IOC_GL_LRPCNT;
}
```

```
int get_lrpcnt_i ( void )
{
  globalref int SGN$GL_LRPCNT;

  return SGN$GL_LRPCNT;
}


int get_npaged_c ( void )
{
  globalref int MMG$GL_NPAGEDYN, MMG$GL_NPAGNEXT;

  return  MMG$GL_NPAGNEXT - MMG$GL_NPAGEDYN;
}


int get_npaged_i ( void )
{
  globalref int SGN$GL_NPAGEDYN;

  return  SGN$GL_NPAGEDYN;
}


int get_paged_c ( void )
{
  globalref int SGN$GL_PAGEDYN;

  return  SGN$GL_PAGEDYN;
}
int get_paged_i ( void )
{
  globalref int SGN$GL_PAGEDYN;

  return  SGN$GL_PAGEDYN;
}
```

DEFINE_MEMORY_STATS.C

```c
#include <stdio.h>
#include <starlet.h>
#include <libdtdef.h>
#include <lib$routines.h>
#include <stdlib.h>
#include <descrip.h>
#include "memory:check_memory"

#define    INITIAL  0   /* offset to initial value */
#define    CURRENT  1   /* offset to current value */
#define    LINE_LEN 80

define_memory_stats ( int flags[] )
{
  static $DESCRIPTOR( fao_format, "!8UL" );
  static $DESCRIPTOR( srp_s, "SRP_NEEDED" );
  static $DESCRIPTOR( irp_s, "IRP_NEEDED" );
  static $DESCRIPTOR( lrp_s, "LRP_NEEDED" );
  static $DESCRIPTOR( npg_s, "NPG_NEEDED" );

  int  srp[2], irp[2], lrp[2], npg[2]; /* holds current and initial
*/
  int  get_memory_stats (), temp;
  short int i;
  int  report_line_len;

  char report_line_buff[LINE_LEN];

  $DESCRIPTOR( report_line, report_line_buff );

  if ( check_mask.check$v_srp ||
      check_mask.check$v_irp ||
      check_mask.check$v_lrp ||
```

```
            check_mask.check$v_npg )
  {
    get_memory_stats ( srp, irp, lrp, npg );


      if ( check_mask.check$v_srp )
        if ( srp[CURRENT] != srp[INITIAL] || check_mask.check$v_always
)
          {
            sys$fao ( &fao_format, &i, &report_line, srp[CURRENT] -
srp[INITIAL] );
            report_line_buff[i] = '\0';
            report_line.dsc$w_length = i;
            lib$set_symbol (
              &srp_s,
              &report_line,
              &2);
    }
  if ( check_mask.check$v_irp )
    if ( irp[CURRENT] != irp[INITIAL] || check_mask.check$v_always )
    {
        sys$fao ( &fao_format, &i, &report_line, irp[CURRENT] -
irp[INITIAL] );
            report_line_buff[i] = '\0';
            report_line.dsc$w_length = i;
            lib$set_symbol (
              &irp_s,
              &report_line,
              &2);
    }
  if ( check_mask.check$v_lrp )
    if ( lrp[CURRENT] != lrp[INITIAL] || check_mask.check$v_always )
    {
      sys$fao ( &fao_format, &i, &report_line, lrp[CURRENT] -
lrp[INITIAL] );
```

```
            report_line_buff[i] = '\0';

            report_line.dsc$w_length = i;

            lib$set_symbol (

              &srp_s,

              &report_line,

              &2);

        }

    if ( check_mask.check$v_npg )

      if ( npg[CURRENT] != npg[INITIAL] || check_mask.check$v_always )

      {

        sys$fao ( &fao_format, &i, &report_line, npg[CURRENT] -
npg[INITIAL] );

            report_line_buff[i] = '\0';

            report_line.dsc$w_length = i;

            lib$set_symbol (

              &srp_s,

              &report_line,

              &2);

        }


      }

  }
```

CHECK_MEMORY.LNK_DEF

```
memory:check_memory
memory:print_memory_stats
memory:get_node_name
memory:get_memory_stats
memory:define_memory_stats
#ifdef VAX
sys$share:vaxcrtl/lib
sys$system:sys.stb/sel
#endif
```

CHECK_MEMORY OUTPUT SCREENS

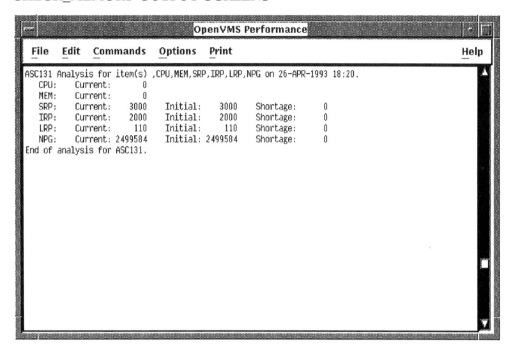

MSCP Information Program

DSRVDEF.H

```
#ifndef DSRVDEF_H
#define DSRVDEF_H
/*
** To update this for future releases of OpenVMS:
** Get library copy — lib/ext=$DSRVDEF sys$share:lib.mlb
** Insure offsets match the offsets in this file.
*/

#pragma nostandard

#ifdef DEC_ARA
#pragma member_alignment __save
#pragma nomember_alignment
#endif

/*
**+
** DSRV Definitions
**
** This module defines the main data structure of the MSCP
** server. This structure contains the values specified in
** the startup qualifiers when the server was loaded, the
** UQB vector table, and statistics that are kept for server
** performance measurements.
**
** CHECKED for  OpenVMS VAX 5.5-2
** CHECKED for  OpenVMS AXP 1.5
**-
*/
#define DSRV$M_LOG_ENABLD 0x1
#define DSRV$M_LOG_PRESENT 0x2
#define DSRV$M_PKT_LOGGED 0x4
#define DSRV$M_PKT_LOST 0x8
```

```
#define DSRV$M_LBSTEP1 0x10
#define DSRV$M_LBSTEP2 0x20
#define DSRV$M_LBEVENT 0x40
#define DSRV$M_HULB_DEL 0x80
#define DSRV$M_MON_ACTIVE 0x100
#define DSRV$M_LB_REQ 0x200
#define DSRV$M_CONFIG_WAIT 0x400
#define DSRV$C_LENGTH 1900
#define DSRV$K_LENGTH 1900
#define DSRV$K_AR_ADD 2                        /* Action routine code */
struct DSRVDEF {
  unsigned int DSRV$L_FLINK;                   /* Field maintained for */
  unsigned int DSRV$L_BLINK;                   /*  compatability */
  unsigned short int DSRV$W_SIZE;              /* Structure size in bytes*/
  unsigned char DSRV$B_TYPE;                   /* MSCP type structure */
  unsigned char DSRV$B_SUBTYPE;                /*  with a DSRV subtype (1) */
  variant_union {
    unsigned short int DSRV$W_STATE;    /* Current state of the server */
    variant_struct {
      unsigned DSRV$V_LOG_ENABLD : 1; /* Logging is enabled */
      unsigned DSRV$V_LOG_PRESENT : 1; /* Logging code is present */
      unsigned DSRV$V_PKT_LOGGED : 1; /* A packet has been logged */
      unsigned DSRV$V_PKT_LOST : 1;   /* One or more packets over- */
                                      /* written since last read */
      unsigned DSRV$V_LBSTEP1 : 1;    /* Load balancing step1 active */
      unsigned DSRV$V_LBSTEP2 : 1;    /* Load balancing step2 active */
      unsigned DSRV$V_LBEVENT : 1;    /* An event of interest to LB has */
                                      /* occured while STEP1 was active */
      unsigned DSRV$V_HULB_DEL : 1;   /* One or more HULBs to be deleted */
      unsigned DSRV$V_MON_ACTIVE : 1; /* The load monitor thread is active */
      unsigned DSRV$V_LB_REQ : 1; /* A load balance request has been sent */
      unsigned DSRV$V_CONFIG_WAIT : 1;
/* Waiting for STACONFIG to complete */
      unsigned DSRV$V_FILL_2 : 5;
      } DSRV$R_FILL_1;
    } DSRV$R_FILL_0;
  unsigned short int DSRV$W_BUFWAIT;    /* I/Os that had to wait */
  unsigned int DSRV$L_LOG_BUF_START;    /* Address of start of buffer */
  unsigned int DSRV$L_LOG_BUF_END;      /* Address of end of buffer */
  unsigned int DSRV$L_NEXT_READ;        /* Adrs of next packet to read */
  unsigned int DSRV$L_NEXT_WRITE;       /* Adrs of next packet to write */
  unsigned short int DSRV$W_INC_LOLIM;  /* Low unit number to log */
  unsigned short int DSRV$W_INC_HILIM;  /* High unit number to log */
  unsigned short int DSRV$W_EXC_LOLIM;  /* Low unit number not to log */
```

294

```
  unsigned short int DSRV$W_EXC_HILIM; /* High unit number not to log */
  unsigned int DSRV$L_SRVBUF;          /* Address of preallocated pool */
  unsigned int DSRV$L_FREE_LIST;       /* Pointer to head of free pool */
  unsigned int DSRV$L_AVAIL;           /* Sum of bytes available in buffer */
  unsigned int DSRV$L_BUFFER_MIN;      /* Min xfer size based on buffer */
  unsigned int DSRV$L_SPLITXFER;       /* Fragmented I/O count */
  variant_struct  {                    /* Info returned in GCI cmd */
    unsigned short int DSRV$W_VERSION; /* Server software version */
    unsigned short int DSRV$W_CFLAGS;  /* Controller flags */
    unsigned short int DSRV$W_CTIMO;   /* Controller timeout */
    unsigned short int DSRV$w_reserved;/* Reserved for alignment */
    } DSRV$R_CTRL_INFO;
  unsigned int DSRV$Q_CTRL_ID [2];     /* Unique MSCP device identifier */
  unsigned int DSRV$L_MEMW_TOT;        /* Number of I/Os that had to wait */
  unsigned short int DSRV$W_MEMW_CNT;  /* Requests in memory wait queue */
  unsigned short int DSRV$W_MEMW_MAX;  /* Most requests ever in MEMWAIT */
  unsigned int DSRV$L_MEMW_FL;         /* Queue listhead for requests */
  unsigned int DSRV$L_MEMW_BL;         /*  in memory wait state */
  unsigned short int DSRV$W_NUM_HOST;  /* Count of hosts being served */
  unsigned short int DSRV$W_NUM_UNIT;  /* Count of disks being served */
  unsigned int DSRV$L_HQB_FL;          /* Host queue block list head */
  unsigned int DSRV$L_HQB_BL;          /*                            */
  unsigned int DSRV$L_UQB_FL;          /* Unit queue block list head */
  unsigned int DSRV$L_UQB_BL;          /*                            */
/*                                                                    */
/* new fields should be added here, after the UQB linkages            */
/*                                                                    */
/*                                                                    */
/* Server Load Balancing fields                                       */
/*                                                                    */
/* The following fields contain working information and statistics    */
/* for the server load balancing function. Load balancing status bits*/
/* are defined in DSRV$STATE above. Time fields are in EXE$GL_ABSTIM  */
/* format.                                                            */
/*                                                                    */
  unsigned short int DSRV$W_LOAD_AVAIL; /* Current load available */
  unsigned short int DSRV$W_LOAD_CAPACITY; /* Server load capacity */
  unsigned short int DSRV$W_LBLOAD;     /* Target load for LB request */
  unsigned short int DSRV$W_LBRESP;     /* Load available from other server */
  unsigned short int DSRV$W_LM_LOAD1;   /* previous interval load 1 */
  unsigned short int DSRV$W_LM_LOAD2;   /* previous interval load 2 */
  unsigned short int DSRV$W_LM_LOAD3;   /* previous interval load 3 */
  unsigned short int DSRV$W_LM_LOAD4;   /* previous interval load 4 */
```

```
  unsigned short int DSRV$W_LBINIT_CNT;/* Count of LB requests we have sent */
  unsigned short int DSRV$W_LBFAIL_CNT; /* Count of LB requests that failed */
  unsigned short int DSRV$W_LBREQ_CNT;
/* Count of LB requests from other servers */
  unsigned short int DSRV$W_LBRESP_CNT;
/* Count of LB requests we to which we responded */
  unsigned int DSRV$L_LBREQ_TIME;      /* Time last LB request was sent */
  unsigned int DSRV$L_LBMON_TIME;      /* Time of last LB monitor pass */
  unsigned int DSRV$L_LM_FKB;          /* Address of load monitor thread FKB */
  unsigned int DSRV$L_LB_FKB;          /* Address of load balance thread FKB */
  unsigned short int DSRV$W_LM_INTERVAL; /* Load monitoring interval */
  unsigned char DSRV$B_LB_COUNT1;      /* Counter for load balancing thread */
  unsigned char DSRV$B_LB_COUNT2;      /* Counter for load balancing thread */
  unsigned int DSRV$L_HULB_FL;         /* HULB queue listhead        */
  unsigned int DSRV$L_HULB_BL;         /*                            */
  unsigned char DSRV$B_HOSTS [32];     /* Bit array of hosts served */
  unsigned int DSRV$L_UNITS [256];     /* Table of UQB addresses     */
/*                                                                  */
/* Statistics gathering fields                                      */
/*                                                                  */
/* Two tables are maintained below. The first table is made up of the  */
/* frequency count for each of the opcodes received since the server   */
/* was loaded. The opcode is used as an index into the table to its own */
/* frequency count (the zeroeth element contains a total count). The   */
/* second table is made up of the frequency counters for all the      */
/* different sized block transfers. For this table, the size of the    */
/* transfer is the index into the table.                             */
/*                                                                  */
  variant_struct {                     /* Op-code counters        */
    unsigned int DSRV$L_OPCOUNT;       /* Total operations count */
    unsigned int DSRV$L_ABORT_CNT;     /*  - 1 -                 */
    unsigned int DSRV$L_GET_CMD_CNT;   /*  - 2 -                 */
    unsigned int DSRV$L_GET_UNT_CNT;   /*  - 3 -                 */
    unsigned int DSRV$L_SET_CON_CNT;   /*  - 4 -                 */
    unsigned int DSRV$l_reserved;      /*  - 5 -                 */
    unsigned short int DSRV$l_reserved1; /*  - 6 -                 */
    unsigned int DSRV$l_reserved2;     /*  - 7 -                 */
    unsigned int DSRV$L_AVAIL_CNT;     /*  - 8 -                 */
    unsigned int DSRV$L_ONLIN_CNT;     /*  - 9 -                 */
    unsigned int DSRV$L_SET_UNT_CNT;   /*  - 10 -                */
    unsigned int DSRV$L_DET_ACC_CNT;   /*  - 11 -                */
    unsigned int DSRV$l_reserved3;     /*  - 12 -                */
    unsigned int DSRV$l_reserved4;     /*  - 13 -                */
    unsigned int DSRV$l_reserved5;     /*  - 14 -                */
```

```
        unsigned int DSRV$l_reserved6;    /*  - 15 -            */
        unsigned int DSRV$L_ACCES_CNT;    /*  - 16 -            */
        unsigned int DSRV$L_CMP_CON_CNT;  /*  - 17 -            */
        unsigned int DSRV$L_ERASE_CNT;    /*  - 18 -            */
        unsigned int DSRV$L_FLUSH_CNT;    /*  - 19 -            */
        unsigned int DSRV$L_REPLC_CNT;    /*  - 20 -            */
        unsigned int DSRV$l_reserved7;    /*  - 21 -            */
        unsigned int DSRV$l_reserved8;    /*  - 22 -            */
        unsigned int DSRV$l_reserved9;    /*  - 23 -            */
        unsigned int DSRV$l_reserved10;   /*  - 24 -            */
        unsigned int DSRV$l_reserved11;   /*  - 25 -            */
        unsigned int DSRV$l_reserved12;   /*  - 26 -            */
        unsigned int DSRV$l_reserved13;   /*  - 27 -            */
        unsigned int DSRV$l_reserved14;   /*  - 28 -            */
        unsigned int DSRV$l_reserved15;   /*  - 29 -            */
        unsigned int DSRV$l_reserved16;   /*  - 30 -            */
        unsigned int DSRV$l_reserved17;   /*  - 31 -            */
        unsigned int DSRV$L_CMP_HST_CNT;  /*  - 32 -            */
        unsigned int DSRV$L_READ_CNT;     /*  - 33 -            */
        unsigned int DSRV$L_WRITE_CNT;    /*  - 34 -            */
        unsigned int DSRV$l_reserved18;   /*  - 35 -            */
        unsigned int DSRV$l_reserved19;   /*  - 36 -            */
        unsigned int DSRV$l_reserved20;   /*  - 37 -            */
        unsigned int DSRV$l_reserved21;   /*  - 38 -            */
        unsigned int DSRV$l_reserved22;   /*  - 39 -            */
#ifndef DEC_ARA
        unsigned int DSRV$l_reserved23;
        unsigned int DSRV$l_reserved24;
        unsigned int DSRV$l_reserved25;
        unsigned int DSRV$l_reserved26;
        unsigned int DSRV$l_reserved27;
        unsigned int DSRV$l_reserved28;
        unsigned int DSRV$l_reserved29;
        unsigned int DSRV$l_reserved30;
        unsigned int DSRV$l_reserved31;
        unsigned int DSRV$l_reserved32;
#endif
        } DSRV$R_OPCODE_CNTRS;
  unsigned int DSRV$L_VCFAIL_CNT;     /* Count of VC failures */
  unsigned int DSRV$L_BLKCOUNT [129]; /* Counters for block xfer reqs */
  } ;

#pragma standard
```

```
#ifdef DEC_ARA
#pragma member_alignment __restore
#endif

#endif
```

UQBDEF.H

```
#ifndef UQBDEF_H
#define UQBDEF_H
/*
** To update this for future releases of OpenVMS:
** Get library copy - lib/ext=$UQBDEF sys$share:lib.mlb
** Insure offsets match the offsets in this file.
*/

#pragma nostandard

#ifdef DEC_ARA
#pragma member_alignment __save
#pragma nomember_alignment
#endif

/*+
** UQB  (Unit Queue Block)  MSCP Server
**
** This data structure has all the information pertaining to a unit that
** is currently being served.
**
*/
#define UQB$M_SEQ 0x1
#define UQB$M_WRTPH 0x2
#define UQB$M_WRTPS 0x4
#define UQB$M_C 0x1F
#define UQB$M_D1 0x3E0
#define UQB$M_D0 0x7C00
#define UQB$C_LENGTH 112
#define UQB$K_LENGTH 112
/* Unit state definitions                                          */
#define UQB$K_ST_ONLINE 2              /*  Unit is online to some host */
#define UQB$K_ST_OFFLINE 3             /*  Unit is offline */
#define UQB$K_ST_AVAILABLE 4          /*  Unit is available */
struct UQBDEF {
  unsigned int UQB$L_FLINK;           /* Used to link together all */
```

```
unsigned int UQB$L_BLINK;           .   /*   UQBs being served */
unsigned short int UQB$W_SIZE;          /* Structure size in bytes */
unsigned char UQB$B_TYPE;               /* MSCP type structure */
unsigned char UQB$B_SUBTYPE;            /*  with a UQB subtype      (5) */
unsigned short int UQB$W_STATE;         /* Current state of this unit */
variant_union {
  unsigned short int UQB$W_FLAGS;       /* Unit usage */
  variant_struct {
    unsigned UQB$V_SEQ : 1;      /* Sequential command executing */
    unsigned UQB$V_WRTPH : 1;    /* Unit is writelocked */
    unsigned UQB$V_WRTPS : 1;    /* Unit was mounted /NOWRITE */
    unsigned UQB$V_FILL_6 : 5;
    } UQB$R_FILL_1;
  } UQB$R_FILL_0;
unsigned short int UQB$W_OLD_UNIT;    /* "Old Style" unit number */
unsigned short int UQB$W_CURRENT;     /* Commands active on this unit */
unsigned short int UQB$W_MULT_UNIT;   /* This information is set up */
unsigned short int UQB$W_UNIT_FLAGS;  /*  in ADDUNIT when the device */
variant_union {
  unsigned int UQB$Q_UNIT_ID [2];     /*  is set /SERVED. */
  variant_struct {
    unsigned int UQB$L_ALLOCLS;        /* The unit identifier is made up */
    unsigned short int UQB$W_UNIT;     /*  of the allocation class, the */
    variant_union {
      unsigned short int UQB$W_DEVNAME; /*                         */
      variant_struct {
        unsigned UQB$V_C : 5;          /* UCB unit number, the controller */
        unsigned UQB$V_D1 : 5;         /*  letter, and the D1 D0 fields */
        unsigned UQB$V_D0 : 5;         /*  from the media ID field */
        unsigned UQB$V_FILL_7 : 1;
        } UQB$R_FILL_5;
      } UQB$R_FILL_4;
    } UQB$R_FILL_3;
  } UQB$R_FILL_2;
unsigned int UQB$l_reserved;          /*                         */
unsigned int UQB$L_UCB;               /* UCB address for this unit */
unsigned short int UQB$W_NUM_QUE;     /* Host requests pending */
unsigned short int UQB$W_MAX_QUE;     /* Most requests ever pending */
unsigned int UQB$L_BLOCKED_FL;        /* List head for HRBs pending */
unsigned int UQB$L_BLOCKED_BL;        /*  sequential cmd completion */
unsigned char UQB$B_ONLINE [32];      /* Array of hosts with unit online */
unsigned int UQB$L_EXTRA_IO;          /* Splinter requests */
unsigned int UQB$L_IOCNT;             /* Server contribution to total */
unsigned short int UQB$W_QLEN;        /* Server queue length for unit */
```

```
   unsigned short int UQB$W_SLUN;        /* Server local unit number */
/* max chars in Cluster unique                                                */
/* device name ( dependency in                                                */
/* PEDRIVER's PEM_DEF.SDL)                                                     */
   unsigned char UQB$B_UNIQUE_DNAME_CNT; /* .ASCIC string with             */
   char UQB$T_UNIQUE_DNAME [15];          /*  Cluster unique name for disk */
/* unit (obtained VIA GETDVI                                                  */
/* ALLDEVNAM item)                                                            */
/* Align to a quadword                                                        */
   } ;


#ifdef DEC_ARA
#pragma member_alignment __restore
#endif

#pragma standard
#endif
```

MSCP_INFO.C

```
/*
**++
** FACILITY:  OpenVMS Tools
**
** Copyright (c) 1993 James W. Coburn
** Copyright (c) 1993 Cardinal Business Media
** This program may be copied for noncommercial purposes. Use of this
** program for any other purpose without the express written consent
** of the publisher is prohibited.
**
** MODULE DESCRIPTION:
**
** This module implements a program that dumps out the entire MSCP
** data base for performance analysis.
**
** AUTHORS:
**
** Jim Coburn
**
** CREATION DATE:  May, 1993
**
** DESIGN ISSUES:
**
** This module requires CMEXEC privs for OpenVMS VAX and OpenVMS
** AXP.  This could be implemented on OpenVMS AXP without privs,
```

300

```
** but to keep this a single program we will do it this way.
**
**
** MODIFICATION HISTORY:
**
** {@tbs@}...
**-
*/

/*
**
** INCLUDE FILES
**
*/

#include <descrip.h>
#include <string.h>
#include <stdio.h>
#include <stdio.h>
#include <starlet.h>
#include <libdtdef.h>
#include <lib$routines.h>
#include <stdlib.h>

#include <mscp/dsrvdef.h>
#include <mscp/uqbdef.h>

#ifdef DEC_ARA
extern struct DSRVDEF *SCS$GL_MSCP;
#else
globalref struct DSRVDEF *SCS$GL_MSCP;
#endif

struct DSRVDEF *SCS$GL_MSCP_LOCAL;
struct UQBDEF *device;
unsigned int ExtraIOs;
/*
**++
** FUNCTIONAL DESCRIPTION:
**
** This is the main line driver program. It calls the procedure that
** runs in executive mode and then dumps out the MSCP data for the
** user.
**
** FORMAL PARAMETERS:
```

```
**
** Normal, standard C main line interface.
**
** RETURN VALUE:
**
** None
**
** SIDE EFFECTS:
**
** None
**
** DESIGN:
**
** Change mode to Executive (CMEXEC) privilege is needed to access the
** data structures in the system executive.
**
**—
*/
main (int argc, char *argv[], char *envp[])
{
  int i;
  int get_data( );

/*
** Allocate local space for temp copy of system data that is protected by
** an Executive read access
*/
  SCS$GL_MSCP_LOCAL = (struct DSRVDEF *) calloc( (size_t) 1,
      (size_t) sizeof( struct DSRVDEF ) );

/*
** Call routine from Executive mode.
*/
  sys$cmexec ( get_data, 0);

/*
** Now that we have a copy of the data that we can access format it for
** general use.
*/

  if( SCS$GL_MSCP_LOCAL->DSRV$W_LOAD_AVAIL == 65535 )
  {
    printf(
          " Serving only Local Disk.  No Load balance data available \n" );
```

```
      SCS$GL_MSCP_LOCAL->DSRV$L_GET_UNT_CNT = 0;
      SCS$GL_MSCP_LOCAL->DSRV$L_SET_CON_CNT = 0;
   }
   else
   {
        printf( " Load is calculated as number of I/O operations per
Second\n");
        printf( " Collection interval is %d seconds\n\n",
            SCS$GL_MSCP_LOCAL->DSRV$W_LM_INTERVAL);
     printf( " Load Available is         %10.10d \n",
            SCS$GL_MSCP_LOCAL->DSRV$W_LOAD_AVAIL);
     printf( " Load Capacity is          %10.10d \n",
            SCS$GL_MSCP_LOCAL->DSRV$W_LOAD_CAPACITY);
     printf( " Load in last interval was  %10.10d \n",
            SCS$GL_MSCP_LOCAL->DSRV$W_LM_LOAD1);
     printf( " Load in interval -1 was    %10.10d \n",
            SCS$GL_MSCP_LOCAL->DSRV$W_LM_LOAD2);
     printf( " Load in interval -2 was    %10.10d \n",
            SCS$GL_MSCP_LOCAL->DSRV$W_LM_LOAD3);
     printf( " Load in interval -3 was    %10.10d \n\n",
            SCS$GL_MSCP_LOCAL->DSRV$W_LM_LOAD4);
     }
     printf( " I/Os that had to wait      %10.10d \n",
            SCS$GL_MSCP_LOCAL->DSRV$W_BUFWAIT);
     printf( " I/Os that had extra I/Os   %10.10d \n",
            ExtraIOs);
     printf( " I/Os that were split       %10.10d \n",
            SCS$GL_MSCP_LOCAL->DSRV$L_SPLITXFER);

/*
**   Complete data breakout
*/

     printf( "\n Total operations count is   %10.10d\n",
            SCS$GL_MSCP_LOCAL->DSRV$L_OPCOUNT );
     printf( " Read count is               %10.10d\n",
            SCS$GL_MSCP_LOCAL->DSRV$L_READ_CNT );
     printf( " Write count is              %10.10d\n",
            SCS$GL_MSCP_LOCAL->DSRV$L_WRITE_CNT );

     printf( " Abort Count is              %10.10d\n",
            SCS$GL_MSCP_LOCAL->DSRV$L_ABORT_CNT);
     printf( " Get Command Status Count is  %10.10d\n",
            SCS$GL_MSCP_LOCAL->DSRV$L_GET_CMD_CNT);
```

```
    printf( " Get Unit Status Count is      %10.10d\n",
        SCS$GL_MSCP_LOCAL->DSRV$L_GET_UNT_CNT);
    printf( " Set Controller Char Count is  %10.10d\n",
        SCS$GL_MSCP_LOCAL->DSRV$L_SET_CON_CNT);
    printf( " Available Count is            %10.10d\n",
        SCS$GL_MSCP_LOCAL->DSRV$L_AVAIL_CNT);
    printf( " Online Count is               %10.10d\n",
        SCS$GL_MSCP_LOCAL->DSRV$L_ONLIN_CNT);
    printf( " Set Unit Char                 %10.10d\n",
        SCS$GL_MSCP_LOCAL->DSRV$L_SET_UNT_CNT);
    printf( " Determine Access Path Count   %10.10d\n",
        SCS$GL_MSCP_LOCAL->DSRV$L_DET_ACC_CNT);
    printf( " Access Data Count             %10.10d\n",
        SCS$GL_MSCP_LOCAL->DSRV$L_ACCES_CNT);
  printf( " Compare controller data Count %10.10d\n",
        SCS$GL_MSCP_LOCAL->DSRV$L_CMP_CON_CNT);
    printf( " Erase data Count              %10.10d\n",
        SCS$GL_MSCP_LOCAL->DSRV$L_ERASE_CNT);
    printf( " Flush host buffers Count      %10.10d\n",
        SCS$GL_MSCP_LOCAL->DSRV$L_FLUSH_CNT);
    printf( " Replace data Count            %10.10d\n",
        SCS$GL_MSCP_LOCAL->DSRV$L_REPLC_CNT);
    printf( " Compare host data Count       %10.10d\n",
        SCS$GL_MSCP_LOCAL->DSRV$L_CMP_HST_CNT);

    printf( "\n\n\n Blocks per I/O \t\t\t\tCounts\n");
    printf( "———— \t\t————————————\n");
    for( i = 0; i < 128; i += 4)
    {
       printf( " %2.2d - %2.2d\t\t\t %10.10d %10.10d %10.10d %10.10d \n", i,
i+3,
        SCS$GL_MSCP_LOCAL->DSRV$L_BLKCOUNT[ i ],
        SCS$GL_MSCP_LOCAL->DSRV$L_BLKCOUNT[ i+1 ],
        SCS$GL_MSCP_LOCAL->DSRV$L_BLKCOUNT[ i+2 ],
        SCS$GL_MSCP_LOCAL->DSRV$L_BLKCOUNT[ i+3 ] );


    }
    printf( "\nI/O Forced to Split due to size >= 128 blocks %10.10d\n",
        SCS$GL_MSCP_LOCAL->DSRV$L_BLKCOUNT[ 127 ] );


}


/*
**++
```

```
**   FUNCTIONAL DESCRIPTION:
**
** The routine copies the MSCP data structure from system protected
** area to a local user area.  Also the UQB structures are walked to
** get the number of Extra I/Os due to MSCP service.
**
** FORMAL PARAMETERS:
**
** None.
**
** RETURN VALUE:
**
** Always return success.
**
** SIDE EFFECTS:
**
** Global value of ExtraIOs is set.
**
** DESIGN:
**
** For more info check out the listing for MSCP and Monitor.
**
**—
*/
int get_data( )
{

/*
** Set no extra ios.
*/
  ExtraIOs = 0;

  *SCS$GL_MSCP_LOCAL = *SCS$GL_MSCP;
  device = ( struct UQBDEF *) SCS$GL_MSCP->DSRV$L_UQB_FL;
  do
  {
      ExtraIOs += device->UQB$L_EXTRA_IO;
      device = (struct UQBDEF * )device->UQB$L_FLINK;
  } while ( device != ( struct UQBDEF *) SCS$GL_MSCP->DSRV$L_UQB_FL );
  return 1;
}
```

MSCP_INFO.LNK_DEF

```
MSCP:mscp_info.obj
#ifdef VAX
sys$share:vaxcrtl/lib
sys$system:sys.stb/sel
#endif
```

MSCP_INFO OUTPUT SCREENS

Since the output is so large, it is broken out into two screens.

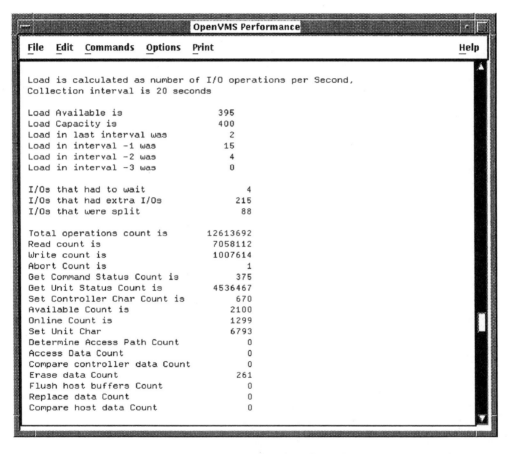

Figure J-1. MSCP Info Listing (Part 1)

```
┌─────────────────────────────────────────────────────────────────────────┐
│ ▭                        OpenVMS Performance                         ◄ ▯  │
├─────────────────────────────────────────────────────────────────────────┤
│  File   Edit   Commands   Options   Print                          Help   │
├─────────────────────────────────────────────────────────────────────────┤
│  Blocks per I/O                              Counts                      ▲ │
│  ---------------              ------------------------------------------   │
│    0 -   3                           0   3722521     552165     507192     │
│    4 -   7                      397593    480063     707308      77934     │
│    8 -  11                      314632     77434     103685      49240     │
│   12 -  15                       59404     53298      30900      53962     │
│   16 -  19                      432024     10695      10215       8760     │
│   20 -  23                        8893      8171       6955       8022     │
│   24 -  27                       10678      6911       8474       5156     │
│   28 -  31                        8616      5369       7194       7873     │
│   32 -  35                       46181      3523       3957       3725     │
│   36 -  39                        4063      5642       3862       4916     │
│   40 -  43                        5496      3856       3756       2730     │
│   44 -  47                        5615      3429       4794       3033     │
│   48 -  51                        9532      2253       2548       2270     │
│   52 -  55                        5362      2084       2624       2683     │
│   56 -  59                        3471      2162       2888       2409     │
│   60 -  63                        3109      2725      17381       2736     │
│   64 -  67                       62863      1398        846        743     │
│   68 -  71                         833      1128        967        990     │
│   72 -  75                        2245      1987       3055      13302     │
│   76 -  79                         106       117        474        399     │
│   80 -  83                        1626       124        100       1186     │
│   84 -  87                          97      2028        164         35     │
│   88 -  91                         180        66        216        131     │
│   92 -  95                          72       229        738        232     │
│   96 -  99                        1449        26        126          9     │
│  100 - 103                       27377        69         40        205     │
│  104 - 107                         268       102          2          2     │
│  108 - 111                         122       241        169        249     │
│  112 - 115                        4084        77          4        160     │
│  116 - 119                          28        33         77         82     │
│  120 - 123                         986        28         10       1325     │
│  124 - 127                         665      2040        319      10513     │
│                                                                           │
│  I/O Forced to Split due to size >= 128 blocks      10513               ▼ │
└─────────────────────────────────────────────────────────────────────────┘
```

Figure J-2. MSCP Info Listing (Part 2)

Monitor System Program

PROGRAM OVERVIEW

There are several programs included in this appendix that can be used to collect the data needed to analyze the performance of your system. The next several sections will explain how to use these programs to collect and analyze performance data.

PROGRAM OPERATION

The program in this appendix is a real-time data collection utility that must be run on each node for which you want to collect data. The program accesses various system performance database locations and structures. Using a user-specified time interval, all data requested is sampled and written to a binary file. The program is started using the commands:

```
$!  Uncomment Line if you want to collect that data set.
$! COLLECTMSCP = "TRUE"
$! COLLECTPAGE
$! COLLECTDISK
$! COLLECTSCS
$! COLLECTMISC
$! COLLECPMS
$ DELTATIME="0-00:00:10.00"  ! 10 second collection interval
$ Set Process/priv=all
$ Set Process/prior=17
$ Run  MONITOR.EXE
```

For most cases, a delta-time of 10 seconds is a good value. The binary file for output is created by opening the file specified by the logical MONITOR$DATA. If MONITOR$DATA is not defined, a file is created in the current directory with the file name MONITOR$DATA. You must have at least CMKRNL privileges for this program to execute correctly. Currently, the program is stopped using the command:

```
$ stop /id = xxxxxxxx
```

Warning: If you use the program with the sizing parameters set to large values, there will be a nontrivial I/O and disk space load due to running this program. Currently, these sizing parameters are set to 50 in the code lines:

```
#define MAXDISKS 50
#define MAXSCS 50
#define MAXPROCESS 50
```

This program was used to collect most of the data for the charts and plots included in this book.

AXP_PHDDEF.H

```
#ifndef AXP_PHDDEF_H
#define AXP_PHDDEF_H
/*
** To update this for future releases of OpenVMS:
** Get library copy — lib/ext=$PHDDEF sys$share:lib.mlb
** Insure offsets match the offsets in this file.
*/
#pragma nostandard
#pragma member_alignment __save
#pragma nomember_alignment
/*   */
/* Process Header Definitions.  The process header contains the swappable  */
/* scheduler and memory management data bases for a process in the balance */
/* set. */
/*   */
#define PHD$M_ASTEN 0xF
#define PHD$M_ASTSR 0xF0
#define PHD$M_ASTEN_KEN 0x1
#define PHD$M_ASTEN_EEN 0x2
#define PHD$M_ASTEN_SEN 0x4
#define PHD$M_ASTEN_UEN 0x8
#define PHD$M_ASTSR_KPD 0x10
#define PHD$M_ASTSR_EPD 0x20
#define PHD$M_ASTSR_SPD 0x40
#define PHD$M_ASTSR_UPD 0x80
#define PHD$M_FEN 0x1
#define PHD$M_PME 0x4000000000000000
#define PHD$M_DATFX 0x8000000000000000
#define PHD$C_HWPCBLEN 128 /* Length of HWPCB  */
#define PHD$K_HWPCBLEN 128 /* Length of HWPCB  */
/*   */
#define PHD$C_FPR_COUNT 32 /* Count of saved FP registers  */
#define PHD$K_FPR_COUNT 32 /* Count of saved FP registers  */
#define PHD$C_PHDPAGCTX 8  /* Size of context for PHD pages  */
#define PHD$M_PFMFLG 0x1
```

```
#define PHD$M_DALCSTX 0x2
#define PHD$M_WSPEAKCHK 0x4
#define PHD$M_NOACCVIO 0x8
#define PHD$M_IWSPEAKCK 0x10
#define PHD$M_IMGDMP 0x20
#define PHD$M_NO_WS_CHNG 0x40
#define PHD$M_PGFLACC 0x80
#define PHD$M_LOCK_HEADER 0x100
#define PHD$M_SW_FEN 0x1
#define PHD$M_AST_PENDING 0x80000000
#define PHD$K_LENGTH 760    /* Length of fixed part of process header  */
#define PHD$C_LENGTH 760    /* Length of fixed part of the process header  */
struct PHDDEF {
  unsigned int PHD$Q_PRIVMSK [2]; /* Privilege mask  */
  unsigned short int PHD$W_SIZE;  /* Structure size  */
  unsigned char PHD$B_TYPE;       /* Dynamic structure type (PHD)  */
  char PHDDEF$$_SPARE_1;          /* Spare  */
/*  */
/* Working set list pointers - these contain longword offsets from the */
/* beginning of the process header.  */
/*  */
  unsigned int PHD$L_WSLIST; /* 1st working set list entry  */
  unsigned int PHD$L_WSLOCK; /* 1st locked working set list entry  */
  unsigned int PHD$L_WSDYN;  /* 1st dynamic working set list entry  */
  unsigned int PHD$L_WSNEXT; /* Last WSL entry replaced  */
  unsigned int PHD$L_WSLAST; /* Last WSL entry in list  */
/*  */
/* The following three longwords specify the maximum and initial working set */
/* sizes for the process. Rather than containing the count of pages, they    */
/* contain the longword index to what would be the last working set list     */
/* entry.  */
/*  */
  unsigned int PHD$L_WSEXTENT; /* Max working set size against borrowing  */
  unsigned int PHD$L_WSQUOTA; /* Quota on working set size  */
  unsigned int PHD$L_DFWSCNT; /* Default working set size  */
  unsigned int PHD$L_CPULIM; /* Limit on CPU time for process  */
/*  */
/* Process Section Table data base - PSTBASOFF is the byte offset  */
/* from the beginning of the process header to the first longword beyond  */
/* the process section table.  PSTLAST and PSTFREE are the section  */
/* table indices which are the negative longword index from the end of the   */
/* section table to the section table entry.  */
/*  */
  unsigned int PHD$L_PSTBASOFF; /* Byte offset to base of PST  */
```

```
                                 /*  First longword not in PST  */
                                 /*  PST grows backwards from here  */
  unsigned int PHD$L_PSTLAST;    /* End of process section table  */
                                 /*  (Address of last PSTE allocated)  */
  unsigned int PHD$L_PSTFREE;    /* Head of free PSTE list  */
/*  */
/* Create/Delete Page Context  */
/*  */
  unsigned int PHD$L_P0LENGTH;  /* Byte length of P0 portion of L3 page table */
  unsigned int PHD$L_P1LENGTH;  /* Byte length of P1 portion of L3 page table */
  int PHD$L_FREP0VA; /* 1st free virtual address at end of P0 space  */
  unsigned int PHD$L_FREPTECNT; /* Count of free PTEs between the ends  */
                                /*  of the P0 and P1 page tables  */
  int PHD$L_FREP1VA; /* 1st free virtual address at end of P1 space  */
  unsigned int PHD$L_DFPFC;      /* Default page fault cluster  */
  unsigned int PHD$L_PGTBPFC;    /* Page table cluster factor  */
/*  */
/* Quotas and Limits  */
/*  */
  unsigned int PHD$L_QUANT; /* Accumulated CPU time since last quantum */
                           /* overflow */
  unsigned int PHD$L_ASTLM; /* AST limit  */
  unsigned int PHD$L_WSLX;  /* Pointer to working set list index save area  */
  union  {
    unsigned int PHD$L_BAK;     /* Pointer to backup address vector for  */
                                /* process header pages  */
    int PHD$L_PSTBASMAX;        /* LW offset to top PST address  */
    } PHD$R_BAK_OVERLAY;
  unsigned int PHD$L_WSSIZE;   /* Current allowed working set size  */
  unsigned int PHD$L_DIOCNT;    /* Direct I/O count  */
  unsigned int PHD$L_BIOCNT;    /* Buffered I/O count  */
  unsigned int PHD$L_PHVINDEX; /* Process header vector index  */
  union  {
    unsigned int PHD$Q_PAGFIL [2]; /* Template to assign page file backing */
                                   /* store  */
    struct  {
      unsigned int PHD$l_fill_5;   /* Must Be Zero  */
      char PHDDEF$$_FILL_28 [3];
      unsigned char PHD$B_PAGFIL;  /* Current SYSTEM page file index  */
      } PHD$R_PAGFIL_QW_OVERLAY;
    } PHD$R_PAGFIL_OVERLAY;
/*  */
/* Hardware Privileged Context Block (HWPCB) - This structure must be aligned */
/* to a 128 byte boundary. Natural alignment prevents the structure from */
```

```
/* crossing a page boundary.  */
/*  */
/* NOTE WELL: There are bit symbols defined here for accessing the saved */
/* ASTEN, ASTSR, FEN and DATFX values in the HWPCB. These symbols are NOT to
*/
/* be used when interfacing to the ASTEN, ASTSR, FEN or DATFX internal */
/* processor registers directly. See the specific internal register */
/* definitions for bitmasks and constants to be used when interfacing to the
*/ /* IPRs directly.  */
/*  */
  union {
    unsigned int PHD$Q_HWPCB [2];    /* Base of HWPCB  */
    unsigned int PHD$Q_KSP [2];      /* Kernel stack pointer  */
    } PHD$R_HWPCB_OVERLAY;
  unsigned int PHD$Q_ESP [2];        /* Executive stack pointer  */
  unsigned int PHD$Q_SSP [2];        /* Supervisor stack pointer  */
  unsigned int PHD$Q_USP [2];        /* User stack pointer  */
  unsigned int PHD$Q_PTBR [2];       /* Page Table Base Register  */
  unsigned int PHD$Q_ASN [2];        /* Address Space Number  */
  union {
    unsigned int PHD$Q_ASTSR_ASTEN [2]; /* ASTSR / ASTEN quadword  */
    struct {
      unsigned PHD$V_ASTEN : 4;      /* AST Enable Register  */
      unsigned PHD$V_ASTSR : 4;      /* AST Pending Summary Register  */
      } PHD$R_AST_BITS0;
    struct {
      unsigned PHD$V_ASTEN_KEN : 1; /* Kernel AST Enable = 1  */
      unsigned PHD$V_ASTEN_EEN : 1; /* Executive AST Enable = 1  */
      unsigned PHD$V_ASTEN_SEN : 1; /* Supervisor AST Enable = 1  */
      unsigned PHD$V_ASTEN_UEN : 1; /* User AST Enable = 1  */
      unsigned PHD$V_ASTSR_KPD : 1; /* Kernel AST Pending = 1  */
      unsigned PHD$V_ASTSR_EPD : 1; /* Executive AST Pending = 1  */
      unsigned PHD$V_ASTSR_SPD : 1; /* Supervisor AST Pending = 1  */
      unsigned PHD$V_ASTSR_UPD : 1; /* User AST Pending = 1  */
      } PHD$R_AST_BITS1;
    } PHD$R_AST_OVERLAY;
  union {
    unsigned int PHD$Q_FEN_DATFX [2]; /* Floating Point Enable  */
    struct {
      unsigned PHD$V_FEN : 1;         /* Floating Point Enable = 1  */
      unsigned PHD$v_fill_31 : 31;
      unsigned PHD$v_fill_30 : 30;
      unsigned PHD$V_PME : 1;         /* Performance Monitor Enable  */
      unsigned PHD$V_DATFX : 1;       /* Data Alignment Trap Fixup  */
```

```
      } PHD$R_FEN_DATFX_OVERLAY;
    } PHD$R_FEN_OVERLAY;
  unsigned int PHD$Q_CC [2];          /* Cycle Counter  */
  unsigned int PHD$Q_UNQ [2];         /* Process Unique Value  */
  int PHD$Q_PAL_RSVD [2] [6];         /* Reserved for PAL Scratch  */
/* End of Hardware Privileged Context Block (HWPCB).  */
/*  */
/*  */
/* Floating Point Register Save Area. There is space for 32 floating  */
/* point registers, F0 through F30, and the FPCR. Note that F31 is a  */
/* fixed sink register that doesn't need to be saved.  */
/*  */
  union  {
    int PHD$Q_FPR [2] [32];  /* Space for 32 floating point registers  */
    struct  {
      unsigned int PHD$Q_F0 [2];  /* Floating Point Register F0  */
      unsigned int PHD$Q_F1 [2];  /* F1  */
      unsigned int PHD$Q_F2 [2];  /* F2  */
      unsigned int PHD$Q_F3 [2];  /* F3  */
      unsigned int PHD$Q_F4 [2];  /* F4  */
      unsigned int PHD$Q_F5 [2];  /* F5  */
      unsigned int PHD$Q_F6 [2];  /* F6  */
      unsigned int PHD$Q_F7 [2];  /* F7  */
      unsigned int PHD$Q_F8 [2];  /* F8  */
      unsigned int PHD$Q_F9 [2];  /* F9  */
      unsigned int PHD$Q_F10 [2];  /* F10  */
      unsigned int PHD$Q_F11 [2];  /* F11  */
      unsigned int PHD$Q_F12 [2];  /* F12  */
      unsigned int PHD$Q_F13 [2];  /* F13  */
      unsigned int PHD$Q_F14 [2];  /* F14  */
      unsigned int PHD$Q_F15 [2];  /* F15  */
      unsigned int PHD$Q_F16 [2];  /* F16  */
      unsigned int PHD$Q_F17 [2];  /* F17  */
      unsigned int PHD$Q_F18 [2];  /* F18  */
      unsigned int PHD$Q_F19 [2];  /* F19  */
      unsigned int PHD$Q_F20 [2];  /* F20  */
      unsigned int PHD$Q_F21 [2];  /* F21  */
      unsigned int PHD$Q_F22 [2];  /* F22  */
      unsigned int PHD$Q_F23 [2];  /* F23  */
      unsigned int PHD$Q_F24 [2];  /* F24  */
      unsigned int PHD$Q_F25 [2];  /* F25  */
      unsigned int PHD$Q_F26 [2];  /* F26  */
      unsigned int PHD$Q_F27 [2];  /* F27  */
      unsigned int PHD$Q_F28 [2];  /* F28  */
```

```
      unsigned int PHD$Q_F29 [2]; /* F29  */
      unsigned int PHD$Q_F30 [2]; /* F30  */
      unsigned int PHD$Q_FPCR [2]; /* FPCR  */
      } PHD$R_FPR_NUMS;
    } PHD$R_FPR_OVERLAY;
/*  */
/* End of Floating Point Register Save Area.  */
/*  */
  unsigned int PHD$Q_ASNSEQ [2];   /* Address Space Number Sequence  */
  union {
    unsigned int PHD$Q_LEFC [2];   /* Local event flags  */
    struct {
      unsigned int PHD$L_LEFC_0;   /* Cluster 0  */
      unsigned int PHD$L_LEFC_1;   /* Cluster 1  */
      } PHD$R_LEFC_CLUSTERS;
    } PHD$R_LEFC_OVERLAY;
  int PHD$L_L2PT_VA;     /* Virtual address of Level 2 Page Table  */
  int PHD$L_L3PT_VA;     /* Virtual address of Level 3 Page Tables  */
  int PHD$L_L3PT_VA_P1; /* Virtual address of "P1" Level 3 Page Tables
*/
  unsigned int PHD$L_PAGEFLTS;  /* Count of page faults  */
  unsigned int PHD$L_FOW_FLTS;  /* Count of Fault On Write faults incurred  */
  unsigned int PHD$L_FOR_FLTS;  /* Count of Fault On Read faults incurred  */
  unsigned int PHD$L_FOE_FLTS;  /* Count of Fault On Execute faults incurred  */
  unsigned int PHD$L_CPUTIM;    /* Accumulated CPU time charged  */
  unsigned int PHD$L_CPUMODE;   /* Access mode to notify about cputime  */
  unsigned int PHD$L_AWSMODE;   /* Access mode flag for auto WS AST  */
  unsigned int PHD$L_PRCPAGFIL; /* Current PROCESS page file index  */
  unsigned int PHD$L_PGFLCNT;   /* Number of assigned page files  */
/*  */
/* Page Table Statistics  */
/*  */
  unsigned int PHD$L_PTWSLELCK; /* Byte offset to longword array of counts  */
                                /*  of locked WSLE's in this page table  */
  unsigned int PHD$L_PTWSLEVAL; /* Byte offset to longword array of counts  */
                                /*  of valid WSLE's in this page table  */
  unsigned int PHD$L_PTCNTLCK;  /* Count of page tables containing  */
                                /*  1 or more locked WSLE  */
  unsigned int PHD$L_PTCNTVAL;  /* Count of page tables containing  */
                                /*  1 or more valid WSLE  */
  unsigned int PHD$L_PTCNTACT;  /* Count of active page tables  */
  unsigned int PHD$L_PTCNTMAX;  /* Max count of page tables  */
                                /*  which have non-zero PTEs  */
  int PHD$L_WSFLUID;            /* Guaranteed number of fluid WS pages  */
```

```
   unsigned int PHD$L_EMPTPG;      /* Count of empty working set pages  */
   unsigned int PHD$L_EXTDYNWS;   /* Extra dynamic working set list entries  */
                                  /*  above required WSFLUID minimum  */
   unsigned int PHD$L_PRCPGFLPAGES; /* Remaining number of reserved pages in  */
                                  /*  the current process page file  */
   unsigned int PHD$L_PRCPGFLOPAGES;/*Original number of reserved pages in  */
                                  /*  the current process page file  */
   unsigned char PHD$B_PRCPGFL [4]; /* Current SYSTEM page file assignments  */
   unsigned int PHD$L_WSAUTH;      /* Authorized working set size  */
   unsigned int PHD$L_WSAUTHEXT;   /* Authorized WS extent  */
   int PHD$L_RESLSTH;              /* Pointer to resource list  */
   unsigned int PHD$L_AUTHPRI;     /* Initial process priority  */
   unsigned int PHD$Q_AUTHPRIV [2]; /* Authorized privileges mask  */
   unsigned int PHD$Q_IMAGPRIV [2]; /* Installed image privileges mask  */
   unsigned int PHD$L_IMGCNT;      /* Image counter bumped by SYSRUNDWN  */
   unsigned int PHD$L_PFLTRATE;    /* Page fault rate  */
   unsigned int PHD$L_PFLREF;      /* Page faults at end of last interval  */
   unsigned int PHD$L_TIMREF;      /* Time at end of last interval  */
   unsigned int PHD$L_PGFLTIO;     /* Count of pagefault I/O  */
   struct {                        /* Minimum authorized security clearance  */
     unsigned char PHD$$$_FILL_3 [20];
     } PHD$R_MIN_CLASS;
   struct {    /* Maximum authorized security clearance  */
     unsigned char PHD$$$_FILL_4 [20];
     } PHD$R_MAX_CLASS;
   unsigned int PHD$L_PRCPGFLREFS [4];/* # pages currently being used  */
                                  /* in each process page file  */
   unsigned int PHD$L_PPGFLVA;     /* "Quota" of available pages which may  */
                                  /* have page file backing store  */
/*  */
  union {
    unsigned int PHD$L_FLAGS; /* Flags longword  */
    struct {
      unsigned PHD$V_PFMFLG : 1;     /* Page fault monitoring enabled  */
      unsigned PHD$V_DALCSTX : 1;    /* Need to deallocate section indices  */
      unsigned PHD$V_WSPEAKCHK : 1; /* Check for new working set size (proc)  */
      unsigned PHD$V_NOACCVIO : 1;  /* Set after inswap of process header  */
      unsigned PHD$V_IWSPEAKCK : 1; /* Check for new working set size (image) */
      unsigned PHD$V_IMGDMP : 1;    /* Take image dump on error exit  */
      unsigned PHD$V_NO_WS_CHNG : 1;/* No change to working set or swapping  */
                                  /* (Transient use by MMG code only)  */
      unsigned PHD$V_PGFLACC : 1; /* Page file reservation accounting enabled*/
      unsigned PHD$V_LOCK_HEADER : 1;/* Do not swap process header  */
                                  /* (Transient use by MMG code only)  */
```

```
      unsigned PHD$V_FILL_0 : 7;
      } PHD$R_FLAGS_BITS;
    } PHD$R_FLAGS_OVERLAY;
/*  */
/*  Note: The Alpha architecture defines that the FEN bit in HWPCB cannot  */
/*  be read, so a separate software FEN bit must be kept. For performance  */
/*  reasons, we make this bit the low-bit.  */
/*  */
  union  {
    unsigned int PHD$L_FLAGS2;          /* Flags2 longword  */
    struct  {
      unsigned PHD$V_SW_FEN : 1;        /* Software FEN bit  */
      unsigned PHD$v_fill_flags2 : 30;
      unsigned PHD$V_AST_PENDING : 1;  /* AST pending optimization  */
      } PHD$R_FLAGS2_BITS;
    } PHD$R_FLAGS2_OVERLAY;
/*  */
/* Cluster-Wide Process Services  */
/*  */
  unsigned int PHD$Q_PSCANCTX_QUEUE [2]; /* Queue of PSCAN blocks  */
  unsigned int PHD$L_PSCANCTX_SEQNUM;    /* PSCAN sequence number  */
  unsigned int PHD$L_EXTRACPU;  /* Accumulated CPU time limit extension  */
/*  */
/* End of the fixed portion of the process header.  */
/*  */
  int PHD$L_WSL;                       /* First working set list entry  */
  } ;



#pragma standard
#pragma member_alignment __restore
#endif
```

AXP_PCBDEF.H

```
#ifndef AXP_PCBDEF_H
#define AXP_PCBDEF_H
/*
** To update this for future releases of OpenVMS:
** Get library copy — lib/ext=$PCBDEF sys$share:lib.mlb
** Insure offsets match the offsets in this file.
*/
#pragma nostandard
#pragma member_alignment __save
#pragma nomember_alignment
```

```
/*  */
/* Software Process Control Block Definitions  */
/*  */
#define PCB$M_RES 0x1
#define PCB$M_DELPEN 0x2
#define PCB$M_FORCPEN 0x4
#define PCB$M_INQUAN 0x8
#define PCB$M_PSWAPM 0x10
#define PCB$M_RESPEN 0x20
#define PCB$M_SSFEXC 0x40
#define PCB$M_SSFEXCE 0x80
#define PCB$M_SSFEXCS 0x100
#define PCB$M_SSFEXCU 0x200
#define PCB$M_SSRWAIT 0x400
#define PCB$M_SUSPEN 0x800
#define PCB$M_WAKEPEN 0x1000
#define PCB$M_WALL 0x2000
#define PCB$M_BATCH 0x4000
#define PCB$M_NOACNT 0x8000
#define PCB$M_NOSUSPEND 0x10000
#define PCB$M_ASTPEN 0x20000
#define PCB$M_PHDRES 0x40000
#define PCB$M_HIBER 0x80000
#define PCB$M_LOGIN 0x100000
#define PCB$M_NETWRK 0x200000
#define PCB$M_PWRAST 0x400000
#define PCB$M_NODELET 0x800000
#define PCB$M_DISAWS 0x1000000
#define PCB$M_INTER 0x2000000
#define PCB$M_RECOVER 0x4000000
#define PCB$M_SECAUDIT 0x8000000
#define PCB$M_HARDAFF 0x10000000
#define PCB$M_ERDACT 0x20000000
#define PCB$M_SOFTSUSP 0x40000000
#define PCB$M_PREEMPTED 0x80000000
#define PCB$M_QUANTUM_RESCHED 0x1
#define PCB$M_PHDLOCK 0x8
#define PCB$M_EPID_WILD 0x80000000
#define PCB$K_LENGTH 572          /* Length of PCB  */
#define PCB$C_LENGTH 572          /* Length of PCB  */
struct PCBDEF {
  int PCB$L_SQFL;                 /* State queue forward link  */
  int PCB$L_SQBL;                 /* State queue backward link  */
  unsigned short int PCB$W_SIZE;  /* Size, in bytes  */
```

```
unsigned char PCB$B_TYPE;        /* Structure type code for PCB  */
unsigned char PCB$b_fill_1;
unsigned int PCB$L_AST_PENDING; /* AST pending mask  */
unsigned int PCB$Q_PHYPCB [2];  /* Physical address of HWPCB  */
variant_union  {
  unsigned int PCB$Q_LEFC_SWAPPED [2]; /* Local event flags - swapped  */
  variant_struct  {
    unsigned int PCB$L_LEFC_0_SWAPPED; /* Cluster 0  */
    unsigned int PCB$L_LEFC_1_SWAPPED; /* Cluster 1  */
    } PCB$R_LEFC_CLUSTERS_SWAPPED;
  } PCB$R_LEFC_OVERLAY_SWAPPED;
int PCB$L_ASTQFL_SPK;  /* Special kernel AST queue  */
                       /*  forward link (head)  */
int PCB$L_ASTQBL_SPK;  /* Special kernel AST queue back link (tail)  */
int PCB$L_ASTQFL_K;    /* Kernel AST queue forward link (head)  */
int PCB$L_ASTQBL_K;    /* Kernel AST queue back link (tail)  */
int PCB$L_ASTQFL_E;    /* Executive AST queue forward link (head)  */
int PCB$L_ASTQBL_E;    /* Executive AST queue back link (tail)  */
int PCB$L_ASTQFL_S;    /* Supervisor AST queue forward link (head)  */
int PCB$L_ASTQBL_S;    /* Supervisor AST queue back link (tail)  */
int PCB$L_ASTQFL_U;    /* User AST queue forward link (head)  */
int PCB$L_ASTQBL_U;    /* User AST queue back link (tail)  */
int PCB$L_PRVCPU;      /* Previous CPU (not current CPU)  */
int PCB$L_CPU_ID;      /* Current CPU (last one to load context)  */
unsigned int PCB$Q_PRVASN [2];     /* Previous Address Space Number (ASN)  */
unsigned int PCB$Q_PRVASNSEQ [2]; /* Previous ASN Sequence Number  */
unsigned int PCB$Q_ONCPUCNT [2];  /* Count of threads in CUR state  */
unsigned int PCB$L_ASTACT;         /* Access modes with active ASTs  */
unsigned int PCB$L_STATE;          /* Process state  */
unsigned int PCB$L_PRI;            /* Process current priority  */
unsigned int PCB$L_PRIB;           /* Base priority  */
unsigned int PCB$L_AFFINITY_SKIP; /* Affinity skip count  */
unsigned int PCB$L_OWNER;          /* PID of creator  */
variant_union  {
  unsigned int PCB$L_STS;          /* Process status flags  */
  variant_struct  {
    unsigned PCB$V_RES : 1;        /* Resident, in balance set  */
    unsigned PCB$V_DELPEN : 1;     /* Delete pending  */
    unsigned PCB$V_FORCPEN : 1;    /* Force exit pending  */
    unsigned PCB$V_INQUAN : 1;     /* Initial quantum in progress  */
    unsigned PCB$V_PSWAPM : 1;     /* Process swap mode, 1=NOSWAP  */
    unsigned PCB$V_RESPEN : 1;     /* Resume pending, skip suspend  */
    unsigned PCB$V_SSFEXC : 1;     /* System service exception enable (K)  */
    unsigned PCB$V_SSFEXCE : 1;    /* System service exception enable (E)  */
```

319

```
      unsigned PCB$V_SSFEXCS : 1;    /* System service exception enable (S)  */
      unsigned PCB$V_SSFEXCU : 1;    /* System service exception enable (U)  */
      unsigned PCB$V_SSRWAIT : 1;   /* System service resource wait disable  */
      unsigned PCB$V_SUSPEN : 1;     /* Suspend pending */
      unsigned PCB$V_WAKEPEN : 1;    /* Wake pending, skip hibernate  */
      unsigned PCB$V_WALL : 1;       /* Wait for all events in mask  */
      unsigned PCB$V_BATCH : 1;      /* Process is a batch job  */
      unsigned PCB$V_NOACNT : 1;     /* No accounting for process  */
      unsigned PCB$V_NOSUSPEND : 1; /* Process cannot be suspended  */
      unsigned PCB$V_ASTPEN : 1;     /* AST pending  */
      unsigned PCB$V_PHDRES : 1;     /* Process header resident  */
      unsigned PCB$V_HIBER : 1;       /* Hibernate after initial image activate */
      unsigned PCB$V_LOGIN : 1;      /* Login without reading UAF  */
      unsigned PCB$V_NETWRK : 1;     /* Network connect job  */
      unsigned PCB$V_PWRAST : 1;     /* Power fail AST  */
      unsigned PCB$V_NODELET : 1;    /* No delete  */
      unsigned PCB$V_DISAWS : 1;     /* Disable automatic WS adjustment  */
      unsigned PCB$V_INTER : 1;      /* Process is an interactive job  */
      unsigned PCB$V_RECOVER : 1;    /* Process can recover locks  */
      unsigned PCB$V_SECAUDIT : 1;   /* Mandatory security auditing enabled  */
      unsigned PCB$V_HARDAFF : 1;    /* Process is bound to particular CPU  */
      unsigned PCB$V_ERDACT : 1;     /* Exec mode rundown active  */
      unsigned PCB$V_SOFTSUSP : 1;   /* Process is in "soft" suspend  */
      unsigned PCB$V_PREEMPTED : 1; /* Hard suspend has preempted soft  */
      } PCB$R_FILL_1;
    } PCB$R_FILL_0;
  variant_union {
    unsigned int PCB$L_STS2; /* Process status flags (2nd LW) */
    variant_struct {
      unsigned PCB$V_QUANTUM_RESCHED : 1;/* Quantum-oriented  */
                                      /*process reschedule  */
      unsigned PCB$v_fill_2 : 2;
      unsigned PCB$V_PHDLOCK : 1;           /* Don't swap PHD */
                                            /*  process has $LCKPAG pages  */
      unsigned PCB$V_FILL_14 : 4;
      } PCB$R_FILL_3;
    } PCB$R_FILL_2;
  unsigned int PCB$L_PRISAV; /* Saved current priority  */
  unsigned int PCB$L_PRIBSAV; /* Saved base priority  */
  unsigned int PCB$L_AUTHPRI; /* Initial process priority  */
  unsigned int PCB$L_ONQTIME; /* Abs time when placed on COM/COMO */
                             /* queue, adjusted for process wait time  */
  unsigned int PCB$L_WAITIME; /* Abs time of last process event  */
  unsigned int PCB$L_ASTCNT; /* AST count remaining  */
```

```
  unsigned int PCB$L_BIOCNT;    /* Buffered I/O count remaining  */
  unsigned int PCB$L_BIOLM;     /* Buffered I/O limit  */
  unsigned int PCB$L_DIOCNT;    /* Direct I/O count remaining  */
  unsigned int PCB$L_DIOLM;     /* Direct I/O count limit  */
  unsigned int PCB$L_PRCCNT;    /* Subprocess count  */
  char PCB$T_TERMINAL [8];      /* Terminal device name string  */
                                /*  for interactive jobs  */
  unsigned int PCB$L_WEFC;      /* Waiting EF cluster number  */
  variant_union {
    unsigned int PCB$L_EFWM;    /* Event flag wait mask  */
    int PCB$L_PQB;              /* Pointer to Process Quota Block  */
                                /*  (process creation only)  */
    } PCB$R_PQB_OVERLAY;
  unsigned int PCB$L_EFCS;      /* Local event flag cluster, system  */
  unsigned int PCB$L_EFCU;      /* Local event flag cluster, user  */
  variant_union {
    variant_struct   {
      int PCB$L_EFC2P;          /* Pointer to global cluster #2  */
      int PCB$L_EFC3P;          /* Pointer to global cluster #3  */
      } PCB$R_CEFC_OVERLAY_1;
    variant_struct   {          /* (used only until SHELL runs)  */
      unsigned short int PCB$W_PGFLCHAR; /* Page file characteristics  */
      unsigned char PCB$B_PGFLINDEX;    /* Desired SYSTEM page file index  */
      } PCB$R_CEFC_OVERLAY_2;
    } PCB$R_CEFC_OVERLAY;
  unsigned int PCB$L_PID;       /* Process ID used by exec on local node only. */
  variant_union {
    unsigned int PCB$L_EPID;  /* Cluster-wide process ID seen by the world  */
    variant_struct   {
    unsigned PCB$V_EPID_PROC : 21;      /* Process ID field, can convert to  */
                                        /* PCB$l_pid  */
      unsigned PCB$V_EPID_NODE_IDX : 8;  /* IDX - index to table of node */
                                         /*  identifications  */
      unsigned PCB$V_EPID_NODE_SEQ : 2;  /* SEQ - sequence number for node */
                                         /*  table entry reuse  */
      unsigned PCB$V_EPID_WILD : 1;      /* Flag that EPID is wildcard context*/
                                         /* for $GETJPI,  */

      } PCB$R_FILL_5;
    } PCB$R_FILL_4;
/*  and not a valid EPID */
  unsigned int PCB$L_EOWNER;    /* EPID of process owner  */
  unsigned int PCB$L_APTCNT;    /* Active page table count  */
  unsigned int PCB$L_MTXCNT;    /* Count of mutex semaphores owned  */
  unsigned int PCB$L_GPGCNT;    /* Global page count in WS  */
```

```
unsigned int PCB$L_PPGCNT;    /* Process page count in WS  */
unsigned int PCB$L_WSSWP;     /* Swap file disk address  */
unsigned int PCB$L_SWAPSIZE;  /* Swap block allocation  */
struct PHDDEF *PCB$L_PHD;     /* Address of Process Header  */
int PCB$L_JIB;                /* Address of Job Information Block  */
  variant_struct  {
  unsigned int PCB$Q_PRIV [2];      /* Current privilege mask  */
  int PCB$L_ARB;                    /* Address of Access Rights Block  */
  char PCB$$$_ARB_FILL_1 [48];      /* Rights list descriptors, etc.  */
  variant_union  {
    unsigned int PCB$L_UIC;         /* Logon UIC of process  */
    variant_struct  {
      unsigned short int PCB$W_MEM; /* Member number in UIC  */
      unsigned short int PCB$W_GRP; /* Group number in UIC  */
      } PCB$R_FILL_7;
        } PCB$R_FILL_6;
      char PCB$$$_ARB_FILL_2 [60];  /* Remainder of ARB  */
      } PCB$R_PCBARB;
  int PCB$L_ORB;                    /* Address of process ORB  */
  unsigned int PCB$L_TMBU;          /* Termination mailbox unit number  */
  int PCB$L_LOCKQFL;                /* Lock queue forward link  */
  int PCB$L_LOCKQBL;                /* Lock queue backward link  */
  int PCB$L_DLCKPRI;                /* Deadlock resolution priority  */
  unsigned int PCB$L_DEFPROT;       /* Process default protection  */
  int PCB$L_PMB;                    /* PMB address  */
  int PCB$L_AFFINITY;               /* CPU ID for affinity  */
  unsigned int PCB$L_CAPABILITY;    /* CPU capability selection bitmask  */
  unsigned int PCB$L_CPUTIM;        /* Accumulated CPU time at last outswap */
  char PCB$T_LNAME [16];            /* Process name  */
  int PCB$L_PRCPDB;                 /* Address of process */
                                    /*  Performance Data Block  */
  unsigned int PCB$L_PIXHIST;       /* PIXSCAN history summary LW (bitmask) */
  int PCB$L_AFFINITY_CALLBACK;      /* Callback for breaking affinity  */
  unsigned int PCB$L_PERMANENT_CAPABILITY; /* Permanent capability mask  */
  int PCB$L_PERMANENT_CPU_AFFINITY;  /* Permanent CPU affinity  */
  unsigned int PCB$Q_CWPSSRV_QUEUE [2];   /* CWPS service block queue  */
  unsigned int PCB$L_CURRENT_AFFINITY;    /* Current CPU mask  */
  int PCB$L_CAPABILITY_SEQ;               /* Copy of last sequence number  */
  unsigned int PCB$Q_BUFOBJ_LIST [2]; /* Defined buffer objects queue head  */
  unsigned int PCB$L_AST_BLOCKED;    /* AST blocked bits  */
  int PCB$L_ADB_LINK;                /* Address of AST Data Blocks */
  unsigned int PCB$L_TOTAL_EVTAST;   /* Total AST quota in use for event */
  int *PCB$A_CURRENT_TX;     /* Pointer to process default transaction  */
```

```
    int *PCB$A_CURRENT_CD;        /* Pointer to process default commit domain  */
    int *PCB$A_CURRENT_VERTEX;  /* Pointer to process default execution vertex */
    variant_union  {
      unsigned int PCB$Q_XSCB_QUE [2];  /* Transaction Segment list  */
      variant_struct   {
        int *PCB$A_XSCB_FLINK;
        int *PCB$A_XSCB_BLINK;
        } PCB$R_FILL_9;
      } PCB$R_FILL_8;
    variant_union  {
      unsigned int PCB$Q_RMCB_QUE [2]; /* Declared resource manager list  */
      variant_struct   {
        int *PCB$A_RMCB_FLINK;
        int *PCB$A_RMCB_BLINK;
        } PCB$R_FILL_11;
      } PCB$R_FILL_10;
    variant_union  {
      unsigned int PCB$Q_CD_QUE [2];    /* Commit domain membership list  */
      variant_struct   {
        int *PCB$A_CD_FLINK;
        int *PCB$A_CD_BLINK;
        } PCB$R_FILL_13;
      } PCB$R_FILL_12;
    unsigned int PCB$L_DPC;                  /* Delete pending count  */
    unsigned int PCB$L_CPUTIME_REF;    /* CPUTIME at last TICK time  */
    unsigned int PCB$L_ACC_WAITIME;    /* Accumulated wait time  */
    int PCB$L_XPCB;                          /* address of the POSIX extended PCB  */
    int PCB$L_PSX_SPARE_L1;            /* POSIX spare longword  */
    unsigned int PCB$Q_PSX_SPARE_Q1 [2]; /* POSIX spare quadword  */
    unsigned int PCB$L_KERNEL_COUNTER; /* Per-process kernel mode counters  */
    unsigned int PCB$L_EXEC_COUNTER;   /* Per-process exec mode counters  */
    unsigned int PCB$L_SUPER_COUNTER;  /* Per-process super mode counters  */
    unsigned int PCB$L_USER_COUNTER;   /* Per-process user mode counters  */
    } ;

#pragma standard
#pragma member_alignment __restore
#endif
```

GETSPIDEF.H

```
#ifndef GETSPIDEF_H
#define GETSPIDEF_H
/*
** To update this for future releases of OpenVMS:
** Get library copy – lib/ext=$SPIDEF sys$share:lib.mlb
** Insure offsets match the offsets in this file.
*/
#pragma nostandard
#pragma member_alignment __save
#pragma nomember_alignment
/* DEFINE TABLE TYPES  */
#define SPI$C_EXETYPE 1  /* Executive cells  */
#define SPI$C_EWSTYPE 2  /* Executive writable storage area  */
#define SPI$C_MONTYPE 3  /* Monitor specific items  */
#define SPI$C_RMSTYPE 4  /* Monitor RMS specific items  */
#define SPI$C_LISTEND Ø  /* End of table list  */
/*  */
/* The following section defines items collected during initialization. */
/* The items include general system information and server version number.  */
/* The server version number is also defined here.  */
/*  */
#define spi$_initial -1         /* Initialization item list  */
#define spi$_data_collection -2 /* Data collection item list  */
#define spi$_sysinfo -3         /* System information item  */
#define spi$_version_number -4  /* Monitor version number  */
#define spi$_rms_file -5        /* Parse file name  */
#define spi$_rms_gs -6          /* Get global section address  */
#define spi$_last_type -7
#define spi$_server_version 3
/*  */
/* Define bits in the PMS flags field PMS$GL_FLAGS. These are used to  */
/* synchronize access to some PMS field and enable other activity.  */
/*  */
struct pms_flags {
  struct {                      /* Class qualifier flags for CDB (Active)  */
    unsigned spi$v_disk_enable : 1;/* YES => Enable disk queue collection */
    unsigned spi$v_disk_sync : 1;  /* YES => Synchronize access to PMS */
    unsigned spi$v_filler : 30;    /* Fill out remainder of field  */
    } spi$l_flags;
  } ;
/* Define item identifier numbers.  Each data item has an associated  */
/* value which is used to find its entry in the EXETBL. The item table  */
/* is defined by the macros SPI_GENERATE_TABLE which makes multiple calls  */
```

```
/* to the macro SPI_ITEM_CODE defined in the SYSGETSPI module.  */
/*   */
#define spi$_MODES 4096              /* All modes counters on all CPU's  */
#define spi$_INTERRUPT 4097          /* time on interrupt stack - primary  */
#define spi$_KERNEL 4098             /* time in kernel mode - primary  */
#define spi$_EXEC 4099               /* time in exec mode - primary  */
#define spi$_SUPER 4100              /* time in supervisor mode - primary  */
#define spi$_USER 4101               /* time in user mode - primary  */
#define spi$_COMPAT 4102             /* time in compat. mode - primary  */
#define spi$_INTERRUPT_BUSY 4103 /* Time spent spinning on the interrupt stack*/
#define spi$_KERNEL_BUSY 4104        /* Time spent spinning on the lernel stack  */
#define spi$_IDLE 4105               /* idle time - primary  */
#define spi$_CPUBUSY 4106            /* RETIRED ITEM - RETURNS 0  */
#define spi$_COLPG 4107              /* collided page wait  */
#define spi$_MWAIT 4108              /* memory wait  */
#define spi$_CEF 4109                /* common event flag wait  */
#define spi$_PFW 4110                /* page wait  */
#define spi$_LEF 4111                /* local event flag wait  */
#define spi$_LEFO 4112               /* lef wait out of bal. set  */
#define spi$_HIB 4113                /* hibernating  */
#define spi$_HIBO 4114               /* hibernating outswapped  */
#define spi$_SUSP 4115               /* suspended  */
#define spi$_SUSPO 4116              /* suspended outswapped  */
#define spi$_FPG 4117                /* free page wait  */
#define spi$_COM 4118                /* computing  */
#define spi$_COMO 4119               /* computable outswapped  */
#define spi$_CUR 4120                /* current  */
#define spi$_OTHSTAT 4121            /* RETIRED ITEM - RETURNS 0  */
#define spi$_PROCS 4122              /* process count for SYSTEM class  */
#define spi$_PROC 4123               /* collect all process information  */
#define spi$_FRLIST 4124             /* size of free list  */
#define spi$_MODLIST 4125            /* size of modified list  */
#define spi$_FAULTS 4126             /* page fault count  */
#define spi$_PREADS 4127             /* page reads  */
#define spi$_PWRITES 4128            /* page writes  */
#define spi$_PWRITIO 4129            /* physical page write I/O's  */
#define spi$_PREADIO 4130            /* physical page read I/O's  */
#define spi$_GVALFLTS 4131           /* global valid faults  */
#define spi$_WRTINPROG 4132          /* faults from write in progress  */
#define spi$_FREFLTS 4133            /* faults from free list  */
#define spi$_MFYFLTS 4134            /* faults from modified list  */
#define spi$_DZROFLTS 4135           /* demand zero faults  */
#define spi$_SYSFAULTS 4136          /* system page faults  */
#define spi$_LRPCNT 4137             /* number of LRP packets available  */
```

```
#define spi$_LRPINUSE 4138      /* number of LRPs in use  */
#define spi$_IRPCNT 4139        /* number of IRP packets available  */
#define spi$_IRPINUSE 4140      /* number of IRPs in use  */
#define spi$_SRPCNT 4141        /* number of SRP packets available  */
#define spi$_SRPINUSE 4142      /* number of SRPs in use  */
#define spi$_HOLECNT 4143       /* number of blocks in dyn. memory  */
#define spi$_BIGHOLE 4144       /* largest hole  */
#define spi$_SMALLHOLE 4145     /* smallest hole  */
#define spi$_HOLESUM 4146       /* total space in dyn. memory available  */
#define spi$_DYNINUSE 4147      /* dynamic memory space in use  */
#define spi$_SMALLCNT 4148      /* number of blocks < 32 bytes in size  */
#define spi$_ISWPCNT 4149       /* total inswaps  */
#define spi$_DIRIO 4150         /* count of direct I/Os  */
#define spi$_BUFIO 4151         /* count of buffered I/Os  */
#define spi$_MBREADS 4152       /* total mailbox reads  */
#define spi$_MBWRITES 4153      /* total mailbox writes  */
#define spi$_LOGNAM 4154        /* logical name translations  */
#define spi$_FCPCALLS 4155      /* total fcp calls  */
#define spi$_FCPREAD 4156       /* number of disk reads by FCP  */
#define spi$_FCPWRITE 4157      /* number of disk writes by FCP  */
#define spi$_FCPCACHE 4158      /* number of FCP cache hits  */
#define spi$_FCPCPU 4159        /* number of CPU tics by FCP  */
#define spi$_FCPHIT 4160        /* number of window hits  */
#define spi$_FCPSPLIT 4161      /* number of split transfers  */
#define spi$_FCPFAULT 4162      /* number of FCP page faults  */
#define spi$_ENQNEW 4163        /* number of ENQ's (new)  */
#define spi$_ENQCVT 4164        /* number of ENQ's (conversions)  */
#define spi$_DEQ 4165           /* number of DEQ's  */
#define spi$_BLKAST 4166        /* number of blocking AST's  */
#define spi$_ENQWAIT 4167       /* number of ENQ's forced to wait  */
#define spi$_ENQNOTQD 4168      /* number of ENQ's not queued  */
#define spi$_DLCKSRCH 4169      /* number of deadlock searches  */
#define spi$_DLCKFND 4170       /* number of deadlocks found  */
#define spi$_NUMLOCKS 4171      /* total locks  */
#define spi$_NUMRES 4172        /* total resources  */
#define spi$_ARRLOCPK 4173      /* arriving local packets  */
#define spi$_DEPLOCPK 4174      /* departing local packets  */
#define spi$_ARRTRAPK 4175      /* arriving transit packets  */
#define spi$_TRCNGLOS 4176      /* transit congestion loss  */
#define spi$_RCVBUFFL 4177      /* receiver buffer failures  */
#define spi$_RESERVED1 4178     /* Reserved PMS location 1  */
                                /* Through  Location 18  */

#define spi$_RESERVED18 4195    /* Reserved PMS location 18  */
#define spi$_FID_TRIES 4196     /* count of File Id cache attempts  */
```

```
#define spi$_FILHDR_TRIES 4197      /* count of File header cache attempts   */
#define spi$_DIRFCB_TRIES 4198      /* count of Directory block cache attempts   */
#define spi$_DIRDATA_TRIES 4199     /* count of Directory data cache attempts   */
#define spi$_EXT_TRIES 4200         /* count of Extent cache attempts   */
#define spi$_QUO_TRIES 4201         /* count of Quota cache attempts   */
#define spi$_STORAGMAP_TRIES 4202   /* count of storage bitmap cache attempts   */
#define spi$_DISKS 4203             /* all disk data   */
#define spi$_TOTAL_LOCKS 4204       /* Total of all locking activity -*/
#define spi$_ENQNEWLOC 4205         /* new lock requests (local)   */
#define spi$_ENQNEWIN 4206          /* new lock requests (incoming)   */
#define spi$_ENQNEWOUT 4207         /* new lock requests (outgoing)   */
#define spi$_ENQCVTLOC 4208         /* lock conversion requests (local)   */
#define spi$_ENQCVTIN 4209          /* lock conversion requests (incoming)   */
#define spi$_ENQCVTOUT 4210         /* lock conversion requests (outgoing)   */
#define spi$_DEQLOC 4211            /* dequeues (local)   */
#define spi$_DEQIN 4212             /* dequeues (incoming)   */
#define spi$_DEQOUT 4213            /* dequeues (outgoing)   */
#define spi$_BLKLOC 4214            /* blocking ASTs queued (local)   */
#define spi$_BLKIN 4215             /* blocking ASTs queued (incoming)   */
#define spi$_BLKOUT 4216            /* blocking ASTs queued (outgoing)   */
#define spi$_DIRIN 4217             /* directory operations (incoming)   */
#define spi$_DIROUT 4218            /* directory operations (outgoing)   */
#define spi$_DLCKMSGS 4219          /* deadlock detection messages (in & out)   */
#define spi$_SCS 4220               /* All SCS information   */
#define spi$_SYSTIME 4221           /* Current system time   */
#define spi$_MSCP_REQUEST 4222      /* IO request rate to the MSCP server   */
#define spi$_MSCP_READ 4223         /* Read request rate to the MSCP server   */
#define spi$_MSCP_WRITE 4224        /* Write request rate to the MSCP server   */
#define spi$_MSCP_FRAGMENT 4225     /* Rate at which I/O's are fragmented   */
#define spi$_MSCP_SPLIT 4226        /* Rate at which I/O's are split   */
#define spi$_MSCP_BUFWAIT 4227      /* Rate at which incoming requests */
                                    /* have to wait for a buffer   */
#define spi$_MSCP_SIZE1 4228        /* I/O rate for sizes 1-2 blocks   */
#define spi$_MSCP_SIZE2 4229        /* I/O rate for sizes 2-3 blocks   */
#define spi$_MSCP_SIZE3 4230        /* I/O rate for sizes 4-7 blocks   */
#define spi$_MSCP_SIZE4 4231        /* I/O rate for sizes 8-15 blocks   */
#define spi$_MSCP_SIZE5 4232        /* I/O rate for sizes 16-31 blocks   */
#define spi$_MSCP_SIZE6 4233        /* I/O rate for sizes 32-63 blocks   */
#define spi$_MSCP_SIZE7 4234        /* I/O rate for sizes 64-127 blocks   */
#define spi$_MSCP_ALL 4235          /* All MSCP server class items   */
#define spi$_DDTM_STARTS 4236       /* Local Transaction starts   */
#define spi$_DDTM_PREPARES 4237     /* Local Transaction prepare event   */
#define spi$_DDTM_ONE_PHASE 4238    /* Transaction ONE_PHASE commit event   */
#define spi$_DDTM_COMMITS 4239      /* Local Transaction commit event   */
```

```
#define spi$_DDTM_ABORTS 4240      /* Local Transaction abort event  */
#define spi$_DDTM_ENDS 4241        /* Local Transaction ends  */
#define spi$_DDTM_BRANCHS 4242      /* Start branch event  */
#define spi$_DDTM_ADDS 4243        /* Add branch event  */
#define spi$_DDTM_BUCKETS1 4244     /* TPS rate for < 1  */
#define spi$_DDTM_BUCKETS2 4245     /* TPS rate for 1-2  */
#define spi$_DDTM_BUCKETS3 4246     /* TPS rate for 2-3  */
#define spi$_DDTM_BUCKETS4 4247     /* TPS rate for 3-4  */
#define spi$_DDTM_BUCKETS5 4248     /* TPS rate for 4-5  */
#define spi$_DDTM_BUCKETS6 4249     /* TPS rate for > 6  */
#define spi$_DDTM_ALL 4250         /* All TRANSACTION class items  */
#define spi$_VECTORP 4251          /* Vector Processor tics scheduled  */
#define spi$_RESERVEDEXE1 4252      /* Reserved EXE items  */
                                   /* Through */
#define spi$_RESERVEDEXE84 4335     /* Reserved EXE items  */
#define spi$_LASTEXE 4336          /* Last item in the EXE table  */
/*   */
/* These next items are located in an executive writable page in memory  */
/*   */
#define spi$_ACCESS 8432           /* number of file accesses  */
#define spi$_ALLOC 8433            /* number of file extends  */
#define spi$_FCPCREATE 8434         /* number of file creations  */
#define spi$_VOLWAIT 8435          /* # of times XQP waited for volume lock  */
#define spi$_FCPTURN 8436          /* number of window turns  */
#define spi$_FCPERASE 8437         /* number of erase calls  */
#define spi$_OPENS 8438            /* number of file opens  */
#define spi$_FIDHIT 8439           /* count of File Id cache hits  */
#define spi$_FIDMISS 8440          /* count of File Id cache misses  */
#define spi$_FILHDR_HIT 8441        /* count of File header cache hits  */
#define spi$_DIRFCB_HIT 8442        /* count of Directory block cache hits  */
#define spi$_DIRFCB_MISS 8443       /* count of Directory block cache misses  */
#define spi$_DIRDATA_HIT 8444       /* count of Directory data cache hits  */
#define spi$_EXTHIT 8445           /* count of Extent cache hits  */
#define spi$_EXTMISS 8446          /* count of Extent cache misses  */
#define spi$_QUOHIT 8447           /* count of Quota cache hits  */
#define spi$_QUOMISS 8448          /* count of Quota cache misses  */
#define spi$_STORAGMAP_HIT 8449     /* count of storage bitmap cache hits  */
#define spi$_VOLLCK 8450           /* Volume synch locks  */
#define spi$_SYNCHLCK 8451         /* directory and file synch locks  */
#define spi$_SYNCHWAIT 8452        /* # of times XQP waited for a directory */
                                   /* or file synch lock  */
#define spi$_ACCLCK 8453           /* access locks  */
#define spi$_XQPCACHEWAIT 8454      /* # of times XQP had to wait for free space */
                                   /*in a cache  */
```

```
#define spi$_RESERVEDEWS1 8455    /* Reserved EWS items  */
                                  /* Through  100 */
#define spi$_RESERVEDEWS100 8554 /* Reserved EWS items  */
#define spi$_LASTEWS 8555         /* Last item in the exec writable table  */
/*  */
/* Begin monitor specific data items. The items listed below are  */
/* NOT collected by the SPI as individual items. Some are NOT collected  */
/* at all but are computed by MONITOR.  */
/*  */
#define spi$_FIDHITPCNT 12651 /* percentage of file id cache hits/hits+misses */
#define spi$_FILHDR_HITPCNT 12652   /* percentage of file header cache /*
                                    /*hits/hits+misses  */
#define spi$_DIRFCB_HITPCNT 12653   /* percentage of directory block cache /*
                                    /*hits/hits+misses  */
#define spi$_DIRDATA_HITPCNT 12654   /* percentage of directory data cache */
                                     /*hits/hits+misses  */
#define spi$_EXTHITPCNT 12655 /* percentage of extent cache hits/hits+misses */
#define spi$_QUOHITPCNT 12656 /* percentage of quota cache hits/hits+misses  */
#define spi$_STORAGMAP_HITPCNT 12657 /* percentage of storage map cache */
                                     /*hits/hits+misses  */
#define spi$_OPCNT 12658          /* disk io operation count  */
#define spi$_IOQUELEN 12659       /* disk io queue length  */
#define spi$_IOAQUELEN 12660      /* Accurate disk io queue length  */
#define spi$_DISKRESPTIM 12661    /* disk io response time  */
#define spi$_JNLIOCNT 12662       /* journaling io operation count (for disks) */
#define spi$_JDNQLEN 12663        /* jdevice normal io queue length  */
#define spi$_JDWQLEN 12664        /* jdevice wait irp queue length  */
#define spi$_JDFQLEN 12665        /* jdevice force io queue length  */
#define spi$_JDEXCNT 12666        /* jdevice extend count  */
#define spi$_JNLWRTSS 12667       /* obsolete  */
#define spi$_JNLBUFWR 12668       /* obsolete  */
#define spi$_DGSENT 12669         /* SCS application datagrams sent  */
#define spi$_DGRCVD 12670         /* SCS application datagrams received  */
#define spi$_DGDISCARD 12671      /* SCS application datagrams discarded  */
#define spi$_MSGSENT 12672        /* SCS application messages sent  */
#define spi$_MSGRCVD 12673        /* SCS application messages received  */
#define spi$_SNDATS 12674         /* SCS block send datas initiated  */
#define spi$_KBYTSENT 12675       /* SCS kbytes sent via send datas  */
#define spi$_REQDATS 12676        /* SCS block request datas initiated  */
#define spi$_KBYTREQD 12677       /* SCS kbytes received via request datas  */
#define spi$_KBYTMAPD 12678       /* SCS kbytes mapped for block transfer  */
#define spi$_QCR_CNT 12679        /* SCS times connection queued for */
                                  /*  send credit*/
#define spi$_QBDT_CNT 12680       /* SCS times connection queued for buffer */
```

329

```
                                        /* descriptor   */
#define spi$_DIRLOOK 12681              /* directory lookups   */
#define spi$_DIRINS 12682              /* directory inserts   */
#define spi$_DIRDEL 12683              /* directory deletes   */
#define spi$_PACKETS 12684             /* Ethernet packets/second   */
#define spi$_KBYTES 12685              /* Kbytes/second   */
#define spi$_PACKETSIZE 12686          /* Packets size (bytes)   */
#define spi$_MPACKETS 12687            /* Multicast packets/second   */
#define spi$_MKBYTES 12688             /* Multicast Kbytes/second   */
#define spi$_MPACKETSIZE 12689         /* Multicast packet size (bytes)   */
#define spi$_SINGLECOLL 12690          /* Transmit single collision detected   */
#define spi$_MULTICOLL 12691           /* Transmit multi collisions detected   */
#define spi$_INITDEFER 12692           /* Transmit initially deferred   */
#define spi$_INTERNALBUFERR 12693      /* Receive internal buffer error   */
#define spi$_LOCBUFERR 12694           /* Receive local buffer error   */
#define spi$_BUFFUNAVAIL 12695         /* System buffer unavailable   */
#define spi$_FILLER 12696              /* Dummy pad item   */
#define spi$_RESERVEDMON1 12697        /* Reserved MON items   */
                                        /* Through 100 */
#define spi$_RESERVEDMON100 12796      /* Reserved MON items   */
#define spi$_LASTMON 12797             /* Last item in the monitor specific table   */
/*   */
/* Begin items specific to Monitor RMS class. These items are maintained by   */
/* RMS and collected from a global section with the following naming scheme: */
/* _RMS$xxxxxxxxyyyyy where x is the volume lock id and y is the fid of the */
/* file being monitored.   */
/*   */
#define spi$_RMS_STATS 16893           /* All of the following rms statistics   */
#define spi$_SEQGETS 16894             /* Total # of sequential gets   */
#define spi$_KEYGETS 16895             /* Total # of keyed gets   */
#define spi$_RFAGETS 16896             /* Total # of gets by RFA   */
#define spi$_GETBYTES 16897            /* Total size in bytes of all GETS   */
#define spi$_SEQPUTS 16898             /* Total # of sequential puts   */
#define spi$_KEYPUTS 16899             /* Total # of puts by key   */
#define spi$_PUTBYTES 16900            /* Total # of bytes put to file   */
#define spi$_UPDATES 16901             /* Total # of updates to the file   */
#define spi$_UPDATEBYTES 16902         /* Total # of bytes updated in file   */
#define spi$_DELETES 16903             /* Total # of deletes to file   */
#define spi$_TRUNCATES 16904           /* Total # of times file has been truncated   */
#define spi$_TRUNCBLKS 16905           /* Total # of blocks file has been truncated */
#define spi$_SEQFINDS 16906            /* Total # of sequential finds   */
#define spi$_KEYFINDS 16907            /* Total # of keyed finds   */
#define spi$_RFAFINDS 16908            /* Total # of RFA finds   */
#define spi$_READS 16909               /* Total # of $READS   */
```

```
#define spi$_READBYTES 16910        /* Total # of bytes read from $READS  */
#define spi$_CONNECTS 16911          /* Total connect requests  */
#define spi$_DISCONNECTS 16912       /* Total disconnect requests  */
#define spi$_EXTENDS 16913           /* Total extends  */
#define spi$_EXTBLOCKS 16914         /* Total number of blocks file has been */
                                     /* extended*/
#define spi$_FLUSHES 16915           /* Total number of calls to flush  */
#define spi$_REWINDS 16916           /* Total number of calls to REWIND  */
#define spi$_WRITES 16917            /* Total number of calls to $WRITE  */
#define spi$_WRITEBYTES 16918        /* Total bytes written using $WRITE  */
#define spi$_FLCKENQS 16919          /* Total number of file lock ENQ's  */
#define spi$_FLCKDEQS 16920          /* Total number of file lock DEQ's  */
#define spi$_FLCKCNVS 16921          /* Total number of file lock conversions  */
#define spi$_LBLCKENQS 16922         /* Total number of local buffer lock ENQ's  */
#define spi$_LBLCKDEQS 16923         /* Total number of local buffer lock DEQ's  */
#define spi$_LBLCKCNVS 16924         /* Total number of local buffer lock */
                                     /* conversions*/
#define spi$_GBLCKENQS 16925         /* Total number of global buffer lock ENQ's  */
#define spi$_GBLCKDEQS 16926         /* Total number of global buffer lock DEQ's  */
#define spi$_GBLCKCNVS 16927         /* Total number of global buffer lock */
                                     /* conversions  */
#define spi$_GSLCKENQS 16928         /* Total number of global section lock ENQ's */
#define spi$_GSLCKDEQS 16929         /* Total number of global section lock DEQ's */
#define spi$_GSLCKCNVS 16930         /* Total number of global section lock */
                                     /* conversions  */
#define spi$_RLCKENQS 16931          /* Total number of record lock ENQ's  */
#define spi$_RLCKDEQS 16932          /* Total number of record lock DEQ's  */
#define spi$_RLCKCNVS 16933          /* Total number of record lock conversions  */
#define spi$_APPLCKENQS 16934        /* Total number of append lock ENQ's  */
#define spi$_APPLCKDEQS 16935        /* Total number of append lock DEQ's  */
#define spi$_APPLCKCNVS 16936        /* Total number of append lock conversions  */
#define spi$_FLBLKASTS 16937         /* Total number of file lock blocking ASTs  */
#define spi$_LBLBLKASTS 16938        /* Total number of local buffer */
                                     /*  lock blocking ASTs  */
#define spi$_GBLBLKASTS 16939        /* Total number of global buffer lock */
                                     /* blocking ASTs  */
#define spi$_APPBLKASTS 16940        /* Total number of shared append lock */
                                     /*  blocking ASTs  */
#define spi$_LCACHEHITS 16941 /* Total cache hits on buckets in local buffers */
#define spi$_LCACHETRIES 16942/* Total cache attempts on buckets in local */
                              /* buffers  */
#define spi$_GCACHEHITS 16943 /* Total cache hits on buckets in global buffers*/
#define spi$_GCACHETRIES 16944/* Total cache attempts on buckets in global */
                              /* buffers  */
```

```
#define spi$_GBRDIRIOS 16945   /* Total direct IO's causes by global buffer */
                               /* cache reads  */
#define spi$_GBWDIRIOS 16946   /* Total direct IO's causes by global buffer */
                               /*  cache writes  */
#define spi$_LBRDIRIOS 16947   /* Total direct IO's causes by local buffer */
                               /*  cache reads  */
#define spi$_LBWDIRIOS 16948   /* Total direct IO's causes by local buffer */
                               /*  cache writes  */
#define spi$_BKTSPLT 16949     /* Total number of 2 bucket splits done for */
                               /*  this file  */
#define spi$_MBKTSPLT 16950    /* Total number of multi-bucket splits done */
                               /*  for this file  */
#define spi$_RMSOPENS 16951    /* Total number of times file has been opened*/
#define spi$_CLOSES 16952      /* Total number of times file has been closed  */
#define spi$_GSBLKASTS 16953   /* Global Section Blocking ASTS  */
#define spi$_FLWAITS 16954     /* File lock ENQs forced to wait  */
#define spi$_LBWAITS 16955     /* Local buffer ENQs forced to wait  */
#define spi$_GBWAITS 16956     /* Global buffer ENQs forced to wait  */
#define spi$_GSWAITS 16957     /* Global section ENQs forced to wait  */
#define spi$_RLWAITS 16958     /* Record lock ENQs forced to wait  */
#define spi$_APWAITS 16959     /* Append lock ENQs forced to wait  */
#define spi$_TOTWAITS 16960    /* Total ENQs forced to wait  */
#define spi$_OUTBUFQUO 16961   /* Number of times a process runs out of */
                               /*  buffer quota  */
#define spi$_RMSDEV1 16962     /* Reserved for RMS  */
                               /* Through 15 */
#define spi$_RMSDEV15 16976    /* Reserved for RMS   */
#define spi$_XQPQIOS 16977     /* Number of XQP operations for this*/
                               /* file by RMS  */
#define spi$_LCACHEHITPCNT 16978 /* Local RMS buffer hit percent  */
#define spi$_GCACHEHITPCNT 16979 /* Global RMS buffer hit percent  */
#define spi$_TOTALGET 16980      /* Total $GET call rate  */
#define spi$_TOTALPUT 16981      /* Total $PUT call rate  */
#define spi$_TOTALFIND 16982     /* Total $FIND call rate  */
#define spi$_BYTESGET 16983      /* Bytes per $GET  */
#define spi$_BYTESPUT 16984      /* Bytes per $PUT  */
#define spi$_BYTESUPDATE 16985   /* Bytes per $UPDATE  */
#define spi$_BYTESREAD 16986     /* Bytes per $READ  */
#define spi$_BYTESWRITE 16987    /* Bytes per $WRITE  */
#define spi$_BLOCKSTRUNCATE 16988/* Bytes per $TRUNCATE  */
#define spi$_BLOCKSEXTEND 16989  /* Bytes per $EXTEND  */
#define spi$_ACTIVE_STREAMS 16990/* Active connects to file  */
#define spi$_TOTAL_ENQS 16991    /* Total new ENQs  */
#define spi$_TOTAL_DEQS 16992    /* Total DEQs  */
```

```
#define spi$_TOTAL_CNVS 16993      /* Total ENQ conversions  */
#define spi$_TOTAL_BLKAST 16994    /* Total blocking ASTs  */
#define spi$_RMS_ORG 16995         /* RMS File org  */
#define spi$_RESERVEDRMS1 16996    /* Reserved RMS items  */
                                   /* Through 100 */
#define spi$_RESERVEDRMS100 17095  /* Reserved RMS items  */
#define spi$_LASTRMS 17096         /* Last item in the monitor specific table  */
/*  */
/* Add new data items specific to MONITOR (not collected by the SPI on a per  */
/* item basis) above this point.  */
/*  */
#define spi$_tablesize 712
/*  */
/* End of MONITOR specific data items.  */
/*  */
struct item_list_descriptor {
  short int ild$W_LENGTH;  /* Word containing length of destination buffer  */
  short int ild$w_item_id; /* Word containing the item identifier  */
  int *ild$a_item_buf;     /* Address of destination buffer  */
  int *ild$a_length_buf;   /* Address of a longword to receive the */
                           /*  resulting length of the item  */
                           /* Size of one item descriptor  */
  } ;
#define item_list_descriptor_size 12
#define item_table_size 8544
struct scs_offsets {           /* SCS class information  */
  char spi$b_scs_nodecount;
  char spi$b_scs_nodename [7]; /* System node name  */
  int spi$l_scs_dgsent;        /* Application datagrams sent  */
  int spi$l_scs_dgrcvd;        /* Application datagrams received  */
  int spi$l_scs_dgdiscard;     /* Application datagrams discarded  */
  int spi$l_scs_msgsent;       /* Application messages sent  */
  int spi$l_scs_msgrcvd;       /* Application messages received  */
  int spi$l_scs_snddats;       /* Block send datas initiated  */
  int spi$l_scs_kbytsent;      /* Kbytes sent via send datas  */
  int spi$l_scs_reqdats;       /* Block request datas initiated  */
  int spi$l_scs_kbytreqd;      / * Kbytes received via request datas  */
  int spi$l_scs_kbyt.mapd;     /* Kbytes mapped for block transfers  */
  int spi$l_scs_qcr_cnt;       /* Times connection queued for send credit  */
  int spi$l_scs_qbdt_cnt;      /* Times connection queued for buffer */
                               /*  descriptor*/
  } ;
#define spi$c_scs_minsize 56   /* Size of one collection block for scs class  */
struct disk_offsets {          /* DISK class information  */
```

333

```
  char spi$b_disk_alloclass;    /* Allocation class  */
  char spi$b_disk_devcount;
  char spi$b_disk_devname[3];   /* Device name  */
  short int spi$w_disk_unitnum;/* Unit number  */
  char spi$b_disk_flags;        /* Flags byte (low bit indicates served disk  */
  char spi$b_disk_nodecount;
  char spi$b_disk_nodename [7];/* Nodename  */
  char spi$b_disk_volcount;
  char spi$b_disk_volnamel [11];/* Volume name (low)  */
  int spi$l_disk_optcnt;        /* Operation count  */
  int spi$l_disk_qcount;        /* Queue length accumulator  */
  } ;
#define spi$c_disk_minsize 36   /* Size of one block  */
struct proc_class {             /* PROCESSES Class Data Block  */
  int spi$l_proc_ipid;          /* Internal PID  */
  int spi$l_proc_uic;           /* UIC (Member is low-order word)  */
  short int spi$w_proc_state;   /* State value  */
  char spi$b_proc_pri;          /* Priority (negative value)  */
  int spi$o proc_lname [4];     /* Process name (counted string)  */
  int spi$l_proc_gpgcnt;        /* Global page count  */
  int spi$l_proc_ppgcnt;        /* Process page count  */
  int spi$l_proc_sts;           /* PCB Status Vector  */
/* (PCB$V_RES bit clear => swapped out)  */
  int spi$l_proc_diocnt;        /* Direct I/O count  */
  int spi$l_proc_pageflts;      /* Page fault count  */
  int spi$l_proc_cputim;        /* Accumulated CPU time (in ticks)  */
  int spi$l_proc_biocnt;        /* Buffered I/O count  */
  int spi$l_proc_epid;          /* Extended PID  */
  int spi$l_proc_efwm;          /* Event flag wait mask (for MWAITs)  */
  } ;

#define spi$c_proc_minsize 63

#pragma standard
#pragma member_alignment __restore
#endif
```

DSRVDEF.H

```
#ifndef DSRVDEF_H
#define DSRVDEF_H
/*
** To update this for future releases of OpenVMS:
** Get library copy — lib/ext=$EWDATADEF sys$share:lib.mlb
```

```
** Insure offsets match the offsets in this file.
*/

#pragma nostandard

#ifdef DEC_ARA
#pragma member_alignment __save
#pragma nomember_alignment
#endif

/*
**+
** DSRV Definitions
**
** This module defines the main data structure of the MSCP server. This
** structure contains the values specified in the start-up qualifiers when
** the server was loaded, the  UQB vector table, and statistics that are
** kept for server performance measurements.
**
** CHECKED for  OpenVMS VAX 5.5-2
** CHECKED for  OpenVMS AXP 1.5
**-
*/
#define DSRV$M_LOG_ENABLD 0x1
#define DSRV$M_LOG_PRESENT 0x2
#define DSRV$M_PKT_LOGGED 0x4
#define DSRV$M_PKT_LOST 0x8
#define DSRV$M_LBSTEP1 0x10
#define DSRV$M_LBSTEP2 0x20
#define DSRV$M_LBEVENT 0x40
#define DSRV$M_HULB_DEL 0x80
#define DSRV$M_MON_ACTIVE 0x100
#define DSRV$M_LB_REQ 0x200
#define DSRV$M_CONFIG_WAIT 0x400
#define DSRV$C_LENGTH 1900
#define DSRV$K_LENGTH 1900
#define DSRV$K_AR_ADD 2              /* Action routine code  */
struct DSRVDEF {
  unsigned int DSRV$L_FLINK;        /* Field maintained for  */
  unsigned int DSRV$L_BLINK;        /*  compatability  */
  unsigned short int DSRV$W_SIZE; /* Structure size in bytes*/
  unsigned char DSRV$B_TYPE;        /* MSCP type structure   */
  unsigned char DSRV$B_SUBTYPE;     /*  with a DSRV subtype (1)*/
  variant_union  {
```

335

```
  unsigned short int DSRV$W_STATE;    /* Current state of the server*/
  variant_struct {
    unsigned DSRV$V_LOG_ENABLD : 1;   /* Logging is enabled  */
    unsigned DSRV$V_LOG_PRESENT : 1;  /* Logging code is present  */
    unsigned DSRV$V_PKT_LOGGED : 1;   /* A packet has been logged  */
    unsigned DSRV$V_PKT_LOST : 1;     /* One or more packets over-  */
                                      /*  written since last read  */
    unsigned DSRV$V_LBSTEP1 : 1;      /* Load balancing step1 active  */
    unsigned DSRV$V_LBSTEP2 : 1;      /* Load balancing step2 active  */
    unsigned DSRV$V_LBEVENT : 1;      /* An event of interest to LB has  */
                                      /*  occured while STEP1 was active*/
    unsigned DSRV$V_HULB_DEL : 1;     /* One or more HULBs to be deleted  */
    unsigned DSRV$V_MON_ACTIVE : 1;   /* The load monitor thread is active  */
    unsigned DSRV$V_LB_REQ : 1;       /* A load balance request has been */
                                      /*  sent*/
    unsigned DSRV$V_CONFIG_WAIT : 1;  /* Waiting for STACONFIG to */
                                      /*  complete  */
    unsigned DSRV$V_FILL_2 : 5;
    } DSRV$R_FILL_1;
  } DSRV$R_FILL_0;
unsigned short int DSRV$W_BUFWAIT;    /* I/Os that had to wait  */
unsigned int DSRV$L_LOG_BUF_START;    /* Address of start of buffer  */
unsigned int DSRV$L_LOG_BUF_END;      /* Address of end of buffer  */
unsigned int DSRV$L_NEXT_READ;        /* Adrs of next packet to read  */
unsigned int DSRV$L_NEXT_WRITE;       /* Adrs of next packet to write  */
unsigned short int DSRV$W_INC_LOLIM;  /* Low unit number to log  */
unsigned short int DSRV$W_INC_HILIM;  /* High unit number to log  */
unsigned short int DSRV$W_EXC_LOLIM;  /* Low unit number not to log  */
unsigned short int DSRV$W_EXC_HILIM;  /* High unit number not to log  */
unsigned int DSRV$L_SRVBUF;           /* Address of preallocated pool  */
unsigned int DSRV$L_FREE_LIST;        /* Pointer to head of free pool  */
unsigned int DSRV$L_AVAIL;            /* Sum of bytes available in buffer  */
unsigned int DSRV$L_BUFFER_MIN;       /* Min xfer size based on buffer  */
unsigned int DSRV$L_SPLITXFER;        /* Fragmented I/O count  */
variant_struct {                      /* Info returned in GCI cmd  */
  unsigned short int DSRV$W_VERSION;  /* Server software version  */
  unsigned short int DSRV$W_CFLAGS;   /* Controller flags  */
  unsigned short int DSRV$W_CTIMO;    /* Controller timeout  */
  unsigned short int DSRV$w_reserved; /* Reserved for alignment  */
  } DSRV$R_CTRL_INFO;
unsigned int DSRV$Q_CTRL_ID [2];      /* Unique MSCP device identifier  */
unsigned int DSRV$L_MEMW_TOT;         /* Number of I/Os that had to wait  */
unsigned short int DSRV$W_MEMW_CNT;   /* Requests in memory wait queue  */
unsigned short int DSRV$W_MEMW_MAX;   /* Most requests ever in MEMWAIT  */
```

336

```
    unsigned int DSRV$L_MEMW_FL;          /* Queue listhead for requests  */
    unsigned int DSRV$L_MEMW_BL;          /*  in memory wait state  */
    unsigned short int DSRV$W_NUM_HOST;   /* Count of hosts being served  */
    unsigned short int DSRV$W_NUM_UNIT;   /* Count of disks being served  */
    unsigned int DSRV$L_HQB_FL;           /* Host queue block list head  */
    unsigned int DSRV$L_HQB_BL;           /*  */
    unsigned int DSRV$L_UQB_FL;           /* Unit queue block list head  */
    unsigned int DSRV$L_UQB_BL;           /*  */
/*  */
/*  */
/*  */
/* Server Load Balancing fields  */
/*  */
/* The following fields contain working information and statistics  */
/* for the server load balancing function. Load balancing status bits  */
/* are defined in DSRV$STATE above. Time fields are in EXE$GL_ABSTIM  */
/* format.  */
/*  */
    unsigned short int DSRV$W_LOAD_AVAIL;    /* Current load available  */
    unsigned short int DSRV$W_LOAD_CAPACITY;/* Server load capacity  */
    unsigned short int DSRV$W_LBLOAD;        /* Target load for LB request  */
    unsigned short int DSRV$W_LBRESP;        /* Load available from other server  */
    unsigned short int DSRV$W_LM_LOAD1;      /* previous interval load 1  */
    unsigned short int DSRV$W_LM_LOAD2;      /* previous interval load 2  */
    unsigned short int DSRV$W_LM_LOAD3;      /* previous interval load 3  */
    unsigned short int DSRV$W_LM_LOAD4;      /* previous interval load 4  */
    unsigned short int DSRV$W_LBINIT_CNT;    /* Count of LB requests we have sent */
    unsigned short int DSRV$W_LBFAIL_CNT;    /* Count of LB requests that failed  */
    unsigned short int DSRV$W_LBREQ_CNT;     /* Count of LB requests from other */
                                             /*  servers  */
    unsigned short int DSRV$W_LBRESP_CNT;    /* Count of LB requests we to which */
                                             /*  we responded  */
    unsigned int DSRV$L_LBREQ_TIME;          /* Time last LB request was sent  */
    unsigned int DSRV$L_LBMON_TIME;          /* Time of last LB monitor pass  */
    unsigned int DSRV$L_LM_FKB;              /* Address of load monitor thread */
                                             /*  FKB*/
    unsigned int DSRV$L_LB_FKB;              /* Address of load balance thread */
                                             /*  FKB*/
    unsigned short int DSRV$W_LM_INTERVAL;   /* Load monitoring interval  */
    unsigned char DSRV$B_LB_COUNT1;          /* Counter for load balancing thread */
    unsigned char DSRV$B_LB_COUNT2;          /* Counter for load balancing thread */
    unsigned int DSRV$L_HULB_FL;             /* HULB queue listhead  */
    unsigned int DSRV$L_HULB_BL;             /*  */
    unsigned char DSRV$B_HOSTS [32];         /* Bit array of hosts served  */
```

337

```
  unsigned int DSRV$L_UNITS [256];          /* Table of UQB addresses  */
/*  */
/* Statistics gathering fields  */
/*  */
/* Two tables are maintained below. The first table is made up of the   */
/* frequency count for each of the opcodes received since the server   */
/* was loaded. The opcode is used as an index into the table to its own   */
/* frequency count (the zeroeth element contains a total count). The   */
/* second table is made up of the frequency counters for all the   */
/* different sized block transfers. For this table, the size of the   */
/* transfer is the index into the table.  */
/*  */
  variant_struct  {                      /* Op-code counters  */
    unsigned int DSRV$L_OPCOUNT;        /* Total operations count  */
    unsigned int DSRV$L_ABORT_CNT;     /*  - 1 -  */
    unsigned int DSRV$L_GET_CMD_CNT; /*  - 2 -  */
    unsigned int DSRV$L_GET_UNT_CNT; /*  - 3 -  */
    unsigned int DSRV$L_SET_CON_CNT; /*  - 4 -  */
    unsigned int DSRV$l_reserved;      /*  - 5 -  */
    unsigned int DSRV$l_reserved1;     /*  - 6 -  */
    unsigned int DSRV$l_reserved2;     /*  - 7 -  */
    unsigned int DSRV$L_AVAIL_CNT;     /*  - 8 -  */
    unsigned int DSRV$L_ONLIN_CNT;     /*  - 9 -  */
    unsigned int DSRV$L_SET_UNT_CNT; /*  - 10 -  */
    unsigned int DSRV$L_DET_ACC_CNT; /*  - 11 -  */
    unsigned int DSRV$l_reserved3;     /*  - 12 -  */
    unsigned int DSRV$l_reserved4;     /*  - 13 -  */
    unsigned int DSRV$l_reserved5;     /*  - 14 -  */
    unsigned int DSRV$l_reserved6;     /*  - 15 -  */
    unsigned int DSRV$L_ACCES_CNT;     /*  - 16 -  */
    unsigned int DSRV$L_CMP_CON_CNT; /*  - 17 -  */
    unsigned int DSRV$L_ERASE_CNT;     /*  - 18 -  */
    unsigned int DSRV$L_FLUSH_CNT;     /*  - 19 -  */
    unsigned int DSRV$L_REPLC_CNT;     /*  - 20 -  */
    unsigned int DSRV$l_reserved7;     /*  - 21 -  */
    unsigned int DSRV$l_reserved8;     /*  - 22 -  */
    unsigned int DSRV$l_reserved9;     /*  - 23 -  */
    unsigned int DSRV$l_reserved10;    /*  - 24 -  */
    unsigned int DSRV$l_reserved11;    /*  - 25 -  */
    unsigned int DSRV$l_reserved12;    /*  - 26 -  */
    unsigned int DSRV$l_reserved13;    /*  - 27 -  */
    unsigned int DSRV$l_reserved14;    /*  - 28 -  */
    unsigned int DSRV$l_reserved15;    /*  - 29 -  */
    unsigned int DSRV$l_reserved16;    /*  - 30 -  */
```

```
        unsigned int DSRV$l_reserved17;   /*   - 31 -   */
        unsigned int DSRV$L_CMP_HST_CNT; /*   - 32 -   */
        unsigned int DSRV$L_READ_CNT;     /*   - 33 -   */
        unsigned int DSRV$L_WRITE_CNT;    /*   - 34 -   */
        unsigned int DSRV$l_reserved18;   /*   - 35 -   */
        unsigned int DSRV$l_reserved19;   /*   - 36 -   */
        unsigned int DSRV$l_reserved20;   /*   - 37 -   */
        unsigned int DSRV$l_reserved21;   /*   - 38 -   */
        unsigned int DSRV$l_reserved22;   /*   - 39 -   */
#ifndef DEC_ARA
        unsigned int DSRV$l_reserved23;
        unsigned int DSRV$l_reserved24;
        unsigned int DSRV$l_reserved25;
        unsigned int DSRV$l_reserved26;
        unsigned int DSRV$l_reserved27;
        unsigned int DSRV$l_reserved28;
        unsigned int DSRV$l_reserved29;
        unsigned int DSRV$l_reserved30;
        unsigned int DSRV$l_reserved31;
        unsigned int DSRV$l_reserved32;
#endif
    } DSRV$R_OPCODE_CNTRS;
    unsigned int DSRV$L_VCFAIL_CNT;  /* Count of VC failures  */
    unsigned int DSRV$L_BLKCOUNT [129]; /* Counters for block xfer reqs  */
    } ;

#pragma standard

#ifdef DEC_ARA
#pragma member_alignment __restore
#endif

#endif
```

EWDATADEF.H

```
#ifndef EWDATADEF_H
#define EWDATADEF_H
/*
** To update this for future releases of OpenVMS:
** Get library copy — lib/ext=$EWDATADEF sys$share:lib.mlb
** Insure offsets match the offsets in this file.
*/
#pragma nostandard
```

```
#pragma member_alignment __save
#pragma nomember_alignment
/*+   */
/* $EWDATADEF - Symbolic offsets within the exec-writable page  */
/*   */
#define EW$K_LENGTH 378
#define EW$C_LENGTH 378
struct EWDATADEF {
  variant_struct  {
    char EW_PMS$GL_FCP [];            /* start of the FCP counters  */
    char EW_PMS$GL_FCP2 [];           /* start of the FCP2 counters  */
    unsigned int EW_PMS$AL_COUNT [10]; /* number of operations  */
    unsigned int EW_PMS$AL_MCNT [10];  /* number of modifiers  */
    unsigned int EW_PMS$AL_READ [10];  /* number of disk reads  */
    unsigned int EW_PMS$AL_WRITE [10]; /* number of disk writes  */
    unsigned int EW_PMS$AL_CACHE [10]; /* number of cache hits  */
    unsigned int EW_PMS$AL_CPU [10];   /* accumulated cpu times  */
    unsigned int EW_PMS$AL_PFA [10];   /* accumulated page faults  */
    unsigned int FW_PMS$GL_TURN;       /* number of window turns  */
    unsigned int EW_PMS$GL_DIRHIT;     /* count of directory LRU hits  */
    unsigned int EW_PMS$GL_DIRMISS;    /* count of directory LRU misses  */
    unsigned int EW_PMS$GL_QUOHIT;     /* count of quota cache hits  */
    unsigned int EW_PMS$GL_QUOMISS;    /* count of quota cache misses  */
    unsigned int EW_PMS$GL_FIDHIT;     /* count of file ID cache hits  */
    unsigned int EW_PMS$GL_FIDMISS;    /* count of file ID cache misses  */
    unsigned int EW_PMS$GL_EXTHIT;     /* count of extent cache hits  */
    unsigned int EW_PMS$GL_EXTMISS;    /* count of extent cache misses  */
    unsigned int EW_PMS$GL_FILHDR_HIT; /* count of file header cache hits  */
    unsigned int EW_PMS$GL_FILHDR_MISS;/* count of file header cache misses  */
    unsigned int EW_PMS$GL_DIRDATA_HIT;/* count of directory data block hits  */
    unsigned int EW_PMS$GL_DIRDATA_MISS; /* count of directory data block */
                                         /*  misses*/
    unsigned int EW_PMS$GL_STORAGMAP_HIT; /* count of storage bit map cache */
                                          /*  hits*/
    unsigned int EW_PMS$GL_STORAGMAP_MISS;/* count of storage bit map cache */
                                          /*  misses  */
    unsigned int EW_PMS$GL_OPEN;       /* number of currently open files  */
    unsigned int EW_PMS$GL_OPENS;      /* total count of opens  */
    unsigned int EW_PMS$GL_ERASEIO;    /* total count of erase QIO's issued*/
    unsigned int EW_PMS$GL_VOLLCK;     /* count of XQP volume synch locks  */
    unsigned int EW_PMS$GL_VOLWAIT;    /* # of times XQP had to wait for a */
                                       /* volume synch lock  */
    unsigned int EW_PMS$GL_SYNCHLCK;   /* count of XQP directory and  */
                                       /* file synch locks  */
```

```
      unsigned int EW_PMS$GL_SYNCHWAIT;        /* # of times XQP had to wait for a */
                                               /* directory or file synch lock   */
      unsigned int EW_PMS$GL_ACCLCK;           /* count of XQP access locks   */
      unsigned int EW_PMS$GL_XQPCACHEWAIT;  /* # of times XQP had to wait for  */
                                               /* free space in a cache  */
    } EW$R_PMSEWDATA;
  variant_struct{
    unsigned short int EW_RMS$GW_GBLBUFQUO; /* current global buffer quota */
                                            /*  remaining  */

    } EW$R_RMSEWDATA;
  } ;


#pragma member_alignment __restore
#pragma standard

#endif
```

MONITOR.H

```
#ifndef MONITOR_H
#define MONITOR_H

#pragma nostandard
#pragma member_alignment __save
#pragma member_alignment

#define MAXDISKS  50
#define MAXSCS 50
#define MAXPROCESS 50

struct DATE_TIME
{
  unsigned int time[2];
};



struct HEADER
{
unsigned long int gen$l_flink;    /* Forward link to next list in the queue  */
  unsigned long int gen$l_blink;  /* Back link to previous list in queue  */
  unsigned short int gen$w_size;  /* Total size of the list  */
  unsigned char gen$b_type;       /* Structure type code  */
};
```

```
#define PAGEDATA 1
#define MSCPDATA 2
#define DISKDATA 3
#define SCSDATA  4
#define MISCDATA 5
#define PMSDATA 6
struct GOT_DATA
{
  struct HEADER Header;
  variant_union
  {

  struct DATAPAGE
  {
    struct PCBDEF *process_header, **process_index_array;
    struct page_offsets
    {
        unsigned int page_faults, page_fault_ios;
        unsigned int process_pages, global_pages;
        unsigned int pid, diocnt, biocnt, wssize;
    }processdata[MAXPROCESS];
    unsigned int free_size, mod_size;
    struct DATE_TIME current_time;
  }PageInfo;
  struct DATAMSCP
  {
    int TotalIOCount;
    int ReadCount;
    int WriteCount;
    int ExtraIOCount;
    int SplitCount;
    int WaitIOCount;
    int ForceCounts;
    struct DATE_TIME current_time;
  }MSCPInfo;
  struct DATADISK
  {
    int NumberDisks;
    struct disk_offsets diskdata[MAXDISKS];
    struct DATE_TIME current_time;
  }Diskinfo;
  struct DATASCS
  {
    int NumberSCSNodes;
```

```
      struct scs_offsets scsdata[MAXSCS];
      struct DATE_TIME current_time;
}SCSInfo;
struct DATASPECIAL
{
  unsigned int LockCount;
  unsigned int ResourceCount;
  unsigned int FreeListSize;
  unsigned int ModListSize;
  unsigned int WindowTurns;
  unsigned int DirectoryHits;
  unsigned int DirectoryMisses;
  unsigned int QuotaHits;
  unsigned int QuotaMisses;
  unsigned int FileCacheHits;
  unsigned int FileCacheMisses;
  unsigned int ExtentHits;
  unsigned int ExtentMisses;
  unsigned int FileHeaderHits;
  unsigned int FileHeaderMisses;
  unsigned int DirectoryBlockHits;
  unsigned int DirectoryBlockMisses;
  unsigned int BitMapHits;
  unsigned int BitMapMisses;
  unsigned int OpenFiles;
  unsigned int Opens;
  unsigned int Erase;
  unsigned int VolumeSyncLocks;
  unsigned int VolumeSyncLocksWaits;
  unsigned int DirectoryandFileSynchLocks;
  unsigned int DirectoryandFileSynchLocksWAits;
  unsigned int AccessLocks;
  unsigned int XQPCacheWait;
  struct DATE_TIME current_time;
}MISCInfo;
struct DATAPMS
{
  unsigned int PMS$GL_PREADIO;    /* count page read i/o requests */
  unsigned int PMS$GL_PREADS;     /* number of pages read */
  unsigned int PMS$GL_PWRITES;    /* Modified pages written */
  unsigned int PMS$GL_PWRITIO;    /* I/Os to write the modified pages */
  unsigned int PMS$GL_FAULTS;     /* count all the page faults */
  unsigned int PMS$GL_FREEFLTS;   /* Free list page faults al_transflt[0] */
  unsigned int PMS$GL_MODFLTS;    /* Modified list page faults */
```

343

```
      unsigned int PMS$GL_GVALID;      /* Global valid faults */
      unsigned int PMS$GL_SCH_0_PAGE;
      /* Zeroed pages created in scheduler idle loop */
      unsigned int PMS$GL_PAGES;
      /* number of pages of memory on configuration */
      unsigned int PMS$GL_DZROFLTS;    /* demand zero page faults */
      unsigned int PMS$GL_DPTSCN;      /* dead page table scans */
      unsigned int PMS$AL_CRF[2];      /* copy on reference private/global*/
      unsigned int PMS$AL_CRFIO[2];    /* and the I/Os */
      struct DATE_TIME current_time;
    }PMSInfo;
   }NotUsed;
}LocalCopy;


#pragma standard
#pragma member_alignment __restore


#endif
```

MONITOR.C

```
/*
**++
**   FACILITY:  VMS_TOOLS
**
** Copyright (c) 1993 James W. Coburn
** Copyright (c) 1993 Cardinal Business Media
** This program may be copied for noncommercial purposes. Use of this
** program for any other purpose without the express written consent
** of the publisher is prohibited.
**
** MODULE DESCRIPTION:
**
** This program collects System Performance data for a clustered
** system.  The data is collected using the ****Undocumented**
** system call EXE$GETSPI.  In some cases EXE$GETSPI does not
** collect the data we need, so direct calls are made to OS data
** structures.
**
** TEST on a single node cluster before running in a productions
** environment.  This code uses kernel mode access and thus will
** crash your system if there are coding bugs or if changes to
** VMS introduce new bugs.
**
** This code has been tested on:
```

```
** OpenVMS AXP 1.5
**
**
** AUTHORS:
**
** Jim Coburn
**
** CREATION DATE:  June 1993
**
** DESIGN ISSUES:
**
**
**
** MODIFICATION HISTORY:
**
**
**—
*/


/*
**
** INCLUDE FILES
**
*/

#include <descrip.h>
#include <string.h>
#include <stdio.h>
#include <rms.h>
#include <descrip.h>
#include <stdio.h>
#include <starlet.h>
#include <libdtdef.h>
#include <lib$routines.h>
#include <stdlib.h>

#include <pfm/AXP_phddef.h>
#include <pfm/AXP_pcbdef.h>
#include <mscp/dsrvdef.h>
#include <pfm/getspidef.h>
#include <pfm/ewdatadef.h>
#include <pfm/monitor.h>
```

345

```
/*
**
**   Prototypes
**
*/

void OpenFile( void );
int GetMSCPInfo( struct GOT_DATA *LocalCopy );
int GetPageInfo( struct GOT_DATA *LocalCopy );
int GetDiskInfo( struct GOT_DATA *LocalCopy );
int GetSCSInfo( struct GOT_DATA *LocalCopy );
int GetMISCInfo( struct GOT_DATA *LocalCopy );
int GetPMSInfo( struct GOT_DATA *LocalCopy );
int spi$dskini( int );


/*
**   Globals from System.
*/

#pragma nostandard
globalref unsigned int SCH$GL_MAXPIX;
globalref struct PCBDEF **SCH$GL_PCBVEC;
globalref struct PCBDEF *SCH$AR_NULLPCB;
globalref unsigned int SCH$GL_MFYCNT;
globalref unsigned int SCH$GL_FREECNT;
globalref struct DATE_TIME EXE$GQ_SYSTIME;
globalref struct DSRVDEF *SCS$GL_MSCP;
globalref unsigned int LCK$GL_LCKCNT;
globalref unsigned int LCK$GL_RSBCNT;
globalref struct EWDATADEF *EXE$AR_EWDATA;
globalref unsigned int PMS$GL_PREADIO;  /* count page read i/o requests */
globalref unsigned int PMS$GL_PREADS;   /* number of pages read */
globalref unsigned int PMS$GL_PWRITES;  /* Modified pages written */
globalref unsigned int PMS$GL_PWRITIO;  /* I/O requests to write the modified pa
ges */
globalref unsigned int PMS$GL_FAULTS;   /* count all the page faults */
globalref unsigned int PMS$AL_TRANSFLT[2]; /* Free/Mod faults */
globalref unsigned int PMS$GL_GVALID;   /* Global valid faults */
globalref unsigned int PMS$GL_SCH_0_PAGE;
/* Zeroed pages created in scheduler idle loop */
globalref unsigned int PMS$GL_PAGES;
/* number of pages of memory on configuration */
globalref unsigned int PMS$GL_DZROFLTS; /* demand zero page faults */
globalref unsigned int PMS$GL_DPTSCN;   /* dead page table scans */
```

```
globalref unsigned int PMS$AL_CRF[2];    /* copy on reference private/global */
globalref unsigned int PMS$AL_CRFIO[2]; /* and the I/Os */

#pragma standard

/*
**   For output
*/

struct FAB fblock;  /* Declare a fab structure  */
struct RAB rblock;  /* Declare a rab structure  */

#pragma nostandard
#define __unknown_params
int EXE$GETSPI( __unknown_params);
#pragma standard

struct item_list_descriptor SPIList[2];

struct IOSB
{
  short cond, count;
  int other;
} iosb;


main (int argc, char *argv[], char *envp[])
{

  struct DATE_TIME wake_up_time;
/*
**   Only collect data requested.
**   To make collect data enter the following before running this program.
**   $ COLLECTdata=="TRUE"
**   or
**   $ define/xxx COLLECTdata "TRUE"
**   Where xxx is any table that is accessable to this program.
*/
  int GetMSCP = ( int ) getenv("COLLECTMSCP");
  int GetPAGE = ( int ) getenv("COLLECTPAGE");
  int GetDISK = ( int ) getenv("COLLECTDISK");
  int GetSCS  = ( int ) getenv("COLLECTSCS");
  int GetMISC = ( int ) getenv("COLLECTMISC");
  int GetPMS = ( int ) getenv("COLLECPMS");
```

347

```
/*
**   Default collection interval is 3 seconds.
**   Change via $ DELTATIME="Valid delta time"
*/

  $DESCRIPTOR( delta_time, "0 00:00:03.00" );
  char *NewTime = getenv("DELTATIME");

  int status;

/*
**   Debug to insure getenv is working correctly on AXP.
*/
  printf( "MSCP = %d, PAGE = %d, DISK = %d, SCS = %d MISC = % d NewTime = %d \
n",
       GetMSCP, GetPAGE, GetDISK, GetSCS, GetMISC, NewTime );

  if( GetMSCP == 0 && GetPAGE == 0 && GetDISK == 0 &&
      GetSCS == 0 && GetMISC == 0 && GetPMS == 0)
  {
      printf( "Usage error, no data to collect.\n");
      exit (1 );
  }
/*
**   Open the file and setup for output
*/

  OpenFile();

  rblock.rab$l_rbf = (char *) &LocalCopy;      /* Set up the buffer  */
  rblock.rab$w_rsz = sizeof(struct GOT_DATA); /* Number of bytes to write  */

/*
**   If collecting disk data you must initialize the collector.
**   If you don't collect within 903 seconds the collection stops.
**   (Part of MONITOR).
*/
  if( GetDISK != 0 )
  {
      status = spi$dskini( 903);
  }


  /*
```

```
**  If user specified new collection interval use it.
*/
  if( NewTime != NULL )
  {
      delta_time.dsc$a_pointer = NewTime;
  }
  sys$bintim( &delta_time, &wake_up_time );
  sys$schdwk( 0, 0, &wake_up_time, &wake_up_time );

/*
** Program works by
** schedule wakeup in n second,
** collect data and write to file
** hiber until wakeup.
*/
  for( ; ; )
  {

/*
**  If class of data is wanted then collect
**  classes are: PAGE, MSCP, DISK, SCS,
*/
    if( GetPAGE != 0 )
    {
      status = GetPageInfo( &LocalCopy );
    }
    if( GetDISK != 0 )
    {
      status = GetDiskInfo( &LocalCopy );
    }
    if( GetSCS != 0 )
    {
      status = GetSCSInfo( &LocalCopy );
    }
    if( GetMSCP != 0 )
    {
      status = GetMSCPInfo( &LocalCopy );
    }
    if( GetMISC != 0 )
    {
      status = GetMISCInfo( &LocalCopy );
    }
    if( GetPMS != 0 )
    {
```

```
      status = GetPMSInfo( &LocalCopy );
    }
    sys$hiber();
  .}
}


/*
**++
**   FUNCTIONAL DESCRIPTION:
**
**   This function collects Process stats and writes them to the file.
**
**   FORMAL PARAMETERS:
**
**   None:  We assume that LocalData is where the data goes.
**
**   RETURN VALUE:
**
**   1 if data is collected, 0 if not.
**
**   SIDE EFFECTS:
**
**   Data is read from system protected memory into user space.
**   Thus we are running in Kernel mode.  Be very very careful here.
**   The GETSPI would work but it does not collect the data we need.
**
**—
*/
int GetPageData( int loop_count )
{

/*
**   Walk the list is processes getting data.
*/
  LocalCopy.PageInfo.process_header =
      LocalCopy.PageInfo.process_index_array[loop_count];

/*
**   Skip unused slots, swapped out, and deleting processes.
*/

  if ( ( LocalCopy.PageInfo.process_header == SCH$AR_NULLPCB ) ||
      (LocalCopy.PageInfo.process_header->PCB$L_PHD == 0 ) ||
      ( ( 1 & LocalCopy.PageInfo.process_header->PCB$L_STS) != 1 ) )
```

```
  {
      LocalCopy.PageInfo.processdata[loop_count].page_faults = 0;
      LocalCopy.PageInfo.processdata[loop_count].page_fault_ios = 0;
      LocalCopy.PageInfo.processdata[loop_count].pid = 0;
      LocalCopy.PageInfo.processdata[loop_count].process_pages = 0;
      LocalCopy.PageInfo.processdata[loop_count].global_pages = 0;
      LocalCopy.PageInfo.processdata[loop_count].diocnt = 0;
      LocalCopy.PageInfo.processdata[loop_count].biocnt = 0;
      LocalCopy.PageInfo.processdata[loop_count].wssize = 0;
      return 0;
  }
/*
**   Get stuff we need.
*/
  if( loop_count < MAXPROCESS)
  {
    LocalCopy.PageInfo.processdata[loop_count].page_faults =
      LocalCopy.PageInfo.process_header->PCB$L_PHD->PHD$L_PAGEFLTS;
    LocalCopy.PageInfo.processdata[loop_count].page_fault_ios =
      LocalCopy.PageInfo.process_header->PCB$L_PHD->PHD$L_PGFLTIO;
    LocalCopy.PageInfo.processdata[loop_count].pid =
      LocalCopy.PageInfo.process_header->PCB$L_EPID;
    LocalCopy.PageInfo.processdata[loop_count].process_pages =
      LocalCopy.PageInfo.process_header->PCB$L_PPGCNT;
    LocalCopy.PageInfo.processdata[loop_count].global_pages =
      LocalCopy.PageInfo.process_header->PCB$L_GPGCNT;
    LocalCopy.PageInfo.processdata[loop_count].diocnt =
      LocalCopy.PageInfo.process_header->PCB$L_PHD->PHD$L_DIOCNT;
    LocalCopy.PageInfo.processdata[loop_count].biocnt =
      LocalCopy.PageInfo.process_header->PCB$L_PHD->PHD$L_BIOCNT;
    LocalCopy.PageInfo.processdata[loop_count].wssize =
      LocalCopy.PageInfo.process_header->PCB$L_PHD->PHD$L_WSSIZE;
}

    return 1;
}


/*
**++
** FUNCTIONAL DESCRIPTION:
**
** This routine uses kernel mode code to collect Process page data
** for our monitor.
```

```
**
** FORMAL PARAMETERS:
**
**    struct GOT_DATA *DataCopy :
**       Pointer to master area to store the data you collect.
**
** RETURN VALUE:
**
**    Alway return 1, success.
**
** SIDE EFFECTS:
**
**    Process Page performance data is collected and stored in the file.
**
**
**_
*/
int GetPageInfo( struct GOT_DATA *DataCopy )
{
  int loop_count, got_one;
  int status, GetPageData();
  struct
  {
      int count;
      int value;
  }arglist;
/*
** Initialize page data structur.
*/
  DataCopy->PageInfo.process_index_array = SCH$GL_PCBVEC;
/*
** Process all active/valid processes
*/

  arglist.count = 1;
  for( loop_count = 0; loop_count <= SCH$GL_MAXPIX; loop_count++)
  {
      arglist.value = loop_count;
      status = sys$cmexec ( GetPageData, &arglist);
  }
/*
** Mark header with type and data and also save
** Size for freelist and modified list.
*/
```

```
  DataCopy->PageInfo.free_size = SCH$GL_FREECNT;
  DataCopy->PageInfo.mod_size = SCH$GL_MFYCNT;
  DataCopy->PageInfo.current_time = EXE$GQ_SYSTIME;
  DataCopy->Header.gen$b_type = PAGEDATA;

  status = sys$put(&rblock);
  if (status != RMS$_NORMAL)
  {
      lib$stop(status);
  }
  return ( 1 );
}

/*
**++
** FUNCTIONAL DESCRIPTION:
**
** Collect MSCP performance data without kernel calls.
**
** FORMAL PARAMETERS:
**
**   struct GOT_DATA *DataCopy :
**     Pointer to master area to store the data you collect.
**
** RETURN VALUE:
**
**   Alway return 1, success.
**
** SIDE EFFECTS:
**
**   MSCP performance data is collected and stored in the file.
**
**
**--
*/
int GetMSCPInfo( struct GOT_DATA *DataCopy )
{

/*
**   Struct to hold the MSCP data we want.  It is not the
**   same as what GETSPI returns.  We use GETSPI to avoid
**   kernel code and reduce amount of work needed with each
**   VMS system release.
*/
```

```
    struct MSCPSPI
    {
        int TotalIOCount;
        int ReadCount;
        int WriteCount;
        int ExtraIOCount;
        int SplitCount;
        int WaitIOCount;
        int Sizes[7];
    }MSCPspi;

    int status, retval, ctx= 0;

/*
**  Set up item list for call.
*/
    SPIList[0].ild$W_LENGTH      = sizeof( struct MSCPSPI);
    SPIList[0].ild$w_item_id     = spi$_MSCP_ALL;
    SPIList[0].ild$a_item_buf    = (int * )&( MSCPspi);
    SPIList[0].ild$a_length_buf  = &retval;

    SPIList[1].ild$W_LENGTH      = 0;
    SPIList[1].ild$w_item_id     = 0;

/*
**  Since GETSPI is not a "supported call" there is not version
**  with wait.
*/
    status = EXE$GETSPI( 9, &ctx, 0, (struct ItemList *)&SPIList,
        (struct IOSB *) &iosb, 0, 0);
    sys$waitfr (9);

    if( status )
    {
/*
**  Mark header with type and time.
*/
        DataCopy->Header.gen$b_type = MSCPDATA;
        DataCopy->MSCPInfo.current_time = EXE$GQ_SYSTIME;
/*
**  Move data from our are to the data struct
*/
        DataCopy->MSCPInfo.TotalIOCount = MSCPspi.TotalIOCount;
```

354

```
       DataCopy->MSCPInfo.ReadCount = MSCPspi.ReadCount;
       DataCopy->MSCPInfo.WriteCount = MSCPspi.WriteCount;
       DataCopy->MSCPInfo.ExtraIOCount = MSCPspi.ExtraIOCount;
       DataCopy->MSCPInfo.SplitCount = MSCPspi.SplitCount;
       DataCopy->MSCPInfo.WaitIOCount = MSCPspi.WaitIOCount;
#ifdef VAX
/*
**   Cannot read on VAX with kernel code so skip for now.
*/
       DataCopy->MSCPInfo.ForceCounts = 0;
#else
       DataCopy->MSCPInfo.ForceCounts = SCS$GL_MSCP-
>DSRV$L_BLKCOUNT[127];
#endif

/*
**   Save data to file.
*/
       status = sys$put(&rblock);
       if (status != RMS$_NORMAL)
       {
         lib$stop(status);
       }
  }
  return 1;
}


/*
**++
** FUNCTIONAL DESCRIPTION:
**
** Collect SCS performance data without kernel calls.
**
** FORMAL PARAMETERS:
**
**    struct GOT_DATA *DataCopy :
**      Pointer to master area to store the data you collect.
**
** RETURN VALUE:
**
**    Alway return 1, success.
**
** SIDE EFFECTS:
**
```

355

```
** SCS performance data is collected and stored in the file.
**
**
**—
*/
int GetSCSInfo( struct GOT_DATA *DataCopy )
{

  int status, retval, ctx= 0;

/*
**  Set up item list for call.
*/

  SPIList[0].ild$W_LENGTH    =  MAXSCS*spi$c_scs_minsize+4;
  SPIList[0].ild$w_item_id   =  spi$_SCS;
  SPIList[0].ild$a_item_buf  =  (int * )&(DataCopy->SCSInfo);
  SPIList[0].ild$a_length_buf =  &retval;

  SPIL1st[1].ild$W_LENGTH   =  0;
  SPIList[1].ild$w_item_id  =  0;

  status = EXE$GETSPI( 9, &ctx, 0, (struct ItemList *)&SPIList,
      (struct IOSB *) &iosb, 0, 0);
  sys$waitfr (9);


  if( status )
  {
/*
**  Mark header with type and time.
*/
      DataCopy->SCSInfo.current_time = EXE$GQ_SYSTIME;
      DataCopy->Header.gen$b_type = SCSDATA;

/*
**  Save data to file.
*/
      status = sys$put(&rblock);
      if (status != RMS$_NORMAL)
      {
        lib$stop(status);
      }
  }
```

356

```
  return 1;
}


/*
**++
** FUNCTIONAL DESCRIPTION:
**
** Collect DISK performance data without kernel calls.
**
** FORMAL PARAMETERS:
**
**   struct GOT_DATA *DataCopy :
**     Pointer to master area to store the data you collect.
**
** RETURN VALUE:
**
**   Alway return 1, success.
**
** SIDE EFFECTS:
**
** DISK performance data is collected and stored in the file.
**
**
**—
*/
int GetDiskInfo( struct GOT_DATA *DataCopy )
{
  int status;
  int ctx, proc_l;
  static int FirstTime = TRUE;

  SPIList[0].ild$W_LENGTH    = MAXDISKS*spi$c_disk_minsize+4;
  SPIList[0].ild$w_item_id   = spi$_DISKS;
  SPIList[0].ild$a_item_buf  = (int * )&(LocalCopy.Diskinfo);
  SPIList[0].ild$a_length_buf = &proc_l;

  SPIList[1].ild$W_LENGTH    = 0;
  SPIList[1].ild$w_item_id   = 0;

  status = EXE$GETSPI(9, &ctx, 0, (struct ItemList *)&SPIList,
      (struct IOSB *) &iosb, 0, 0);
  sys$waitfr (9);

  if( FirstTime && LocalCopy.Diskinfo.NumberDisks >= MAXDISKS )
```

357

```
  {
      printf( "MAXDISK value of %d is to small\n", MAXDISKS);
      FirstTime = FALSE;
  }



/*
**   Mark header with type and time.
*/
  if ( status )
  {
      LocalCopy.Header.gen$b_type = DISKDATA;
      LocalCopy.Diskinfo.current_time = EXE$GQ_SYSTIME;
/*
**   Save data to file.
*/
      status = sys$put(&rblock);
      if (status != RMS$_NORMAL)
      {
        lib$stop(status);
      }
  }

  return 1;
}

void OpenFile( void )
{
  int status;
  char *fname="monitor$data";   /* File name to be accessed  */
  fblock = cc$rms_fab;          /* Initialize fab structure  */
  rblock = cc$rms_rab;          /* Initialize rab structure  */

/* Declare file access options.  In this case the file will be opened with
   write, read, and update (respectively).  */

  fblock.fab$b_fac = FAB$M_PUT | FAB$M_GET | FAB$M_UPD;
  rblock.rab$l_fab = &fblock;   /* Point the rab to the fab  */
  fblock.fab$l_fna = fname;     /* file name  */
  fblock.fab$b_fns = strlen(fname);  /* length of file name  */
  fblock.fab$b_rfm = FAB$C_FIX; /* variable length records  */
  fblock.fab$b_rat = FAB$M_CR;  /* carriage return attribute*/
  fblock.fab$w_mrs = sizeof( struct GOT_DATA);
```

358

```
    status = sys$create(&fblock);
    if (status != RMS$_NORMAL)
    {
        lib$stop(status);
    }
    status = sys$connect(&rblock);
    if (status != RMS$_NORMAL)
    {
        lib$stop(status);
    }

/*
**  Specify sequential access
*/
    rblock.rab$b_rac = RAB$C_SEQ;
}

close_file()
{
  int status;
  status = sys$close(&fblock);  /* Close the file  */
  if (status != RMS$_NORMAL)
  {
        lib$stop(status);
  }
}

/*
**++
** FUNCTIONAL DESCRIPTION:
**
** This routine uses kernel mode code to collect Process page data
** for our monitor.
**
** FORMAL PARAMETERS:
**
**   struct GOT_DATA *DataCopy :
**      Pointer to master area to store the data you collect.
**
** RETURN VALUE:
**
**   Alway return 1, success.
**
** SIDE EFFECTS:
```

```
**
** Process Page performance data is collected and stored in the file.
**
**
**_
*/
int GetMISCInfo( struct GOT_DATA *DataCopy )
{
  int loop_count, got_one;
  int status;

/*
**   Mark header with type and data and also save
**   Size for freelist and modified list.
*/
  DataCopy->MISCInfo.FreeListSize = SCH$GL_FREECNT;
  DataCopy->MISCInfo.ModListSize = SCH$GL_MFYCNT;
  DataCopy->MISCInfo.LockCount = LCK$GL_LCKCNT;
  DataCopy->MISCInfo.ResourceCount = LCK$GL_RSBCNT;
  DataCopy->MISCInfo.WindowTurns = EXE$AR_EWDATA->EW_PMS$GL_TURN;
  DataCopy->MISCInfo.DirectoryHits = EXE$AR_EWDATA->EW_PMS$GL_DIRHIT;
  DataCopy->MISCInfo.DirectoryMisses =
    EXE$AR_EWDATA->EW_PMS$GL_DIRMISS;
  DataCopy->MISCInfo.QuotaHits = EXE$AR_EWDATA->EW_PMS$GL_QUOHIT;
  DataCopy->MISCInfo.QuotaMisses = EXE$AR_EWDATA->EW_PMS$GL_QUOMISS;
  DataCopy->MISCInfo.FileCacheHits = EXE$AR_EWDATA->EW_PMS$GL_FIDHIT;
  DataCopy->MISCInfo.FileCacheMisses =
    EXE$AR_EWDATA->EW_PMS$GL_FIDMISS;
  DataCopy->MISCInfo.ExtentHits = EXE$AR_EWDATA->EW_PMS$GL_EXTHIT;
  DataCopy->MISCInfo.ExtentMisses = EXE$AR_EWDATA->EW_PMS$GL_EXTMISS;
  DataCopy->MISCInfo.FileHeaderHits =
    EXE$AR_EWDATA->EW_PMS$GL_FILHDR_HIT;
  DataCopy->MISCInfo.FileHeaderMisses =
    EXE$AR_EWDATA->EW_PMS$GL_FILHDR_MISS;
  DataCopy->MISCInfo.DirectoryBlockHits =
    EXE$AR_EWDATA->EW_PMS$GL_DIRDATA_HIT;
  DataCopy->MISCInfo.DirectoryBlockMisses =
    EXE$AR_EWDATA->EW_PMS$GL_DIRDATA_MISS;
  DataCopy->MISCInfo.BitMapHits =
    EXE$AR_EWDATA->EW_PMS$GL_STORAGMAP_HIT;
  DataCopy->MISCInfo.BitMapMisses =
    EXE$AR_EWDATA->EW_PMS$GL_STORAGMAP_MISS;
  DataCopy->MISCInfo.OpenFiles = EXE$AR_EWDATA->EW_PMS$GL_OPEN;
  DataCopy->MISCInfo.Opens = EXE$AR_EWDATA->EW_PMS$GL_OPENS;
```

```
  DataCopy->MISCInfo.Erase = EXE$AR_EWDATA->EW_PMS$GL_ERASEIO;
  DataCopy->MISCInfo.VolumeSyncLocks =
    EXE$AR_EWDATA->EW_PMS$GL_VOLLCK;
  DataCopy->MISCInfo.VolumeSyncLocksWaits =
    EXE$AR_EWDATA->EW_PMS$GL_VOLWAIT;
  DataCopy->MISCInfo.DirectoryandFileSynchLocks =
    EXE$AR_EWDATA->EW_PMS$GL_SYNCHLCK;
  DataCopy->MISCInfo.DirectoryandFileSynchLocksWaits =
    EXE$AR_EWDATA->EW_PMS$GL_SYNCHWAIT;
  DataCopy->MISCInfo.AccessLocks = EXE$AR_EWDATA->EW_PMS$GL_ACCLCK;
  DataCopy->MISCInfo.XQPCacheWait =
    EXE$AR_EWDATA->EW_PMS$GL_XQPCACHEWAIT;

  DataCopy->MISCInfo.current_time = EXE$GQ_SYSTIME;
  DataCopy->Header.gen$b_type = MISCDATA;

  status = sys$put(&rblock);
  if (status != RMS$_NORMAL)
  {
      lib$stop(status);
  }
  return ( 1 );
}
/*
**++
** FUNCTIONAL DESCRIPTION:
**
** This routine collects PMS page fault data
** for our monitor.
**
** FORMAL PARAMETERS:
**
**    struct GOT_DATA *DataCopy :
**       Pointer to master area to store the data you collect.
**
** RETURN VALUE:
**
**    Alway return 1, success.
**
** SIDE EFFECTS:
**
** Process Page performance data is collected and stored in the file.
**
**
```

```
**—
*/
int GetPMSInfo( struct GOT_DATA *DataCopy )
{
  int status;
/*
**  Mark header with type and data
*/
  DataCopy->PMSInfo.PMS$GL_PREADIO = PMS$GL_PREADIO;
  DataCopy->PMSInfo.PMS$GL_PREADS = PMS$GL_PREADS;
  DataCopy->PMSInfo.PMS$GL_PWRITES = PMS$GL_PWRITES;
  DataCopy->PMSInfo.PMS$GL_PWRITIO  = PMS$GL_PWRITIO ;
  DataCopy->PMSInfo.PMS$GL_FAULTS = PMS$GL_FAULTS;
  DataCopy->PMSInfo.PMS$GL_FREEFLTS  =  PMS$AL_TRANSFLT[0];
  DataCopy->PMSInfo.PMS$GL_MODFLTS  = PMS$AL_TRANSFLT[1];
  DataCopy->PMSInfo.PMS$GL_GVALID = PMS$GL_GVALID;
  DataCopy->PMSInfo.PMS$GL_SCH_0_PAGE  = PMS$GL_SCH_0_PAGE ;
  DataCopy->PMSInfo.PMS$GL_PAGES = PMS$GL_PAGES;
  DataCopy->PMSInfo.PMS$GL_DZROFLTS  = PMS$GL_DZROFLTS ;
  DataCopy->PMSInfo.PMS$GL_DPTSCN = PMS$GL_DPTSCN;
  DataCopy->PMSInfo.PMS$AL_CRF[0] = PMS$AL_CRF[0];
  DataCopy->PMSInfo.PMS$AL_CRF[1] = PMS$AL_CRF[1];
  DataCopy->PMSInfo.PMS$AL_CRFIO[0] = PMS$AL_CRFIO[0];
  DataCopy->PMSInfo.PMS$AL_CRFIO[1] = PMS$AL_CRFIO[1];

  DataCopy->PMSInfo.current_time = EXE$GQ_SYSTIME;
  DataCopy->Header.gen$b_type = PMSDATA;

  status = sys$put(&rblock);
  if (status != RMS$_NORMAL)
  {
      lib$stop(status);
  }
  return ( 1 );
```

MONITOR.LNK_DEF

```
pfm:monitor.obj
sys$share:spishr.exe/share
#ifdef VAX
sys$share:vaxcrtl/lib
sys$system:sys.stb/sel
#endif
```

DUMP_PMS.C

```c
#include <descrip.h>
#include <string.h>
#include <stdio.h>
#include <rms.h>
#include <descrip.h>
#include <stdio.h>
#include <starlet.h>
#include <libdtdef.h>
#include <lib$routines.h>
#include <stdlib.h>

#include <pfm/Axp_phddef.h>
#include <pfm/Axp_pcbdef.h>
#include <mscp/dsrvdef.h>
#include <pfm/getspidef.h>
#include <pfm/monitor.h>

void open_file( void );
void close_file( void );

char out_string[133];
$DESCRIPTOR( fao_string_header, " Collection start time !%D");
$DESCRIPTOR( fao_string, " !10UL!_!8UL!_!8UL!_!8UL!_!8UL!_!8UL!_!8UL");
$DESCRIPTOR( string_desc, out_string );
unsigned short out_len;

/*
**  For output
*/

struct FAB fblock;              /* Declare a fab structure  */
struct RAB rblock;              /* Declare a rab structure */

main()
{
  struct GOT_DATA *LastPMS;
  int firsttime = 1;
  int status;
  int DumpTimes= (int ) getenv("DUMPTIMES");

  LastPMS = ( struct GOT_DATA *) calloc( (size_t) 1,
      (size_t ) sizeof( struct GOT_DATA ));
  open_file();
```

363

```
  rblock.rab$l_ubf = (char *) &LocalCopy;       /* Set up the buffer */
  rblock.rab$w_usz = sizeof(struct GOT_DATA); /* Number of bytes to write
*/
  for(;;)
  {
      status = sys$get(&rblock);                      /* Read a record sequentially */
      if (status != RMS$_NORMAL)
      {
        return;
      }
      if( LocalCopy.Header.gen$b_type == PMSDATA )
      {
        if( firsttime == 1 )
        {
            firsttime = 0;
            status = sys$fao( &fao_string_header, &out_len, &string_desc,
              &LocalCopy.PMSInfo.current_time );

            out_string[ out_len] = 0;
            printf( "%s\n", out_string );

            printf( " ");
            printf( " \t Hard Faults " );
            printf( " \t Hard Fault Pages" );
            printf( " \t Modified pages written" );
            printf( " \t Modified I/O requests " );
            printf( " \t Page Faults" );
            printf( " \t Free list page faults " );
            printf( " \t Modified list page faults" );
            printf( " \t Global valid faults" );
            printf( " \t Zeroed pages created" );
            printf( " \t Pages of Memory " );
            printf( " \t Demand Zero page faults" );
            printf( " \t Dead Page table scans" );
            printf( " \t CRF private" );
            printf( " \t CRF global" );
            printf( " \t CRF private I/O" );
            printf( " \t CRF global I/O" );
            printf( "\n");

        }

        if( DumpTimes != 0 )
```

```
    {
        status = sys$fao( &fao_string_header, &out_len,
        &string_desc, &LocalCopy.Diskinfo.current_time );

    out_string[ out_len] = 0;
    printf( "%s^t", out_string );
    }
printf( " %10.10d", LocalCopy.PMSInfo.PMS$GL_PREADIO -
    LastPMS->PMSInfo.PMS$GL_PREADIO );
printf( " \t%10.10d", LocalCopy.PMSInfo.PMS$GL_PREADS -
    LastPMS->PMSInfo.PMS$GL_PREADS );
printf( " \t%10.10d", LocalCopy.PMSInfo.PMS$GL_PWRITES -
    LastPMS->PMSInfo.PMS$GL_PWRITES );
printf( " \t%10.10d", LocalCopy.PMSInfo.PMS$GL_PWRITIO -
    LastPMS->PMSInfo.PMS$GL_PWRITIO );
printf( " \t%10.10d", LocalCopy.PMSInfo.PMS$GL_FAULTS -
    LastPMS->PMSInfo.PMS$GL_FAULTS );
printf( " \t%10.10d", LocalCopy.PMSInfo.PMS$GL_FREEFLTS   -
    LastPMS->PMSInfo.PMS$GL_FREEFLTS   );
printf( " \t%10.10d", LocalCopy.PMSInfo.PMS$GL_MODFLTS   -
    LastPMS->PMSInfo.PMS$GL_MODFLTS   );
printf( " \t%10.10d", LocalCopy.PMSInfo.PMS$GL_GVALID   -
    LastPMS->PMSInfo.PMS$GL_GVALID   );
printf( " \t%10.10d", LocalCopy.PMSInfo.PMS$GL_SCH_0_PAGE   -
    LastPMS->PMSInfo.PMS$GL_SCH_0_PAGE   );
printf( " \t%10.10d", LocalCopy.PMSInfo.PMS$GL_PAGES   -
    LastPMS->PMSInfo.PMS$GL_PAGES   );
printf( " \t%10.10d", LocalCopy.PMSInfo.PMS$GL_DZROFLTS   -
    LastPMS->PMSInfo.PMS$GL_DZROFLTS   );
printf( " \t%10.10d", LocalCopy.PMSInfo.PMS$GL_DPTSCN   -
    LastPMS->PMSInfo.PMS$GL_DPTSCN   );
printf( " \t%10.10d", LocalCopy.PMSInfo.PMS$AL_CRF[0] -
    LastPMS->PMSInfo.PMS$AL_CRF[0] );
printf( " \t%10.10d", LocalCopy.PMSInfo.PMS$AL_CRF[1] -
    LastPMS->PMSInfo.PMS$AL_CRF[1] );
printf( " \t%10.10d", LocalCopy.PMSInfo.PMS$AL_CRFIO[0] -
    LastPMS->PMSInfo.PMS$AL_CRFIO[0] );
printf( " \t%10.10d", LocalCopy.PMSInfo.PMS$AL_CRFIO[1] -
    LastPMS->PMSInfo.PMS$AL_CRFIO[1] );

printf( "\n" );
*LastPMS = LocalCopy;
}
```

```
  }

  close_file();
}
void open_file()
{
  int status;

  char *fname="monitor$data";   /* File name to be accessed */
  fblock = cc$rms_fab;          /* Initialize fab structure */
  rblock = cc$rms_rab;          /* Initialize rab structure */

/* Declare file access options.  In this case the file will be opened for
read. */

  fblock.fab$b_fac = FAB$M_GET ;
  rblock.rab$l_fab = &fblock;             /* Point the rab to the fab */
  fblock.fab$l_fna = fname;               /* file name */
  fblock.fab$b_fns = strlen(fname);       /* length of file name  */
  fblock.fab$b_rfm = FAB$C_FIX;           /* variable length records */
  fblock.fab$b_rat = FAB$M_CR;            /* carriage return attribute*/
  printf("opening %s\n",fname);
  status = sys$open(&fblock);             /* Create the file */
  if (status != RMS$_NORMAL) lib$stop(status);
  status = sys$connect(&rblock);          /* Connect record attributes blk */
  rblock.rab$b_rac = RAB$C_SEQ;           /* Specify sequential access */
  if (status != RMS$_NORMAL) lib$stop(status);
}
void close_file()
{
   int status;
   status = sys$close(&fblock);           /* Close the file */
   if (status != RMS$_NORMAL) lib$stop(status);
}
```

DUMP_PMS.LNK_DEF

```
pfm:dump_pms.obj
#ifdef VAX
sys$share:vaxcrtl/lib
sys$system:sys.stb/sel
#endif
```

Dump Resources Names

RSBDEF.H

```
#ifndef RSBDEF_H
#define RSBDEF_H
/*
** To update this for future releases of OpenVMS:
** Get library copy — lib/ext=$RSBDEF sys$share:lib.mlb
** Insure offsets match the offsets in this file.
*/
#pragma member_alignment __save
#pragma nomember_alignment
/*+                                                              */
/* RSB - RESOURCE BLOCK
*/
/*                                                               */
/* Resource blocks represent resources for which there are locks outstanding.*/
/* Each Resource Block May Have One Or More Lock Blocks (Lkb) Queued To It.  */
/*-                                                              */
#define RSB$M_DIRENTRY 0x1
#define RSB$M_VALINVLD 0x2
#define RSB$M_DIR_RQD 0x4
#define RSB$M_RM_PEND 0x8
#define RSB$M_RM_IP 0x10
#define RSB$M_RM_ACCEPT 0x20
#define RSB$M_RM_RBLD 0x40
#define RSB$M_RM_WAIT 0x80
#define RSB$M_RM_DEFLECT 0x100
#define RSB$M_DIR_IP 0x200
#define RSB$M_RBLD_IP 0x400
#define RSB$M_RBLD_RQD 0x800
#define RSB$M_RBLD_ACT 0x1000
#define RSB$M_CHK_BTR 0x2000
#define RSB$K_LENGTH 120             /*LENGTH OF FIXED PART OF RSB */
#define RSB$C_LENGTH 120             /*LENGTH OF FIXED PART OF RSB */
#define RSB$K_MAXLEN 31              /*MAXIMUM LENGTH OF RESOURCE NAME */
struct RSBDEF {
```

```
struct RSBDEF *RSB$L_HSHCHN;        /*HASH CHAIN */
struct RSBDEF *RSB$L_HSHCHNBK;      /*HASH CHAIN BACK POINTER */
unsigned short int RSB$W_SIZE;      /*SIZE OF RSB */
unsigned char RSB$B_TYPE;           /*STRUCTURE TYPE */
unsigned char RSB$B_DEPTH;          /*DEPTH IN TREE */
unsigned char RSB$B_GGMODE;         /*GROUP GRANT MODE */
unsigned char RSB$B_CGMODE;         /*CONVERSION GRANT MODE */
short int RSB$W_FILL_100;           /*Align */
variant_union {
  unsigned int RSB$L_STATUS;        /*STATUS */
  variant_struct {
    unsigned RSB$V_DIRENTRY : 1;    /* ENTERED IN DIR. DURING FAILOVER */
    unsigned RSB$V_VALINVLD : 1;    /* VALUE BLOCK INVALID */
    unsigned RSB$V_DIR_RQD : 1;     /* DIRECTORY ENTRY REQUIRED */
    unsigned RSB$V_RM_PEND : 1;     /* RESOURCE REMASTER OP PENDING */
    unsigned RSB$V_RM_IP : 1;       /* RESOURCE BEING REMASTERED */
    unsigned RSB$V_RM_ACCEPT : 1;   /* NEW MASTER ACCEPTS */
    unsigned RSB$V_RM_RBLD : 1;     /* ALWAYS REBUILD TREE */
    unsigned RSB$V_RM_WAIT : 1;     /* BLOCK LOCAL ACTIVITY */
    unsigned RSB$V_RM_DEFLECT : 1;  /* DEFLECT REMOTE INTEREST */
    unsigned RSB$V_DIR_IP : 1;      /* DIRECTORY ENTRY BEING CREATED */
    unsigned RSB$V_RBLD_IP : 1;     /* REBUILD IN PROGRESS */
    unsigned RSB$V_RBLD_RQD : 1;    /* REBUILD REQUIRED FOR THIS TREE */
    unsigned RSB$V_RBLD_ACT : 1;    /* LOCK RBLD ACTIVE FOR TREE */
    unsigned RSB$V_CHK_BTR : 1;     /* CHECK FOR BETTER MASTER */
    unsigned RSB$V_FILL_0 : 2;
    } RSB$R_STATUS_BITS;
  } RSB$R_STATUS_OVERLAY;
unsigned int RSB$L_GRQFL;           /*GRANTED QUEUE FORWARD LINK */
unsigned int RSB$L_GRQBL;           /*GRANTED QUEUE BACKWARD LINK */
unsigned int RSB$L_CVTQFL;          /*CONVERSION QUEUE FORWARD LINK */
unsigned int RSB$L_CVTQBL;          /*CONVERSION QUEUE */
                                    /*BACKWARD LINK */
unsigned int RSB$L_WTQFL;           /*WAIT QUEUE FORWARD LINK */
unsigned int RSB$L_WTQBL;           /*WAIT QUEUE BACKWARD LINK */
int RSB$L_FILL_101;                 /*Align */
unsigned int RSB$Q_VALBLK [2];      /*VALUE BLOCK */
int RSBDEF$$_FILL_1 [2];            /*MORE VALUE BLOCK */
unsigned int RSB$L_CSID;            /*SYSTEM ID OF MASTER SYS.*/
unsigned int RSB$L_RRSFL;           /*ROOT LIST FORWARD LINK */
unsigned int RSB$L_RRSBL;           /*ROOT LIST BACKWARD LINK */
unsigned int RSB$L_SRSFL;           /*TREE LIST FORWARD LINK */
unsigned int RSB$L_SRSBL;           /*TREE LIST BACKWARD LINK */
unsigned int RSB$L_RM_CSID;         /*PENDNG REMASTER CSID */
```

```
    unsigned int RSB$L_RTRSB;           /*POINTER TO ROOT RSB */
    unsigned int RSB$L_CLURCB;          /*REMASTER CONTROL BLOCK */
    unsigned short int RSB$W_ACTIVITY;/*RESOURCE ACTIVITY COUNTER */
    unsigned short int RSB$W_LCKCNT;    /*COUNT OF LOCKS ON RESOURCE */
    unsigned int RSB$L_VALSEQNUM;       /*VALUE BLOCK SEQ. NUMBER */
    unsigned short int RSB$W_REFCNT;    /*SUB RSB REFERENCE COUNT */
    unsigned short int RSB$W_BLKASTCNT; /*BLOCKING AST COUNT */
    unsigned short int RSB$W_HASHVAL;   /*HASH VALUE */
    unsigned short int RSB$W_RQSEQNM;   /*REQUEST SEQUENCE NUMBER */
    unsigned int RSB$L_PARENT;          /*ADDRESS OF PARENT RSB */
    unsigned short int RSB$W_GROUP;     /*GROUP NUMBER */
    unsigned char RSB$B_RMOD;           /*ACCESS MODE OF RESOURCE */
    unsigned char RSB$B_RSNLEN;         /*RESOURCE NAME LENGTH */
    char RSB$T_RESNAM [];               /*START OF RESOURCE NAME */
    } ;

#pragma member_alignment __restore
#endif
```

DUMP_RESOURCE.C

```
/*
**++
**   FACILITY:  VMS_TOOLS
**
**   MODULE DESCRIPTION:
**
** Copyright (c) 1991 James W. Coburn
** Copyright (c) 1992 James W. Coburn
** Copyright (c) 1993 James W. Coburn
** Copyright (c) 1992 Professional Press Books.
** Copyright (c) 1993 Cardinal Business Media
** This program may be copied for noncommercial purposes. Use of this
** program for any other purpose without the express written consent
** of the publisher is prohibited.
**
** This program searches the Resource tables and lists the current size
** average queue depth and the top 16 queue entries.
**
** TEST on a single node cluster before running in a productions
** environment.  This code uses kernel mode access and thus will
** crash your system if there are coding bugs or if changes to
** VMS introduce new bugs.
**
** This code has been tested on:
```

369

```
** OpenVMS AXP 1.5
**
**
** AUTHORS:
**
** Jim Coburn
**
** CREATION DATE:  Jan 1991
**
** DESIGN ISSUES:
**
**
**
**
** MODIFICATION HISTORY:
**
** Updated for OpenVMS AXP.
**—
*/


/*
**
** INCLUDE FILES
**
*/

#include <stdio.h>
#include <stddef.h>
#include <starlet.h>

#pragma nostandard
#include "RESHASHTBL:rsbdef.h"
#pragma standard

#define MAXQUEUE 4*4

struct STATUS_BLOCK
{
    struct RSBDEF *resource_hash;
    int table_size;
    int free_entries;
    int total;
    float average_length;
```

```
    int max_length[MAXQUEUE];
    struct RSBDEF *where[MAXQUEUE];
} status_block;

struct RSBDEF **pointer, *pointer2;

#pragma nostandard
globalref struct RSBDEF **LCK$GL_HASHTBL;
globalref unsigned int LCK$GL_HTBLSIZ;
#pragma standard

void print_it( char *type1, char *type2 );

main()
{
      int resource_lookup();
      int loop;

      sys$cmexec ( resource_lookup, 0 );

      print_it( "RESHASHTBL", "System" );-

}
resource_lookup()
{

int count, this_time, loop, loop1, loop2;
int slot, update;

status_block.resource_hash = *LCK$GL_HASHTBL;
status_block.table_size = LCK$GL_HTBLSIZ;

pointer = LCK$GL_HASHTBL;
for( count = 0; count < status_block.table_size; count++ )
{
    pointer2 = *pointer;
    for( this_time = 0; pointer2 != 0; pointer2 = pointer2->RSB$L_HSHCHN )
    {
      this_time++;
    }
    status_block.total += this_time;
    if( this_time == 0 )
          status_block.free_entries++;
    else
```

```
    {
      update = 0;

      for( loop = 0; loop < MAXQUEUE ; loop++ )
      {
        if( this_time > status_block.max_length[loop] )
            {
        update = 1;
              break;
    }
  }
    if( update == 1 )
    {
        slot = loop;
        for( loop1 = MAXQUEUE-1; loop1 > slot ; loop1-);
      {
          status_block.max_length[loop1] = status_block.max_length[loop1-1];
          status_block.where[loop1] = status_block.where[loop1-1];
      }
        status_block.max_length[slot] = this_time;
        status_block.where[slot] = *pointer;
    }
  }
        pointer = pointer++;
  }


}
void print_it( char *type1, char *type2 )
{
    int loop, used;

    used = status_block.table_size - status_block.free_entries;
    used = used > 0 ? used : 1;
    status_block.average_length = ( (float) status_block.total / (float) used );

    printf( "\n\n %s = %d\n", type1, status_block.table_size );
    printf( " There are %d free entries\n", status_block.free_entries);
    printf( " There are a Total of %d %s Resources\n",
      status_block.total, type2   );
    printf( " Average queue length is %3.3f\n", status_block.average_length );

    printf( "\nTop %d queue depths (queue depth/queue header)\n", MAXQUEUE );

    for( loop = 0; loop < MAXQUEUE; )
```

```
{
  printf( "    %4.4d %08.8X %4.4d %08.8X %4.4d %08.8X %4.4d %08.8X\n",
      status_block.max_length[ loop],
      status_block.where[ loop],
      status_block.max_length[ loop+1],
      status_block.where[ loop+1],
      status_block.max_length[ loop+2],
      status_block.where[ loop+2],
      status_block.max_length[ loop+3],
      status_block.where[ loop+3]);
  loop += 4;
}

}
```

DUMP_RESOURCE SAMPLE OUTPUT

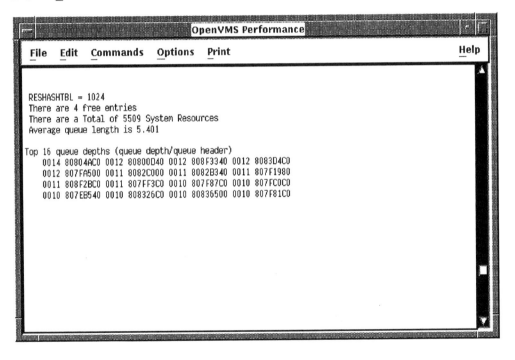

DUMP_RESOURCE_NAME.C

```
/*
**++
**   FACILITY:  VMS_TOOLS
**
**   MODULE DESCRIPTION:
**
** Copyright (c) 1991 James W. Coburn
** Copyright (c) 1992 James W. Coburn
** Copyright (c) 1993 James W. Coburn
** Copyright (c) 1992 Professional Press Books.
** Copyright (c) 1993 Cardinal Business Media
** This program may be copied for noncommercial purposes. Use of this
** program for any other purpose without the express written consent
** of the publisher is prohibited.
**
** This program dumps all resource names hashed to a resource hash
** address.  Get the address using the program above.
**
** TEST on a single node cluster before running in a productions
** environment.  This code uses kernel mode access and thus will
** crash your system if there are coding bugs or if changes to
** VMS introduce new bugs.
**
** This code has been tested on:
** OpenVMS AXP 1.5
**
**
** AUTHORS:
**
** Jim Coburn
**
** CREATION DATE:  Jan 1991
**
** DESIGN ISSUES:
**
**
**
**
** MODIFICATION HISTORY:
**
** Updated for OpenVMS AXP.
**—
*/
/*
**
```

```
**  INCLUDE FILES
**
*/

#include <stdio.h>
#include <stddef.h>
#include <starlet.h>
#include <descrip.h>
#include <lib$routines.h>

#include "RESHASHTBL:rsbdef.h"

struct RSBDEF *resource_name;
struct RSB_LOCAL
{
  unsigned char RSB$B_RSNLEN;          /* RESOURCE NAME LENGTH */
  char RSB$T_RESNAM[ 31 ];             /* START OF RESOURCE NAME */
}resource_name_local;

$DESCRIPTOR(fao_control, "\"!AF\"");
char output_line[80];
unsigned short output_length;
struct dsc$descriptor_s output_descriptor;
main()
{
  int resource_lookup();
  unsigned int address;
  int loop;

  output_descriptor.dsc$a_pointer = output_line;
  output_descriptor.dsc$w_length = 80;
  output_descriptor.dsc$b_class = DSC$K_CLASS_S;
  output_descriptor.dsc$b_dtype = DSC$K_DTYPE_T;

  printf( "enter starting address in HEX " );
  scanf( "%x", &address );
  resource_name = (struct RSBDEF *) address;

  printf( "Resource names for hash entry %x\n", address );
  for( loop = 0; resource_name != 0;loop++ )
  {
      sys$cmexec ( resource_lookup, 0 );
      sys$fao( &fao_control, &output_length, &output_descriptor,
        resource_name_local.RSB$B_RSNLEN,
        &resource_name_local.RSB$T_RESNAM );
```

```
        printf( "%2.2d — %s\n", loop, output_line );
    }

}
resource_lookup()
{

    int i;

    resource_name_local.RSB$B_RSNLEN = resource_name->RSB$B_RSNLEN;
    for (i = 0; i < resource_name_local.RSB$B_RSNLEN; i++)
    {
        resource_name_local.RSB$T_RESNAM[i] = resource_name-
>RSB$T_RESNAM[i];

    }
    resource_name = resource_name->RSB$L_HSHCHN;
}
```

DUMP_RESOURCE_NAMES SAMPLE OUTPUT

```
┌──────────────────────────────────────────────────────────────────────┐
│  ──                    OpenVMS Performance                         ┌┐  │
├──────────────────────────────────────────────────────────────────────┤
│    File   Edit   Commands   Options   Print                    Help    │
├──────────────────────────────────────────────────────────────────────┤
│ enter starting address in HEX Resource names for hash entry 80804ac0 ▲ │
│ 00 --- "SYS$_ASC385$DKA300:"                                           │
│ 01 --- "F11B$vDSK003        " "                                        │
│ 02 --- "F11B$s...."3        " "                                        │
│ 03 --- "F11B$s...."3        " "                                        │
│ 04 --- "F11B$s...."3        " "                                        │
│ 05 --- "F11B$skr.."3        " "                                        │
│ 06 --- "F11B$sI´.."3        " "                                        │
│ 07 --- "F11B$s?..."3        " "                                        │
│ 08 --- "F11B$ss..."3        " "                                        │
│ 09 --- "F11B$s.m.."3        " "                                        │
│ 10 --- "F11B$ss..."3        " "                                        │
│ 11 --- "F11B$sA..."3        " "                                        │
│ 12 --- "F11B$sZ..."3        " "                                        │
│ 13 --- "F11B$sA..."3        " "                                        │
│                                                                     ▼  │
└──────────────────────────────────────────────────────────────────────┘
```

AST Control

AST CODE LISTING

```
.TITLE AST_routine Routine to Adjust your working set
.IDENT /VAX Version/


;++
; FACILITY: Special Code for System Performance Work
;
; Copyright (c) 1993 James W. Coburn
; Copyright (c) 1993 Cardinal Business Media
; This program may be copied for noncommercial purposes.
; Use of this program for any other purpose without the
; express written consent of the publisher is prohibited.
;
; FUNCTIONAL DESCRIPTION:
;
; These routines are:
;    (1) AST code to adjust the working set of a process
;    (2) code to load the AST code into system space.
;
; The purpose of these routines is really just to show how
; to make the code work, not to do any really useful work.
;
; ENVIRONMENT: VAX/VMS
;
; AUTHOR: Jim Coburn, CREATION-DATE: January, 1993
;
; MODIFIED BY:
;
;-
;
 .SUBTITLE AST Code


;++
; FUNCTIONAL DESCRIPTION:
```

```
;
; Adjust the working set of the current process either up or down
; depending on the value of first input parameter
;
; CALLING SEQUENCE:
;
; Called by the system as an AST
;
; PUSHL  #1 ;Adjust up (use #0 to adjust down)
; CALLS  #1, AST_routine
;
; INPUT PARAMETERS:
;
; Either a 1 to adjust up or 0 to adjust down
;
; IMPLICIT INPUTS:
;
; None
;
; OUTPUT PARAMETERS:
;

; None
;
; IMPLICIT OUTPUTS:
;
; None
;
; COMPLETION CODES:
;
; We will always just return success.
;
; SIDE EFFECTS:
;
; The working set of the current process is either increased
; or decreased.
;
;—
;

  .library /sys$share:lib.mlb/
  $ARCH_DEFS
  $ACBDEF
  $DYNDEF
```

```
      $PRIDEF
      $PSLDEF

      .PSECT $CODE,pic, shr, nowrt, long

AST_START:  .ENTRY AST_routine,^M<r2,r3,r4,r5,r6>

;
; Invoke the service and get the current size
; (set Pagcnt == 0 )
;

  pushal Currentsize
  pushl #0
  calls #2, g^sys$adjwsl

;
; Now either adjust up or down
;
  movl #-256, r2
  tstl 4(AP)
  beql Skip
;
; Parameter was 1 so convert -256 to +256
;
  MNEGL r2,r2
Skip:

;
; Invoke the service and adjust
;
;

; Invoke the service, adjust working set and get the new
; size
;
  pushal Aftersize
  pushl r2
  calls #2, g^sys$adjwsl

  movl #SS$_NORMAL,r0  ;just return normal
  ret
;
; Used to insure code is working.  Not needed for any other
```

```
; purpose.
;
Currentsize: .long. Ø
Aftersize: .long Ø
;
AST_CODE_LENGTH = . - AST_START

  .SUBTITLE Loader Code
;++
; FUNCTIONAL DESCRIPTION:
;
; Allocate pool space and load the AST_routine into pool.
; Place the starting address of the AST_routine into SYSGEN
; parameter USERD2, SGN$GL_USERD2
;
; CALLING SEQUENCE:
;
; CALLS  #Ø, Load_routine ;Load AST_routine into pool
;
; INPUT PARAMETERS:
;
; None.
;
; IMPLICIT INPUTS:
;
; None
;
; OUTPUT PARAMETERS:
;
; None
;
; IMPLICIT OUTPUTS:
;
; None
;
; COMPLETION CODES:
;
; SS$_Normal if loaded, else failing reason.
;
; SIDE EFFECTS:
;
; AST_routine is placed into system space.  The AST must
; be called in kernel mode since the code itself is mapped
; to memory that is protected as kernel read.  No lower
```

```
; access mode can even read this code.
;
;-
;
   .PSECT $CODE,pic, shr, nowrt, long

   .ENTRY Load_routine,^M<r2,r3,r4,r5,r6>

   movl #AST_CODE_LENGTH,r1 ; # of bytes in ACB to
                             ; allocate
   jsb g^EXE$ALONONPAGED     ; allocate from non-paged
                             ;pool
   blbc r0,50$ ; if error,
                             ;return w/ status
   movl r2, sgn$gl_userd2    ; Save starting address
   movc3 #AST_CODE_LENGTH, AST_routine, (r2)
                             ;Load the routine
   movl #SS$_NORMAL, r0
50$: ret

   .SUBTITLE Driver Code
;++
; FUNCTIONAL DESCRIPTION:
;
; Allocate pool space for the AST and queue the AST_routine
; in pool to run in the context of the requested process.
;
; CALLING SEQUENCE:
;
; PUSHL  #IPID
; CALLS  #1, Driver_routine
;
; INPUT PARAMETERS:
;
; None.
;
; IMPLICIT INPUTS:
;
; None
;
; OUTPUT PARAMETERS:
;
; None
;
```

```
; IMPLICIT OUTPUTS:
;
; None
;
; COMPLETION CODES:
;
; SS$_Normal
;
; SIDE EFFECTS:
;
; AST_routine in system space is executed in the context of
; process specified by IPID. (I don't accept EPID, to make
; the code shorter.  Use EXEC$ routine to convert EPID to
; IPID or look it up using $ ana/system.)
;
;-
;
  .PSECT long,gbl
IPID: .long Ø
UporDown: .long Ø

  .PSECT $CODE,pic, shr, nowrt, long

  .ENTRY Driver_routine,^M<r2,r3,r4,r5,r6>

  movl 4(ap), UporDown
  movl 8(ap), IPID

  pushl #0
  pushl #InKernel
  calls #2, sys$cmkrnl
  movl #ss$_normal,rØ
  ret ;back to the caller

  .ENTRY InKernel,^M<r2,r3,r4,r5,r6>
  movl #acb$k_length,r1   ; # of bytes in ACB to allocate
  jsb g^EXE$ALONONPAGED  ; allocate from non-paged pool
  blbc rØ,1$ ; if error, return w/ status
  movw r1,acb$w_size(r2) ;move size into block
  movb #dyn$c_acb,acb$b_type(r2) ;set the block type
  movb #psl$c_kernel,acb$b_rmod(r2)
                                ;queue a kernel level ast
  movl IPID,acb$l_pid(r2)        ;to this process
  movl g^sgn$gl_userd2,acb$l_ast(r2)
```

```
                                   ;location of ast routine
  movl UporDown,acb$l_astprm(r2) ;incr or decr
  movl r2,r5 ;set acb address sch$qast
  movl #pri$_resavl,r2
                                   ;give the process a priority boost
  jsb g^sch$qast ;queue the ast up to the process
1$: movl #ss$_normal,rØ ;get out clean anyway
  ret ;back to the caller

  .END
```

USER EXECUTIVE IMAGE ROUTINES

```
  .TITLE AST_routine Routine to Adjust your working set
  .IDENT /VAX UEI Version/
;++
; FACILITY: Special Code for System Performance Work
;
; Copyright (c) 1993 James W. Coburn
; Copyright (c) 1993 Cardinal Business Media
; This program may be copied for noncommercial purposes.
; Use of this program for any other purpose without the
; express written consent of the publisher is prohibited.
;
; FUNCTIONAL DESCRIPTION:
;
; The purpose of this routine is really just to show how to
; make the code work, not to do any really useful work.
;
; ENVIRONMENT: VAX/VMS
;
; AUTHOR: Jim Coburn, CREATION-DATE: January, 1993
;
; MODIFIED BY:
;
; Code has been modified to be used as a user executive
; image.
;—
;
  .SUBTITLE AST Code

;++
; FUNCTIONAL DESCRIPTION:
;
; Adjust the working set of the current process either up
```

```
; or down depending on the value of first input parameter
;
; CALLING SEQUENCE:
;
; Called by the system as an AST
;    PUSHL  #1 ;Adjust up (use #0 to adjust down)
;    CALLS  #1, AST_routine
;
; INPUT PARAMETERS:
;
; Either a 1 to adjust up or 0 to adjust down
;
; IMPLICIT INPUTS:
;
; None
;
; OUTPUT PARAMETERS:
;
; None
;
; IMPLICIT OUTPUTS:
;

; None
;
; COMPLETION CODES:
;
; We will always just return success.
;
; SIDE EFFECTS:
;
; The working set of the current process is either
; increased or decreased
;
; Since the code is now a User Executive Image, the code is
; protected in memory as user readable/no write.
;
;-
;

    .library /sys$share:lib.mlb/
    $ARCH_DEFS
    $ACBDEF
    $DYNDEF
```

```
    $PRIDEF
    $PRTDEF
    $PSLDEF

    declare_psect EXEC$NONPAGED_CODE ; the code section

    .ENTRY AST_routine,^M<r2,r3,r4,r5,r6>


;
; Invoke the service and get the current size
; (set Pagcnt == 0 )
;

do_ast:
    pushal Currentsize
    pushl #0
    calls #2, g^sys$adjwsl

;
; Now either adjust up or down
;
    movl #-256, r2
    tstl 4(AP)
    beql Skip
;
; Parameter was 1 so convert -256 to +256
;
    MNEGL r2,r2
Skip:

;
;

; Invoke the service, adjust working set and get the
; new size
;
    pushal Aftersize
    pushl r2
    calls #2, g^sys$adjwsl

    movl #SS$_NORMAL,r0 ;just return normal
    ret
;
```

```
    declare_psect EXEC$NONPAGED_DATA
;
; Since the data is now part of a User Executive Image,
; the data is protected in memory as kernel write only.
;
; Used to insure code is working.  Not needed for any other
; purpose.
;
Currentsize: .long -1
Aftersize: .long 1234


    .end
```

NEW DRIVER FOR USER EXECUTIVE IMAGE

```
    .SUBTITLE Driver Code
;++
; FUNCTIONAL DESCRIPTION:
;
; Copyright (c) 1993 James W. Coburn
; Copyright (c) 1993 Cardinal Business Media
; This program may be copied for noncommercial purposes.
; Use of this program for any other purpose without the
; express written consent of the publisher is prohibited.
;
; Allocate pool space and queue the AST_routine in pool to
; run in the requested process's context.
;
; CALLING SEQUENCE:
;
; PUSHL   #0 or #1  to increase or decrease
; PUSHL   #IPID
; CALLS   #2, Driver_routine
;
; INPUT PARAMETERS:
;
; None.
;
; IMPLICIT INPUTS:
;
; None
;
; OUTPUT PARAMETERS:
;
; None
```

```
;
; IMPLICIT OUTPUTS:
;

; None
;
; COMPLETION CODES:
;
; SS$_Normal
;
; SIDE EFFECTS:
;
; AST_routine in system space is executed in the context
; of process specified by IPID. (I don't accept EPID, to
; make the code shorter.  Use exe$ routine to convert EPID
; to IPID or look it up using $ ana/system.)
;
;-
;
  .library /sys$share:lib.mlb/
  $ARCH_DEFS
  $ACBDEF
  $DYNDEF
  $PRIDEF
  $PSLDEF


  .PSECT long,gbl
IPID: .long 0
UporDown: .long 0
Mode: .byte psl$c_kernel
  .PSECT $CODE,pic, shr, nowrt, long

  .ENTRY Driver_routine,^M<r2,r3,r4,r5,r6>

  movl 4(ap), UporDown
  movl 8(ap), IPID

  pushl #0
  pushl #InKernel
  calls #2, sys$cmkrnl
  movl #ss$_normal,r0
  ret ;back to the caller

  .ENTRY InKernel,^M<r2,r3,r4,r5,r6>
```

```
  movl #acb$k_length,r1          ; # of bytes in ACB to allocate
  jsb g^EXE$ALONONPAGED          ; allocate from non-paged pool
  blbc  r0,1$ ; if error, return w/ status
  movw r1,acb$w_size(r2)         ;move size into block
  movb #dyn$c_acb,acb$b_type(r2) ;set the block type
;
; if you wish to debug (ie set value for currentsize and
; aftersize in pool), then change psl$c_super to
; psl$c_kernel.
;
  movb #psl$c_super,acb$b_rmod(r2)
                                 ;queue a super level ast
  movl IPID,acb$l_pid(r2)        ;to this process

  movl g^sgn$gl_userd2,acb$l_ast(r2)
                                 ;location of ast routine
  movl UporDown,acb$l_astprm(r2) ;incr or decr
  movl r2,IPID
  movl r2,r5 ;set acb address sch$qast
  movl #pri$_resavl,r2           ;give the process a priority
                                 ;boost
  jsb g^sch$qast                 ;queue the ast up to the process
1$: movl #ss$_normal,r0          ;return success
ret ;back to the caller

  .END
```

ACCESSING LOADABLE IMAGE DATA STRUCTURES

```c
#include "sys$share:string.h"
#include "sys$share:stdio.h"

#pragma member_alignment __save
#pragma nomember_alignment

/*
**   This structure was built using information from
**   VMS for ALPHA Platforms, Internals and Data Structures
*/
struct LDRDEF
{
    struct LDRDEF *next;
    struct LDRDEF *previous;
    unsigned short size;
```

```
        unsigned char   type;
        unsigned char   filler;
        unsigned char   namelength;
        char    name[39];
        unsigned int    ast_routine;
};


#pragma member_alignment __restore

struct LDRDEF *first, *current;
struct LDRDEF usedata;
int Initialized = FALSE;
/*
**   List header in system space.
*/
globalref struct LDRDEF *LDR$GQ_IMAGE_LIST;

/*
**   Number of entries in the list header
*/
globalref int EXE$GL_LDR_CNT;

/*
**   SYSGEN parameter location to save the AST routine
**   address in.
*/
globalref int SGN$GL_USERD2;

struct ExecData
{
    char *ImageToFind;
    unsigned int routine;
};



/*
**   Prototype
*/
int FindExecutiveImage( struct ExecData *FindExec );

main()
{
    struct ExecData FindExec =
```

```
    {
     <SYS$LDR>"SYS$AST_ROUTINE.EXE",
      0
    };


/*
**  Find the specified image's Base Virtual Address
**  when found set into USERD2
*/
    FindExecutiveImage( &FindExec);

}
int FindExecutiveImage( struct ExecData *FindExec )
{
    int GetNextImage();
    int SetAddress();
    int i, count;

    count = strlen( FindExec->ImageToFind);
    for( i = 0; i EXE$GL_LDR_CNT; i++)
{
        sys$cmexec(GetNextImage, 0);

#ifdef PRINTDATA
/*
**  If compiled with cc/define=PRINTDATA
**  Print out relevant info from data structure.
*/
        printf( " %*.*s %x %x\n", usedata.namelength,
            usedata.namelength, usedata.name,
            usedata.ast_routine, usedata);
#endif

/*
**
**  Determine if this is the image we were looking for.
**
*/
    if( count == usedata.namelength)
    {
        if( !strcmp( FindExec->ImageToFind, usedata.name))
        {
```

```
#ifdef    PRINTDATA
          printf( " Found address\n");
#endif

/*
**   This is the one we wanted, so save
**   starting address
*/
          sys$cmkrnl(SetAddress, 0);
          break;
        }
      }
    }
}
/*
**
**   Copy data from Protected memory to user memory
**   Walk down the linked list
**
*/
int GetNextImage()
{

    if( !Initialized )
    {
      first = LDR$GQ_IMAGE_LIST;
      Initialized = TRUE;
    }
    memcpy( &usedata, first, sizeof( struct LDRDEF) );
    first = first->next;
    return 1;
}
/*
**
**   Set system parameter with routine start address.
**
*/

int SetAddress()
{
    SGN$GL_USERD2 = usedata.ast_routine;
}
```

AST ROUTINE FOR AXP

```
      .TITLE  AST_routine Routine to Adjust your working set
      .IDENT  /AXP Version/


;++
; FACILITY: Special Code for System Performance Work
;
;Copyright (c) 1993 James W. Coburn
;Copyright (c) 1993 Cardinal Business Media
;This program may be copied for noncommercial purposes.
;Use of this program for any other purpose without the
;express written consent of the publisher is prohibited.
;
; FUNCTIONAL DESCRIPTION:
;
;The purpose of this routine is really just to show how
;to make the code work, not to do any really useful work.
;
; ENVIRONMENT: VAX/VMS
;
; AUTHOR: Jim Coburn, CREATION-DATE: January, 1993
;
; MODIFIED BY:
;
;Code has been modified to be used as a user executive
;image running on the AXP platform.
;-
;
.SUBTITLE AST Code


;++
; FUNCTIONAL DESCRIPTION:
;
;Adjust the working set of the current process either up or down
;depending on the value of first input parameter
;
; CALLING SEQUENCE:
;
;Called by the system as an AST in either
;PUSHL  #1 ;Adjust up (use #0 to adjust down)
;CALLS  #1, AST_routine
;
; INPUT PARAMETERS:
```

```
;
;Either a 1 to adjust up or 0 to adjust down
;
; IMPLICIT INPUTS:
;
;None
;
; OUTPUT PARAMETERS:
;
;None
;
; IMPLICIT OUTPUTS:
;

;None
;
; COMPLETION CODES:
;
;We will always just return success.
;
; SIDE EFFECTS:
;
;The working set of the current process is either increased
;or decreased
;
;Since the code is now a User Executive Image, the code is
;protected in memory as user readable/no write.
;
;-
;

    .library /sys$share:lib.mlb/
    $ARCH_DEFS
    $ACBDEF
    $DYNDEF
    $LDRIMGDEF
    $PRIDEF
    $PSLDEF

    declare_psect   EXEC$NONPAGED_CODE ; the code section

AST_routine: .CALL_ENTRY
   PRESERVE=<>,MAX_ARGS=1,HOME_ARGS=FALSE, OUTPUT=<R0>
```

```
;
; Invoke the service and get the current size
; (set Pagcnt == 0 )
;

  pushal Currentsize
  pushl  #0
  calls  #2, g^sys$adjwsl


;
;Now either adjust up or down
;
  movl #-256, r2
  tstl 4(AP)
  beql Skip
;
;Parameter was 1 so convert -256 to +256
;
  MNEGL r2,r2
Skip:


;
;Invoke the service, adjust working set and get the
;new size
;

  pushal Aftersize
  pushl r2
  calls #2, g^sys$adjwsl

  movl #SS$_NORMAL,r0 ;just return normal
  ret
;
  declare_psect EXEC$NONPAGED_DATA


;
;Since the data is now part of a User Executive Image,
;the data is protected in memory as kernel write only.
;
; Used to insure code is working.  Not needed for any other
; purpose.

Currentsize: .long 0
```

```
Aftersize: .long 0

.SUBTITLE Loader Code
;++
; FUNCTIONAL DESCRIPTION:
;
;Set the starting address of the AST_routine into SYSGEN
;parameter USERD2, SGN$GL_USERD2.  Work is done by the
;system when it loads the user executive image.
;
; CALLING SEQUENCE:
;
;Done at system boot time.
;
; INPUT PARAMETERS:
;
;None.
;
; IMPLICIT INPUTS:
;
;None
;
; OUTPUT PARAMETERS:
;
;None
;
; IMPLICIT OUTPUTS:
;
;None
;
; COMPLETION CODES:
;
;SS$_Normal if loaded, else failing reason.
;
;-
;

  DECLARE_PSECT    EXEC$INIT_CODE

  INITIALIZATION_ROUTINE   TEST_INIT

TEST_INIT: .CALL_ENTRY PRESERVE=<>,MAX_ARGS=0,HOME_ARGS=FALSE,
OUTPUT=<R0>
```

```
moval    AST_routine,g^sgn$gl_userd2
movl #SS$_NORMAL, RØ

ret

.END
```

DRIVER FOR USER EXECUTIVE IMAGE (AXP)

```
.SUBTITLE Driver Code
;++
; FUNCTIONAL DESCRIPTION:
;
;Copyright (c) 1993 James W. Coburn
;Copyright (c) 1993 Cardinal Business Media
;This program may be copied for noncommercial purposes.
;Use of this program for any other purpose without the
;express written consent of the publisher is prohibited.
;
;Allocate pool space and queue the AST_routine in pool to
;run in the requested process's context.
;
; CALLING SEQUENCE:
;
;PUSHL   #Ø or #1  to increase or decrease
;PUSHL   #IPID
;CALLS   #2, Driver_routine
;
; INPUT PARAMETERS:
;
;None.
;
; IMPLICIT INPUTS:
;
;None
;
; OUTPUT PARAMETERS:
;
;None
;
; IMPLICIT OUTPUTS:
;
;None
```

```
;
; COMPLETION CODES:
;
;SS$_Normal
;
; SIDE EFFECTS:

;
;AST_routine in system space is executed in the context
;of process specified by IPID. (I don't accept EPID, to
;make the code shorter.  Use exe$ routine to convert EPID
;to IPID or look it up using $ ana/system.)
;-
;
  .library /sys$share:lib.mlb/
  $ARCH_DEFS
  $ACBDEF
  $DYNDEF
  $PRIDEF
  $PSLDEF


  .PSECT DATA page,rd,wrt,noexe,noshr
IPID: .long Ø
UporDown: .long Ø


  .PSECT $CODE,pic, shr, nowrt, long

Driver_routine:: .CALL_ENTRY PRESERVE=, <r2,r3,r4,r5,r6>-
MAX_ARGS=2,HOME_ARGS=FALSE,OUTPUT=<RO>

  movl 4(ap), UporDown
  movl 8(ap), IPID

  pushl #Ø
  pushl #InKernel
  calls #2, sys$cmkrnl
  movl #ss$_normal,rØ
  ret ;back to the caller

InKernel: .CALL_ENTRY PRESERVE=,MAX_ARGS=Ø, <r2,r3,r4,r5,r6>-
          HOME_ARGS=FALSE,OUTPUT=<RO>

  movl #acb$k_length,r1 ; # of bytes in ACB to allocate
```

```
     jsb g^EXE$ALONONPAGED  ; allocate from non-paged pool
     blbc rØ,1$ ; if error, return w/ status
     movw r1,acb$w_size(r2) ;move size into block
     movb #dyn$c_acb,acb$b_type(r2) ;set the block type
;
;If you wish to debug (ie set value for currentsize
;and aftersize in pool), then change psl$c_super to
;psl$c_kernel.
;
     movb #psl$c_kernel,acb$b_rmod(r2)
                              ;queue a super level ast
     movl IPID,acb$l_pid(r2) ;to this process
     movl g^sgn$gl_userd2,acb$l_ast(r2)
                              ;location of ast routine
     movl UporDown,acb$l_astprm(r2) ;incr or decr
     movl r2,r5 ;set acb address sch$qast
     movl #pri$_resavl,r2
                              ;give the process a priority boost
     jsb g^sch$qast           ;queue the ast up to the process
1$: movl #ss$_normal,rØ    ;get out clean anyway

     ret                      ;back to the caller

     .END
```

TEST ROUTINE FOR VAX

```
/*
**   Quick and dirty program to test AST_code.
*/
main()

{

    int AST_routine( int );
    int Load_routine( void );
    int Driver_routine( int, int );
    int j, ipid;

    j = AST_routine ( 1 );

    sys$cmkrnl( Load_routine, Ø);

    printf( " enter IPID( in hex ) " );
```

398

```
    scanf ("%x", &ipid );
    while (ipid != 0)
    {
        j = Driver_routine( 1, ipid );
      printf( " enter IPID( in hex ) " );
      scanf ("%x", &ipid );
    }

}
```

TEST ROUTINE FOR AXP

```
/*
**  Quick and dirty program to test AST_code.
*/
main()

{

    int Driver_routine( int, int );
    int j, ipid;

    printf( " enter IPID( in hex ) " );
    scanf ("%x", &ipid );

    while (ipid != 0)
    {
        j = Driver_routine( 1, ipid );
      printf( " enter IPID( in hex ) " );
      scanf ("%x", &ipid );
    }

}
```

Dump Home Block

FIBDEF.H

```
#ifndef FIBDEF_H
#define FIBDEF_H

#ifdef DEC_ARA
#pragma nostandard
#pragma member_alignment __save
#pragma nomember_alignment
#endif

#ifdef __cplusplus
    extern "C" {
#define __unknown_params ...
#define __struct struct
#define __union union
#else
#define __unknown_params
#define __struct variant_struct
#define __union variant_union
#endif

/*    */
#define FIB$M_NOWRITE 0x1
#define FIB$M_DLOCK 0x2
#define FIB$M_BLK_LOCK 0x4
#define FIB$M_SPOOL 0x10
#define FIB$M_WRITECK 0x20
#define FIB$M_SEQONLY 0x40
#define FIB$M_WRITE 0x100
#define FIB$M_READCK 0x200
#define FIB$M_NOREAD 0x400
#define FIB$M_NOTRUNC 0x800
#define FIB$M_CONTROL 0x1000
#define FIB$M_NO_READ_DATA 0x2000
```

```
#define FIB$M_EXECUTE 0x10000
#define FIB$M_PRSRV_ATR 0x20000
#define FIB$M_RMSLOCK 0x40000
#define FIB$M_WRITETHRU 0x80000
#define FIB$M_NOLOCK 0x100000
#define FIB$M_NORECORD 0x200000
#define FIB$M_NOVERIFY 0x400000
#define FIB$M_REWIND 0x8
#define FIB$M_CURPOS 0x10
#define FIB$M_UPDATE 0x40
#define FIB$K_ACCDATA 10 /* ABOVE DATA NECESSARY FOR ACCESS  */
#define FIB$C_ACCDATA 10 /* ABOVE DATA NECESSARY FOR ACCESS  */
#define FIB$K_DIRDATA 22
/* ABOVE DATA NECESSARY FOR DIRECTORY OPS  */
#define FIB$C_DIRDATA 22
/* ABOVE DATA NECESSARY FOR DIRECTORY OPS  */
#define FIB$M_ALLVER 0x8
#define FIB$M_ALLTYP 0x10
#define FIB$M_ALLNAM 0x20
#define FIB$M_WILD 0x100
#define FIB$M_NEWVER 0x200
#define FIB$M_SUPERSEDE 0x400
#define FIB$M_FINDFID 0x800
#define FIB$M_LOWVER 0x4000
#define FIB$M_HIGHVER 0x8000
#define FIB$M_ALCON 0x1
#define FIB$M_ALCONB 0x2
#define FIB$M_FILCON 0x4
#define FIB$M_ALDEF 0x8
#define FIB$M_ALLOCATR 0x10
#define FIB$M_EXTEND 0x80
#define FIB$M_TRUNC 0x100
#define FIB$M_NOHDREXT 0x200
#define FIB$M_MARKBAD 0x400
#define FIB$M_NOPLACE 0x4000
#define FIB$M_NOCHARGE 0x8000
#define FIB$K_EXTDATA 32
/* ABOVE NECESSARY FOR BASIC FILE EXTENSION  */
#define FIB$C_EXTDATA 32
/* ABOVE NECESSARY FOR BASIC FILE EXTENSION  */
#define FIB$M_EXACT 0x1
#define FIB$M_ONCYL 0x2
#define FIB$C_CYL 1 /* CYLINDER ADDRESS SPECIFIED*/
#define FIB$C_LBN 2 /* LBN SPECIFIED        */
```

```
#define FIB$C_VBN 3 /* PROXIMATE VBN SPECIFIED    */
#define FIB$C_RFI 4 /* RELATED FILE ID SPECIFIED */
#define FIB$K_ALCDATA 44
/* ABOVE DATA NECESSARY FOR PLACEMENT   */
#define FIB$C_ALCDATA 44
/* ABOVE DATA NECESSARY FOR PLACEMENT   */
#define FIB$M_ALT_REQ 0x1
#define FIB$M_ALT_GRANTED 0x2
#define FIB$M_DIRACL 0x4
#define FIB$M_PROPAGATE 0x8
#define FIB$K_MOVEFILE 72 /* end of FIB required by MOVEFILE */
#define FIB$C_MOVEFILE 72 /* end of FIB required by MOVEFILE */
#define FIB$K_LENGTH 72
#define FIB$C_LENGTH 72
struct FIBDEF {
  __union  {
    unsigned int fib$l_acctl;        /* ACCESS CONTROL BIT */
    __struct  {
      unsigned fib$v_nowrite : 1;    /* NO OTHER WRITERS*/
      unsigned fib$v_dlock : 1;      /* ENABLE DEACCESS LOCK*/
      unsigned fib$v_blk_lock : 1;
/* ENABLE RMS-11 BLOCK LOCKING       */
      unsigned fibdef$$_fill_1 : 1; /* UNUSED */
      unsigned fib$v_spool : 1;      /* SPOOL FILE ON CLOSE/
      unsigned fib$v_writeck : 1;    /* ENABLE WRITE CHECK /
      unsigned fib$v_seqonly : 1;
/* SEQUENTIAL ONLY ACCESS*/
      unsigned fibdef$$_fill_2 : 1; /* SPARE */
      unsigned fib$v_write : 1;      /* WRITE ACCESS */
      unsigned fib$v_readck : 1;     /* ENABLE READ CHECK */
      unsigned fib$v_noread : 1;     /* NO OTHER READERS */
      unsigned fib$v_notrunc : 1;
/* FILE MAY NOT BE TRUNCATED */
      unsigned fib$v_control : 1;
/* CONTROL ACCESS TO FILE     */
      unsigned fib$v_no_read_data : 1;
/* NO READ ACCESS TO FILE DATA */
      unsigned fibdef$$_fill_3 : 2; /* SPARE*/
/* THE HIGH 8 BITS CANNOT BE COPIED */
/* INTO THE ACCESS MODE WORD IN THE WINDOW */
      unsigned fib$v_execute : 1;
/* ACCESS FOR EXECUTE (USE EXECUTE PROTECTION)  */
      unsigned fib$v_prsrv_atr : 1;
/* PRESERVE ORIGINAL ATTRIBUTES OF FILE  */
```

403

```
    unsigned fib$v_rmslock : 1;
/* OPEN WITH RMS RECORD LOCKING     */
    unsigned fib$v_writethru : 1;
/* FORCE CACHE WRITE-THROUGH ON OPERATION  */
    unsigned fib$v_nolock : 1;
/* OVERRIDE ACCESS INTERLOCKS*/
    unsigned fib$v_norecord : 1;
/* DO NOT RECORD FILE ACCESS*/
    unsigned fib$v_noverify : 1;
/* Do not perform compare on move. */
    unsigned fibdef$$_fill_4 : 2; /* SPARE */
    unsigned fib$v_fill_1 : 7;
    } fib$r_acctl_bits0;
  __struct {
    unsigned fibdef$$_fill_5 : 3;
    unsigned fib$v_rewind : 1;     /* REWIND TAPE  */
    unsigned fib$v_curpos : 1;
/* CREATE AT CURRENT TAPE POSITION  */
    unsigned fibdef$$_fill_6 : 1;
    unsigned fib$v_update : 1;
/* UPDATE MODE (POSITION TO START OF FILE)  */
    unsigned fib$v_fill_2 : 1;
    } fib$r_acctl_bits1;
  __struct {
    char fibdef$$_fill_13 [3];
    char fib$b_wsize;              /* WINDOW SIZE */
    } fib$r_acctl_fields2;
  } fib$r_acctl_overlay;
 __union {
  unsigned short int fib$w_fid [3]; /* FILE ID   */
  __struct {
    unsigned short int fib$w_fid_num;
/* FILE NUMBER */
    unsigned short int fib$w_fid_seq;
/* FILE SEQUENCE NUMBER*/
    __union {
      unsigned short int fib$w_fid_rvn;
/* RELATIVE VOLUME NUMBER  */
      __struct {
        unsigned char fib$b_fid_rvn;
/* SHORT FORM RVN   */
        unsigned char fib$b_fid_nmx;
/* EXTENDED FILE NUMBER    */
      } fib$r_fid_rvn_fields;
```

404

```
        } fib$r_fid_rvn_overlay;
      } fib$r_fid_fields;
    __struct { /* File ID fields for ISO 9660     */
      unsigned short int fib$w_fid_dirnum;
/* Directory number of File-Id */
      unsigned int fib$l_fid_recnum;
/* Record number of File-ID     */
      } fib$r_fid_iso_9660_fields;
    } fib$r_fid_overlay;
  __union {
    unsigned short int fib$w_did [3];
/* DIRECTORY ID      */
    __struct {
      unsigned short int fib$w_did_num;   /* FILE NUMBER  */
      unsigned short int fib$w_did_seq;   /* FILE SEQUENCE NUMBER*/
      __union {
        unsigned short int fib$w_did_rvn; /* RELATIVE VOLUME NUMBER  */
        __struct {
          unsigned char fib$b_did_rvn;    /* SHORT FORM RVN     */
          unsigned char fib$b_did_nmx;    /* EXTENDED FILE NUMBER    */
          } fib$r_did_rvn_fields;
        } fib$r_did_rvn_overlay;
      } fib$r_did_fields;
    __struct {                            /* Directory ID fields for ISO 9660 */
      unsigned short int fib$w_did_dirnum;/* Directory number of File-Id */
      unsigned int fib$l_did_recnum;      /* Record number of File-ID    */
      } fib$r_did_iso_9660_fields;
    } fib$r_did_overlay;
  unsigned int fib$l_wcc;                 /* WILD CARD CONTEXT  */
  __union {
    unsigned short int fib$w_nmctl; /* NAME CONTROL BITS  */
    __struct {
      unsigned fibdef$$_fill_7 : 3;
      unsigned fib$v_allver : 1;    /* MATCH ALL VERSIONS */
      unsigned fib$v_alltyp : 1;    /* MATCH ALL TYPES    */
      unsigned fib$v_allnam : 1;    /* MATCH ALL NAMES    */
      unsigned fibdef$$_fill_8 : 2;
      unsigned fib$v_wild : 1;      /* WILD CARDS IN FILE NAME   */
      unsigned fib$v_newver : 1;    /* MAXIMIZE VERSION NUMBER   */
      unsigned fib$v_supersede : 1; /* SUPERSEDE EXISTING FILE */
      unsigned fib$v_findfid : 1;   /* SEARCH FOR FILE ID */
      unsigned fibdef$$_fill_9 : 2;
      unsigned fib$v_lowver : 1;    /* LOWER VERSION OF FILE EXISTS    */
      unsigned fib$v_highver : 1;   /* HIGHER VERSION OF FILE EXISTS   */
```

405

```
        } fib$r_nmctl_bits;
      } fib$r_nmctl_overlay;
   __union {
     unsigned short int fib$w_exctl; /* EXTEND CONTROL     */
     __struct {
       unsigned fib$v_alcon : 1;      /* ALLOCATE CONTIGUOUS*/
       unsigned fib$v_alconb : 1;     /* CONTIGUOUS BEST EFFORT   */
       unsigned fib$v_filcon : 1;     /* MARK FILE CONTIGUOUS     */
       unsigned fib$v_aldef : 1;      /* ALLOCATE DEFAULT AMOUNT   */
       unsigned fib$v_allocatr : 1;
/* PLACEMENT DATA PRESENT IN ATTRIBUTE LIST  */
       unsigned fibdef$$_fill_10 : 2;
       unsigned fib$v_extend : 1;     /* ENABLE EXTENSION   */
       unsigned fib$v_trunc : 1;      /* ENABLE TRUNCATION  */
       unsigned fib$v_nohdrext : 1;   /* INHIBIT EXTENSION HEADERS*/
       unsigned fib$v_markbad : 1;    /* MARK BLOCKS BAD    */
       unsigned fibdef$$_fill_11 : 3;
       unsigned fib$v_noplace : 1;
  /* DON'T ADD PLACEMENT POINTERS IN MOVEFILE */
       unsigned fib$v_nocharge : 1;  /* DON'T CHARGE DISKQUOTA   */
      } fib$r_exctl_bits;
    } fib$r_exctl_overlay;
   unsigned int fib$l_exsz;             /* EXTEND SIZE */
   unsigned int fib$l_exvbn;            /* EXTENSION VBN      */
   __union {
     unsigned char fib$b_alopts;      /* ALLOCATION OPTIONS */
     __struct {
       unsigned fib$v_exact : 1;     /* EXACT PLACEMENT REQUIRED  */
       unsigned fib$v_oncyl : 1;     /* PUT ALLOCATION ON ONE CYLINDER   */
       unsigned fib$v_fill_3 : 6;
      } fib$r_alopts_bits;
    } fib$r_alopts_overlay;
   unsigned char fib$b_alalign;                 /* ALLOCATION ALIGNMENT */
   __union {
     unsigned short int fib$w_alloc [5];        /* ALLOCATION LOCATION */
     __struct {
       __union {
         unsigned short int fib$w_loc_fid [3]; /* RELATED FILE ID */
         __struct {
           unsigned short int fib$w_loc_num;   /* RELATED FILE NUMBER */
           unsigned short int fib$w_loc_seq;   /* FILE SEQUENCE NUMBER */
           __union {
             unsigned short int fib$w_loc_rvn; /* RELATED RVN */
             __struct {
```

```
                unsigned char fib$b_loc_rvn;      /* SHORT FORM RVN */
                unsigned char fib$b_loc_nmx;      /* EXTENDED FILE NUMBER */
                } fib$r_loc_rvn_fields;
              } fib$r_loc_rvn_overlay;
            } fib$r_loc_fid_fields;
          } fib$r_loc_fid_overlay;
      unsigned int fib$l_loc_addr;    /* LOCATION ADDRESS (VBN, LBN, CYL)  */
      } fib$r_alloc_fields;
    } fib$r_alloc_overlay;
  unsigned short int fib$w_verlimit; /* DIRECTORY ENTRY VERSION LIMIT     */
  unsigned char fib$b_agent_mode;    /* AGENTS ACCESS MODE */
  unsigned char fib$b_ru_facility;   /* RECOVERABLE-FACILITY CODE */
  unsigned int fib$l_aclctx;         /* ACL CONTEXT FOR READ       */
  unsigned int fib$l_acl_status;     /* RETURN STATUS FROM ACL OPERATION */
  __union {
    unsigned int fib$l_status;       /* GENERAL STATUS LONGWORD    */
    __struct {
      unsigned fib$v_alt_req : 1;     /* ALTERNATE ACCESS REQUIRED */
      unsigned fib$v_alt_granted : 1;/* ALTERNATE ACCESS GRANTED      */
      unsigned fib$v_diracl : 1;      /* DO DIRECTORY ACL PROPAGATION    */
      unsigned fib$v_propagate : 1;   /* DO PROPAGATION ON ENTER */
      unsigned fib$v_fill_4 : 4;
      } fib$r_status_bits;
    } fib$r_status_overlay;
  unsigned int fib$l_alt_access;     /* ALTERNATE ACCESS MASK       */
  __union {
    __struct {
      unsigned int fib$l_mov_svbn;    /* starting VBN (MOVEFILE)  */
      unsigned int fib$l_mov_vbncnt; /* count of VBNs (MOVEFILE)       */
      } fib$r_movfildp;
    } fib$r_funcdepend;
  } ;
#ifdef __cplusplus
#define fib$l_acctl fib$r_acctl_overlay.fib$l_acctl
#define fib$v_nowrite fib$r_acctl_overlay.fib$r_acctl_bits0.fib$v_nowrite
#define fib$v_dlock fib$r_acctl_overlay.fib$r_acctl_bits0.fib$v_dlock
#define fib$v_blk_lock fib$r_acctl_overlay.fib$r_acctl_bits0.fib$v_blk_lock
#define fib$v_spool fib$r_acctl_overlay.fib$r_acctl_bits0.fib$v_spool
#define fib$v_writeck fib$r_acctl_overlay.fib$r_acctl_bits0.fib$v_writeck
#define fib$v_seqonly fib$r_acctl_overlay.fib$r_acctl_bits0.fib$v_seqonly
#define fib$v_write fib$r_acctl_overlay.fib$r_acctl_bits0.fib$v_write
#define fib$v_readck fib$r_acctl_overlay.fib$r_acctl_bits0.fib$v_readck
#define fib$v_noread fib$r_acctl_overlay.fib$r_acctl_bits0.fib$v_noread
#define fib$v_notrunc fib$r_acctl_overlay.fib$r_acctl_bits0.fib$v_notrunc
```

407

```
#define fib$v_control fib$r_acctl_overlay.fib$r_acctl_bits0.fib$v_control
#definefib$v_no_read_datafib$r_acctl_overlay.fib$r_acctl_bits0.fib$v_no_read_data
#define fib$v_execute fib$r_acctl_overlay.fib$r_acctl_bits0.fib$v_execute
#define fib$v_prsrv_atr fib$r_acctl_overlay.fib$r_acctl_bits0.fib$v_prsrv_atr
#define fib$v_rmslock fib$r_acctl_overlay.fib$r_acctl_bits0.fib$v_rmslock
#define fib$v_writethru fib$r_acctl_overlay.fib$r_acctl_bits0.fib$v_writethru
#define fib$v_nolock fib$r_acctl_overlay.fib$r_acctl_bits0.fib$v_nolock
#define fib$v_norecord fib$r_acctl_overlay.fib$r_acctl_bits0.fib$v_norecord
#define fib$v_noverify fib$r_acctl_overlay.fib$r_acctl_bits0.fib$v_noverify
#define fib$v_rewind fib$r_acctl_overlay.fib$r_acctl_bits1.fib$v_rewind
#define fib$v_curpos fib$r_acctl_overlay.fib$r_acctl_bits1.fib$v_curpos
#define fib$v_update fib$r_acctl_overlay.fib$r_acctl_bits1.fib$v_update
#define fib$b_wsize fib$r_acctl_overlay.fib$r_acctl_fields2.fib$b_wsize
#define fib$w_fid fib$r_fid_overlay.fib$w_fid
#define fib$w_fid_num fib$r_fid_overlay.fib$r_fid_fields.fib$w_fid_num
#define fib$w_fid_seq fib$r_fid_overlay.fib$r_fid_fields.fib$w_fid_seq
#define fib$w_fid_rvn fib$r_fid_overlay.fib$r_fid_fields.fib$r_\
fid_rvn_overlay.fib$w_fid_rvn
#define fib$h_fid_rvn
fib$r_fid_overlay.fib$r_fid_fields.fib$r_fid_rvn_overlay.fib$r_\
fid_rvn_fields.fib$b_fid_rvn
#define fib$b_fid_nmx
fib$r_fid_overlay.fib$r_fid_fields.fib$r_fid_rvn_overlay.fib$r_\
fid_rvn_fields.fib$b_fid_nmx
#define fib$w_fid_dirnum
fib$r_fid_overlay.fib$r_fid_iso_9660_fields.fib$w_fid_dirnum
#define fib$l_fid_recnum
fib$r_fid_overlay.fib$r_fid_iso_9660_fields.fib$l_fid_recnum
#define fib$w_did fib$r_did_overlay.fib$w_did
#define fib$w_did_num fib$r_did_overlay.fib$r_did_fields.fib$w_did_num
#define fib$w_did_seq fib$r_did_overlay.fib$r_did_fields.fib$w_did_seq
#define fib$w_did_rvn fib$r_did_overlay.fib$r_did_fields.fib$r_\
did_rvn_overlay.fib$w_did_rvn
#define fib$b_did_rvn
fib$r_did_overlay.fib$r_did_fields.fib$r_did_rvn_overlay.fib$r_\
did_rvn_fields.fib$b_did_rvn
#define fib$b_did_nmx
fib$r_did_overlay.fib$r_did_fields.fib$r_did_rvn_overlay.fib$r_\
did_rvn_fields.fib$b_did_nmx
#define fib$w_did_dirnum
fib$r_did_overlay.fib$r_did_iso_9660_fields.fib$w_did_dirnum
#define fib$l_did_recnum
fib$r_did_overlay.fib$r_did_iso_9660_fields.fib$l_did_recnum
#define fib$w_nmctl fib$r_nmctl_overlay.fib$w_nmctl
```

```
#define fib$v_allver fib$r_nmctl_overlay.fib$r_nmctl_bits.fib$v_allver
#define fib$v_alltyp fib$r_nmctl_overlay.fib$r_nmctl_bits.fib$v_alltyp
#define fib$v_allnam fib$r_nmctl_overlay.fib$r_nmctl_bits.fib$v_allnam
#define fib$v_wild fib$r_nmctl_overlay.fib$r_nmctl_bits.fib$v_wild
#define fib$v_newver fib$r_nmctl_overlay.fib$r_nmctl_bits.fib$v_newver
#define fib$v_supersede fib$r_nmctl_overlay.fib$r_nmctl_bits.fib$v_supersede
#define fib$v_findfid fib$r_nmctl_overlay.fib$r_nmctl_bits.fib$v_findfid
#define fib$v_lowver fib$r_nmctl_overlay.fib$r_nmctl_bits.fib$v_lowver
#define fib$v_highver fib$r_nmctl_overlay.fib$r_nmctl_bits.fib$v_highver
#define fib$w_exctl fib$r_exctl_overlay.fib$w_exctl
#define fib$v_alcon fib$r_exctl_overlay.fib$r_exctl_bits.fib$v_alcon
#define fib$v_alconb fib$r_exctl_overlay.fib$r_exctl_bits.fib$v_alconb
#define fib$v_filcon fib$r_exctl_overlay.fib$r_exctl_bits.fib$v_filcon
#define fib$v_aldef fib$r_exctl_overlay.fib$r_exctl_bits.fib$v_aldef
#define fib$v_allocatr fib$r_exctl_overlay.fib$r_exctl_bits.fib$v_allocatr
#define fib$v_extend fib$r_exctl_overlay.fib$r_exctl_bits.fib$v_extend
#define fib$v_trunc fib$r_exctl_overlay.fib$r_exctl_bits.fib$v_trunc
#define fib$v_nohdrext fib$r_exctl_overlay.fib$r_exctl_bits.fib$v_nohdrext
#define fib$v_markbad fib$r_exctl_overlay.fib$r_exctl_bits.fib$v_markbad
#define fib$v_noplace fib$r_exctl_overlay.fib$r_exctl_bits.fib$v_noplace
#define fib$v_nocharge fib$r_exctl_overlay.fib$r_exctl_bits.fib$v_nocharge
#define fib$b_alopts fib$r_alopts_overlay.fib$b_alopts
#define fib$v_exact fib$r_alopts_overlay.fib$r_alopts_bits.fib$v_exact
#define fib$v_oncyl fib$r_alopts_overlay.fib$r_alopts_bits.fib$v_oncyl
#define fib$w_alloc fib$r_alloc_overlay.fib$w_alloc
#define fib$w_loc_fid fib$r_alloc_overlay.fib$r_alloc_fields.fib$r_\
loc_fid_overlay.fib$w_loc_fid
#define fib$w_loc_num fib$r_alloc_overlay.fib$r_alloc_fields.fib$r_\
loc_fid_overlay.fib$r_loc_fid_fields.fib$w_loc_num
#define fib$w_loc_seq
fib$r_alloc_overlay.fib$r_alloc_fields.fib$r_loc_fid_overlay.fib$r_\
loc_fid_fields.fib$w_loc_seq
#define fib$w_loc_rvn
fib$r_alloc_overlay.fib$r_alloc_fields.fib$r_loc_fid_overlay.fib$r_\
loc_fid_fields.fib$r_loc_rvn_overlay.fib$w_loc_rvn
#define fib$b_loc_rvn
fib$r_alloc_overlay.fib$r_alloc_fields.fib$r_loc_fid_overlay.fib$r_\
loc_fid_fields.fib$r_loc_rvn_overlay.fib$r_loc_rvn_fields.fib
#define fib$b_loc_nmx
fib$r_alloc_overlay.fib$r_alloc_fields.fib$r_loc_fid_overlay.fib$r_\
loc_fid_fields.fib$r_loc_rvn_overlay.fib$r_loc_rvn_fields.fib
#define fib$l_loc_addr fib$r_alloc_overlay.fib$r_alloc_fields.fib$l_loc_addr
#define fib$l_status fib$r_status_overlay.fib$l_status
#define fib$v_alt_req fib$r_status_overlay.fib$r_status_bits.fib$v_alt_req
```

```
#define fib$v_alt_granted fib$r_status_overlay.fib$r_status_bits.fib$v_alt_granted
#define fib$v_diracl fib$r_status_overlay.fib$r_status_bits.fib$v_diracl
#define fib$v_propagate fib$r_status_overlay.fib$r_status_bits.fib$v_propagate
#define fib$l_mov_svbn fib$r_funcdepend.fib$r_movfildp.fib$l_mov_svbn
#define fib$l_mov_vbncnt fib$r_funcdepend.fib$r_movfildp.fib$l_mov_vbncnt
#endif
#define FIB$C_REWINDVOL 1                        /* REWIND VOLUME SET   */
#define FIB$C_POSEND 2                           /* POSITION TO END OF VOLUME SET    */
#define FIB$C_NEXTVOL 3                          /* FORCE NEXT VOLUME  */
#define FIB$C_SPACE 4                            /* SPACE MAGNETIC TAPE*/
#define FIB$C_ILLEGAL 5                          /*       */
#define FIB$C_REWINDFIL 6                        /* REWIND FILE */
#define FIB$C_LOCK_VOL 7                         /* LOCK VOLUME AGAINST ALLOCATION
*/
#define FIB$C_UNLK_VOL 8                         /* UNLOCK VOLUME        */
/* QUOTA FILE OPERATIONS    */
#define FIB$C_ENA_QUOTA 9                        /* ENABLE QUOTA FILE  */
#define FIB$C_DSA_QUOTA 10                       /* DISABLE QUOTA FILE */
#define FIB$C_ADD QUOTA 11                       /* ADD QUOTA FILE ENTRY       */
#define FIB$C_EXA_QUOTA 12                       /* EXAMINE QUOTA FILE ENTRY  */
#define FIB$C_MOD_QUOTA 13                       /* MODIFY QUOTA FILE ENTRY   */
#define FIB$C_REM_QUOTA 14                       /* REMOVE QUOTA FILE ENTRY   */
#define FIB$C_USEREOT 15                         /* ENABLE USER END OF TAPE HANDLING  */
#define FIB$C_REMAP 16                           /* REMAP FILE WINDOW  */
#define FIB$C_CLSEREXCP 17                       /* ALLOW THE USER TO CLEAR A SERIOUS
EXCP FROM A TAPE DRIVE */
#define FIB$C_FLUSH_CACHE 18                     /* FLUSH SELECTED CACHE        */
#define FIB$C_FORCE_MV 19                        /* FORCE MOUNT VERIFICATION TO OCCUR */
#define FIB$K_MTALEN 28                          /* LENGTH OF MTAACP DATA      */
#define FIB$C_MTALEN 28                          /* LENGTH OF MTAACP DATA      */
/*    */
#define FIB$C_FID_CACHE 1                        /* FLUSH THE FID CACHE*/
#define FIB$C_EXTENT_CACHE 2                     /* FLUSH THE EXTENT CACHE   */
#define FIB$C_QUOTA_CACHE 3                      /* FLUSH THE QUOTA CACHE    */
#define FIB$C_BFRD_CACHE 4                       /* FLUSH THE BFRD CACHE      */
/*    */
#define FIB$M_ALL_MEM 0x1
#define FIB$M_ALL_GRP 0x2
#define FIB$M_MOD_USE 0x4
#define FIB$M_MOD_PERM 0x8
#define FIB$M_MOD_OVER 0x10
struct fibdef1 {
  char fibdef$$_fill_14 [22];
  unsigned short int fib$w_cntrlfunc; /* ACP CONTROL FUNCTION      */
```

```
/* DEFINE ACP CONTROL FUNCTION CODES     */
/*    */
  __union {
    unsigned int fib$l_cntrlval;  /* ACP CONTROL FUNCTION VALUE PARAMETER */
/* CACHE IDENTIFIER CODES FOR FLUSH_CACHE*/
/*    */
/* CONTROL BITS FOR QUOTA FILE OPERATIONS*/
/*    */
    __struct {
      unsigned fib$v_all_mem : 1;  /* MATCH ALL MEMBER NUMBERS   */
      unsigned fib$v_all_grp : 1;  /* MATCH ALL GROUP NUMBERS    */
      unsigned fib$v_mod_use : 1;  /* MODIFY USAGE DATA  */
      unsigned fib$v_mod_perm : 1; /* MODIFY PERMANENT QUOTA    */
      unsigned fib$v_mod_over : 1; /* MODIFY OVERDRAFT LIMIT    */
      unsigned fib$v_fill_5 : 3;
      } fib$r_cntrlval_bits;
    } fib$r_cntrlval_overlay;
  } ;
#ifdef __cplusplus
#define fib$l_cntrlval fib$r_cntrlval_overlay.fib$l_cntrlval
#define fib$v_all_mem fib$r_cntrlval_overlay.fib$r_cntrlval_bits.fib$v_all_mem
#define fib$v_all_grp fib$r_cntrlval_overlay.fib$r_cntrlval_bits.fib$v_all_grp
#define fib$v_mod_use fib$r_cntrlval_overlay.fib$r_cntrlval_bits.fib$v_mod_use
#define fib$v_mod_perm fib$r_cntrlval_overlay.fib$r_cntrlval_bits.fib$v_mod_perm
#define fib$v_mod_over fib$r_cntrlval_overlay.fib$r_cntrlval_bits.fib$v_mod_over
#endif

#ifdef __cplusplus
  }
#endif

#ifdef DEC_ARA
#pragma standard
#pragma member_alignment __restore
#endif

#endif /* __FIBDEF_LOADED */
```

411

FH2DEF.H

```
#ifndef FH2DEF_H
#define FH2DEF_H

#ifdef DEC_ARA
#pragma member_alignment __save
#pragma nostandard
#pragma nomember_alignment
#endif

#ifdef __cplusplus
  extern "C" {
#define __unknown_params ...
#define __struct struct
#define __union union
#else
#define __unknown_params
#define __struct variant_struct
#define __union variant_union
#endif

#include "expired_files/fatdef.H"

/*+                                              */
/*                                               */
/* File header definitions for Files-11 Structure Level 2  */
/*                                               */
/*-                                              */
#define FH2$C_LEVEL1 257   /* 401 octal = structure level 1 */
#define FH2$C_LEVEL2 512   /* 1000 octal = structure level 2*/
#define FH2$M_VCC_STATE 0x700
#define FH2$M_ALM_STATE 0xC0000
#define FH2$M_WASCONTIG 0x1
#define FH2$M_NOBACKUP 0x2
#define FH2$M_WRITEBACK 0x4
#define FH2$M_READCHECK 0x8
#define FH2$M_WRITCHECK 0x10
#define FH2$M_CONTIGB 0x20
#define FH2$M_LOCKED 0x40
#define FH2$M_CONTIG 0x80
#define FH2$M_BADACL 0x800
#define FH2$M_SPOOL 0x1000
#define FH2$M_DIRECTORY 0x2000
#define FH2$M_BADBLOCK 0x4000
```

```
#define FH2$M_MARKDEL 0x8000
#define FH2$M_NOCHARGE 0x10000
#define FH2$M_ERASE 0x20000
#define FH2$M_ALM_AIP 0x40000
#define FH2$M_ALM_ARCHIVED 0x80000
#define FH2$M_SCRATCH 0x100000
#define FH2$M_NOMOVE 0x200000
#define FH2$M_ONLY_RU 0x1
#define FH2$M_RUJNL 0x2
#define FH2$M_BIJNL 0x4
#define FH2$M_AIJNL 0x8
#define FH2$M_ATJNL 0x10
#define FH2$M_NEVER_RU 0x20
#define FH2$M_JOURNAL_FILE 0x40
#define FH2$C_RU_FACILITY_RMS 1            /* RMS */
#define FH2$C_RU_FACILITY_DBMS 2           /* DBMS */
#define FH2$C_RU_FACILITY_RDB 3            /* Rdb/VMS */
#define FH2$C_RU_FACILITY_CHKPNT 4         /* Checkpoint/Restart */
#define FH2$K_LENGTH 80                    /* length of header area */
#define FH2$C_LENGTH 80                    /* length of header area */
#define FH2$K_SUBSET0_LENGTH 88            /* length of header area */
#define FH2$C_SUBSET0_LENGTH 88            /* length of header area */
#define FH2$K_FULL_LENGTH 108              /* length of full header */
#define FH2$C_FULL_LENGTH 108              /* length of full header */
struct FH2DEF {
  unsigned char FH2$B_IDOFFSET;            /* ident area offset in words */
  unsigned char FH2$B_MPOFFSET;            /* map area offset in words */
  unsigned char FH2$B_ACOFFSET;            /* access control list offset in words */
  unsigned char FH2$B_RSOFFSET;            /* reserved area offset in words */
  unsigned short int FH2$W_SEG_NUM;        /* file segment number */
  __union {
    unsigned short int FH2$W_STRUCLEV;     /* file structure level */
    __struct {
      unsigned char FH2$B_STRUCVER;        /* file structure version */
      unsigned char FH2$B_STRUCLEV;        /* principal file structure level  */
      } FH2$R_STRUCLEV_FIELDS;
    } FH2$R_STRUCLEV_OVERLAY;
  __union {
    unsigned short int FH2$W_FID [3];      /* file ID */
    __struct {
      unsigned short int FH2$W_FID_NUM;    /* file number */
      unsigned short int FH2$W_FID_SEQ;    /* file sequence number */
      __union {
        unsigned short int FH2$W_FID_RVN;  /* relative volume number */
```

413

```
         __struct  {
           unsigned char FH2$B_FID_RVN; /* alternate format RVN */
           unsigned char FH2$B_FID_NMX; /* alternate format file number extension */
           } FH2$R_FID_RVN_FIELDS;
          } FH2$R_FID_RVN_OVERLAY;
         } FH2$R_FID_FIELDS;
        } FH2$R_FID_OVERLAY;
    __union  {
      unsigned short int FH2$W_EXT_FID [3];    /* extension file ID */
      __struct {
        unsigned short int FH2$W_EX_FIDNUM;    /* extension file number */
        unsigned short int FH2$W_EX_FIDSEQ;    /* extension file sequence number */
        __union {
          unsigned short int FH2$W_EX_FIDRVN; /* extension relative volume number  */
          __struct {
            unsigned char FH2$B_EX_FIDRVN; /* alternate format extension RVN */
            unsigned char FH2$B_EX_FIDNMX;
 /* alternate format extension file number extension */
           } FH2$R EX FIDRVN_FIELDS;
          } FH2$R_EX_FIDRVN_OVERLAY;
         } FH2$R_EXT_FID_FIELDS;
        } FH2$R_EXT_FID_OVERLAY;
   unsigned short int FH2$W_RECATTR [16];    /* file record attributes */
   __union  {
     unsigned int FH2$L_FILECHAR;               /* file characteristics */
     __struct {
       unsigned FH2DEF$$_FILL_21 : 8;          /* reserved */
       unsigned FH2$V_VCC_STATE : 3;           /* VCC state bits */
       unsigned FH2DEF$$_FILL_22 : 7;          /* reserved */
/***********The following line is different from FH2 */
       unsigned FH2$V_ALM_STATE : 2;           /* ALM state bits */
       unsigned FH2$V_FILL_0 : 4;
       } FH2$R_FILECHAR_CHUNKS;
     __struct {
       unsigned FH2$V_WASCONTIG : 1;    /* file was (and should be) contiguous */
       unsigned FH2$V_NOBACKUP : 1;     /* file is not to be backed up */
       unsigned FH2$V_WRITEBACK : 1;    /* file may be write-back cached */
       unsigned FH2$V_READCHECK : 1;    /* verify all read operations */
       unsigned FH2$V_WRITCHECK : 1;    /* verify all write operations */
       unsigned FH2$V_CONTIGB : 1;      /* keep file as contiguous as possible  */
       unsigned FH2$V_LOCKED : 1;       /* file is deaccess locked */
       unsigned FH2$V_CONTIG : 1;       /* file is contiguous */
       unsigned FH2DEF$$_FILL_2 : 3;    /* reserved */
       unsigned FH2$V_BADACL : 1;       /* ACL is invalid */
```

```
      unsigned FH2$V_SPOOL : 1;          /* intermediate spool file */
      unsigned FH2$V_DIRECTORY : 1;      /* file is a directory */
      unsigned FH2$V_BADBLOCK : 1;       /* file contains bad blocks */
      unsigned FH2$V_MARKDEL : 1;        /* file is marked for delete */
      unsigned FH2$V_NOCHARGE : 1;       /* file space is not to be charged */
      unsigned FH2$V_ERASE : 1;          /* erase file contents before deletion */
/***********The following two lines are different from FCH */
      unsigned FH2$V_ALM_AIP : 1;        /* Archive in progress - ALM proj cancelled
*/
      unsigned FH2$V_ALM_ARCHIVED : 1;   /* File archived - ALM proj cancelled */
      unsigned FH2$V_SCRATCH : 1;        /* Scratch Header used by movefile */
      unsigned FH2$V_NOMOVE : 1;         /* Disable movefile on this file */
/* Note: The high 8 bits of this longword */
/* are reserved for user and CSS use. */
      unsigned FH2$V_FILL_1 : 2;
      } FH2$R_FILECHAR_BITS;
    } FH2$R_FILECHAR_OVERLAY;
  unsigned short int FH2$W_RECPROT;    /* record protection */
  unsigned char FH2$B_MAP_INUSE;       /* number of map area words in use */
  unsigned char FH2$B_ACC_MODE;        /* least privileged access mode */
  __union {
    unsigned int FH2$L_FILEOWNER;      /* file owner UIC */
    __struct {
      unsigned short int FH2$W_UICMEMBER;  /* UIC member number */
      unsigned short int FH2$W_UICGROUP;   /* UIC group number */
      } FH2$R_FILEOWNER_FIELDS;
    } FH2$R_FILEOWNER_OVERLAY;
  unsigned short int FH2$W_FILEPROT;     /* file protection */
  __union {
    unsigned short int FH2$W_BACKLINK [3]; /* back link pointer */
    __struct {
      unsigned short int FH2$W_BK_FIDNUM;  /* back link file number */
      unsigned short int FH2$W_BK_FIDSEQ;  /* back link file sequence number */
      __union {
        unsigned short int FH2$W_BK_FIDRVN;/* back link relative volume number */
        __struct {
          unsigned char FH2$B_BK_FIDRVN;   /* alternate format back link RVN */
          unsigned char FH2$B_BK_FIDNMX;
/* alternate format back link file number extension */
          } FH2$R_BK_FIDRVN_FIELDS;
        } FH2$R_BK_FIDRVN_OVERLAY;
      } FH2$R_BACKLINK_FIELDS;
    } FH2$R_BACKLINK_OVERLAY;
  __union {
```

415

```
   unsigned char FH2$B_JOURNAL;       /* journal control flags */
   __struct {
     unsigned FH2$V_ONLY_RU : 1;      /* file is accessible only in recovery unit  */
     unsigned FH2$V_RUJNL : 1;        /* enable recovery unit journal */
     unsigned FH2$V_BIJNL : 1;        /* enable before image journal */
     unsigned FH2$V_AIJNL : 1;        /* enable after image journal */
     unsigned FH2$V_ATJNL : 1;        /* enable audit trail journal */
     unsigned FH2$V_NEVER_RU : 1;     /* file is never accessible in recovery unit */
     unsigned FH2$V_JOURNAL_FILE : 1; /* this is a journal file */
     unsigned FH2$V_FILL_2 : 1;
     } FH2$R_JOURNAL_BITS;
   } FH2$R_JOURNAL_OVERLAY;
  unsigned char FH2$B_RU_ACTIVE;      /* If non-zero, file has active recovery units
*/
/* (value is recoverable facility id number) */
/* 1-99 reserved to DEC, 100-127 reserved for */
/* CSS, 128-255 reserved for customers. */
  short int FH2DEF$$_FILL_3;          /* reserved */
  unsigned int FH2$L_HIGHWATER;       /* high-water mark in filc */
  int FH2$L_FILL_6 [2];               /* reserved  */
  __struct {                          /* security classification mask */
    char FH2$B_FILL_5 [20];           /* see structure in $CLSDEF */
    } FH2$R_CLASS_PROT;
  char FH2DEF$$_FILL_4 [402];         /* rest of file header */
  unsigned short int FH2$W_CHECKSUM;/* file header checksum */
  } ;

#ifdef __cplusplus
  }
#endif

#ifdef DEC_ARA
#pragma standard
#pragma member_alignment __restore
#endif

#endif
```

HM2DEF.H

```
#ifndef HM2DEF_H
#define HM2DEF_H

#ifdef DEC_ARA
#pragma member_alignment __save
#pragma nostandard
#pragma nomember_alignment
#endif

#ifdef __cplusplus
  extern "C" {
#define __unknown_params ...
#define __struct struct
#define __union union
#else
#define __unknown_params
#define __struct variant_struct
#define __union variant_union
#endif

/*+                                               */
/*                                                */
/* Home block definitions for Files-11 Structure Level 2   */
/*                                                */
/*-                                               */
#define HM2$C_LEVEL1 257 /* 401 octal = structure level 1  */
#define HM2$C_LEVEL2 512 /* 1000 octal = structure level 2 */
#define HM2$M_READCHECK 0x1
#define HM2$M_WRITCHECK 0x2
#define HM2$M_ERASE 0x4
#define HM2$M_NOHIGHWATER 0x8
#define HM2$M_CLASS_PROT 0x10
struct HM2DEF {
  unsigned int HM2$L_HOMELBN;          /* LBN of home (i.e., this) block */
  unsigned int HM2$L_ALHOMELBN;        /* LBN of alternate home block */
  unsigned int HM2$L_ALTIDXLBN;        /* LBN of alternate index file header */
  __union  {
    unsigned short int HM2$W_STRUCLEV; /* volume structure level */
    __struct  {
      unsigned char HM2$B_STRUCVER;    /* structure version number */
      unsigned char HM2$B_STRUCLEV;    /* main structure level */
      } HM2$R_STRUCLEV_FIELDS;
    } HM2$R_STRUCLEV_OVERLAY;
```

```
        unsigned short int HM2$W_CLUSTER;      /* storage bitmap cluster factor */
        unsigned short int HM2$W_HOMEVBN;      /* VBN of home (i.e., this) block */
        unsigned short int HM2$W_ALHOMEVBN;    /* VBN of alternate home block */
        unsigned short int HM2$W_ALTIDXVBN;    /* VBN of alternate index file header */
        unsigned short int HM2$W_IBMAPVBN;     /* VBN of index file bitmap */
        unsigned int HM2$L_IBMAPLBN;           /* LBN of index file bitmap */
        unsigned int HM2$L_MAXFILES;           /* maximum ! files on volume */
        unsigned short int HM2$W_IBMAPSIZE;    /* index file bitmap size, blocks */
        unsigned short int HM2$W_RESFILES;     /* ! reserved files on volume */
        unsigned short int HM2$W_DEVTYPE;      /* disk device type */
        unsigned short int HM2$W_RVN;          /* relative volume number of this volume  */
        unsigned short int HM2$W_SETCOUNT;     /* count of volumes in set */
    __union {
      unsigned short int HM2$W_VOLCHAR;        /* volume characteristics */
      __struct {
        unsigned HM2$V_READCHECK : 1;          /* verify all read operations */
        unsigned HM2$V_WRITCHECK : 1;          /* verify all write operations */
        unsigned HM2$V_ERASE : 1;              /* erase all files on delete */
        unsigned HM2$V_NOHIGHWATER : 1;        /* turn off high water marking */
        unsigned HM2$V_CLASS_PROT : 1;
/* enable classification checks on the volume */
        unsigned HM2$V_FILL_0 : 3;
        } HM2$R_VOLCHAR_BITS;
      } HM2$R_VOLCHAR_OVERLAY;
      unsigned int HM2$L_VOLOWNER;             /* volume owner UIC */
      unsigned int HM2$L_SEC_MASK;             /* volume security mask */
      unsigned short int HM2$W_PROTECT;        /* volume protection */
      unsigned short int HM2$W_FILEPROT;       /* default file protection */
      unsigned short int HM2$W_RECPROT;        /* default file record protection */
      unsigned short int HM2$W_CHECKSUM1;      /* first checksum */
      unsigned int HM2$Q_CREDATE [2];          /* volume creation date */
      unsigned char HM2$B_WINDOW;              /* default window size */
      unsigned char HM2$B_LRU_LIM;             /* default LRU limit */
      unsigned short int HM2$W_EXTEND;         /* default file extend */
      unsigned int HM2$Q_RETAINMIN [2];        /* minimum file retention period */
      unsigned int HM2$Q_RETAINMAX [2];        /* maximum file retention period */
      unsigned int HM2$Q_REVDATE [2];          /* volume revision date */
    __struct {                                 /* volume minimum security class */
      char HM2$B_FILL_2 [20];
      } HM2$R_MIN_CLASS;
    __struct {                                 /* volume maximum security class */
      char HM2$B_FILL_3 [20];
      } HM2$R_MAX_CLASS;
      unsigned short int HM2$W_FILETAB_FID [3]; /* file lookup table FID */
```

```
  __union {
    unsigned short int HM2$W_LOWSTRUCLEV;    /* lowest struclev on volume */
    __struct {
      unsigned char HM2$B_LOWSTRUCVER; /* structure version number */
      unsigned char HM2$B_LOWSTRUCLEV; /* main structure level */
      } HM2$R_LOWSTRUCLEV_FIELDS;
    } HM2$R_LOWSTRUCLEV_OVERLAY;
  __union {
    unsigned short int HM2$W_HIGHSTRUCLEV; /* highest struclev on volume */
    __struct {
      unsigned char HM2$B_HIGHSTRUCVER;/* structure version number */
      unsigned char HM2$B_HIGHSTRUCLEV;/* main structure level */
      } HM2$R_HIGHSTRUCLEV_FIELDS;
    } HM2$R_HIGHSTRUCLEV_OVERLAY;
  char HM2DEF$$_FILL_1 [310];           /* spare */
  unsigned int HM2$L_SERIALNUM;         /* pack serial number */
  char HM2$T_STRUCNAME [12];            /* structure (volume set name) */
  char HM2$T_VOLNAME [12];              /* volume name */
  char HM2$T_OWNERNAME [12];            /* volume owner name */
  char HM2$T_FORMAT [12];               /* volume format type */
  char HM2DEF$$_FILL_2 [2];             /* spare */
  unsigned short int HM2$W_CHECKSUM2;   /* second checksum */
  } ;

#ifdef __cplusplus
    }
#endif

#ifdef DEC_ARA
#pragma standard
#pragma member_alignment __restore
#endif

#endif
```

FI2DEF.H

```
#ifndef FI2DEF_H
#define FI2DEF_H

#ifdef DEC_ARA
#pragma member_alignment __save
#pragma nomember_alignment
#pragma nostandard
#endif

#ifdef __cplusplus
  extern "C" {
#define __unknown_params ...
#define __struct struct
#define __union union
#else
#define __unknown_params
#define __struct variant_struct
#define __union variant_union
#endif

#define FI2$K_LENGTH 120                /* length of ident area */
#define FI2$C_LENGTH 120                /* length of ident area */
struct FI2DEF {
  char FI2$T_FILENAME [20];             /* file name, type, and version (ASCII) */
  unsigned short int FI2$W_REVISION;    /* revision number (binary) */
  unsigned int FI2$Q_CREDATE [2];       /* creation date and time */
  unsigned int FI2$Q_REVDATE [2];       /* revision date and time */
  unsigned int FI2$Q_EXPDATE [2];       /* expiration date and time */
  unsigned int FI2$Q_BAKDATE [2];       /* backup date and time */
  char FI2$T_FILENAMEXT [66];           /* extension file name area */
  char FI2$T_USERLABEL [80];            /* optional user file label */
  } ;

#ifdef __cplusplus
  }
#endif

#ifdef DEC_ARA
#pragma standard
#pragma member_alignment __restore
#endif

#endif
```

FAODEFS.H

```
#include <descrip.h>

$DESCRIPTOR( fm00, "   LBN of home (i.e., this) block      !8UL ");
$DESCRIPTOR( fm01, "   LBN of alternate home block         !8UL ");
$DESCRIPTOR( fm02, "   LBN of alternate index file header !8UL ");
$DESCRIPTOR( fm04, "   Structure version number           !8UB ");
$DESCRIPTOR( fm05, "    Main structure level              !8UB ");
$DESCRIPTOR( fm06, "     Storage bitmap cluster factor     !8UW ");
$DESCRIPTOR( fm07, "   VBN of home (i.e., this) block      !8UW ");
$DESCRIPTOR(·fm08, "   VBN of alternate home block         !8UW ");
$DESCRIPTOR( fm09, "   VBN of alternate index file header !8UW ");
$DESCRIPTOR( fm10, "   VBN of index file bitmap            !8UW ");
$DESCRIPTOR( fm11, "   LBN of index file bitmap            !8UL ");
$DESCRIPTOR( fm12, "   Maximum number files on volume      !8UL ");
$DESCRIPTOR( fm13, "   Index file bitmap size, blocks      !8UW ");
$DESCRIPTOR( fm14, "   Number reserved files on volume     !8UW ");
$DESCRIPTOR( fm15, "   Disk device type                    !8UW ");
$DESCRIPTOR( fm16, "   Relative volume number of this volume !8UW ");
$DESCRIPTOR( fm17, "   Count of volumes in set             !8UW ");
$DESCRIPTOR( fm24, "   Volume owner UIC                    !%U ");
$DESCRIPTOR( fm25, "   Volume security mask                !08XL");
$DESCRIPTOR( fm26, "   Volume protection                   !04XW");
$DESCRIPTOR( fm27, "   Default file protection             !04XW");
$DESCRIPTOR( fm28, "   Default file record protection      !04XW");
$DESCRIPTOR( fm29, "   First checksum                      !04XW");
$DESCRIPTOR( fm30, "   Volume creation date                !%D ");
$DESCRIPTOR( fm31, "   Default window size                 !8UB");
$DESCRIPTOR( fm32, "   Default LRU limit                   !8UB");
$DESCRIPTOR( fm34, "   Default file extend                 !8UW");
$DESCRIPTOR( fm35, "   Minimum file retention period       !%D ");
$DESCRIPTOR( fm36, "   Maximum file retention period       !%D ");
$DESCRIPTOR( fm37, "   Volume revision date                !%D ");
$DESCRIPTOR( fm38, "   Volume minimum security class       !8UL");
$DESCRIPTOR( fm39, "   Volume maximum security class       !8UL");
$DESCRIPTOR( fm40, "   File lookup table FID               !04ZW,!04ZW,!04ZW ");
$DESCRIPTOR( fm45, "   Structure version number            !8UB");
$DESCRIPTOR( fm46, "   Main structure level                !8UB");
$DESCRIPTOR( fm48, "   Pack serial number                  !8UL");
$DESCRIPTOR( fm49, "   Structure (volume set name)         !AD");
$DESCRIPTOR( fm50, "   Volume name                         !AD");
$DESCRIPTOR( fm51, "   Volume owner name                   !AD");
$DESCRIPTOR( fm52, "   Volume format type                  !AD");
$DESCRIPTOR( fm54, "   Second checksum                     !8UW");
```

DUMPHOME.C

```
/*
**++
**   FACILITY:  VMS_TOOLS
**
** Copyright (c) 1993 James W. Coburn
** Copyright (c) 1993 Cardinal Business Media
** This program may be copied for noncommercial purposes. Use of this
** program for any other purpose without the express written consent
** of the publisher is prohibited.
**


** MODULE DESCRIPTION:
**
** This program opens the master index file for the specified
** disk and dumps out the home block information.
**
** TEST on a single node cluster before running in a productions
** environment.  This code uses kernel mode access and thus will
** crash your system if there are coding bugs or if changes to
** VMS introduce new bugs.
**
** This code has been tested on:
** OpenVMS AXP 1.5
**
**
** AUTHORS:
**
** Jim Coburn
**
** CREATION DATE:  June 1993
**
** DESIGN ISSUES:
**
**
**
**
** MODIFICATION HISTORY:
**
**
**—
*/
```

```
/*
**
**   INCLUDE FILES
**
*/

#include <descrip.h>
#include <string.h>
#include <stdio.h>
#include <rms.h>
#include <dvidef.h>
#include <ssdef.h>
#include <iodef.h>
#include <starlet.h>
#include <libdtdef.h>
#include <lib$routines.h>
#include <stdlib.h>
#include <str$routines.h>

#include "expired_files/fibdef.h"
#include "expired_files/fh2def.h"
#include "expired_files/hm2def.h"
#include "expired_files/fi2def.h"
#include "expired_files/faodefs.h"

struct FH2DEF fh2, file_header;
struct HM2DEF hm2;
struct FI2DEF *ident_area;
struct FIBDEF fib;

struct ITEMLIST
{
  short buffer_length, item_code;
  int *buffer_address;
  int *return_len_address;
};
struct ITEMLIST getdvi_list[2];

struct dsc$descriptor device = {0, DSC$K_DTYPE_T, DSC$K_CLASS_D, 0};
struct dsc$descriptor command_line = {0, DSC$K_DTYPE_T, DSC$K_CLASS_D, 0};

int cli_get_value( char *s1, struct dsc$descriptor *s2 );
int cli_present( char *s1 );
void open_file( void );
```

```
void get_eof( void );
void initialize( void);
int cli$dcl_parse( struct dsc$descriptor *full_command_line,
  int DumpHome_cld(), int i, int j, int k);

void DumpHomeBlocks( void )
{
  char output_line[80];
  unsigned short output_length;
  struct dsc$descriptor_s output_descriptor;

  printf("\n\n  Start of Home Block Data for %*.*s\n\n", device.dsc$w_length,
      device.dsc$w_length, device.dsc$a_pointer );

  output_descriptor.dsc$b_class = DSC$K_CLASS_S;
  output_descriptor.dsc$b_dtype = DSC$K_DTYPE_T;

  output_descriptor.dsc$a_pointer = output_line;
  output_descriptor.dsc$w_length.h = 80;
  sys$fao( &fm00, &output_length, &output_descriptor,
      hm2.HM2$L_HOMELBN );

  output_line[ (int) output_length ] = '\0';
  printf( "%s\n", output_line );

  output_descriptor.dsc$a_pointer = output_line;
  output_descriptor.dsc$w_length = 80;
  sys$fao( &fm01, &output_length, &output_descriptor,
      hm2.HM2$L_ALHOMELBN );

  output_line[ (int) output_length ] = '\0';
  printf( "%s\n", output_line );

  output_descriptor.dsc$a_pointer = output_line;
  output_descriptor.dsc$w_length = 80;
  sys$fao( &fm02, &output_length, &output_descriptor,
      hm2.HM2$L_ALTIDXLBN );

  output_line[ (int) output_length ] = '\0';
  printf( "%s\n", output_line );

  printf("  Volume structure level \n");

  output_descriptor.dsc$a_pointer = output_line;
```

```
output_descriptor.dsc$w_length = 80;
sys$fao( &fm04, &output_length, &output_descriptor,
    hm2.HM2$B_STRUCVER );

output_line[ (int) output_length ] = '\0';
printf( "%s\n", output_line );

output_descriptor.dsc$a_pointer = output_line;
output_descriptor.dsc$w_length = 80;
sys$fao( &fm05, &output_length, &output_descriptor,
    hm2.HM2$B_STRUCLEV );

output_line[ (int) output_length ] = '\0';
printf( "%s\n", output_line );

output_descriptor.dsc$a_pointer = output_line;
output_descriptor.dsc$w_length = 80;
sys$fao( &fm06, &output_length, &output_descriptor,
    hm2.HM2$W_CLUSTER );

output_line[ (int) output_length ] = '\0';
printf( "%s\n", output_line );

output_descriptor.dsc$a_pointer = output_line;
output_descriptor.dsc$w_length = 80;
sys$fao( &fm07, &output_length, &output_descriptor,
    hm2.HM2$W_HOMEVBN );

output_line[ (int) output_length ] = '\0';
printf( "%s\n", output_line );

output_descriptor.dsc$a_pointer = output_line;
output_descriptor.dsc$w_length = 80;
sys$fao( &fm08, &output_length, &output_descriptor,
    hm2.HM2$W_ALHOMEVBN );

output_line[ (int) output_length ] = '\0';
printf( "%s\n", output_line );

output_descriptor.dsc$a_pointer = output_line;
output_descriptor.dsc$w_length = 80;
sys$fao( &fm09, &output_length, &output_descriptor,
    hm2.HM2$W_ALTIDXVBN );

output_line[ (int) output_length ] = '\0';
```

425

```
printf( "%s\n", output_line );

output_descriptor.dsc$a_pointer = output_line;
output_descriptor.dsc$w_length = 80;
sys$fao( &fm10, &output_length, &output_descriptor,
    hm2.HM2$W_IBMAPVBN  );

output_line[ (int) output_length ] = '\0';
printf( "%s\n", output_line );

output_descriptor.dsc$a_pointer = output_line;
output_descriptor.dsc$w_length = 80;
sys$fao( &fm11, &output_length, &output_descriptor,
    hm2.HM2$L_IBMAPLBN );

output_line[ (int) output_length ] = '\0';
printf( "%s\n", output_line );

output_descriptor.dsc$a_pointer = output_line;
output_descriptor.dsc$w_length = 80;
sys$fao( &fm12, &output_length, &output_descriptor,
    hm2.HM2$L_MAXFILES );

output_line[ (int) output_length ] = '\0';
printf( "%s\n", output_line );

output_descriptor.dsc$a_pointer = output_line;
output_descriptor.dsc$w_length = 80;
sys$fao( &fm13, &output_length, &output_descriptor,
    hm2.HM2$W_IBMAPSIZE  );

output_line[ (int) output_length ] = '\0';
printf( "%s\n", output_line );

output_descriptor.dsc$a_pointer = output_line;
output_descriptor.dsc$w_length = 80;
sys$fao( &fm14, &output_length, &output_descriptor,
    hm2.HM2$W_RESFILES  );

output_line[ (int) output_length ] = '\0';
printf( "%s\n", output_line );

output_descriptor.dsc$a_pointer = output_line;
output_descriptor.dsc$w_length = 80;
```

```
sys$fao( &fm15, &output_length, &output_descriptor,
    hm2.HM2$W_DEVTYPE  );

output_line[ (int) output_length ] = '\0';
printf( "%s\n", output_line );


output_descriptor.dsc$a_pointer = output_line;
output_descriptor.dsc$w_length = 80;
sys$fao( &fm16, &output_length, &output_descriptor,
    hm2.HM2$W_RVN  );

output_line[ (int) output_length ] = '\0';
printf( "%s\n", output_line );


output_descriptor.dsc$a_pointer = output_line;
output_descriptor.dsc$w_length = 80;
sys$fao( &fm17, &output_length, &output_descriptor,
    hm2.HM2$W_SETCOUNT  );

output_line[ (int) output_length ] = '\0';
printf( "%s\n", output_line );

printf( "  Volume characteristics " );

if( hm2.HM2$V_READCHECK )
    printf( "\n     Verify all read operations ");
if( hm2.HM2$V_WRITCHECK )
    printf( "\n     Verify all write operations ");
if( hm2.HM2$V_ERASE )
    printf( "\n     Erase all files on delete ");
if( hm2.HM2$V_NOHIGHWATER )
    printf( "\n     Turn off high-water marking ");
if( hm2.HM2$V_CLASS_PROT )
    printf( "\n     Enable classification checks on the volume ");

printf( "\n");

output_descriptor.dsc$a_pointer = output_line;
output_descriptor.dsc$w_length = 80;
sys$fao( &fm24, &output_length, &output_descriptor,
    hm2.HM2$L_VOLOWNER );

output_line[ (int) output_length ] = '\0';
printf( "%s\n", output_line );
```

427

```
output_descriptor.dsc$a_pointer = output_line;
output_descriptor.dsc$w_length = 80;
sys$fao( &fm25, &output_length, &output_descriptor,
    hm2.HM2$L_SEC_MASK );

output_line[ (int) output_length ] = '\0';
printf( "%s\n", output_line );

output_descriptor.dsc$a_pointer = output_line;
output_descriptor.dsc$w_length = 80;
sys$fao( &fm26, &output_length, &output_descriptor,
    hm2.HM2$W_PROTECT );

output_line[ (int) output_length ] = '\0';
printf( "%s\n", output_line );

output_descriptor.dsc$a_pointer = output_line;
output_descriptor.dsc$w_lenqth = 80;
sys$fao( &fm27, &output_length, &output_descriptor,
    hm2.HM2$W_FILEPROT );

output_line[ (int) output_length ] = '\0';
printf( "%s\n", output_line );

output_descriptor.dsc$a_pointer = output_line;
output_descriptor.dsc$w_length = 80;
sys$fao( &fm28, &output_length, &output_descriptor,
    hm2.HM2$W_RECPROT );

output_line[ (int) output_length ] = '\0';
printf( "%s\n", output_line );

output_descriptor.dsc$a_pointer = output_line;
output_descriptor.dsc$w_length = 80;
sys$fao( &fm29, &output_length, &output_descriptor,
    hm2.HM2$W_CHECKSUM1 );

output_line[ (int) output_length ] = '\0';
printf( "%s\n", output_line );

output_descriptor.dsc$a_pointer = output_line;
output_descriptor.dsc$w_length = 80;
sys$fao( &fm30, &output_length, &output_descriptor,
```

```
        &hm2.HM2$Q_CREDATE   );

output_line[ (int) output_length ] = '\0';
printf( "%s\n", output_line );

output_descriptor.dsc$a_pointer = output_line;
output_descriptor.dsc$w_length = 80;
sys$fao( &fm31, &output_length, &output_descriptor,
    hm2.HM2$B_WINDOW   );

output_line[ (int) output_length ] = '\0';
printf( "%s\n", output_line );

output_descriptor.dsc$a_pointer = output_line;
output_descriptor.dsc$w_length = 80;
sys$fao( &fm32, &output_length·, &output_descriptor,
    hm2.HM2$B_LRU_LIM   );

output_line[ (int) output_length ] = '\0';
printf( "%s\n", output_line );

output_descriptor.dsc$a_pointer = output_line;
output_descriptor.dsc$w_length = 80;
sys$fao( &fm34, &output_length, &output_descriptor,
    hm2.HM2$W_EXTEND   );

output_line[ (int) output_length ] = '\0';
printf( "%s\n", output_line );

output_descriptor.dsc$a_pointer = output_line;
output_descriptor.dsc$w_length = 80;
sys$fao( &fm35, &output_length, &output_descriptor,
    &hm2.HM2$Q_RETAINMIN );

output_line[ (int) output_length ] = '\0';
printf( "%s\n", output_line );

output_descriptor.dsc$a_pointer = output_line;
output_descriptor.dsc$w_length = 80;
sys$fao( &fm36, &output_length, &output_descriptor,
    &hm2.HM2$Q_RETAINMAX );

output_line[ (int) output_length ] = '\0';
printf( "%s\n", output_line );
```

```
output_descriptor.dsc$a_pointer = output_line;
output_descriptor.dsc$w_length = 80;
sys$fao( &fm37, &output_length, &output_descriptor,
    &hm2.HM2$Q_REVDATE );

output_line[ (int) output_length ] = '\0';
printf( "%s\n", output_line );

output_descriptor.dsc$a_pointer = output_line;
output_descriptor.dsc$w_length = 80;
sys$fao( &fm40, &output_length, &output_descriptor,
    hm2.HM2$W_FILETAB_FID[0], hm2.HM2$W_FILETAB_FID[1],
    hm2.HM2$W_FILETAB_FID[2] );

output_line[ (int) output_length ] = '\0';
printf( "%s\n", output_line );

printf( "  Lowest struclev on volume \n" );

output_descriptor.dsc$a_pointer = output_line;
output_descriptor.dsc$w_length = 80;
sys$fao( &fm45, &output_length, &output_descriptor,
    hm2.HM2$B_LOWSTRUCVER );

output_line[ (int) output_length ] = '\0';
printf( "%s\n", output_line );

output_descriptor.dsc$a_pointer = output_line;
output_descriptor.dsc$w_length = 80;
sys$fao( &fm46, &output_length, &output_descriptor,
    hm2.HM2$B_LOWSTRUCLEV );

output_line[ (int) output_length ] = '\0';
printf( "%s\n", output_line );

printf( "  Highest struclev on volume \n" );

output_descriptor.dsc$a_pointer = output_line;
output_descriptor.dsc$w_length = 80;
sys$fao( &fm45, &output_length, &output_descriptor,
    hm2.HM2$B_HIGHSTRUCVER );

output_line[ (int) output_length ] = '\0';
printf( "%s\n", output_line );

output_descriptor.dsc$a_pointer = output_line;
```

```
output_descriptor.dsc$w_length = 80;
sys$fao( &fm46, &output_length, &output_descriptor,
    hm2.HM2$B_HIGHSTRUCLEV );

output_line[ (int) output_length ] = '\0';
printf( "%s\n", output_line );

printf( "  Spare (310 bytes) \n");

output_descriptor.dsc$a_pointer = output_line;
output_descriptor.dsc$w_length = 80;
sys$fao( &fm48, &output_length, &output_descriptor,
    hm2.HM2$L_SERIALNUM );

output_line[ (int) output_length ] = '\0';
printf( "%s\n", output_line );

output_descriptor.dsc$a_pointer = output_line;
output_descriptor.dsc$w_length = 80;
sys$fao( &fm49, &output_length, &output_descriptor,
    12, hm2.HM2$T_STRUCNAME );

output_line[ (int) output_length ] = '\0';
printf( "%s\n", output_line );

output_descriptor.dsc$a_pointer = output_line;
output_descriptor.dsc$w_length = 80;
sys$fao( &fm50, &output_length, &output_descriptor,
    12, hm2.HM2$T_VOLNAME  );

output_line[ (int) output_length ] = '\0';
printf( "%s\n", output_line );

output_descriptor.dsc$a_pointer = output_line;
output_descriptor.dsc$w_length = 80;
sys$fao( &fm51, &output_length, &output_descriptor,
    12, hm2.HM2$T_OWNERNAME  );

output_line[ (int) output_length ] = '\0';
printf( "%s\n", output_line );

output_descriptor.dsc$a_pointer = output_line;
output_descriptor.dsc$w_length = 80;
sys$fao( &fm52, &output_length, &output_descriptor,
    12, hm2.HM2$T_FORMAT  );

output_line[ (int) output_length ] = '\0';
```

```
   printf( "%s\n", output_line );

   printf( "  Spare (2 bytes) \n");

   output_descriptor.dsc$a_pointer = output_line;
   output_descriptor.dsc$w_length = 80;
   sys$fao( &fm54, &output_length, &output_descriptor,
       hm2.HM2$W_CHECKSUM2  );
   output_line[ (int) output_length ] = '\0';
   printf( "%s\n", output_line );

   printf("\n\n  End of Home Block Data for %*.*s\n\n", device.dsc$w_length,
device.dsc$w_length, device.dsc$a_pointer );

}

main()
{

   int DumpHome_cld();
   long int offset=1;
   struct dsc$descriptor fib_desc;
   static struct dsc$descriptor dynstr = {0, DSC$K_DTYPE_T, DSC$K_CLASS_D, 0};
   static $DESCRIPTOR(null,"\0");
   static $DESCRIPTOR(command,"DumpHome ");
   static struct dsc$descriptor full_command_line  =
       {0, DSC$K_DTYPE_T, DSC$K_CLASS_D, 0};

   int iosb[2], status;
   short int channel;
   int func, index;

   char *access[] = { "w", "a+" };
   status = lib$get_foreign( &command_line );
   str$append (&full_command_line, &command );
   str$append (&full_command_line, &command_line);
   status = cli$dcl_parse( &full_command_line, &DumpHome_cld, 0, 0, 0 );

   if (cli_present("OUTPUT") & 1)
   {
   /* we should see if they want output to go to a file or to SYS$OUTPUT */
       status = cli_get_value("OUTPUT",&dynstr);
       if (status & 1)
       {
         if (cli_present("APPEND") & 1)
             index = 1;
```

```
        else
            index = 0;

        str$append(&dynstr,&null);
        freopen(dynstr.dsc$a_pointer, access[index],stdout,"rfm=var","rat=cr");
    }
}
fib_desc.dsc$a_pointer = (char *) &fib;
fib_desc.dsc$w_length = FIB$C_LENGTH;

/* get the name of the device which we're planning on checking */
status = cli_get_value("P1",&device);
if (!(status & 1)) return(status);

get_eof();
sys$assign( &device, &channel, 0, 0 );

fib.fib$w_fid[0] = 1;
fib.fib$w_fid[1] = 1;
fib.fib$w_fid[2] = 0;
fib.fib$l_acctl = FIB$M_NOWRITE + FIB$M_WRITE;

func = IO$_ACCESS + IO$M_ACCESS;
status = sys$qio( 0, channel, func, &iosb,
    0, 0, &fib_desc, 0, 0, 0, 0, 0 );

/*  Read in the home block - 2 */

offset = 2;
status = sys$qiow( 0,  channel, IO$_READVBLK, &iosb,
    0, 0, &hm2, 512, offset, 0, 0, 0 );

if (hm2.HM2$B_STRUCLEV != 2) {
    printf("Sorry, Expired_files only works for ODS-2 disks\n");
    return;
}

DumpHomeBlocks( );

sys$dassgn ( channel );
}
```

RMS_OPEN.C

```c
/*
**
**   INCLUDE FILES
**
*/

#include <descrip.h>
#include <string.h>
#include <stdio.h>
#include <rms.h>
#include <dvidef.h>
#include <ssdef.h>
#include <iodef.h>
#include <starlet.h>
#include <libdtdef.h>
#include <lib$routines.h>
#include <stdlib.h>
#include <str$routines.h>

#include "expired_files:fibdef.h"

int rms_status;

static struct FAB fab;
static struct NAM nam;
static struct RAB rab;
static struct XABFHC xab;
int last_header;

static struct dsc$descriptor device = {0, DSC$K_DTYPE_T, DSC$K_CLASS_D, 0};

void initialize( void);
void open_file( void );

void get_eof( void )
{

  initialize();
  open_file();
  last_header = xab.xab$l_ebk;
  sys$close ( &fab );
}
```

```
void initialize( void)
{

  fab = cc$rms_fab;
  nam = cc$rms_nam;
  rab = cc$rms_rab;
  xab = cc$rms_xabfhc;

  fab.fab$l_dna = device.dsc$a_pointer;
  fab.fab$b_dns = device.dsc$w_length;

  fab.fab$l_fna = "[000000]indexf.sys";
  fab.fab$b_fns = strlen(fab.fab$l_fna);
  fab.fab$b_fac = FAB$M_GET;
  fab.fab$l_nam = &nam;
  fab.fab$l_xab = (char *) &xab;

}

void open_file( void )
{
  rms_status = sys$open( &fab );
}
```

DUMPHOME_CLD.CLD

```
module DumpHome_cld
define verb DUMPHOME
  parameter P1
    default
    value (default="SYS$DISK",type=$infile)
  qualifier OUTPUT
    value (default="DUMPHOME.LIS",type=$outfile)
  qualifier APPEND
```

DUMPHOME.LNK_DEF

```
EXPIRED_FILES:dumphome.obj
EXPIRED_FILES:cli.obj
EXPIRED_FILES:rms_open.obj
EXPIRED_FILES:dumphome_cld.obj
#ifdef VAX
sys$share:vaxcrtl/lib
#eneif
```

435

DUMP HOME OUTPUT SCREENS

LBN of home (that is, this) block	1
LBN of alternate home block	767
LBN of alternate index file header	409986
Volume structure level	
Structure version number	1
Main structure level	2
Storage bitmap cluster factor	3
VBN of home (that is, this) block	2
VBN of alternate home block	9
VBN of alternate index file header	10
VBN of index file bitmap	13
LBN of index file bitmap	409221
Maximum number files on volume	102287
Index file bitmap size, in blocks	25
Number reserved files on volume	9
Disk device type	0
Relative volume number of this volume	0
Count of volumes In set	0
Volume characteristics	
Turn off high-water marking	
Volume owner UIC	[1,4]
Volume security mask	00000000
Volume protection	0000
Default file protection	FA00
Default file record protection	FE00
First checksum	0CF8
Volume creation date	30-DEC-1991 13:35:44.81
Default window size	7
Default LRU limit	3
Default file extend	5
Minimum file retention period	20 00:00:00.00
Maximum file retention period	30 00:00:00.00
Volume revision date	17-NOV-1858 00:00:00.00
File lookup table FID	0000
Lowest struclev on volume	
Structure version number	0
Main structure level	0
Highest struclev on volume	
Structure version number	0
Main structure level	0
Spare (310 bytes)	
Pack serial number	0

```
Structure (volume set name)
Volume name                              ASC513_4609X
Volume owner name
Volume format type                        DECFILE11B
Spare (2 bytes)
Second checksum                                17272
```

Index

Also Available from CBM Books

Special Order from your bookstore or order direct by phone: (215) 957-4265. Prices subject to change.

CBM Books

The Complete Guide to PATHWORKS: PATHWORKS for VMS and DOS
by Kenneth L. Spencer

This definitive, practical guide is for system managers, network managers ... anyone installing or supporting a PATHWORKS network. Includes one 3 1/2-inch disk containing batch file utilities, new logon procedures for DOS and Windows, and the WinBatch language for Windows.

"What has long been needed is a book on PATHWORKS that is accessible to users and useful to system administrators. Ken Spencer has done an excellent job in this regard with The Complete Guide to PATHWORKS, a current and lucid presentation of PATHWORKS overflowing with anecdotes, real-world examples, and tips on customizing PATHWORKS. It's everything you need to know to make PATHWORKS work for you."
—Chris Lord, Senior Software Engineer, Digital Equipment Corp.

1-878956-22-1/$39

Practical Guide to Windows NT by Kenneth L. Spencer

This book provides professional and amateur users with practical advice on how to get up and running in Windows NT. It approaches Windows NT as a network environment. Not bogged down with technical jargon, the text focuses on all interfaces and concentrates on efficient and effective management of the application. This guide features chapters on choosing a platform, installation, security, networks and the future of windows.

1-878956-39-6/$25

TP Software Development for OpenVMS by John M. Willis

"This is an excellent and easy-to-read guide that gives an applications programmer a running start for developing client/server TP applications using ACMS."
— Vijay Trehan, Technical Director, Transaction Processing, Digital Equipment Corp.

This book discusses and demonstrates all aspects of software development using the core software products; ACMS, DECforms, SQL and Rdb. You will be given an in-depth understanding of all the software components of a VMS based TP system, their interaction, dependency and relationship with one another.

1-878956-34-5/$35

Total SNMP: Exploring the Simple Network Management Protocol
by Sean J. Harnedy

This book is intended for anyone interested in the use of the SNMP framework as a Network Management solution. It presents the network manager, the agent, and the protocol for the two to communicate the necessary management information about the network. It includes an in-depth and comprehensive discussion of all the SNMP specifications and associated RFCs.

1-878956-33-7/$45

Introduction to VAX/VMS 3rd Edition by David W. Bynon and Terry C. Shannon

This book provides a step-by-step, hands-on approach to learning VMS, with examples users can try at their terminals. It introduces DECwindows and the Digital Command Language, the primary interface between the user and the computer. It then explains the VMS file and directory system and teaches users how to modify their VMS user accounts and terminal characteristics.

The book describes both the EVE and EDT text editors, VMS utilities and DECwindows FileView. Also covered are symbols, command procedures and selected advanced VMS features.

1-878956-05-1/$35

VAX I/O Subsystems: Optimizing Performance by Ken Bates

Learn how to analyze and improve I/O performance from leading expert Ken Bates, a member of the original development teams for both the HSC and KDM70 controllers, and the developer of the first striping product offered by Digital.

"(This book) explores the right strategies to help system managers obtain the greatest total performance from their systems."

— Grant Saviers, Vice President, PC & Systems Peripherals Group,
Digital Equipment Corp.

"A landmark book."

— DEC Professional

1-878956-02-7/$49

Mastering VMS by David W. Bynon

This handbook uses step-by-step examples and explanations on how to apply VMS system operation and management techniques. Hands-on instruction for system managers, programmers, operators and analysts.

"Provides the reader with information on everything from the rise of the VAX machine and study of the VMS operating system to information on VMS operation management, utilities and commands."

— The Office

"A valuable book for those using the VMS operating system."

— CHOICE

0-9614729-7-9/$40

The Hitchhiker's Guide to VMS by Bruce Ellis

This unusual programmer's guide from VMS internals guru Bruce Ellis transforms hands-on system programming tips into a fast, fun read. From VMS internals and process concepts to system data structures and security, The Hitchhiker's Guide to VMS covers all the bases.

"Bruce Ellis is the only author I've found who can write entertainingly about the low-level details of VMS. The book is amazingly fun to read...you'll learn a lot."

— DECUSCOPE

"... put your thumb up, this hitchhike could be the most enjoyable learning experience you've had."

— ON$DECK Magazine

1-878956-00-0/$17

Special Order from your bookstore, or order direct by calling (215) 957-4265

CBM Books Teaches You All About DEC Computing

From an introduction to the VMS operating system to advanced texts on system management and performance, learn what you need to know from CBM Books.

For experienced VMS professionals like you . . .

A Practical Guide to Windows NT
MIS and end users alike will find this guide an indispensible resource for understanding Windows NT. Essential reading for anyone interested in the future of computing.
224 pages, ISBN 1-878956-39-6

Kenneth L. Spencer	$25

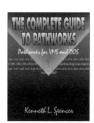

The Complete Guide to Pathworks
". . . A current and lucid presentation. . ."*Chris Lord, Senior Software Engineer, Digital Equipment Corp.*
Put a copy on every network manager's desk. Helpful for all MIS staff members and even end users.
390 pages, ISBN 1-878956-22-1, 3 ½" Disk Included

Kenneth L. Spencer	$39

The *Ethernet Pocket Guide, 2nd Edition* is an updated handbook for designing, installing and trouble-shooting Ethernet networks. A step-by-step guide for network managers, installers, support staff, system managers and administrators.
95 pages, ISBN 1-878956-43-4

Byron Spinney	$15

101 Witmer Road,
Horsham, PA 19044
(215) 957-4265
FAX (215) 957-1050

CBM
B O O K S

For your staff training and education needs . . .

Mastering VMS provides detailed how-to's for VMS system managers and programmers who need to learn more about managing and operating VMS systems.
465 pages, ISBN 0-9614729-7-9

David W. Bynon	$40

Introduction to VAX/VMS, 3rd Edition, is a basic guide to understanding the VMS operating system. Learn how to use VMS utilities, the EVE and EDT text editors, DECwindows, FileView, subprocesses, VAX workstations and more.
316 pages, ISBN 1-878956-05-1

David W. Bynon and Terry C. Shannon	$35

TP Software Development for OpenVMS demonstrates application and database development using Digital Equipment Corporation's Transaction Processing (TP) software ACMS and Rdb, in conjunction with SQL, DECforms and CDD.
360 pages, ISBN 1-878956-34-5

John M. Willis	$35

Total SNMP: Exploring the Simple Network Management Protocol provides useful information on mastering the dynamics of SNMP. It is intended for anyone interested in the use of the SNMP framework as a Network Management Solution. Comprehensive appendix.
656 pages, ISBN 1-878956-33-7

Sean Harnedy	$45

Use the form on the other side to order your copies now.

CBM Books Order Form

CBM BOOKS

For fast, easy ordering . . .
- By Phone (215) 957-4265
- FAX (215) 957-1050
- Through CompuServe Mail ... User ID #76702,1564

Title		Quantity	Subtotal
OpenVMS Performance Management, 2nd Edition			
1-5 copies	$40 ea.		
6-15 copies	$34 ea.		
16-49 copies	$28 ea.		
50+ copies	$24 ea.		
A Practical Guide to Windows NT	$25		
The Complete Guide to Pathworks	$39		
Ethernet Pocket Guide, 2nd Edition	$15		
Mastering VMS	$40		
Introduction to VAX/VMS, 3rd Edition	$35		
TP Software Development for OpenVMS	$35		
Total SNMP: Exploring the Simple Network Management Protocol	$45		
PA residents add 6% sales tax.			
UPS shipping: In the U.S., $4 for the first book, $1 for each additional book. Outside the U.S., please call (215) 957-4265 for shipping information.	**Shipping**		
	Handling Charge		$1.50
TOTAL ORDER			

Save on multiple copies!

Name _____

Title _____

Company _____

Address _____

City _____ State _____ Zip _____

Country _____

Telephone (_____) _____ FAX (_____) _____

Street address required.

☐ Payment enclosed $_____. (payable to Cardinal Business Media, Inc.)

Charge to: ☐ MasterCard MasterCard   ☐ VISA VISA   ☐ American Express American Express

Account #: _____ Exp. Date _____

Signature _____ Date _____

☐ Please send me a FREE CBM Books catalog.

PMBI0594

Mail to: CBM Books
CBM BOOKS 101 Witmer Road, P.O. Box 446
Horsham, PA 19044